Memoirs and Correspondence of Viscount Castlereagh, Second Marquess of Londonderry, Volume 12

CORRESPONDENCE,

DESPATCHES, AND OTHER PAPERS,

OF

VISCOUNT CASTLEREAGH,

SECOND MARQUESS OF LONDONDERRY.

EDITED BY

HIS BROTHER,

CHARLES WILLIAM VANE, MARQUESS OF LONDONDERRY,

G.C.B., G.C.H., G.B.E., ETC.

IN TWELVE VOLUMES.—VOL. XII.

LONDON
JOHN MURRAY, ALBEMARLE STREET.

1853.

CONTENTS

OF

THE TWELFTH VOLUME.

CONGRESS OF AIX-LA-CHAPELLE.

1818. (*Continued.*)

1818.   PAGE

Sept. 2. Lord Castlereagh to Lord Liverpool, proposing that his
     brother should attend at Aix during the Congress   . .   1

   4. Lord Liverpool to Lord Castlereagh, referring to a negocia-
     tion between Prince Metternich and Monsieur, and to the
     good policy of keeping the Emperor of Russia from visit-
     ing England   2

   8. Mr. James Stephen to Lord Castlereagh, transmitting a
     Paper entitled Suggestions relative to Africa and Colonial
     Discussions that may have place in the Congress of Aix-
     la-Chapelle—comprehending considerations on the state
     of St. Domingo, and the probable consequences of its re-
     duction under the dominion of France   .   *ib*

  15. Prince Leopold to Lord Castlereagh, adverting to certain
     territorial exchanges desired by his brother   .   .   35

  18. Lord Clancarty to Lord Castlereagh, returning Papers on
     the negociations with the United States; and mentioning
     preparations making for the reception of the Emperor of
     Austria, on his way down the Rhine to Aix   .   .   36

  18. Lord Liverpool to Lord Castlereagh, relating to the subjects
     in negociation with the United States; adverting to the
     murder of Arbuthnot and Ambrister, to the conduct of
     General Jackson, to the occupation of Pensacola, and to
     the dangerous state of the Queen   .   .   .   38

  22. Mr. W. Hamilton to Mr. Planta, referring to the unwilling-
     ness of the Neapolitan Government to permit the import-
     ation of British goods in ships not British, with enclosure: 39

1818.   PAGE

Sept. 19. Memorandum, relative to an interview with the Duke
de B——   40

25. Lord Bathurst to Lord Castlereagh, transmitting papers
relative to the treatment of Bonaparte at St. Helena, to
prepare him, in case of complaints being made on that
subject to the Sovereigns at Aix   .   .   .   41

27. Lord Castlereagh to Lord Liverpool, communicating the
results of conversations with the Duke de Richelieu   .   42

27. Lord Burghersh to Lord Castlereagh, glancing at members
of the Bonaparte family in Italy, at the Duchess of Lucca,
the Duke of Modena, and at roads in progress, or proposed   43

28. Lord Castlereagh to Lord Clancarty, transmitting instructions   44

30. Lord Clancarty to Lord Castlereagh, announcing the proposed movements of the King, and remarking on the
Bouillon question   45

Oct. 2. Lord Clancarty to Lord Castlereagh, mentioning the impri-
sonment of a proprietor of a libellous journal   .   .   46

2. Lord Clancarty to Lord Castlereagh, adverting to the subject of the additional fortresses   .   .   .   ib.

4. Lord Castlereagh to Lord Liverpool, expressing his belief
in the sincere intention of the Emperor of Russia to pursue a peace policy, and adverting to the fortifications
planned for the defence of the Netherlands   .   .   47

6. Prince Leopold to Lord Castlereagh, recommending to him
the interests of his brother, the Duke of Coburg   .   49

7. Mr. C. Bagot to Lord Castlereagh, respecting the mediation
between Spain and her colonies   .   .   .   50

13. Lord Clancarty to Lord Castlereagh, relative to the Bouillon affair   .   .   .   .   .   .   ib.

17. Lord Bathurst to Lord Castlereagh, conveying a proposal
for an application to the Austrian Government for compensation for funds seized by it belonging to the Ionian
Islands   52

18. Lord Clancarty to Lord Castlereagh, communicating the
sentiments of the Netherlands' Government concerning
the Convention with France for the reduction of the Army
of Occupation   53

20. Lord Castlereagh to Lord Liverpool, on the state of Conferences at Aix-la-Chapelle   54

20. Lord Bathurst to Lord Castlereagh, signifying the disapprobation of the Cabinet of the proposal for announcing
continued meetings of the Allied Sovereigns at fixed
points   55

22. Lord Melville to Lord Castlereagh, on the omission of foreign

1818.

PAGE

ships to fire the customary salutes on entering British
ports, and adverting to the subject of the Barbary
States 58

Oct. 23. Lord Bathurst to Lord Castlereagh, on the subject of farther
meetings of the Allied Sovereigns . . . 60

23. Lord Liverpool to Lord Castlereagh, expressing the sentiments of Government relative to further meetings of the
Sovereigns or their Ministers . . . 61

23. Lord Liverpool to Lord Castlereagh, signifying decided disapprobation of a new treaty to which France might be a
party 63

23. Lord Liverpool to Lord Castlereagh, communicating the
resignation of Lord Mulgrave as Master-General of the
Ordnance, in order that the office, with a seat in the
Cabinet, might be given to the Duke of Wellington . ib.

29. Lord Clancarty to Lord Castlereagh, relative to the seizure
of Kniphausen by the Duke of Oldenburg, and adverting
to an extraordinary Note from the Prussian Chargé
d'Affaires to M. de Nagell 64

31 Mr. C. Bagot to Lord Castlereagh, reporting an interview
with Mr. Adams on the subject of mediation between
Spain and her colonies 66

Nov. 2. Mr. C. Bagot to Lord Castlereagh, transmitting letters from
Colonel Barclay, stating that forts erected by the American Government on Lake Champlain are upon British
territory 69

4. Lord Liverpool to Lord Castlereagh, remarking upon papers
transmitted by him 71

8. Mr. Edward Cooke to Lord Castlereagh, enclosing a letter
from Sir Philip Roche, relative to the state of Spain . ib.

8. Lord Clancarty to Lord Castlereagh, reporting the improved
tone introduced into the communications of the diplomatic
agents of Prussia and the Netherlands, and adverting to
the payment to be made by France under the late Convention 74

9. Lord Castlereagh to Lord Liverpool, remarking on papers
transmitted to and by him, and adverting to the state of
France 75

9. Lord Liverpool to Lord Castlereagh, on the mediation between Spain and her colonies . . . 76

10. Lord Liverpool to Lord Castlereagh, acknowledging receipt
of despatches, and referring to the conduct of Eugene
Beauharnois 78

10. Lord Bathurst to Lord Castlereagh, regretting Capodistrias'
journey to the Ionian Islands . . . 79

1818. PAGE

Nov. 12. Lord Clancarty to Lord Castlereagh, on the subject of a proposed Convention of guarantee; animadverting on a paper of Prince Hardenberg's relative to the position of Prussia; and referring to the efforts of the Netherlands' Government to control the proceedings of French emigrants 79

13. Lord Bathurst to Lord Castlereagh, expressing dislike of the projected treaty 85

15. Lord Clancarty to Lord Castlereagh, remarking upon Prussian complaints against the Netherlands' Government, and adverting to financial matters . . . 86

26. Lord Castlereagh to Lord Melville, reporting that the Allied Sovereigns had decided to instruct their Ministers in London to agree upon a common system of salute, and that France would be required to join in the remonstrance on the Barbary question 89

26. Lord Castlereagh to Lord Liverpool, on the mediation between Spain and her colonies . . . 90

Dec. 9. Alexander Prince of Solms to Lord Castlereagh, transmitting a letter to the Prince Regent, suggesting the policy of his union with a Sardinian princess, and a genealogical table of the Stuart family 91

21. Sir H. Wellesley to Lord Castlereagh, reporting the increased influence of the Russian Ambassador at Madrid, and a strong manifestation of ill-humour against the British Government 94

24. Lord Clancarty to Lord Castlereagh, relative to diplomatic business at Frankfort, and to the Beauharnois establishment 95

1819.

FURTHER NEGOCIATIONS WITH THE UNITED STATES OF AMERICA — AFFAIRS OF RUSSIA, THE NETHERLANDS, FRANCE, GERMANY, ETC.

1819. PAGE

Jan. 1. Mr. Rose to Lord Castlereagh, communicating miscellaneous information 98

4. Mr. C. Bagot to Lord Castlereagh, reporting communications with Mr. Adams relative to the Spanish American colonies, and to General Jackson's invasion of Florida . . 99

22. Lord Castlereagh to Lord Clancarty, relative to the negociations at Frankfort 101

26. Mr. Rose to Lord Castlereagh, asking his advice for Count

1819. PAGE

Bernstorf, respecting a letter from the King of Sweden to the King of Prussia 102

Jan. 30. Mr. Rose to Lord Castlereagh, to the same purport as the preceding 103

Feb. 2. Lord Clancarty to Lord Castlereagh, representing the state of the negociators at Frankfort . . . 104

11. Count de Ludolf to Lord Castlereagh, conveying his Neapolitan Majesty's acknowledgments to the Prince Regent for the communication of the Acts of the Congress of Aix, and the King's firm determination to adhere to his engagements with his Allies the Sovereigns of Great Britain and Austria 106

Mar. 1. The Marquis d'Osmond to Lord Castlereagh, enclosing Extracts of a Letter from the Duc de Richelieu, relative to the plot for assassinating the Duke of Wellington . 108

5. Lord Cathcart to Lord Castlereagh, thanking him for his (Feb. 21.) recommendation of his son for a diplomatic appointment 109

6. Mr. C. Bagot to Lord Castlereagh, signifying his probable return to England in the ensuing month, and adverting to the treaty concluded by the United States with Spain . 111

12. Mr. Joseph Planta to Lord Castlereagh, relative to the Persian Embassy, then on its way to England, enclosing Memoranda respecting its probable objects and expenses 112

19. Mr. Planta to Lord Castlereagh, conveying a second proposition concerning the Persian Embassy . ⁛ 119

Apr. 7. Mr. C. Bagot to Lord Castlereagh, announcing the purposed visit of a Mr. Lowndes to England . . 120

7. Mr. C. Bagot to Lord Castlereagh, reporting the substance of a conversation with Mr. Adams relative to the Spanish American Colonies 121

May Lord Cathcart to Lord Castlereagh, transmitting a speci-
13-1. men of a new Russian Bank paper, with particulars relative to its preparation 123

20-8. Lord Cathcart to Lord Castlereagh, communicating the intended mission of Count Capodistrias to France and England, and adverting to the probable movements of the Emperor 126

28. Lord Strangford to Lord Castlereagh, reporting the accession of the Swedish Government to the propositions for an arrangement with Denmark . . . 127

June 24. Lord Cathcart to Lord Castlereagh, reporting the mission of Count d'Oserey to St. Petersburg . . . ib.

28. Lord Cathcart to Lord Castlereagh, notifying the arrival at

1819.

PAGE

St. Petersburg of intelligence of the prospect of an amicable settlement between Sweden and Denmark . 128

July 1. Mr. Antrobus to Lord Castlereagh, communicating information respecting an expedition preparing by the American Government for exploring the country westward of the United States to the Pacific Ocean . . . 129

10. Sir Robert Liston to Lord Castlereagh, expressing his willingness to remain at his post so long as there was more than routine business to be performed, otherwise, wishing to be recalled in about a year . . . 131

21-9. Lord Cathcart to Lord Castlereagh, referring to Russian documents previously transmitted through Count Lieven, and enclosing an Extract of a despatch from Count d'Engeström to M. de Brandel, expressing the sincere satisfaction of the King of Sweden at the cessation of the differences between the Courts of Stockholm and St. Petersburg 133

August Lord Cathcart to Lord Castlereagh, referring to a circular
6-18. from St. Petersburg to London, Vienna, and Berlin, and to the desire of the Danes to include in the Convention an article to set at rest any question between Norway and Denmark not included in the Treaty of Kiel . . . 136

20. Lord Clancarty to Lord Castlereagh, reporting conversation with M. Falck on the views of his Government in the Eastern seas—referring to the proposed expedition to the coast of Barbary, and to his return to England . . ib.

23. Lord Castlereagh to Sir Charles Stuart, acknowledging receipt of his despatch relative to the claims of the Princess of Montfort, and stating the decided opinion of the Prince Regent that the Treaty of Fontainebleau had been annulled by the subsequent conduct of Bonaparte . 138

24. Sir H. Wellesley to Lord Castlereagh, holding out a prospect of an amicable termination of the negociations between Spain and Portugal, as far as they related to the territory occupied by the Portuguese troops . . 139

28. Count Capodistrias to Lord Castlereagh, transmitting papers on the state of the Ionian Islands . . . 140

28. Lord Castlereagh to Lord Bathurst, relative to the complaints of Capodistrias respecting the Ionian Islands, and enclosing a letter to Lord Castlereagh from the Emperor of Russia on the same subject . . . 141

31. Lord Strangford to Lord Castlereagh, announcing that the next day was fixed for the signature of the Convention between Sweden and Denmark . . . 144

Sept. 3. Lord Bathurst to Lord Castlereagh, giving an account

1819.　　　　　　　　　　　　　　　　　　　　PAGE

　　　of the visit of Capodistrias and Lieven to him in the
　　　country　.　　.　　.　　.　　.　144

Sept. 7. Lord Castlereagh to the Marquis de la Tour-Maubourg,
　　　conveying information respecting Admiral Fremantle and
　　　the English squadron at Toulon　.　　.　　.　146

　.7. Baron Fagel to Lord Castlereagh, enclosing a letter from
　　　Baron Nagell on the affairs of India　.　　.　147

　8. Lord Castlereagh to Baron Fagel, in reply to the preceding　ib.

　8. Lord Castlereagh to Lord Bathurst, approving of the course
　　　which he proposed to pursue in regard to the Ionian
　　　business　.　　.　　.　　.　　.　148

22. Rev. Dr. Curtis to Lord Castlereagh, notifying his appoint-
　　　ment by the Pope as Bishop of Armagh, and professing
　　　his determination to employ all his influence for promoting
　　　peace, concord, and a spirit of conciliation, rather than
　　　controversy, among all classes of people　.　　.　ib.

22-10. Lord Cathcart to Lord Castlereagh, referring to the with-
　　　holding of the payment due by France to Austria till the
　　　latter should liquidate French claims, and to his approach-
　　　ing departure from Russia　.　　.　　.　149

29. Mr. Jacob Bosanquet to Lord Castlereagh, referring to the
　　　alteration of the tariff at Constantinople; soliciting the
　　　appointment of a King's Commissioner for Mr. Cartwright,
　　　Consul General of the Levant Company; expressing ap-
　　　prehensions respecting the state of the country; and
　　　recommending his son for diplomatic employment　.　150

Oct. 7. Lord Strangford to Lord Castlereagh, conveying the ex-
　　　pression of his gratitude to his lordship for his recom-
　　　dation and to the Prince Regent for his appointment to a
　　　new post, and referring to the proposal of a new tariff at
　　　Stockholm　.　　.　　.　　.　　.　153

　9. Lord Cathcart to Lord Castlereagh, expressing his acknow-
　　　ledgment for the marks of confidence and friendly interest
　　　conferred on him for so many years; adverting to his
　　　homeward journey, and to the Emperor's sentiments re-
　　　specting Conferences　.　　.　　.　　.　154

12. Sir William à Court to Lord Castlereagh, conveying his
　　　most sincere thanks for the distinction of the Bath, and
　　　expressing a wish to be brought nearer home　.　155

17. Count Münster to Lord Castlereagh, remarking on German
　　　politics　.　　.　　.　　.　　.　156

Nov. 13. Mr. Louis Casamajor (Secretary of Legation at St. Peters-
　　　burg) to Lord Castlereagh, accounting for the detention
　　　of the messenger with answers to the important matter
　　　contained in Lord Castlereagh's late despatches; and

1819.   **PAGE**

       adverting to the sentiments of the Russian Cabinet in regard to the Spanish and Portuguese negociations   . 157

Nov. 25. Sir Robert Liston to Lord Castlereagh, acknowledging, with sentiments of cordial gratitude, the terms in which he communicated the Prince Regent's permission to retire from public life   .   .   .   158

       Statement of the arrest of General Gourgaud, and execution of the order of the Prince Regent for his departing the kingdom   159

Dec. 29. M. Neumann, Austrian Chargé d'Affaires, to Lord Castlereagh, referring to despatches previously transmitted, expressing the desire of his Government to act in concert with the British Cabinet in regard to the mediation between Spain and Portugal   .   .   161

    29. The Hon. F. Lamb to Mr. Planta, adverting to the instructions of Russia to her agents relative to German affairs . 162

    30. Prince Hardenberg to Lord Castlereagh, animadverting on the policy of Russia in relation to the affairs of Germany 162

1820.

AFFAIRS OF THE CONTINENTAL STATES OF EUROPE IN GENERAL, AND OF SPAIN AND NAPLES IN PARTICULAR—CONFERENCES OF TROPPAU—ADOPTION OF THE PRINCIPLE OF ARMED INTERVENTION BY THE ALLIED MONARCHS.

1820.   **PAGE**

— Jan. 4. The Hon. F. Lamb to Lord Castlereagh, referring to a Circular of Russia to her Ministers, and to the policy of that Power in German affairs; and enclosing conversations with Anstett, the Russian Minister   .   .   165

    6. Sir H. Wellesley to Lord Castlereagh, on the affairs of Spain 170

    9. Sir H. Wellesley to Lord Castlereagh, adverting to the reported conspiracy in the expeditionary army .   .   171

   11. Sir H. Wellesley to Lord Castlereagh, adverting to the insurrection of the military .   .   .   172

— 15. Lord Castlereagh to Prince Hardenberg, referring to the Prince Regent's reply to the overtures of Russia, and to the state of affairs in Paris   .   :   173

   15. Lord Castlereagh to Mr. George Rose, enclosing the preceding letter to Prince Hardenberg, with instructions .   174

   25. Lord Clancarty to Lord Castlereagh, reporting the desire of the Netherlands' Government to postpone the Eastern negociation   175

1820.   PAGE

Jan. 26. Baron Fagel to Lord Castlereagh, with enclosure from
         Baron de Nagel, on the same subject as the preceding . 176

     26. Extract of a despatch from Prince Metternich to M. de
         Neumann conveying instructions relative to a declaration
         to be drawn up at the request of the Portuguese Am-
         bassador   177

Jan. 26. Count Lieven to Lord Castlereagh, communicating French
         translations of two letters of his lordship's   .   . 178

     14. Lord Castlereagh to Count Lieven, on the affairs of Germany   ib.

     14. Lord Castlereagh to Lord Stuart, concerning Continental
         affairs, with instructions regarding Austria   .   . 184

         Lord Castlereagh to Count Capodistrias, confuting com-
         plaints of discontented persons in the Ionian Islands   . 190

Feb. 4. Lord Castlereagh to Sir Charles Stuart, explaining the sub-
         ject of conferences between Great Britain and Russia   . 209

     13. Lord Castlereagh to Lord Stewart communicating the
         King's determination on the subject of a divorce from the
         Queen, and the sentiments of his Ministers on the subject 210

     25. Lord Clancarty to Lord Castlereagh, on the apprehended
         change of Ministers   214

Mar. 4. Mr. G. H. Rose to Lord Castlereagh, announcing the inten-
         tion of the Prussian Court to send a mission to compliment
         George IV. on his accession; enclosing letters from M.
         Ancillon and Prince Hardenberg   ·.   .   . 216

     7. Prince Metternich to Lord Castlereagh, on the danger to
         be apprehended from the influence of France .   . 219

     13. Sir H. Wellesley to Lord Castlereagh, on an absurd report
         relative to the Duke of Wellington   .   ·.   221

     20. Sir H. Wellesley to Lord Castlereagh reporting the recall
         of the Duke of San Carlos   .   .   . 222

     30. Sir Charles Stuart to Lord Castlereagh, on the changes in
         the French Cabinet   .   .   .   . ib.

     31. Prince Hardenberg to Lord Castlereagh, enclosing the copy
         of a despatch from Count de Goltz .   .   . 223

     31. Mr. G. H. Rose to Lord Castlereagh, relative to a despatch
         from Count de Goltz, containing Spanish and French in-
         telligence; and vindicating Sir Charles Stuart from impu-
         tations conveyed therein 234

April 1. Mr. G. H. Rose to Lord Castlereagh, detailing the opinions
         of several statesmen in Berlin relative to the affairs of
         Spain and Portugal   236

     7. Cardinal Consalvi to Lord Castlereagh, advising him of pro-
         posed movements of the Queen   .   .   . 239

     10. Lord Castlereagh to the Duke de Richelieu, transmitting
         copies of two letters of a mysterious character   . ib.

1820.   PAGE

April 17. The Duke de Richelieu to Lord Castlereagh, relative to two letters concerning a plan for promoting the escape of Napoleon from St. Helena 240

17. Lord Castlereagh to George IV., enclosing for his signature a proposed letter to the King of Spain . . 242

17-29. Sir Daniel Bayley to Joseph Planta, Jun., Esq., relative to a ukase for granting a drawback on cottons imported into Russia . . . . . *ib.*

20. Mr. Hamilton to Lord Castlereagh, conveying his opinion of the conduct and sentiments of Sir Charles Stuart; and enclosing a letter from him to Lord Castlereagh in his own vindication, and the copy of one from Sir H. Wellesley to Sir Charles Stuart . . . 243

24. Lord Castlereagh to the Duke de Richelieu, respecting the supposed scheme relative to Napoleon, referred to in former letters 251

24. Sir Charles Stuart to Lord Castlereagh, reporting the substance of an interview with the Duke de Richelieu . 252

27. Sir Charles Stuart to Lord Castlereagh, returning the copies of papers which had passed between the Allied Courts 253

30. Lord Castlereagh to George IV., submitting the sentiments of his Ministers on Continental affairs . . 255

May 1. The Duke de Richelieu to Lord Castlereagh, thanking him for the original letters; and complimenting him upon the example set by the British Parliament . . 257

6. Lord Castlereagh to Prince Metternich, on the improved state of affairs in Great Britain; and on the course likely to be pursued by the Queen . . . 258

9. Lord Clancarty to Lord Castlereagh, announcing his approaching departure from the Hague . . 260

12. Lord Castlereagh to Sir Charles Stuart, conveying instructions for his guidance in his intercourse with the Duke de Richelieu . . . . . *ib.*

12. Lord Castlereagh to Prince Hardenberg, vindicating the policy of the British Government . . . 261

15. Sir H. Wellesley to Lord Castlereagh, on the affairs of Spain 262

28. The Hon. F. Lamb to Lord Castlereagh, reporting the perfect tranquillity and improved state of affairs in the South of Germany; and accounting for the disaffection of the Tyrolese towards Austria . . . 263

29. The Hon. F. Lamb to Lord Castlereagh, on the state of public opinion in Hesse-Darmstadt . . . 268

June 2. Lord Castlereagh to Sir H. Wellesley, on the critical state of affairs in Spain . . . . *ib.*

. 1820. PAGE

June 6. Lord Clancarty to Lord Castlereagh, detailing a private
interview with the King of the Netherlands . . 270

26. The Hon F. Lamb to Lord Castlereagh, enclosing communications relative to the affairs of Germany . . 272

July 5. Extract of a despatch from Sir William à Court, on the defection of the Neapolitan army . . . 278

6. Sir William à Court to Lord Castlereagh, on the same subject as the preceding 279

17. Prince Castelcicala to Prince [no address], on the disastrous
events at Naples, and their probable consequences ib.

19-31. Sir Charles Bagot to Lord Castlereagh, transmitting copies
of papers communicated to him by Count Nesselrode . 280

24. Sir H. Wellesley to Lord Castlereagh, on Spanish affairs . 282

29. Lieut.-Col. Browne to Lord Castlereagh, on the revolutionary spirit prevailing in Italy . . . 283

Aug. 21. Count Lieven to Lord Castlereagh, enclosing copies of
despatches transmitted from St. Petersburg . . 285

26. Lord Castlereagh to Sir William à Court, on the affairs of
Naples and Sicily 295

26. Sir Charles Bagot to Lord Castlereagh, detailing an inter-
(Sept. 7.) view with Count Nesselrode . . . 296

27. The Hon. F. Lamb to Lord Castlereagh, announcing a
report made to a German Court relative to the extension
of the spirit of the Carbonari in Italy . . 298

29. Lieut.-Col. Browne to Lord Castlereagh, communicating
intelligence respecting the insurrection in Sicily . 299

Sept. 1. The Hon. F. Lamb to Lord Castlereagh, on the state of the
fortresses of the German Confederation . . 300

4-16. Sir Charles Bagot to Lord Castlereagh, relative to a despatch
received from M. Saldanha, as to the object of certain
secret societies ; and detailing the reception of the Duke
of Serracapriola at Vienna . . . 301

7. Sir H. Wellesley to Lord Castlereagh, on insurrectionary
movements in Spain and Portugal . . . 302

10. Lieut.-Col. Browne to Lord Castlereagh, on the departure
from Milan of the Neapolitan Consul . . 303

10. Lt.-Col. Browne to Lord Castlereagh, soliciting the appointment of military reporter at the Austrian head-quarters . 304

11. Extract of a despatch from the Duc de Laval on the re-
establishment of tranquillity at Madrid . ib.

13-25. Sir Charles Bagot to Lord Castlereagh, on Continental affairs 307

16. Lieut.-Col Browne to Lord Castlereagh, on the movements
of the Austrians 309

16. The Hon. F. Lamb to Lord Castlereagh, containing M. Anstett's opinions relative to Naples . . . 310

1820.   PAGE

Sept. 16. Lord Castlereagh to Lord Stewart stating his views as to the
    policy which ought to be pursued by the Allied Powers .   311

17-29. Sir Charles Bagot to Lord Castlereagh, exhibiting the
    views of M. Brusasco, the Sardinian Minister, relative to
    the designs of Austria against Italy   .   .   318

21. The Hon. F. Lamb to Lord Castlereagh, referring ot papers
    communicated to him by Anstett   .   .   .   320

Oct. 7. Sir Charles Bagot to Lord Castlereagh, enclosing copies of
(Sept. 25.) papers placed in his hands by the Portuguese Minister .   322

9. Mr. Stratford Canning to Lord Castlereagh, reporting the
    substance of a conversation with Mr. Adams on the Slave
    Trade   324

9. Sir H. Wellesley to Lord Castlereagh, on the pretensions
    of the Duc de Cadaval to the throne of Portugal   .   325

17. The Hon. F. Lamb to Lord Castlereagh, on the state of
    public feeling at Warsaw ; and referring to some inter-
    cepted letters   327

Nov. Sir Charles Bagot to Lord Castlereagh, enclosing the copy
7-19. of a despatch addressed by the new Government of
   -   Portugal to the Portuguese Minister at St. Petersburg .   328

9. Sir Charles Stuart to Lord Castlereagh, on the dulness at
    the French Court, and the King's intimacy with Madame
    de Cayla   329

Dec. 8. Circular relative to the first results of the Conferences of
    Troppau   330

15-27. Count Capodistrias to Count Lieven on the same subject .   333

15-27. Count Capodistrias to Count Lieven, on the same subject .   334

26. Lord Clancarty to Lord Castleragh, relative to the recall
    of Mr. Seymour   335

1821.

AFFAIRS OF SPAIN, PORTUGAL, NAPLES, GREECE, THE NETHER-
LANDS, RUSSIA—CONGRESS OF LAYBACH.

1821.   PAGE

Jan. 1. Extract of a letter from Lord Clancarty to Lord Castlereagh,
    communicating the satisfaction of the King of the Nether-
    lands with his lordship's despatches to Vienna and Naples   337

3. Sir Charles Bagot to Lord Castlereagh, conveying intelli-
(Dec. 22) gence from St. Petersburg   .   .   .   338 -

5. Extract of a letter from Lord Castlereagh to Lord Stewart,
    on the policy of Austria relative to Naples   .   .   340 -

5. Lord Clancarty to Lord Castlereagh, reporting his conver-
    sation with M. Falck on the Slave Trade   .   .   341

1820. PAGE

Claims of British Officers, lately in the service of Portugal, on the Government of that country . 343

Jan. 6. Sir G. H. Rose to Lord Castlereagh, on his indisposition . 349

— 6. The Hon F. Lamb to Lord Castlereagh, on the policy of Austria in regard to Naples . . . *ib.*

— 8. Sir William à Court to Lord Castlereagh, on the affairs of Naples 351

14. Mr. Edward Ward to Lord Castlereagh, on the state of parties in Portugal . . . 352

— 19. Lord Castlereagh to Sir William à Court, transmitting the the copy of a letter from the King of Sicily to George IV. 354

20. Mr. T. Musgrave to Marshal Beresford, on the state of the army in Portugal, and the political aspect of affairs in that country . . . . . *ib.*

Précis of a Russian Memoir on the Conferences in London, on the Slave Trade and the Barbary Powers . . 358

27. Sir H. Wellesley to Lord Castlereagh, on his approaching departure from Madrid . . . 361

30. The Hon. F. Lamb to Lord Castlereagh, enclosing the extract of a despatch from Baron Anstett to his Court, on German affairs 362

Feb. 7. Lord Castlereagh to Sir William à Court, on a proposed reduction of the naval force in the Mediterranean; and referring to Parliamentary proceedings respecting the Queen 364

8. Sir H. Wellesley to Lord Castlereagh, on the affairs of Spain . . . . *ib.*

8. Sir H. Wellesley to Lord Castlereagh, on a report circulated by the Infanta, wife of Don Carlos . . 365

21. Lord Burghersh to Lord Castlereagh, referring to a despatch containing instructions for his guidance . . 366

— 24. The Hon. F. Lamb to Lord Castlereagh, communicating the subjects of Russian letters relative to the affairs of Naples 367

— 25. Sir H. Wellesley to Lord Castlereagh, on the affairs of Naples and Spain . . . 369

— 25. The Hon. R. Gordon to Lord Castlereagh, on the plan for re-constructing the Italian Government . 370

26-18. Mr. Thomas Robinson to Thomas Lach, Esq., expressing his opinion on the intention of the Government of Naples to impose new duties on trade in general . . 373

— Mar. 24. The Hon. F. Lamb to Lord Castlereagh, respecting a Russian Circular, on the strength of the Austrian Army, &c. 374

27. Lord Clancarty to Lord Castlereagh, on his desired audience with the King of the Netherlands respecting the Slave

1821.

PAGE

Trade Treaty; and enclosing copy of his second note to
M. de Nagell 379

Mar. 31. Mr. W. Kenny to Lord Castlereagh, enclosing copy of Sir
William à Court's Note to the King of Sicily, on the sentiments of Great Britain towards that Island . . 381

April 3. The Hon. F. Lamb to Lord Castlereagh, on the public feeling
in Germany relative to Naples . . 385

3. Mr. Edward Thornton to Lord Castlereagh, on the Count
de Palmella's approaching return to Europe . . 386

5. Mr. Edward Thornton to Lord Castlereagh, relating a conversation with Count de Palmella . . . 387

10-22. Sir Charles Bagot to Joseph Planta, Esq., containing intelligence from St. Petersburg, &c. . . . 388

13. Lord Beresford to the Marquess of Londonderry, alluding
to the receipt of news from the Brazils . . 390

17. Lord Clancarty to the Marquess of Londonderry, on the
conduct of the King of the Netherlands . . 391

May 4. Prince Esterhazy to Lord Castlereagh, expressive of his
sentiments, and high regard for his lordship . . 392

7. Mr. Edward Thornton to Lord Castlereagh, relating his
conversation with the King of Portugal on the Slave
Trade 393

13. The Hon. R. Gordon to Lord Castlereagh, on European
politics 396

18-30. Sir Charles Bagot to the Marquess of Londonderry, containing intelligence from St. Petersburg . . 397

21. Sir Charles Bagot to Joseph Planta, Esq., containing news
(June 2.) from St. Petersburg . . . 398

June 5. Mr. Lionel Hervey to the Marquess of Londonderry, on
the state of affairs in Spain . . 399

17. Mr Lionel Hervey to the Marquess of Londonderry, on the
influence of the Cortes 401

28. Mr. Lionel Hervey to the Marquess of Londonderry, on the
breach between the King of Spain and his Ministers . 402

July 16. The Marquess of Londonderry to the Emperor of Russia, on
the affairs of Turkey 403

26. Sir William à Court to the Marquess of Londonderry, enclosing his remarks on Lord W. Bentinck's speech on the
the affairs of Sicily 408

Aug. 3. Lord Clancarty to the Marquess of Londonderry, offering
suggestions for a conference between him and the King
of the Netherlands, on the Slave Trade . . 420

6-18. Sir Charles Bagot to Joseph Planta, Esq., relative to the
illness of Mr. Chamberlain . . . 422

14. Lord Clancarty to the Marquess of Londonderry, enclosing

1821.

PAGE

a Memorandum by the Duke of Wellington of a conversation between his Grace and the King of the Netherlands 242

Sept. 5-17. Sir Charles Bagot to the Marquess of Londonderry, chiefly on the expected War between Russia and Turkey . 429

22. Sir George Rose to the Marquess of Londonderry, principally on Russian affairs . . . 432

28. Mr. Edward Ward to the Marquess of Londonderry, on the proceedings of the Cortes . . . 437

Oct. 2. Lord Clancarty to M. le Comte de Herdt, accompanied by a box presented by George IV. to him . . 438

3. The Hon. R. Gordon to the Marquess of Londonderry, expressing Prince Metternich's desire to have an interview with his Britannic Majesty . . . 439

21. Lord Clancarty to Viscount Sidmouth, on his Majesty's proposed visit to Brussels . . . 441

26. Prince Metternich to the Marquess of Londonderry, on Prussian affairs . . . 442

Dec. 14. The Marquess or Londonderry to Sir Charles Bagot, on the affairs of Greece; and the spread of the revolutionary movement both in Europe and America . 443

18. Mr. Lionel Hervey to the Marquess of Londonderry, on the disgraceful proceedings in the Cortes . . 446

1822.

MISCELLANEOUS.

1822.

PAGE

Jan. 18. Lord Clancarty to the Marquess of Londonderry, on the instructions of the Government of the Netherlands to its Colonies 448

22. Lord Clancarty to the Marquess of Londonderry, containing intelligence from the Hague . . 449

Mar. 25. The Hon. R. Gordon to the Marquess of Londonderry, enclosing a note from Prince Metternich, relating the result of his interview with the Russian Ministers . 450

April 6. Mr. Lionel Hervey to the Marquess of Londonderry, on the conduct of the King of Spain . . . 453

Lord Burghersh to the Marquess of Londonderry, vindicating himself from an accusation in respect to his note to Courts to which he was accredited . . 454

9. The Rev. Dr. Poynter to the Marquess of Londonderry, on liquidating the claims of British subjects on the French Government 458

1822.   PAGE

May 2. Robert Sutherland, Esq., to the Marquess of Londonderry,
on the state of affairs in Hayti . . . 461

16-28. Sir Charles Bagot to the Marquess of Londonderry, on the
affairs of Russia and Turkey . . . 465 ◎

31. Captain Irby, R. N. to the Marquess of Londonderry, enclosing a statement of the claims of certain Naval Officers
employed on the coast of Africa, from 1811 to 1815 . 467

June 3. Lord Clancarty to the Marquess of Londonderry, on the
absence of Mr. Eliot, one of his attahhés; enclosing letter
from his father 474

July 4. The Hon. F. Lamb to the Marquess of Londonderry, on
his proposed excursion . . 476

20. Mr. John Lowe to the Marquess of Londonderry, on the
subject of Trade to Columbia . . . 476

LETTERS AND DESPATCHES

OF

LORD CASTLEREAGH.

___

1818 CONTINUED.

CONGRESS OF AIX-LA-CHAPELLE.

Lord Castlereagh to Lord Liverpool.

Dover, September 2, 1818.

My dear Liverpool—I send you some despatches from my brother, which show enough of the Austrian views to satisfy me that we shall have no difficulty with her. I do not expect much good from Metternich's secret negociation at Paris, and should not wish myself to be mixed in it. The less a British Minister dabbles in Monsieur's politics the better.

Do you see any objection to Charles coming to Aix, as he can *do nothing* at Vienna, and Metternich urges it? I am rather disposed to bring him there. He will be of considerable use to me in keeping Metternich *steady*, and apprising me what he is about. He could also undertake to *furnish you* with a private bulletin of all details, anecdotes, &c. On his own private concerns, it would be an object, as correspondence with Vienna is slow, and unsafe by post. I also feel that, as the Queen is more likely to drop than when we talked over this point, and the appeal may be approaching, there may be many things to decide connected with these proceedings which

I would rather not have the responsibility of deciding in his absence. In truth, I have too many other things to think of. I see no difficulty, as far as concerns our other Ambassadors. Charles, at Aix, is with the Court to which he is accredited; at Vienna, he is utterly useless. Clancarty has his own duty, and no unimportant one, in the Netherlands. Cathcart has decided the point, as you will see, for himself. If, therefore, you concur, I will write to him to come, though certainly contrary to my first intentions. His presence there, I think, cannot be open to any criticism to which the Austrian invitation is not a full answer. In truth, he may be of considerable use there—none, where he otherwise would be.

Ever, my dear Liverpool, &c.,   CASTLEREAGH.

Lord Liverpool to Lord Castlereagh.

London, September 4, 1818.

My dear Castlereagh—The despatches from Vienna are upon the whole satisfactory. I augur no good from Metternich's negociation with Monsieur, and I am very glad you are to be in no way involved in it.

I think you will have no difficulty in keeping the Emperor of Russia from coming here in November; this visit might certainly lead to intrigues, and would, at all events, be very inconvenient; and, from Cathcart's account, he has enough to occupy him at home.

The Queen continues much the same: the disorder gains ground, and it is apprehended that she cannot last many days.

Believe me to be, &c.,   LIVERPOOL.

Mr. James Stephen[1] to Lord Castlereagh.

Kensington Gore, September 8, 1818.

My Lord—Availing myself of your lordship's obliging permission to send you such suggestions as might occur to me

---

[1] Mr. Stephen, a native of the West Indies, was sent at an early age to England, to pursue the profession of the law. By means of a matri-

respecting the interests of the great African cause at the approaching Congress, and the Haytian case in connexion with them, I have drawn up the enclosed paper solely for your lordship's consideration, and beg leave to request your perusal of it. Its length, though great, is not beyond its importance, if any of its reasonings are just ; yet I would abridge it, to save your lordship's time, but for the disadvantage of delay.

The same consideration induces me to send the rough draft as it has come from my own slovenly pen ; for a friend in the house with me, who has been keeping up with me in a copy, has made, though a neater, a much less legible manuscript. I do not like to wait for better clerical help ; I hope, therefore, that your lordship will kindly excuse all its defects.

I called at your house in St. James's Square, the 1st inst., with two Haytian pamphlets, which I left in a parcel, finding that your lordship was engaged, and was soon to set off for your seat in Kent, without returning to town. I hope they were put up, as I desired, with such papers as you might take in your carriage ; for, if your lordship had not before seen them, they may convey useful information as to the state of affairs in Hayti, and I cannot help thinking many of De Vastey's arguments not unworthy of your perusal.

Clarkson still holds his purpose of going to Aix-la-Chapelle, and an address which he means to present to the Emperor of Russia is translating into French. A few copies are to be printed, (not published) and I shall take care that one of the first that is out of the press shall be sent to your lordship. He means to request the Emperor to present copies to the other Sovereigns. We mean also to enlighten the English public a little on the true nature and important bearings of the Haytian case ; but most of the topics and reasonings in the enclosed manuscript are unfit at present for public discussion.

monial alliance with the family of Mr. Wilberforce, he obtained a seat in Parliament, which he resigned on being appointed Master in Chancery, in order to attend to the duties of that office.

I would have submitted to your lordship some suggestions and facts also more immediately relative to the state of affairs in Africa; but I find that Mr. Macaulay, whose information on that branch of our cause is fuller and more accurate than mine, has communicated all that he thought material to Mr. Planta.

You will perceive that I am not unaware of the great difficulties your lordship will have to surmount in effecting anything for us of a decisive kind with Portugal and France. But so much the greater will be the honour of success, or rather let me say the conscious satisfaction and happiness you will derive from it; for, though I have reasoned chiefly or wholly upon political principles, I do your lordship the justice to believe you will feel, in this case, less as a politician than as a man, and I trust I may add, as a Christian.

   I have the honour to be, &c., JAMES STEPHEN.

PS. I will take the liberty of also putting up in this parcel a copy of my pamphlet on the right of compelling Spain to relinquish the Slave Trade in Northern Africa, as it contains several arguments applicable to the remaining questions with France and Portugal, and to what I humbly conceive to be the duties of the European Powers at the approaching Congress.

Suggestions relative to Africa and Colonial Discussions that may have place in the Congress at Aix-la-Chapelle.

HAYTI, OR ST. DOMINGO.

It would be of unspeakable importance to Great Britain, if means could be found to induce France to release her claim of sovereignty in Hayti, or, if this cannot be accomplished, at least to prevent her from asserting that claim by war. The reasons are chiefly these:

1st. If France is left in her present relations to Hayti when the Allied armies are withdrawn, it cannot be expected that she will persist in her present passive line of conduct, permitting

British and American merchants to enjoy without interruption
all the commerce of the country, while she herself derives
nothing from it but a barren title.   Her past forbearance has
probably proceeded from the difficulties of her situation, which
would have made even a blockade of the Haytian ports, and
much more a military invasion of the island, a more expensive
undertaking than she could well sustain.   There might be a
fear, too, of disputes with Great Britain or the United States
from the measures necessary to put a stop to their commerce
with Hayti; and these, while the Allied armies were in France,
might have been productive of much embarrassment and mortification.   No inference, at least, can be drawn from the past,
that she will acquiesce in the practical independence of a
country which she claims as a French colony, when the impediment and the excuse arising from the occupation of her
own territory by foreign armies shall have ceased.

2ndly. It is quite clear that, if Hayti is to be brought again
under the dominion of France, it must be by force of arms.
The voluntary submission of the Negroes cannot possibly be
expected. They know by dreadful experience the gross perfidy
and ruthless cruelty of those who were their former masters.
They will not, and they ought not, to distinguish in this
respect between submission to Buonaparte and submission to
Louis XVIII. In both cases, their inexorable enemies are
the French planters, to whom they once belonged. These
were the instigators of the First Consul; they are equally so
of the King; and these are enemies whom nothing can satisfy
but their submission, not only to the French sceptre, but to
the whip. The Mulattoes and the *anciens libres* among the
Negroes were weak enough to think that antipathy and disdain for their complexion at least might be worn out in the
bosoms of white colonists by the humbling lessons of adversity,
or, if not, would be restrained by the dictates of self-preser-
vation. They, therefore, trusted to the solemn engagements
of Leclerc, and helped him by force and fraud to place Tous-

saint under a necessity of accepting the treacherous pacification which cost him his life. But he was speedily revenged upon them by the perfidy of their French allies. The planters could not wait till they were safe for the indulgence of their inveterate and invincible antipathies, any more than for the recovery of their despotic authority on the plantations. They preferred destruction to equality of rights and society in arms with free Negroes and Mulattoes. They urged Leclerc and Rochambeau, if the latter monster, indeed, required solicitation, to adopt their own frantic views. The coloured leaders and officers were seized and cruelly butchered and destroyed, even in the very towns and forts which their arms had recently rescued from an infuriated enemy, and by the very men whom their bravery had preserved: torture, as well as death, was their reward, and all this without trial, without inquiry, without accusation even, or the rational suspicion of a crime. The only cause was that they had African blood in their veins, and that the men to whom they had given back their property and their power were West Indians. The history of human wickedness has nothing to compare with the horrible ingratitude, perfidy, and cruelty, of which they were the victims, or with the horrors that ensued. For the honour of human nature, one would wish to disbelieve, but the dreadful tale rests not on the credit of the Haytians. It is confirmed through every possible source of evidence. It has never been contradicted, either by the French Government or its agents. It has been publicly attested by some of the French officers who were eye-witnesses, and apparently also unwilling instruments, of those atrocious crimes. The pamphlet of Colonel Malenfaut especially will carry conviction home to the mind of any man who entertains a doubt on the subject.

Driven as the surviving Mulatto leaders and their followers were to cast themselves on the confidence and mercy of the Blacks, and to stimulate the latter to new efforts for their common preservation, the distinction between *les anciens* and *les nouveaux libres* was forgotten in the mutual danger and the mutual thirst for revenge. With their triumph and security it again in some degree revived. It has been the chief source of the schism between the Haytians of the South, under Petion, and those of the North, under Henri Christophe, and of the intestine war which, for several years, was carried on between them. Not that any large proportion of the Negroes in the South can now be *anciens libres*, or persons free before the revolution; but many of them were slaves of the Mulatto planters, and the rest, to whichever description they formerly belonged, have ranged themselves successively under Rigaud and Petion, from local or other attachments. Many also, it is said, have lately emigrated from the North to the South, from the allurements of that comparative laxity of military discipline and civil police which prevailed under Petion's government.

This distinction of parties and division of power has been supposed favourable to the counter-revolutionary purposes of France. But neutral persons, who have resided in the island, or obtained good information of its state, are of a contrary opinion. Though Petion was more moderate in his language than King Henry, both, it is believed, were equally determined rather to perish than ever again submit to the dominion of France. The only difference was that Petion was not indisposed to provide some modified indemnity to the ex-proprietors for the loss of their lands, which Henry indignantly refused. But Petion freely declared that, if he could possibly entertain a disposition to receive the French again into the island, it would be utterly impracticable, because the people under his government would unanimously revolt from him on the suspicion of any such design, and it would be fruitless of everything but his own destruction. There is abundant reason to believe that this is true not only of the Negroes but the remaining Mulattoes and all their leaders; and, indeed, from the experience they have had, it seems impossible that they

should be infatuated enough again to trust themselves and
their families to the faith of any white Government. The
perfidy of Leclerc and Rochambeau was only the last of the
terrible proofs they have had that the antipathy and hatred of
white Creoles towards their unfortunate race are quite incurable; and that, under every form and character of government in France, the influence of those inveterate enemies is
sure to prevail against them, at the expense even of the clearest
policy, as well as humanity and justice. To show the full
force of their experience in this respect, it would be necessary
to write the history of St. Domingo, from the first revolutionary movement to the present hour. The facts are too
little known, or rather they are radically misconceived in
Europe: but, when such a history shall be written by the
light of authentic public documents and other decisive evidence, it will show that all the calamities of the white colonists
—calamities by which they were at length crushed and overwhelmed—were the natural and well-merited effects of their
own crimes against the free people of colour. It will be seen
that St. Domingo was made a slaughter-house and a ruin, not
because slaves were allowed by law, or instigated by conspi-
rators to break their chains, but because white men in the
West Indies hate free Mulattoes more than they love property
or life. Had not the feeling been indulged on the part of *les
petits blancs*, (the white mob) at least to the most desperate
extremes, the insurrection of the slaves would never have taken
place, or would have been strangled at its birth. The Negroes
owed their liberty neither to the good-will of the Mulattoes nor
of the Convention. The former demonstrated to the utmost the
falsehood of their colonial dogma, opposed to all experience and
all reason, that the free coloured people are a dangerous class,
in respect of their natural affinity to the slaves. They proved
that their sympathies, as free men and masters, with their
paternal colour were infinitely stronger than those with their
maternal colour, flowing from the balanced feeling of native

extraction alone. They clung fondly, boldly, and obstinately, to the cause of the Whites, in spite of their contempt, until reiterated perfidy, proscription, and massacre, forced them to abandon it, and to leave those infatuated colonists to their fate.

As to the Convention, the enfranchisement of the Colonial slaves, or any improvement in their state by law, was no part of its innovations. It shrunk, in that instance, from its own principles. To the free of all colours it voted equality of rights, and sent out orders for the imparting that equality to the Mulattoes, and afterwards receded from, modified, retracted, renewed, those orders, with a fatal vacillation of policy, as the clamours of the white colonists (*who were for the most part very good Jacobins*) or the sense of what was due to its own avowed principles, alternately prevailed. But for the *slaves* nothing was done or attempted, till nothing remained to do. The Commissioners Santhonax and Poverel were sent out with legislative powers to conciliate, when the hour of conciliation was past; and, after those Commissioners had tried several other experiments in vain, the former, on whom the sole authority had devolved, wisely put law and liberty on the same side, when he found that bloodshed and anarchy were the only fruits of their opposition. He decreed freedom to the natives, when slavery existed no more. Toussaint had too much judgment to think himself indebted to the Republic for this tardy and constrained recognition of a title won from her by force. Policy, and a sense of duty perhaps also, led him from that time to be loyal to France under every existing Government, but his predilections, it is well known, were in favour of the Royalist party.

The Negroes and Mulattoes must now be equally convinced that any terms of conciliation which the French Government may offer cannot be sincere, if they comprise equality of civil privileges between the different colours, or the abolition of private slavery. They must be still more certain that, even if the Government were sincere in such terms, they would soon

be violated, unless the ex-proprietors and all Creole Frenchmen were prohibited from returning or settling in the island;
but this would be incompatible with the private interests, or
supposed interests, by which the royal counsels always have
been and always will be influenced in colonial affairs.   On the
whole, therefore, a determined resistance by arms to the sovereignty of France is and will be felt to be their only chance
of preserving property, private liberty, or even life itself.
They will be as unanimous and as desperate as they threaten
to be.   France must either acquiesce in their independence, or
plunge into a new Haytian war—a war which cannot be carried
on without means revolting to humanity, and can end only in
the final triumph of the Blacks or their entire extermination.
France, in this new war, will have still more formidable difficulties to conflict with than were found by Buonaparte. Toussaint
was found unprepared.   He had long vanquished his interior
enemies, and he reposed with confidence on the professions and
the laws, but still more, perhaps, on the obvious interests of
the Republic.   He was her Captain General and her faithful
subject.   He was rapidly restoring the island to prosperity for
her benefit.   His services had been acknowledged publicly,
and warmly eulogized in the State papers of Napoleon himself.
It is no impeachment, therefore, of the prudence of that illus-
trious African, that the hostile attack of the usurper took him
by surprise.   He knew the planters, indeed, but could not
rationally suppose that their blind avarice and foolish prejudices would be adopted by a Government that had the reputa-
tion of sagacity and prudence.

The case, in all points, is widely different now.   The Chiefs
both of the north and the south have always foreseen that the
peace of Europe would be the birth of a new French war for
them.   Nor have they been thrown off their guard by the long
pause of France since her last pacification with the Allies.
They comprehend its true causes. King Henry asserts, and it
is believed with truth, that an expedition was actually preparing

against him at the moment of Buonaparte's return from Elba.
He now asserts that he has intelligence from France of the
revival of that design, and that it will be carried into effect
soon after the Allied armies shall be withdrawn. His military
force, therefore, and other preparations, have been kept up and
increased. He knows his enemies, and all their means of annoyance. He knows well, also, from experience, his own
advantages in the climate and the physical qualities of his
troops: and his plan of defence is maturely digested, not
only in its principles but its practical details. Whether the
expectation of invasion is equally strong in the South is not
known; but the means of resistance are there also formidably
great, and the resolution to employ them with vigour and perseverance, and to endure all extremities rather than fall under
the French yoke again, is universal. Such, at least, is the
unanimous opinion of all who have visited the Haytian republic; and there is the same authority for believing that the first
appearance or known approach of a French armament will be
the signal for an immediate coalition between the rival Governments.

It seems probable that this interior schism, instead of
favouring the hostile purposes of France, has, in its consequences, been very propitious to the security of Haytian freedom, because it has obliged both parties to keep up and maintain in constant discipline large regular armies, with all their
necessary equipments and magazines; whereas, if they had
been at peace among themselves, and united under one head,
they would naturally, during the war in Europe, and the
known inability of France to annoy them, have reduced their
military establishments, and have been very sparing in the
purchase of ammunition and arms. It is worthy of remark,
too, that, since the peace in Europe opened to them the prospect of a new contest with France, they have wasted none of
their strength upon each other, but mutually abstained from
all attacks, though without any express agreement.

From these considerations it may with certainty be concluded that, if Hayti is to be re-annexed in possession to France, it must be through the medium of a very arduous and sanguinary war, in which the greater part, if not the whole, of the black population will be destroyed.

3rdly. In whatever way France may attempt the forcible recovery of this colony, the consequences of the attempt will be very disadvantageous to Great Britain, and productive not only of commercial loss but political inconveniences and dangers.

The smallest consideration, perhaps, is the loss of our existing trade with Hayti; and yet this is by no means an inconsiderable object. The exports from that country now are far greater in amount and value than those of any colony we have, Jamaica only excepted. It is difficult or impossible to ascertain the quantities of the coffee, sugar, cotton, and other commodities, annually sent from the various ports of the North and South collectively; but the Baron de Vastey, in a recent official publication, states the number of foreign vessels which loaded with produce at Cape Henry, in 1817, to have been a hundred and fifty, and estimates, from that datum, the whole number from the different ports of Hayti at between four and five hundred.[1] The tonnage is not given; but I have before me an Haytian Gazette of the 14th August, 1817, containing an official return of vessels entered at Cape Henry from the 1st January to the 4th August of that year, with their tonnage, &c., which amount to 70, and make an average of 122 tons, being 8,532 tons in all. The same return states them

---

[1] Reflexions Politiques, p. 79 :—" Ce qui doit étendre proportionnellement le nombre pour *Hayti* de quatre à cinq cens bâtiments." This loose way of expressing himself, by the *Secrétaire du Roi*, was probably intended to comprise the ports of the South, without noticing the indecorous fact that they were in the hands of those whom he must have called *rebels*, and that, therefore, though part of the kingdom of Hayti, he had no return of their trade.

to have exported 17,084,000 pounds of sugar and coffee, but without giving the proportions of each. If we adopt De Vastey's rule of estimate, this would give for all Hayti an export trade, employing 54,840 tons of shipping, and exporting, if they were all equally full, and laden with the same commodities, 109,826,000 pounds of sugar and coffee.   But at Gonaives, the other principal port of King Henry, and in the ports of the South, cotton and coffee are the chief articles of produce exported.   The estimate, also, in other respects, is obviously very loose, and the data, though official, may be suspected of exaggeration. Indeed, the results exceed probability; for the tonnage employed in the whole commerce of St. Domingo, at its most flourishing period, in 1788, if we except the African slave trade and the re-exportation of slaves to Cuba, was only 189,679 tons.   It seems not probable that the exports of the island now approach so near to one-third of the former maximum.

But, after every reasonable deduction shall be made, the commerce of Hayti will be seen to be of very great value, more especially to a manufacturing country, which can pay in its own fabrics for the produce it buys and exports. Jamaica employed in 1788, in all its branches of trade together, 400 vessels, containing together 78,862 tons, and the total value of the products exported by them was, by Mr. B. Edwards' estimate, £2,136,442, and the whole import in British manufactures is valued by him, from official returns, at £686,657. But by far the greater part of these, probably two-thirds, are re-exported to the Spanish and other foreign colonies—Jamaica, in consequence of her free ports and local situation, being the greatest entrepôt of that indirect trade with the South American continent and Cuba.   It would be a very large estimate to suppose that our sugar colonies in general consume in British manufactures and commodities of all kinds sent from this kingdom one-tenth part of the value of their exports; whereas our exports from Hayti are in general the proceeds of

British goods previously imported there for the interior supply and consumption of the island. It is true we at present divide the Haytian trade with the merchants of the United States, and, in some degree, with other foreigners also; but it is because we have been able to give to it no public sanction or encouragement, but, on the contrary, have subjected it to some disadvantageous restraints, and because the British merchants in general have been led, from the political situation of Hayti and calumnious accounts of the conduct of its Chiefs, to suppose the property they may place there in great danger, and the returns for their cargoes uncertain.

Such of them, however, as have made trial of this commerce are found to persevere in it, and their exports of British manufactures are said to have exceeded £700,000 per annum.[1] With the unequivocal and strong disposition manifested by King Henry, and even by the republican Government of the South, to cultivate connexions with England, and to give us commercial privileges at the expense of other nations, it would be our own fault if their recognized independence, or even such a tacit acquiescence in it as France has lately practised, did not soon put the entire trade of the island into our hands. We might, in that case, perhaps have, at no far distant period, a West Indian island worth more to our manufacturers than all our sugar colonies collectively, and without any drawback for the expenses of its government and its protection in time of war.

The political considerations are of much greater moment. They may be more clearly examined by dividing them under three distinct heads of inquiry, viz.:

1st. What consequences affecting Great Britain may be expected from a new war between Hayti and France?

2nd. What would be those consequences in the event of

---

[1] This is taken as the medium of different estimates. I have heard them estimated, by an eminent merchant engaged in the trade, at a million sterling.

France being again repulsed and obliged to abandon the war?

3rd. What in the opposite event?

The first question respects the contest itself, independently of its issue. In all human probability, the struggle would not be short. It would be sustained by national pride on the part of France, however at the outset unpropitious to her object, and long perhaps after a rational hope of final success had failed, unless a foreign quarrel intervened to save her from the mortification of yielding to the unsupported efforts of those whom she calls her own rebellious subjects. But the shortest possible term of the contest would suffice to place us in very embarrassing circumstances. We should in the first place be called upon to abandon all intercourse with the Haytian people, which would be not only to renounce their present amity and predilection, with the commercial advantages that have been noticed, and to transfer them probably to America, but to sacrifice perhaps no small amount of British property already in the hands or within the power of the Haytian Government.

A maritime blockade would, of course, either as preliminary to or concurrent with a military invasion, be one of the first measures on the part of France, and would be enforced by her ships of war in the most rigorous way. Our own precedents and rules of naval blockade, during the two late wars, though consonant to the true principles of international law, were never before so fully drawn out into practice, would be put in action against us. Our merchantmen and ships of war would have to learn their duties as *patients*, under a system in which we have hitherto only been the *active practitioners*. From the course of our Jamaica trade, and still more from that which we now carry on with the agitated Spanish settlements on the Main, it would hardly be possible to avoid the suspicion, in numberless cases, of a blockade-breaking intention, and thereby justifying not only visitation and search, but detention and carrying into port. The fraudulent use of our flag by Americans, by the vessels of the Spanish insurgents, and others, would multiply the causes of interruption to our lawful trade, and the occasions of dispute with the French officers on the Haytian station, or with France herself. Meantime, it would be difficult at once to satisfy her with those offices of hospitality or amity which she might expect from us in the neighbouring ports of Jamaica, and to avoid more than the appearance of taking part with her, in the eyes both of the Haytians and the people of England; while the feelings of the latter would be outraged perhaps by the renewal of all the barbarous and unnatural atrocities of Rochambeau for the extirpation of an unfortunate and injured people, who could not otherwise be subdued into slavery.

We are now on the question of policy alone; but regard to the moral feelings of the country is not foreign to that consideration. It never was less so than in the times we live in, and may be still more important in times near at hand.

2nd. The consequences of a second and final repulsion of the French would be evil in comparison with the present state of things, because whatever is of a dangerous tendency in the existing circumstances of Hayti would be augmented, and whatever is advantageous to ourselves, or of good political promise, would be diminished or lost. Military spirit would be inflamed among the Haytians, and that of pacific improvements, agricultural, commercial, and moral, would be lamentably checked and suspended, if not for ever extinguished. The now remaining buildings and plantation works would be destroyed; all the land still in culture would be laid waste; the schools would be broken up; the churches and other places of worship in ruins; the English and other European settlers, and Americans, who are now engaged there in commercial establishments, or in the beneficent work of advancing civilization and morals by instructing the Blacks in literature and the liberal arts, would have fled for safety from the seat of a ferocious war, if prudent enough to do so in time, or else have perished in a contest in which their complexions would continually expose them to mistaken popular vengeance on the one side, and their siding with rebels to civil or military execution on the other. Their fate would deter others from engaging hereafter in like pursuits.

But the Haytians would in future desire no such inmates. The ideas of a white man and a merciless enemy would be inseparable. Finding themselves again abandoned to the vengeance of France, after fifteen years of inoffensive conduct towards all their neighbours had proved that their independence was not, as their enemies falsely pretended, incompatible with the peace of the West Indies; finding that all their predilection for England, and anxious endeavours to cultivate our friendship, had not obtained for them one effort from us, to avert a new exterminatory war; and that our conduct in it was perhaps rather that of an enemy than a fair and impartial neutral; they would see that they had no security to hope for from the good will of any European Power who has colonies in the Antilles, but least of all from England. They would either abstain from all intercourse with the Whites of an amicable kind, reverse their present maxims by receiving and protecting fugitive slaves from the neighbouring islands, and by a piratical system perhaps build their future strength and security, like the Barbary Powers, on the fears of their commercial neighbours; or they would seek for alliance and protection in the self-interest of some country not governed by colonial prejudices, and give to it the advantages which we had undervalued and renounced. It is probable that the state of the New World, if not that of Europe, would give them the choice of such connexions; or even France herself, making at last a virtue of necessity, might possibly, by a recognition of their independence and the guarantee of it against other Powers, regain their commerce, and even form with them an alliance for mutual assistance in war. Such an alliance, it may be demonstrated, would make her potentially mistress of

Jamaica, whenever she chose to draw the sword against this country. Indeed, the subsidiary arms of the Haytians would give to any maritime Power that could gain even a local and temporary superiority at sea in that part of the world, a certain and easy conquest of any slave colony she might choose to invade, though Jamaica and Cuba would be the most inviting and readiest prey. Whether the Spanish colonies on the Main will be able to establish their independence seems at least extremely doubtful. If they are, Cuba will soon either become their associate or a most troublesome enemy, whom, for the sake of their commerce, at least, if not for their security, they will make every effort to annoy and reduce. To these new States, therefore, Hayti would be a most invaluable ally. But her attachment will soon be bidden for in the opposite event of the Continental struggle, or in any event, perhaps, by a new maritime Power, now in her close vicinage, and not very scrupulous as to the means of gratifying its ambition. The United States of America, now the possessors of Florida and the angry rivals of England, can have no object of policy in the Mexican Gulf so important, whether in the view of annoying England and Spain in future wars, or of securing and extending their own recent usurpations, or of wresting from England hereafter the trade and territory she possesses in the Antilles, as that of obtaining a *point d'appui* in Hayti, more especially if, to the use of its ports as an ally for belligerent purposes could be added the occasional aid of its hardy and formidable troops in attacks upon neighbouring colonies.

Without looking forward more distinctly to probable results from the interesting and critical circumstances of the Western world, we may fairly conclude that Hayti, independent and hostile to England, or disaffected to her and connected with her enemies or rivals, would form a most inconvenient and dangerous novelty in our West Indian position and prospects. The importance of these considerations is greatly enhanced by an approaching consequence of the known situation of the planters and merchants of the Bahamas. The former class, indeed, has almost ceased to exist. They are *proprietors* of lands and slaves, but for the most part *planters* no more. Agriculture is nearly abandoned in all those numerous islands. The soil, after various fruitless experiments, is found utterly unfit for any one of the tropical staples. It is so shallow and barren, that it will yield neither sugar, nor coffee, nor cotton. It is indeed a gross misrepresentation to add (as the Bahama planters have done, in order to obtain permission to remove their slaves to Guiana) that the means of sustaining themselves are gone, and that they and their Negroes had no alternative to famine but migration: for the soil can and does produce a sufficiency of Indian corn, potatoes, yams, and other indigenous articles of food; and the sea, in their numerous channels, abounds with the finest fish. But it cannot be expected that the owners of slaves will be content to employ them merely in earning a subsistence for themselves, or even such a surplus as may give to the masters a bare supply of the necessaries of life, while they may be removed to other places, where they may be sold or employed to much better account. It may, therefore, with certainty be foreseen that the emigration which has begun will rapidly proceed, till the whole cluster of those islands, with the exception perhaps of New Providence, will be nearly unpeopled. The exception will be of no great importance, for that seat of Government, though dependent chiefly on commerce, is also in a rapid and incurable decline. The trade which was connected with agriculture has, of course, shared in its ruin, and much that was incidental to the war is now at a stand. The merchants, therefore, as well as the planters, are quitting the hopeless field. The public establishments at New Providence may still give bread to a few, and require a small portion of import trade to supply the garrison and civil officers with their families. But, in the other islands, the population will probably soon be reduced to a few

wreckers, *i.e.* the owners and crews of small vessels and boats,
which are employed in saving the cargoes or fragments of ships
that are wrecked in their very dangerous and intricate channels. These men, by the profits of salvage, and sometimes by
plunder, earn a subsistence not the less prized by them, perhaps,
from its hazardous nature, and may still remain to prosecute
their old occupation. But the Bahamas in general will become
uninhabited islands, and the largest of them will hardly furnish hands or muskets enough to beat off the boat of the small
privateer or pirate vessel that may resort thither for the
annoyance of our homeward-bound Jamaica trade.

The consequences in time of war, more especially an American war, and most of all a war with the maritime masters of
Louisiana and Florida, will be obviously very mischievous.
An inspection of the map alone will enable any man in some
measure to comprehend them, and to comprehend also how
greatly they would be enhanced or mitigated by our hostile or
amicable relations with Hayti. The Windward passage (the
only resource when that by the Gulf of Florida or Bahama
channel is too dangerous) must be made by working to windward, by a long and often difficult navigation, within sight of
the Haytian shores.

3rd. The last question proposed for consideration was, what
would be the consequences to Great Britain, if France should
succeed in a new invasion of Hayti, and re-establish her dominion in the island. This, if a probable event, would present
by far the most alarming views of the subject. Though not
probable, it would be rash to pronounce that such an event is
impossible, and therefore the consequences likely to ensue from
it are not unworthy of our serious consideration. France will,
of course, hold out the most specious and solemn assurances
of maintaining private freedom. But in these she cannot be
sincere; and, if sincere, she would not be trusted. The reasons have been sufficiently stated. If the national interests
of France, indeed, were to govern her public counsels in this

case, she would not only honestly propose but eagerly desire
and, if accepted, faithfully adhere to that basis of pacification.
But such an adjustment, though it would do everything for
France, would do nothing for the ex-proprietors of St. Domingo; and these are the too powerful party, powerful as the
Court in the legislative bodies and in the commercial towns,
whose delusive and selfish suggestions will prevail with the
King, as they did with the Consul, over the plain interests of
the country at large.   Could the contrary be expected, those
who, from feelings of justice and humanity, are zealous friends
to colonial reformation could wish nothing better for their
cause than such an accommodation between Hayti and France.
A free Black colony of that magnitude, in the centre of the
West Indies, under the French Crown, would offer more for
the speedy reformation and final extinction of slavery in the
whole Western world than the independence of Hayti, however firmly established.   To the political interests of Great
Britain, however, the consequences would be perilous enough,
as may be inferred from the preceding remarks; unless she
were disposed to take the reins from the hands of the Assemblies, and raise slaves into subjects and militia-men by a pretty
speedy reformation.

No such accommodation, however, between the French and
Haytian Governments can be rationally expected.   The authority of France must be restored, if at all, not by a treaty but
by the sword.   Nor will any ordinary severities of war suffice
for the purpose.   The whole or nearly the whole of the population, or that portion of it, at least, which is capable of bearing arms must perish.   With whatever moderation France
may begin, she will be led on to a renewal of all the barbarities
that disgraced her arms under Leclerc and Rochambeau.   The
Haytians have publicly proclaimed that, if again invaded, they
will give no quarter; and, should they keep their word, they
will have more excuse than ever people had for it in the extremity of provocation.   Henri Christophe acted, on the former

invasion, with a far different spirit, and foul was the return he
and his unfortunate followers met with.   But he will not now
wait to learn from the invaders the practices of exterminatory
war.   Nor will the nature of the contest give much room on
either side for moderation or mercy in the field.   Massacre,
cold-blooded murder, and inventive, ostentatious cruelty, will
soon with both parties have their former horrible range.   The
bloodhounds will again perhaps be called in; *les écoles des chiens*
will be reopened, and Frenchmen drawn round in a circle, to
enjoy the spectacle of seeing their naked prisoners torn and
devoured by dogs.   Meantime, the women and children will
perish, as before, in multitudes, from famine, inclemency of the
weather, and other hardships, in the woods and on the mountainous ridges to which they will be obliged to fly.

It is difficult amidst prospects so appalling to humanity, to
adhere to the plan of suggesting political considerations alone.
These horrors, however, if effectual to the purposes of France,
will have political consequences of a most mischievous kind to
England.   The worst of them will be the utter frustration of
all our labours and sacrifices for the general abolition of the
Slave Trade.   France, instead of abandoning that commerce,
will prosecute it more extensively than ever.   Having destroyed, or nearly destroyed, the whole Black population of
St. Domingo, she will have to repeople it from Africa.   Half
a million of seasoned Negroes did not suffice for the lands she
had in culture before the Revolution, and, to form that stock,
a million, at least, had been progressively torn from the Slave
Coast.   A term of fifty years would hardly be enough for its
restitution by new importations.   The relapse in its nature,
indeed, would be final and fatal.   If, after all that France, and
Europe, and America, have done and promised, after all the
generous sacrifices, the zealous, able, and successful negociations
of England, and the declaration of Vienna, France should
undertake the resettlement of that vast island by the Slave
Trade, what hope could possibly remain for Africa?   Not only

would her new-born hopes be cruelly strangled, but the sacred principles which gave life to them, the public morals and the liberal feelings of the nations of Europe would receive a fatal wound.   With such a craving and insatiable slave market in the centre of the Antilles, and with the power and influence of France to protect the traders that supplied it, all the concessions that we have obtained from other Powers would be as useless in the West Indies as in Africa.   They could no more check the free influx of new Negroes into the colonies, than prevent the desolation of the Slave Coast north of the Line. Cuba would be as amply supplied after 1820 as before.   If Spain had any scruple of violating the stipulations we had paid for, she would only have to return to her old habits, as they continued up to the time of the French Revolution, by importing slaves into her grand agricultural colony through the neighbouring ports of St. Domingo.   If France, on the other hand, wished for a while to avoid the reproach of openly repealing her Abolition Law, she might conveniently enough use the Spanish flag, while it lawfully protects the Slave Trade to Cuba, for it would cover the destination to any part of St. Domingo to the very moment of entering the port.   But the French would more probably disdain such an apparent deference for the principles of envied and hated England, and be more proud of braving our feelings and frustrating a work glorious to British philanthropy, than ashamed of an open relapse.   The example would multiply the difficulties, already sufficiently great, of obtaining from other Powers a faithful adherence to their Abolition Laws, and the treaties for suppressing the trade.   This, however, would scarcely amount to an additional evil.   France alone would be able to sustain and perpetuate all the mischiefs of that dreadful commerce on both sides of the Atlantic.   As to the now strong and prosperous colony of Sierra Leone, and all the plan of widely expansive good connected with it, their ruin would be sealed.   Even now the conduct of the French at Senegal and Goree is such that,

if persisted in, the best hope of Africa, an early establishment
of beneficent improvements on the northern or windward coast,
must be inevitably blighted.   But if the orders of the French
Government cannot even now restrain the cupidity of the
traders and the corruption of its own officers, so as to prevent
the open prosecution of a trade prohibited by law, how hopeless will the case be when the supply of St. Domingo, the
grand colonial object of the French Government itself, demands the utmost possible extension of the exports by French
subjects from the coast, and when even the dead letter of the
law, perhaps, is no longer opposed to the practice?   It may
with certainty be predicted that the export will be limited only
by the attainable supply.   Whatever the number of vendible
slaves the *tegria*,[1] or other wars, the kidnappings, the judicial
condemnations for real or pretended crimes, and the other practices which manufacture this shocking commodity, can be
instigated to furnish, the French traders will send away from
the windward coast; and the last state of that unhappy
country will be worse than the first.

It should be remembered that the supply from this part of
the Slave Coast had, even before our abolition, become comparatively very small.   The different witnesses examined
before the House of Lords in 1799 then stated it, on an average
of their different estimates, to have been for several years preceding about 6,000 slaves per annum.   Some accounts reduced
them to 3,000, and even so low as 2,500.   Yet, at that time,
the slaves imported into the British islands from Africa at
large amounted to 36,000.   The latter datum was from official
returns, but the places of export were not distinguished.   The
numbers brought from the windward coast were given only by
the loose estimates of different witnesses; and those called by

---

[1] The African name for those wars, the sole object of which is obtaining slaves for the trade (Park's Travels). He adds, that national wars
waged for conquest or other objects which provoke them among civilized States are called by a different name.

the Liverpool petitioners naturally attempted to magnify the supply from the coast north of Cape Palmas, which the Bill proposed to make the subject of local abolition; yet the best informed of these made it only 5,000 per annum. Some of them thought it a third of the whole; but, when put to give their estimates in numbers, could not sustain that proportion. Yet it is taken into the rough average herein given of the different opinions. All agreed that the supply from the wind-ward coast had been greatly reduced, which some ascribed to the war, but others, with far more probability, to the progres-sive decline of native population on the windward coast, which was the part first and much the longest frequented by Euro-pean slave-traders. The war had certainly some effect, because the trade had been more annoyed by French cruisers there than to the southward of Cape Palmas; but, before the war, and in time of profound peace, the supply from the windward coast had greatly fallen off, and become very small compared to the whole exports at the same periods from the Slave Coast at large.

These facts are of some importance, because they tend to show that the French Slave Trade on the windward coast produces, or is likely to produce, an actual deterioration of the state of that district, compared even with the time when the general trade had reached its maximum, and was open to all nations. The actual export from the windward coast has already, if recent estimates may be trusted, become larger than ever; and, though this perhaps may be no more than loose conjecture, there can be no doubt that, in the case here sup-posed—that of an open relapse by France—the before reduced and declining supply from that district will be progressively increased to the utmost of her power. Now, the miseries and crimes produced by the trade in the interior must obviously be the greatest, when a given supply is an increase upon the former amount, because this is most unquestionably the effect of increased demand and excitement; and the intensity of the cruel practices by which vendible slaves are made must obviously be in proportion to the exciting cause.

What is worse, or at least more revolting still to British feelings, in this deterioration, will be an effect of the very means we have used, and the sacrifices we have made for the benefit of that unfortunate district. By giving a total check there to the demand, we have reduced the price of the commodity. By purchasing out the Portuguese and Spanish trade there, we have given a monopoly of it to the French. Both these results become baits and premiums to the avarice of the French traders. They even perhaps encourage the manufacture of slaves, and aggravate its ordinary means, on the same principle that the exclusive privilege of sporting on a manor tends to increase the game. The French, when they excite the barbarous chiefs to multiply their captives for the next season, either by direct exhortation to the *tegria*, &c., or by what is the same in effect, sales of gunpowder and arms, brandy and tobacco, payable in slaves at a future day, well know they shall reap the harvest they have sown. While Spaniards, Portuguese, and other foreigners, were their rivals, they were not so sure of this. More crimes will be committed then, perhaps, and more miseries sustained, than if this African market had remained open to their brother-ruffians of every flag. If the French could not take all, it would be different, but they will certainly, in the case supposed, take all that can be made for them on the windward coast.

Here again we may seem to be mixing moral with political topics. But the ruin of Northern Africa is the ruin of a country in which Great Britain has commercial interests of no contemptible value. Some of them are in possession, but much more in rational prospect. Besides, it is politic to consider if the people of England are thus to lose their commerce, their money, and their benevolent hopes, by the moral apostacy of France, and her breach of solemn engagements, they may not add to it the loss of their temper; and whether, at some

not far distant crisis, the peace of Europe may not be broken
on the Slave Coast. Provocations, and serious ones too, may
soon be offered to our national pride. The vainest people on
earth, and of late the most haughty, will not easily digest
their own humiliations and the glory of a hated rival. If,
awed by a powerful league, they abstain awhile from any direct
hostile aggression, they will so much the rather give vent to
their spleen, and soothe their mortified pride by an arrogant
and insulting bearing towards us on every question of national
courtesy or right. Our merchantmen may perhaps be insulted
on the ocean or in their ports, and even our triumphant public
flag be treated with disrespect on *safe* occasions. Petty
national trespasses on our side may be litigiously and indignantly complained of, and redress for more serious wrongs on
their side insultingly refused. In short, there will be a hostile
and angry mind in the subjects of France, if not in their
Government or its officers, which may probably make the
duties of peace and amity of difficult practice, and create
frequent occasions of dispute. The British Government will
doubtless feel it a duty, in such cases, to act with great
moderation, and to avoid a quarrel while it can be done
compatibly with the national honour. But the Opposition will
as naturally change its pacific tone, when forbearance and conciliation are found to be the system at Court; and loud
appeals will be made to the honorary feelings of the country,
when Ministers can be represented as having tamely brooked
an affront.

If these anticipations are just, peace may be difficult to
maintain, even while the state of our public burdens and
finances most urgently pleads for its continuance. In such a
case, the weight of the neutral or middle party in the country,
thrown into the scale of Government, may be a salutary and
needful counterpoise to the too irritable pride and military
spirit of the people; and this party, being much influenced by
moral and religious principle, will generally be found on the

side of peace. But, if anything can reverse that disposition and reconcile them to all the evils of a new war with France, it will be a strong sense of indignation against that country for the supposed measures in St. Domingo and Africa; with a conviction that a rupture with her is the only remaining mean of putting a stop to the Slave Trade, and rescuing from hopeless barbarism and misery a whole quarter of the globe.

There are other considerations which would be very forcibly felt by the British statesman as reasons for preventing, even by some important sacrifice, if necessary, a relapse into colonization by the Slave Trade on the part of France, if the premises they rest upon were known. Such a relapse, and in such a field as St. Domingo, would be ruinous in its economical consequences to the British planter. But the explanation of this would require the assumption or the proof of controverted facts, the first of which would be unsatisfactory, and the last too long for the plan and object of these suggestions. A proposition that will be more easily admitted is, that the discontent of our planters with the abolition, and their disinclination to the interior reforms that it so urgently demands, and to the measures necessary for making it effectual, will not be lessened by seeing their neighbours and energetic rivals, the French, return to their old system, and re-settle St. Domingo by the Slave Trade. Whoever doubts this must give them credit for a conversion more entire and a reverse of views more perfect than they or their agents in this country have been led, even by urgent motives of policy, lately to profess. Independently, however, of the inclinations and the conduct of the better sort among them, it is hardly possible that our own change of system can work well in a commercial and a political view, in the circumstances here supposed.

One consequence is too obvious for dispute. Such an adherence by France to the old system would hold out dangerous temptation in time of war to such British colonists as were in distress from the want of slaves—a distress which undoubtedly exists already in every colony in which the Abolition Acts have been effectual—(and this is believed to have been in Trinidad the general case)—but which, unless exterior reformation takes place without further delay, must greatly and progressively increase. To suppose the contrary, except on the admission that slaves are unlawfully and largely imported, would be to suppose that, by some occult or miraculous influence, the ebb of population in the sugar colonies has been suddenly stayed, and a flood-tide produced, rejecting every census or return in the nature of it, and all other direct evidence which we have on that interesting point. It would be to ascribe even to the same mysterious cause a sudden supply to some entire colonies, and to very many individual planters in all, of the numbers in which they were notoriously deficient at the cessation of the lawful trade. No man who knows the case, or reasons upon its admitted facts, can doubt that a great proportion of our planters, at least, must severely feel the loss of a slave-market, if the abolition is an efficient law. With many or most of them, it will be their own fault, or that of the proprietors under whom they claim. But the evil will, nevertheless, be felt, and to all these men a French war would, under the circumstances supposed, hold out, in the permanent or temporary change of flags, the only means of relief. The danger of such a powerful temptation does not rest on the probability of revolt or treasonable practices. The *active* loyalty of the islands is necessary to save them from conquest in a maritime war, as we have experienced on all occasions except when the enemy could not send an armament to the West Indies, or maintain a squadron there, as during our last war with France.

These may be said to be arguments which impeach the policy of our abolition. Moral and religious duty, it may be answered, not policy, was the principle of that measure, and it stands now on so broad a basis of national character also and of good faith to other Powers, that it is too late to inquire into its political merits or demerits. The British statesman must now regard it as an unchangeable part of our system, which, like the Constitution itself, he cannot accommodate to his policy, but must accommodate his policy to it. The inconveniences, however, which may arise from the abolition to us, while our great maritime rival prosecutes the trade, will not fairly be imputable to that measure itself. They will rather be the effect of that adherence to old prejudices and practices, and old abuses in the sugar colonies, which the abolition would have corrected, if followed up, as its principle plainly required, by a registration of slaves. If the planters in general had made the sacrifices necessary to keeping up their gangs by native increase, they would not wish to lose the fruit of those sacrifices by a return of the trade, and, indeed, would soon cease to want any extraneous source of supply. But such sacrifices have not been made, because the abolition, without a registry, was known to be an impotent law. Had there been a parliamentary registration of slaves, with provisions, such as the promoters of the abolition desired, and as were adopted by Government at Trinidad, our planters would, in the case here supposed, have had no temptation to desire a temporary change of flags, even while slaves were still wanted. A duplicate registry in England would have defeated the object of recruiting their gangs, while French subjects, even though the colonial books should have been fortunately burnt or kindly destroyed by their conquerors. The slaves bought during the war must have been lost at the peace, unless the ultimate triumph of the enemy prevented the restitution of the island, and left it finally under the dominion of France—an event which the malecontents might not desire, and which their efforts could not produce.

The political danger in question is one of which the promoters of the abolition, such of them, at least, as looked from the first to a registry, ought not to bear the blame. It would be as reasonable to hinder a surgeon from tying up the blood-vessels after an amputation he had performed, and then blame him for the death of the patient.

In the supposed event of a new Haytian war, which we are now considering, that of a re-establishment of the French Government by force of arms, another, and more alarming, or at least a more imminent, danger, would unavoidably ensue. France would find, not a pretext merely, but an absolute necessity for long maintaining such a force in St. Domingo as would place Jamaica quite at her mercy, whenever she chose to draw the sword against us. We could not maintain a permanent defensive force there large enough to prevent this consequence, without such an enormous sacrifice of men and money as no Government would think it warrantable to incur. The seduction of our planters, or the paralyzation of their active loyalty by the prospect of regaining the Slave Trade, would therefore be no necessary mean of conquest in that quarter; and, at the first commencement of the next French war, our commercial and colonial interests might receive a shock more severe than they ever sustained.

After all, the grand mischief, in a political as well as a moral view, would be the adherence of France to the Slave Trade. In this view her Haytian expedition, however it might terminate, would be fatal at this crisis of the great African cause: nay, the intention of such a measure in the mind of the French Government would at present be decisive. It would be idle to go about to prove that, if those who direct the counsels of France still meditate the recovery of St. Domingo by force, they *must* look forward to the Slave Trade. If so, they will not concur in any really *effectual* means for suppressing that commerce as now carried on by French subjects. Still less will their influence be employed to induce Portugal to accede to an early abolition, and to obtain from her and from other Powers the admission of such sanctions and remedies as would make the universal suppression of the trade the right and duty of every maritime State. On the contrary, French intrigue will be employed to frustrate the negociations of the British Government on this subject at Aix-la-Chapelle, at Madrid, Brazil, and every other Court. The French Ministers will naturally hide their purpose, or, at least, not openly avow it. The very object which influences them will dictate this policy. To avow their adherence to or a design of keeping open a recurrence to the Slave Trade would be declaring to the Haytians that their slavery or extermination is in view; and, though the chiefs seem sufficiently aware of this, it is plain from writings patronized by the French Government that it still hopes to deceive and divide the poor ignorant people. Sincerity on the point cannot be necessary to the French negociators. They will find plausible reasons enough in jealousy of England, tenaciousness of the rights of independent flags in time of peace, &c., to give a colour to their most strenuous opposition; and with such arguments they will not only gloss over their own true motives, but fatally, perhaps, strengthen the scruples and confirm the reluctance of other Powers, who are well disposed towards the great general end, so as to prevent the adoption of the only practicable means for attaining it.

If this reasoning is just, a mediation on behalf of Hayti will not add to the difficulties that may attend our negociations for suppressing the Slave Trade. Its success would remove the most intractable of those difficulties; its failure would only leave them where they stand. If France rejects the mediation, it will be because she is resolved to adhere to the trade; and, if *she* adheres to it, the conventional abandonment of it by all other Powers would be useless. Besides, the concurrence of the Court of Brazil in a total abolition, and the means of making it effectual, cannot rationally be hoped, while such a Power as France stands out. That Court, however well disposed, would find it extremely difficult to accede to our solicitations. It is not in a condition to offer violence to the prejudices of its Brazilian subjects with safety; and their resentment at the sacrifice of a trade vital to their hopes of rapid improvement in the culture of that rich and vast but ill-peopled country, which is now the seat of empire, would naturally be very strong and nearly unanimous; for it is not there, as in Europe, a feeling of public interest, to which moral sentiment is opposed. Habit has obtunded all their sensibilities to the cruelty of the trade and the wrongs of the unfortunate Africans. The best hope of inducing and enabling the Brazilian Government to cope with this great difficulty would be found in the unanimity of all other civilized States in the system of abolishing the Slave Trade universally, and in their real or supposed determination not to permit a solitary exception to frustrate their benevolent object, even if compulsion should be necessary to prevent it.

It rarely happens that a sovereign would wish to be thought by his own subjects to act under the dictation of foreign Powers; but the Court of Brazil might wisely entertain such a wish in the present case, if disposed to abolish the Slave Trade; and the Congress at Aix-la-Chapelle seems to present a happy opportunity of furnishing such a plea with the least possible degree of umbrage to the pride of the Portuguese. A resolution to regard a practice so repugnant to the principles of religion and morality, as contrary to the law of nations, and to treat it as piracy after the year 1820, would, without offensively pointing at Portugal, seem to be a natural consequence of the Declaration of Vienna, and would convince the Brazilians of the strict necessity which their own Government was subjected to of prohibiting the trade, in order to save its own dignity and pacific relations with Europe. But to this best or only hope the opposition of France would be fatal.

It is hoped that these reasons, or some of them, will be thought decisive for the policy of our making every effort to induce the French Government to acquiesce in the independence of Hayti, or, at least, to abandon the design of recovering its authority in St. Domingo by war. The *means*, it is felt, are of a very delicate and difficult kind; and the attempt to form a judgment of what they may and ought to be would be presumptuous in any man who possesses none but public information as to the subjects of the impending negociations, the temper in which they are likely to be met by different Courts, or the questions that may probably arise in them between Great Britain and France.

It is suggested, therefore, with the utmost diffidence, as subjects of consideration which may *possibly* find place—

1st. Whether France may not reasonably be invited to declare herself in regard to her views on St. Domingo, on account of their plain connexion with the abolition of the Slave Trade and the peace of the West Indies?

2nd. Whether, if she meditates new expeditions, the influence of Great Britain and other Powers at the Congress may not be properly employed to induce her to desist from that purpose?

3rd. As to the mediation between France and the Haytian Chiefs, there seems to be little or no chance that it would be effectual on any other basis than the recognition of independence. But, though Henri Christophe has indignantly rejected the idea of compensation to the ex-proprietors, there is some probability that he might be brought to agree to *this*, on terms similar to those which Petion proposed, through his Envoy Garbage, to Lord Liverpool, provided the independence were acknowledged. Might not England, without impropriety, offer her mediation to that end, and might not France be glad so to escape from the dilemma she stands in. The private interests which now urge her to the costly and perilous enterprise of a new Haytian war might, by such an arrangement, be placed on the pacific side, and her credit be in some degree saved.

4th. The commerce of Hayti is a valuable interest, which might be made the price of pacification, but for the extreme difficulty of ever again reconciling the Chiefs or people to any

intercourse with France. The difficulty may be reasonably
regarded as being, under present circumstances, quite insu-
perable. On the other hand, Great Britain might easily secure
this commerce to herself, with all the advantages herein before
pointed out, and even obtain perhaps a conventional monopoly of
it, if this were an object we could inoffensively and decorously
pursue. Of course, any appearance of a self-interested purpose
would spoil all. But, might not France herself, finding she
cannot have the trade, be glad to obtain for her ex-colonists
our guarantee for the compensations to a limited extent, or by
annual instalments for a certain term of years, on the condition that, as a counter-security to us, and means of invest-
ment, we should, for a limited period at least, receive the produce of the island, leaving us to obtain the accession of the
Chiefs to that condition, and making the compact depend on
their acceding to it? This would, in its effects, probably secure
to us their amity and commerce for ever, yet would save to
France the reversionary benefit, if she could hereafter conciliate
their confidence.

5th. Are there no other considerations that we might offer
to France on the same arrangement—*e. g.*, some colonial possession? We have more than one which it would be real
policy and advantage to transfer to her without a consideration,
much more for such a benefit as even the temporary trade of
Hayti. But it is, after all, her concurrence in the abolition to
which we should chiefly look, and that, even in a cold, political
estimate, could hardly be bought too dear.

Prince Leopold to Lord Castlereagh.

Elphinau, près de Berne, ce 15 de Septembre, 1818.

Mon très cher Lord—Il faut que je vous écrive quelques
lignes pour vous informer que j'ai écrit à l'Empereur de Russie
et au Comte de Capodistrias, par rapport aux affaires d'échange
de mon frère ainé. Mon frère s'était aussi rendu à Berlin
pour voir l'Empereur, en sorte que j'espère qu'il ne refusera

pas sa cooperation avec votre Seigneurie aussi loin que les circonstances voudront le permettre.

J'ai passé par la France pour venir ici, et j'ai voyagé très vite m'arrêtant seulement quelques jours à Lyon. Je vous souhaite un séjour bien agréable à Aix-la-Chapelle, et de vous revoir en bien bonne santé en Angleterre. Veuillez offrir mes hommages à Lady Castlereagh. En peu de jours je continuerai mon chemin pour Cobourg; si l'occasion s'en présente je verrai peut-être l'Empereur de Russie quelque part sur son passage.

À présent je vous dirai adieu, en vous priant de vouloir bien croire que je serai toujours avec le dévouement le plus inaltérable, mon très cher Lord, de votre Excellence le bien sincère et dévoué serviteur et ami,

LEOPOLD.

Lord Clancarty to Lord Castlereagh.

Bruxelles, September 18, 1818.

My dear Lord—The bag which will accompany this was forwarded here by the Duke of Wellington's sergeant. I have detained it till the arrival of the London post from Ostend, in order that, if anything should be enclosed in our packets to your address, both might be sent on to you by the same conveyance. The estafette, with the London letters of the 15th, is arrived from Ostend, but there are no parcels directed to you in the bag brought by him. I therefore despatch that received from the Duke's messenger.

Your courier, bearing a box for Hamilton and the packet of papers addressed to me upon the negociations with the United States, arrived here yesterday morning. Not knowing of what consequence the early receipt of the box by Hamilton might be, I thought it best to send the Messenger on by Calais rather than detain his despatches till ours should be forwarded this evening, to go afterwards, perhaps with a foul wind, from Ostend.

I return you the American papers, which came to me, not in a box, as you mention, but under a paper cover, as now sent back. They are very interesting. The very delicate point relating to impressment appears to me handled in the most satisfactory manner which circumstances can admit; and if the ideas upon this subject, as appears probable, shall be ripened into a Convention, the best proof of our disposition to conciliate will be afforded to the citizens of the one and the Anglo-Yankees of the other State; while the express reservation of the right and power, after the experiment shall have been tried, to put an end to the adjournment of its exercise, are well calculated effectually to prevent the objections of those who (and they are, thank God, a numerous class) would not well bear a surrender, or even the placing in doubt the existence of the right itself.

The Emperor of Austria will pass from Mayence to Coblentz by water, in a yacht of the Duke of Nassau's, on the 23rd, 24th, and 25th; and such has been the feeling of that part of Germany, that already every boat at Mayence has been engaged at high prices by those who mean to accompany his voyage. All the peasantry on the shores will turn out to greet his passage: every building in the neighbourhood has been engaged by those coming from a distance to see him pass: his course will be a complete appearance of triumph. All this I learn from the spot. If thus honouring the ancient Chief of Germany proceeded from the unmixed feeling of reverence towards him, it would be well; and, as much of it probably will proceed from this feeling, it is so far well: but I cannot help fearing that some of this apparent enthusiasm for one great Sovereign of Germany may find its motive in an endeavour to detract from another.

If you will detain this messenger till an early hour on Monday morning, and then despatch him with your ordinary letters for England, these will arrive here in time to accompany ours on Tuesday, via Ostend, to London.

Adieu. Yours ever affectionately,

CLANCARTY.

Lord Liverpool to Lord Castlereagh.

London, September 18, 1818.

Dear Castlereagh—I am much obliged to you for your two letters. I am going to Walmer to-morrow, and I have not much to communicate to you of any consequence. We have had a Cabinet to-day, in consequence of the first business interview between our Plenipotentiaries and those of America. Their proposition on the Fisheries appears to me to afford a basis, upon which we may hope a satisfactory adjustment of that question may be made. Upon some of the other points there may be more difficulty; but those questions which cannot be settled might, I think, by mutual consent, for the present, be omitted; and, as far as the negociation itself goes, I see nothing to augur an unfavourable result.

The last mail, however, brings no explanation on the subject of the murder of our countrymen, Arbuthnot and Ambrister. The American Government is certainly shy of the question, and I fear, from all the accounts which transpire, even through the American papers, that it is a most foul transaction. I think it most probable that our countrymen acted *imprudently* and *improperly*, and in such a manner as not to make the case in any respect one which ought to lead to the last extremities; but General Jackson's conduct is represented as savage, cunning, and cruel, in the greatest degree, and as such would make it very difficult for us (if it is not distinctly disavowed) to draw closer the ties of friendship and connexion between the two countries, by concluding the treaties which are in progress.

You will have seen the Note respecting Pensacola. The Americans propose to restore it, but they justify Jackson in attacking it; though, if the restitution is right, there can be no excuse for his conduct. They draw a distinction between the case of St. Mark's and that of Pensacola—a distinction quite intelligible, if the facts which are stated are true: but the distinction is this, that the occupation of St. Mark's was a matter of necessity, that of Pensacola was not. They therefore offer an immediate restitution of the one, but restitution of the other only in case of a sufficient force being sent to occupy it. If necessity did not require the occupation of Pensacola, what possible justification can there be for General Jackson's conduct?

The Queen has been alternately better and worse since you left this. The accounts to-day are very bad, and I should think she cannot last much longer. We are already safe against the meeting of Parliament, so as to begin business before the 29th of November.

Believe me to be, &c.,   LIVERPOOL.

Mr. W. Hamilton to Mr. Planta.

Foreign Office, September 22, 1818.

Dear Planta—Nothing of importance has transpired since we last wrote. The Queen still lives, and that is all the *domestic* news I have.

The steps taken by America for the evacuation of Pensacola you will learn in the despatches. Robinson is very anxious for the next arrival on Fisheries, &c.—You will see by the accompanying Memorandum that I have seen the Duke de B——, who is a complete adventurer, and ready to sell his soul to whoever bids most.

On the subject of the Sicilian papers respecting the unwillingness of the Neapolitan Government to allow British goods to be imported into the ports of Naples on board ships not British, Robinson, on further consideration of the subject, is inclined to be of opinion that it may be much more beneficial to us to accept the interpretation of the treaty as laid down by the Neapolitans than that assumed by À Court, inasmuch as it will be a bonus to our shipping in the Mediterranean; and, if we demand the more extended privilege for ourselves, of course all the other Powers—Spain and France, for instance—

will be entitled to the same. If, therefore, Lord Castlereagh does not object, Robinson is prepared to desist from the claim as put forward by our Minister.

Yours, &c.   W. HAMILTON.

I have had several conferences with the King's Advocate about the appointments under the later Slave Trade Acts, and hope soon to report progress. Sir William Scott is out of reach.

W. H.

[Enclosure.]

Memorandum.

Foreign Office, September 19, 1818.

I have just had an interview with the Duke de B——, who comes to offer his services to the British Government, first, as having the means of paralyzing the operations of Joseph Bonaparte, which, he says, are encouraged by the American Government; and 2ndly, as being able to prepare many of the leading members of Congress for a separation of the States in the event of another [war] with England.

He observed that, as it is on all hands felt that Spain must lose her colonies, Russia was anxious to possess herself of California. Of this the Government of the United States was aware, and the principal object for which they gave countenance to Joseph Bonaparte was to lead him to that quarter, as being a neighbour not so likely to check them in their views as Russia would be, if her designs on the western coast were realized— that Joseph Bonaparte had received two offers of residence in Europe, one from Russia, and one from Austria, but had declined both—he was yet, however, anxious to come back to Europe sooner or later; and, feeling that affairs could not last long in France in their present state, he looked forward to the moment when Austria might be setting up his nephew, the young Napoleon, when he should be ready to lend to England and Austria whatever aid was in his power to forward what he considered would be their joint policy—and Joseph had furnished him with a *blanc signé*, which he showed me, by which he would engage to use all his influence in America to promote the views of England, if such prospects as these could be held out to him of future establishment in Europe—that Lucien had been thwarted in his attempts to go to America, where his brother expected him, and the two families were to be united by marriage, in contemplation of their American projects. The Duke had commanded Murat's body-guard at Naples, had been ruined by the extortions of the French troops, then maintained by a pension from the usurper, and now, being without estate or pension, he had determined to travel, and *faire profiter* his *faibles talens*. He said this was all he had to communicate *en principe*, that, if his services were accepted, he could make himself highly useful, and only waited Lord C.'s permission to begin his operations.

I replied to him generally that I did not think his Majesty's Government would listen to any of his overtures, and that particularly in respect to his project for separating the United States of America—we were at peace with that country, and could entertain no hostile act whatever towards it.

W. H.

Lord Bathurst to Lord Castlereagh.

Downing Street, September 25, 1818.

Dear Lord Castlereagh—By an intercepted letter, a copy of which Monsieur de Neumann was good enough to send me, it appears that it is the intention of Las Casas and some friends of General Bonaparte to bring under the consideration of the Sovereigns assembled at Aix-la-Chapelle the treatment which he experiences at St. Helena. I think, therefore, that it may be desirable for you to be in possession of some papers by which you may be enabled to refute the gross misstatements which are circulated on that subject.

The first Paper contains the existing regulations ; the second, the communications made by General Gourgaud, on his arrival here from St. Helena. I regret that he could not be induced

to say more, which he would have been easily persuaded to do,
I imagine, if hopes could have been given to him that the
French Government would pardon him. The third Paper is
the copy of a letter which Sir Hudson Lowe thought it desirable to send to Count Balmain, in vindication of his conduct, of which he apprehended that the frequent interviews
between Count Balmain and the followers of General Bonaparte
had given to the Count an unfavourable impression. I send
it because it is the most succinct defence of Sir Hudson
Lowe's conduct that I am in possession of. The fourth
Paper is a copy of my letter to Sir Hudson Lowe, which
speaks for itself; and I have added to it the despatch which
accounts for the discharge of the cook by General Bonaparte, and some other particulars which are at least amusing.
The last Paper is the draft of a despatch which I am about to
send to Sir Hudson Lowe, in consequence of what appeared in
one of his last despatches regarding a relaxation in one of the
instructions which I thought it right to notice.

Yours very sincerely,   BATHURST.

Lord Castlereagh to Lord Liverpool.

Aix, September 27, 1818.

My dear Lord—I have not written to you before, knowing
that you were absent from London, and in truth having nothing
of interest to convey to you for the Prince Regent's information.

The Duke de Richelieu, I have reason to believe, took Spa
in his way to this place, expecting to find me there. I had
two conversations with him, in which, as far as I could judge,
(under the reserve which a communication with the Minister
of France before I had seen those of the Allies necessarily
imposed) his two objects will be to press the evacuation, and
the admission of the King into the Alliance. As to the mode
in which the latter purpose is to be effected, his ideas appear

to me to be very little matured; but he obviously perceives
the inconvenience of the King being a contracting party to the
existing stipulations; and his mind is afloat to find some expedient by which France might be brought more in line with
the other Powers.

I do not think that the Duke will urge the reception of a
Spanish Plenipotentiary at Aix-la-Chapelle, or that his views
extend to the introduction of Spain, under any circumstances,
into the Alliance. He seemed to admit the importance of not
suffering the conferences to train into length, and that this evil
could only with certainty be avoided by confining our *formal*
discussions to the single object for which the Sovereigns have
declared that they were to assemble.

Upon Spanish politics, his opinions appeared to me very
much to concur with those of the British Government. I
thought the general tone of his conversation was conciliatory
and reasonable. The Duke of Wellington, who arrived at
Spa before I left it, made the same remark.

In giving you this very general outline, I must, however,
beg you to receive it with caution, as I did not wish, for
obvious reasons, to get to close quarters. It was enough to
create an impression that my instructions were not of a nature
that need excite alarm in his mind.

CASTLEREAGH.

Lord Burghersh to Lord Castlereagh.

Florence, September 27, 1818.

My dear Lord Castlereagh—Since my despatches directed
to you have been sent to the post, I have an offer from General
Kitroff to convey anything for you direct to Aix-la-Chapelle.
I send you therefore duplicates, which will reach you before
the originals, and which you may be kind enough to forward
to England. I have no news for you beyond what you will
find in my official letters. Great expectations here that you
will make every sort of political arrangement of Congress, but

great alarm at the idea of the resuscitation of the French power. Louis Bonaparte and his wife have certainly neither met nor made up their differences. He has taken a villa near this town for a short time, while he is occupied in treating for an estate in Tuscany. She remains still near Leghorn, but, I believe, will return to Germany. Pauline is at the baths at Lucca, surrounded by English, whom she appears to prefer to all others, for the gratification of her desires. She speaks in ecstacies of Lord Bathurst, who has written to her, though she is convinced he means to be the death of her poor brother. The Duchess of Lucca is very gay and very expensive. I fear she will raise to herself many difficulties in the government of her country. She is in very constant correspondence with the King of Spain, and treats his Minister with great distinction. The Duke of Modena has lately been trying very hard with her to get the Lugguese districts I mentioned to you in one of my despatches, and has been anxious to keep the knowledge from Tuscany. These districts are part of what Fossombroni, in his propositions, proposes to retain for the Grand Duke. I fear it will be another obstacle to their acceptation. The roads of which I have written to you as being in progress, or proposed, in Italy, are, I think, all of them essential to the Austrian defence of the country, and as such perhaps may merit your consideration and support. The road through the Roman State from Arezzo, across the Apennines to Ancona or Rimini, might become of considerable consequence. Pray remember me to Lady Castlereagh, and believe me, my dear Lord Castlereagh, most sincerely, &c.,

BURGHERSH.

Lord Castlereagh to Lord Clancarty.

Aix-la-Chapelle, September 28, 1818.

My dear Clancarty—I send you your instructions by the present messenger, on the general questions, and also on that of Bouillon. I hope the King on the latter will act liberally.

As I shall see my way here on the former subject, in some degree, before the next courier goes, I wish you so to arrange your journey as to be ready to move on the following day, but not actually to set out till you hear again from me.

CASTLEREAGH.

Lord Clancarty to Lord Castlereagh.

Brussels, Wednesday morning, September 30, 1818.

My dear Lord—I received yesterday, by the messenger Youres, the instructions on the general question, and also on that of Bouillon, and shall be ready to act on both, whenever your final direction shall reach me. The Ministry have orders to leave the Hague on the 5th of October, to establish themselves at this residence; and probably about the 10th the King will himself be here: nevertheless, under the semblance of a long since proclaimed intention of making a short tour through part of the country north of the Meuse, till the recommencement of business here, I shall, on the receipt of your letter for this purpose, make the best of my way to the Loo, where the King (now on a tour to the Helder) will probably be by the time of my arrival there.

With the regard you have shown to this King's feelings in your instruction to Sir Charles Stuart, and agreeing entirely with you that the Bouillon question, in its present state, is one of jurisprudence rather than of a political nature, I think I shall be well able to render the King more facile than he has hitherto shown himself upon it; and the more so, because I cannot help being of opinion that the difficulties imposed on his part have, at least for the most part, had their origin in the exorbitant demands made by his opponents, and the gross intrigues with which it was endeavoured to realize them.

I do not hesitate to send my messenger forward, although the ordinary courier will probably be sent on to you to-morrow, because it is impossible for me to guess of what importance the early receipt of despatches from Madrid may be at this moment.

Yours, my dear lord, &c.,

CLANCARTY.

Lord Clancarty to Lord Castlereagh.

Bruxelles, half-past seven, A.M., October 2, 1818.

My dear Lord—The principal bundles of which this messenger is the bearer arrived this moment by estafette from Ostend. The Queen better on Tuesday last. · The Government here (I know not on what immediate grounds, though on accumulated provocation amply sufficient) have imprisoned a journalist named Dubar, proprietor of a libellist paper, called *Le Journal des deux Flandres*, at Ghent, and stopped the publication of that paper. This looks like vigour; and, though I have not yet heard how the act is to be defended, under the existing regulations of the law, yet I am not sorry it has taken place, and precisely at this time, when the States-General are about to assemble, that this subject of the Press may, once for all, be looked at, and such practicable regulations made thereon, (and no subject was ever more difficult) as may enable this Government to check the evil of its licentious publications.

Adieu.   Most affectionately yours,   CLANCARTY.

Lord Clancarty to Lord Castlereagh.

Bruxelles, October 2, 1818.

My dear Lord—The messenger with yours of yesterday arrived some three hours after we had sent you the Tuesday's mails from England.

I heartily congratulate you on your prospects of an early and satisfactory termination of your Conferences. As the Duke of Wellington proposes to see the King on the subject of the additional fortresses, which seems to be much the most likely means of obtaining the object, I shall not touch upon

the matter in my intercourse with his Majesty, unless in the
course of conversation he should allude to it, and that as the
private impression of my own mind, the statement of an
opinion on the expediency of some more effectual defences for
covering Bruxelles may seem to me calculated to facilitate the
Duke's plans.

> Ever most affectionately yours,   CLANCARTY.

Lord Castlereagh to Lord Liverpool.

Aix-la-Chapelle, October 4, 1818.

My dear Liverpool—As we agreed, I have thrown as much
of what has occurred as I could, either into official or private
letters, addressing them to Bathurst, but directing the bag to
be sent to you immediately upon its being landed at Dover.
You will probably wish to know my real opinion upon the sincerity of all that is passing around me.   My opinion has
always been that, whether sincere or not, we ought to meet it
as if it was; for there is no real security in dealing in the
language of distrust, where your *measure* cannot be of a pre-
cautionary description, and where we, at least, are out of the
reach of immediate danger; but my belief is that the Emperor
of Russia is, in the main, in earnest in what he says—not that
he has not perhaps had before him projects for other alliances,
&c., and possibly conventions; but I do not believe that he
has himself given any formal encouragement to the one, or
ratified the other; but that, whatever has passed, if anything,
has been the produce of some of his foreign agents, brought
forward as remedies, to meet alleged projects against Russian
influence.   Perhaps in these cases, as in that of the overture
from the French exiles in the Low Countries, the Emperor
has suffered himself to be approached, and has delayed the
moment of his declaration upon them.

I have also reason to think that he has been led to believe
that there are secret engagements making between Great

Britain and Austria; but, with all these ideas working upon a somewhat jealous mind, my persuasion is that he means to pursue a peace policy—that he aims at sway, but that he has no desire to change his connexion, or to render the revolutionary spirit in Europe more active; but, on the contrary, is disposed to watch it.

I observe Prince Metternich's suspicions are much allayed, and now principally pointed at the Russian agents. He mentioned to me the Emperor's personal character the other day, as the only guarantee we had against the danger of Russian power. Upon the whole, it seems working as we could wish; and we have only to encourage the sentiments of attachment, of which all the Sovereigns are so prodigal towards each other, and which, I believe, at this moment, are sincerely entertained. I am quite convinced that past habits, common glory, and these occasional meetings, displays, and repledges, are among the best securities Europe now has for a durable peace.

The wonderful struggle the Queen has made will, I trust, enable you to stave off Parliament till after Christmas: it is most desirable. Let me know what you have finally decided about estimates, &c.

The Duke of Wellington, in his way through Brussels, is to see the King of the Netherlands about fortifications. He is very desirous of bringing the King to decide upon the Waterloo works, and one other, nearer the sea, not included in the first plan. The whole money applicable, viz., £2,500,000 from France, £2,000,000 from us, and a like sum from Holland, will complete and arm what has been settled; but it will require £1,200,000 more to construct and arm the two additional works. We cannot urge this with effect, unless we have something to give: what I should then wish to be authorized to do would be to give up our bad debt upon Holland, if his Majesty will take an engagement to complete these works at his own charge. I am of opinion that it is a favourable mode of getting rid of a claim which is open to dispute, and which will bring upon us a counter-claim for the Dutch fleet, taken possession of for the Stadtholder, besides producing ill-humour.

Let me know, by return of messenger, whether I may give the Duke a discretion. The claim is £3,000 or £4,000, for arms and clothing furnished, but not upon any intimation that they were to be paid for.

CASTLEREAGH.

Prince Leopold to Lord Castlereagh.

Cobourg, ce 6 d'Octobre, 1818.

Mon bien cher Lord—Je suis fâché de vous importuner au milieu des occupations et grandeurs d'Aix ; mais mon frère m'a prié d'accompagner quelques papiers qu'il vous envoye de peu de lignes de ma part. Connaissant votre amitié et indulgence, je prends la liberté de vous recommander de nouveau les affaires de mon pauvre frère. Je vous ai expliqué déjà à Londres avec tant de détail la nature de ses réclamations, que je ne veux pas de nouveau vous les exposer, et me borne seulement à vous prier de leur accorder votre protection.

Il n'y a pas de doute que les Puissances feront quelque chose dans cette affaire, au moins la justice le demande: L'état des choses avec la Bade, le grand-duc étant dangereusement malade, offrirait peut-être une bonne occasion pour engager la Bavière à un échange avec mon frère.

Il y a deux jours que je suis ici : j'avais pris la route la plus détournée, pour ne rencontrer aucun des potentats.

Je suis bien peiné que les nouvelles de la Reine, que mes tantes ont la bonté de me faire parvenir, soyent si excessivement mauvaises. Ce sera une grande perte, que je déplore sincèrement. Veuillez faire mes complimens à Lady Castlereagh, et accordez votre appui à mon frère, qui en aura grand besoin.

Avec l'amitié la plus sincère, et une considération bien distinguée, mon bien cher Lord, de votre Excellence, le bien sincèrement dévoué serviteur,

LEOPOLD.

Mr. C. Bagot to Lord Castlereagh.

Washington, October 7, 1818.

My dear Lord—I received on the 18th of last month your lordship's private and confidential letters of the 8th of August, transmitting to me the papers respecting the mediation between Spain and her colonies. Mr. Adams was then in Massachusetts, and though I was very anxious to make a communication to him upon this subject as soon as possible, I did not think it prudent to do so in any manner by writing. I have, therefore, contented myself with sending him, through the chief Clerk of the department of State, a message, which will give him sufficiently to understand that your lordship has enabled me to make him the communication which he has been expecting, as soon as he returns to Washington, which will be in the course of ten days.

I shall be able to write more fully to your lordship by the next mail. Mr. Martinez, the person despatched by the Spanish Minister to Madrid upon the first invasion of Florida, has just returned from Spain. Much importance is attached to his return, but, as the Spanish Minister is not at Washington, I have not yet been able to learn anything upon the subject.

I must request your lordship's indulgence for all my communications by this mail, which, I fear, are neither sufficiently detailed nor explicit; but I have been forced to make them from my bed, to which I have been confined nearly a fortnight by a severe bilious fever. I believe that I have entirely conquered the disease, but I am necessarily still very weak.

I have the honour to be, &c.,   CHARLES BAGOT.

Lord Clancarty to Lord Castlereagh.

Bruxelles, October 13, 1818.

My dear Lord—The difficulty of finding an honest arbitrator to settle the Bouillon affair is, I really believe, the only one which exists with this Government upon the subject. Nagell, in stating it, told me I could scarcely wonder at its being felt, when informed of a circumstance which had occurred to him, and then repeated an anecdote with which he had before acquainted me, of an attempt that had been made to bribe him, through the agency of his banker here, on behalf of the Prince de Rohan. I believe I mentioned this fact to you while you were here.

Happily, the persons who composed the reunion, and pronounced what is called the *jugement arbitral* at Leipsic, had no other function than that of designating the person entitled to the Duchy of Bouillon, because M. le Baron de Binder, who governed his colleagues on that occasion, and induced them to point out the Prince de Rohan as the person, now makes no secret of his having been the Prince's privy councillor in all the negociation here, and that it was he (the Baron) who occasioned its having been broken off, and the subsequent appeal which was made on the subject to the E. and Ex. at Paris.

There is a M. Turette at this moment here, who, having married a Dutch woman or of Dutch family, has latterly been employed as Consul of this Court at Paris. He states positively, though confidentially, to Nagell, that nothing can equal the profligate corruption of all the departments of the Government in France; that, with the exception of the Duke de Richelieu, whom he fully acquits of all foul practices, everything in every department is to be obtained for money; nay, he goes further, and asserts that, on the late loan, not only M. Corvetto, but our friend Pozzo, received three millions of French livres from the contractors, and adds also that Prince Metternich received from Labouchere one million of florins on the Austrian loan. All this may be, and I should hope is, a foul calumny. I mention it, however, in order to account for those who, like Nagell, believe the statement, possessing fears of unfair play with respect to their concerns in the Bouillon case, and this more especially when conjoined with the attempt made on Nagell himself.

Though you probably will not have time to read it, I send you the statement of this Government on the Bouillon subject: it is drawn and not ill-drawn up by a lawyer of some eminence here, and, with some slight alterations, will probably form the memorandum mentioned in my despatch.

There have been some complaints in Holland of the falling off of the transit trade, and the Crown, which had fixed the transit duties too high, will, I believe, be induced, during the approaching session, to propose their being lowered. This, if it should take place, will be beneficial to us; I should, however, apprehend that Belgic jealousy may induce the Deputies of the southern provinces to give some opposition to the success of a measure of this kind.

Nagell has received some accounts of your projected Declaration, much of which I take to be incorrect: it is to be hoped that whatever you publish of this nature may be clothed in a simple garb, and freed from that verbiage and sentimental trash which disgrace many of the modern State papers.

The King arrives here to-night, and the States-General open on Monday next.

Yours, my dear lord, &c.,   CLANCARTY.

Lord Bathurst to Lord Castlereagh.

Downing Street, October 17, 1818.

Dear Lord Castlereagh—Lord Guilford proposes to go to Aix-la-Chapelle, in order to renew to Prince Metternich the application which he made for some compensation being made to the Ionian States, in lieu of certain funds deposited formerly at Venice, for the education of Ionian young men in a seminary at that place. The Austrian Government has seized these funds, and as the Ionian States are about to establish a university, (of which Lord Guilford is good enough to undertake to be Chancellor) what he wishes is that the Austrian

Government will consent to furnish books, to the amount of what they may fairly be considered as owing to the Ionian States for the funds of which it has taken possession, and which were destined for the education of the Ionian young men.

Prince Metternich seemed well inclined to the proposition when Lord Guilford was at Vienna; and I make no doubt that, if you will countenance this arrangement, the Prince will not be sorry to give this proof to the Ionian States of the favourable disposition of the Austrian Government towards their improvement.

I am ever yours, &c.,   BATHURST.

Lord Clancarty to Lord Castlereagh.

Bruxelles, October 18, 1818.

. My dear Lord—Upon receipt of your despatch of the 15th, I applied to my colleagues, the Ministers from the other three Powers, to know whether similar instructions had yet reached them, and finding this was not the case, I immediately, in communication with them, sent in the note I was directed to press, calling on this Government to accede to the Convention of the 9th inst., and, at the same time, made the verbal communication directed by those instructions. M. de Nagell has been with me this morning, and tells me that this Court will be impatient to accede to the Convention, but wishes first to be assured, though in a private form, from you, through me, that this Convention comprises all the payments due from France, to which this kingdom is entitled under the treaty of November, 1815, and the arrangement made by the Duke of Wellington, last spring, for the liquidation. Have the goodness to state the affirmative of this fact to me by the next messenger. I have not been able to follow this business of the moneys due from France with such certainty as to authorize me to act from myself on this subject when my relief was so near, though I have little doubt how the fact stands.

I am just recovering from my *autumnal* attack, which, while it lasted, was sufficiently strong; it confined me for two days to the house.

I have been asked here whether, instead of sending it back to England, we should not be inclined to sell to this Government some, if not the whole, of the gunpowder at present in the stores of our portion of the Occupation Army. Pray tell this to the Duke of Wellington, if he shall not have left Aix-la-Chapelle before this letter shall reach it; and let me know what answer I shall give.

Ever most affectionately yours,　CLANCARTY.

Lord Castlereagh to Lord Liverpool.

Aix, October 20, 1818.

My dear Liverpool—You will receive by an extra messenger the latest intelligence of the state of things here. Though we are essentially harmonious, we had had, within the few last days, some discussions that may be said to have been critical in their consequences. I hope we are over the worst, and that you will find no reason to be dissatisfied with the result.

You will be glad to find that there has not appeared the slightest disposition to push the discussions here beyond the line that had been chalked out by the circular from Paris; and that we have received notice from the Sovereigns to finish all business before the 15th of November. We have, in consequence, agreed to take up the questions of which I enclose a list, in the order in which they stand, with a view of coming to some understanding upon them. This, with the conclusion of our negociation in the treaties with France, will keep us very busy; but I shall not despair of clearing the table of Conference before that day. At all events, it is satisfactory to observe how little embarrassment and how much solid good grow out of these reunions, which sound so terrible at a distance. It really appears to me to be a new discovery in the

European Government, at once extinguishing the cobwebs with which diplomacy obscures the horizon, bringing the whole bearing of the system into its true light, and giving to the counsels of the great Powers the efficiency and almost the simplicity of a single State.

I rejoice to see your revenue going on so well. Save us from a session before Christmas, for God's sake! It would be a real calamity. I shall, however, not fail you, happen when it may, if I am well.

CASTLEREAGH.

Lord Bathurst to Lord Castlereagh.

Downing Street, October 20, 1818.

My dear Castlereagh—You will be desirous of receiving some account of what has passed in Cabinet, in consequence of the despatch which you will receive from me of this day's date, in order to have the feelings of the members who attended more fully explained than could be well done in an official paper.

The members who attended were Lords Liverpool, Sidmouth, and Melville, Canning, and Vansittart. Robinson was particularly engaged with the American Commissioners. We were all more or less impressed with the apprehension of great inconvenience arising from a decision being now publicly announced of continued meetings at fixed points. It is very natural in you to feel a strong wish that they should continue, from having experienced the advantages which have been derived by this which has taken place; but, even if we could be sure that the subsequent meetings would be equally cordial, is there any advantage in fixing beyond the next period; and we all, without exception, in the Cabinet, concur in thinking it very desirable that the next meeting should be fixed and announced. If I understand you right, the decision of meeting at fixed periods is to be announced in a circular letter to the other Powers, with such declarations as may satisfy them.

Do you think that any general declarations can have that
effect? We approve them (and that with difficulty too) on
this occasion, by assuring them that we only intended to treat
on the simple subject of the evacuation; but, in announcing to
them the system of periodical meetings, we must declare that
they are to be confined to any one given subject, or even
with reference to any one Power, (France) and no engagement
not to interfere in any manner in which the Law of Nations
does not justify interference, will give to the other Powers any
security, as they may apprehend that great Sovereigns, with
large armies, are not always regulated by Sir William Scott's
decisions.

You will understand that the objection which I am now
stating is not to the system, but to the expediency of declaring
it in a circular letter. Even if the circular were to announce
simply another meeting, I should doubt the expediency of
writing it; for such letters seldom do any good whatever, and
are generally productive of much inconvenient discussion in Parliament. The decision itself might be otherwise announced.

The objections which Canning feels on this subject are not
confined to the inexpediency of announcing a decision of meeting at fixed periods, but to the system itself. He does not consider the ninth Article as having been generally understood to
apply to any meetings except for the purpose of watching the
internal state of France, as far as it may endanger the public
tranquillity. He thinks that system of periodical meetings of
the four great Powers, with a view to the general concerns of
Europe, new, and of very questionable policy; that it will
necessarily involve us deeply in all the politics of the Continent, whereas our true policy has always been not to interfere
except in great emergencies, and then with a commanding
force. He thinks that all other States must protest against
such an attempt to place them under subjection; that the
meetings may become a scene of cabal and intrigue; and that
the people of this country may be taught to look with great

jealousy for their liberties, if our Court is engaged in meetings with great despotic monarchs, deliberating upon what degree of revolutionary spirit may endanger the public security, and therefore require the interference of the Alliance. This last, however, he only stated as a popular argument.

I do not subscribe to Canning's opinions, nor did any of the Cabinet who attended. But, if this is felt by him, it is not unreasonable to apprehend it may be felt by many other persons, as well as by our decided opponents. And what I wish to ask you is, why take the bull by the horns? Why, by a premature promulgation, should you, by anticipation, bring for the immediate decision of a new Parliament, of doubtful affections, the propriety of establishing a system which, if it be found to be good, will establish itself by one meeting giving rise to another, as the benefit may be experienced at each meeting. And, as all political systems have their day, it will have a less marked end if periodical meetings have not been previously fixed.

There can be no objection to an understanding with each other that you will continue to meet; and the ninth Article has completely provided for such meetings; so that there is no necessity for any additional engagements. All that you need do now is to fix the next meeting; and you will observe that even Canning does not make any objection to such a decision.

I have written to you fully and without disguise, stating my own objections stronger than I should do in Cabinet, and, I think, not overstating the opinions of others. Had Canning's opinions been less essential, the contents of the despatch might have been consigned to a private letter; but, in order to make what now goes out as little official as the nature of the case will admit, we have not used the Prince Regent's name or submitted it to his consideration.

I am sure you must know enough of our feelings towards you, not to be convinced how much hurt we shall be if this despatch shall find you so far advanced in the decision of

fixing and announcing periodical meetings as to render it difficult
for you to recommend some modification of it: the measure,
you will I am sure see, will bring on great parliamentary difficulties, which will be completely gratuitous; for we all concur
in thinking that another meeting should be fixed: and no
advantage can arise from announcing anything beyond what
the occasion requires.

Liverpool set off for Walmer as soon as the Cabinet broke
up. I promised him I would write to you, and he possibly
may write a line himself from Walmer. As my colleagues
know also that I am writing to you, I shall leave it to you to
decide how much of this letter you will answer for their
eventual reading. But there is no necessity of my making
any communication, and possibly I had better not leave the
whole for a public reply. I have only to add that, if you
write a circular letter to the other Powers, it will be very
desirable for you to have a draft of it sent over here, if possible, as these are compositions which often lead to much unnecessary discussion in Parliament, unless they are carefully
worded.

Yours very sincerely,   BATHURST.

Lord Melville to Lord Castlereagh.

Admiralty, October 22, 1818.

Dear Castlereagh—We have received letters to-day from
Commodore Bowles, and I think it right to send you without
delay a copy of one of them. I have sent the original to Lord
Liverpool at Walmer, to which place Lord Bathurst is also
gone early this morning.

You will probably recollect that when the Russian ships
came to Spithead some time ago, on their way to Cadiz, and
also when one or two American ships came to this country, a
considerable sensation was created by the novel circumstance
of their declining to offer the customary salutes on arriving
in our ports—a proceeding which, half a century ago, would

probably have been settled on the spot, by a broadside from
our ships.   As it is desirable not only to avoid such extremities, but to prevent any feeling of irritation against countries
with which we are and wish to continue at peace, and as the
exchanging of salutes, though apparently unimportant, is really
useful in originating mutual civilities, you would render an
essential service if you could bring the principal Powers to an
understanding on the matter.

   I do not dwell on our offended dignity by the omission of
those long established demonstrations of respect and good-
will, because we have it in our own power to be equally un-
civil, and to refuse any assistance in our ports to vessels in
every case where such omission takes place.   To that alternative we may possibly have to resort, unless the business can
be amicably arranged.   I believe that this will not be attended
with difficulty, provided we give up, as I think we ought to do,
our rule of saluting the foreign *officer*, instead of the foreign *flag*.

   . Count Lieven, in talking over this matter, when the Russian ships came to Spithead, suggested that it might be brought
forward at Aix-la-Chapelle ; and, if you can agree with the
other Powers that their Ministers at London or Paris shall
be authorized to treat respecting it, I have no doubt but we
might bring about a general and satisfactory arrangement, to
which you would probably think it right that the United
States might be invited to accede.

   On looking over the two memoranda on which you are acting as instructions, I perceive that, on the subject of the Barbary Powers, a view of it had been taken by the Cabinet on
one material point, which is different from the impression, as
far as I recollect, on your mind as well as my own, when we
conversed upon it some months ago.   I allude to the paragraph
in which it is stated that the refusal of France to enter into
the Mediterranean league ought not to be a bar, *sine quâ non*,
against our entering into it.   It would be unreasonable in me
to pronounce a different opinion, without having heard the argu-

ments pro and con, which induced the Cabinet to come to that conclusion ; but (without troubling you with the reasons which occur to me) I cannot get rid of my former leaning on that point.

You seem to be very gay and comfortable at Aix-la-Chapelle, drinking probably the old toast of "Happy to meet, sorry to part—happy to meet again."

I remain ever yours sincerely,   MELVILLE.

Lord Bathurst to Lord Castlereagh.

Walmer Castle, October 23, 1818.

My dear Castlereagh—I am in great hopes, by the despatch which I have just received, that the business is taking a shape which will get over our difficulties. I own, I think it would be the safest thing to separate without any declaration, as we know how roughly these State papers are apt to be handled in Parliament, and that if, in defending them, a different construction is given to any part by different members of the Government, advantage is taken of it, and differences of opinion are discovered, which, for any practical object, for the present at least, would be otherwise of no importance. I can understand, however, how difficult it would be for a meeting constituted as yours is to separate without some declaration or other ; and therefore all I can say is, that the more general it is the better.

I think Gentz's paper might do, with some alterations.   He had better not have confirmed the Treaties by adding, "après l'examen le plus rigoureux ;" for that involves an examination of every particular, which might be inconvenient.   Prince Metternich's criticisms have given you a sample of this, and you would have more in Parliament.

The great difficulty is how to invite the King of France to these meetings, keeping in view the prominent object of them, viz., France herself. If you give to them a more general object, we give to the Quadruple Alliance something of a new character, and we shall excite the jealousy of other Powers, who, as the Emperor says in his paper, will have a right to complain, if they are excluded. For this reason, I think that part of Gentz's paper is a little objectionable, and I should like it better if the invitation was given to any meetings which might take place, than say that the King was invited to become a part of the *engagements* to meet under the 6th Article.

Have you received a letter from me, recommending for your protection Lord Guilford's negociation with Prince Metternich, about claims on the part of the Ionian States to some money in the Venetian funds, which we are ready to commute for books for the Ionian university? If not, (as I am apprehensive I mislaid the letter) do not plead ignorance when you see Lord Guilford.

Yours very sincerely, BATHURST.

Lord Liverpool to Lord Castlereagh.

Walmer Castle, October 23, 1818.

My dear Castlereagh—I received yesterday, at this place, your despatches Nos. 13 and 14. Bathurst arrived here on a visit for a few days, and he has likewise read them. His letter of Tuesday will have apprised you of our general sentiments upon the present state of the negociation, and we are happy to find that you are likely to be able to send over the Declaration for our consideration, before it is definitively settled.

We cannot but feel anxious on this subject, on many accounts. In the first place, there is no *practical question*, as formerly, now at issue; it is more a discussion as to *words* than *things*. We are all satisfied with our existing engagements: there are some stipulations in them, to which it would be difficult perhaps to reconcile the minds of some persons in this country, under present circumstances; but there is no necessity nor desire to abrogate them. We must only be cautious in adding to them, and even in bringing the doubtful points too prominently forward. In this view the Emperor of Russia's notions are quite mistaken and inadmissible. Gentz's Paper appears to come near the true state of the case. In short, is it necessary to say more than that we adhere to our existing treaties and engagements, and that, whenever the Sovereigns or their Ministers shall have occasion to deliberate collectively on any of the points growing out of the last peace, the French Government shall be invited to be a party to the deliberations. If it is thought advisable, with a view of keeping France in some order, to fix a period at which the Sovereigns will again assemble, we see no objection to such a decision; and, though it might open to some misrepresentation, the good might perhaps counterbalance the inconveniences of such a proceeding; but it is often as unwise to look too far into futurity as to put narrow and contracted limits to our views.

You should be cautious, likewise, how you agree to *secret* stipulations or Protocols. Details of execution, in furtherance of open engagements, may very properly be kept from the public, but the question will certainly be put to us, whether there are any other engagements than those which are brought forward, and it would be awkward to have to equivocate upon such a matter.

We must recollect ourselves in the whole of this business, and ought to make our Allies feel (who are indirectly, if not directly, interested in it) that the general and European discussion of these questions will be in the British Parliament; that we have a new Parliament to meet, which has not been tried, of a doubtful character, and certainly not accustomed to look at foreign questions as Parliaments were some years ago, when under the pressure or immediate recollection of great foreign danger.

Believe me to be, &c.,   LIVERPOOL.

I return to town on Monday or Tuesday next.

Lord Liverpool to Lord Castlereagh.

Dover, October 23, 1818.

My dear Castlereagh—Bathurst and I came over to Dover, to deliver our letters to the Pacquet Agent, and we met your despatches No. 15, 16, and 17. We have had time only to read them very cursorily, but we have been made very nervous even by the possibility of a *new treaty*, to which France might be a party. We are persuaded such a measure would open every obnoxious topic to discussion in the most invidious manner, and we could not prevent Parliament from pronouncing an opinion upon it; whereas, whilst we keep ourselves to our existing engagements, we have the past authority of Parliament for all we do.

Such a proceeding might besides create serious differences amongst ourselves, as it might certainly be represented as contrary to the clear spirit of your instructions, if not to the letter of them, and unwarranted by any pressing necessity which could preclude your transmitting such a document for the opinion of Government at home.

Bathurst's despatch and letter of Tuesday, and my letter of to-day, will put you entirely in possession of our sentiments upon the present state of the negociations. The Russians must be made to feel that we have a Parliament and a public, to which we are responsible, and that we cannot permit ourselves to be drawn into views of policy which are wholly incompatible with the spirit of our Government.

Ever sincerely yours,   LIVERPOOL.

Lord Liverpool to Lord Castlereagh.

Walmer Castle, October 23, 1818.

My dear Castlereagh—Mulgrave is so strongly impressed with the importance of the Duke of Wellington not only being in the Cabinet, on his return from France, but of his holding the *only* military office connected with the Government, that he authorized me to tender his resignation to the Prince

Regent, and the Prince has commanded me to offer to Wellington the situation of Master-General of the Ordnance. You will be glad to hear, at the same time, that Mulgrave has agreed to continue in the Cabinet, not only from feelings of personal regard, but likewise as it obviates all misconception as to the nature and character of the arrangement. I have written by this mail to Wellington on the subject.

If the Queen should live about six days longer, it will not be necessary to meet before Christmas.

Ever sincerely yours,   LIVERPOOL.

Lord Clancarty to Lord Castlereagh.

Bruxelles, October 29, 1818.

My dear Lord—I have little to add upon the subject of my despatch of this date, except that, in order to effect the complete accession by this Court, it may perhaps be requisite to furnish them officially with a more complete copy of the treaty of the 9th than that conveyed in your circular, for the purpose of having the same set forth in the Act of Accession.

In the list which accompanied one of your despatches to England, purporting to set forth the business you have to conclude at Aix, I do not recollect to have seen one item, which, though small in itself, is, however, of some consequence, inasmuch as some scandal has already been produced by it, all repetition of which it would be highly desirable to prevent—I refer to the little State of Kniphausen. You may recollect that, some time since, this was taken possession of by an armed force by the Duke of Oldenburg, and the proprietor (Bentinck Rhone) expelled. This is not right, nor calculated to speak much in favour of the justice of the associated Powers of Europe. True it is the proprietor may not be the most respectable of men, but still he is the legitimate proprietor, and ought not thus to be driven by force from his possessions, or, at least, without being compensated as well for their value, as for the duress under which, for the purpose of effectuating a better arrangement, he may be compelled to part with his territory. That a more convenient arrangement might be made, both generally and as affecting the Duke, by placing this little dominion under the Duke of Oldenburg, I think clear, and, while at Frankfort, I suggested to the Duke the propriety of satisfying Bentinck by a liberal offer. I found, however, that this Duke, though fully desirous and determined to keep the sovereignty, was very little inclined to pay for it. This matter should now be settled. Enclosed is a Protocol of one of our Frankfort sittings, in which it was brought forward by the Russian Minister. There appears to me no objection sufficiently strong to operate against the mediatisation or other conveyance of the sovereignty sought, except what may arise from the amount of the consideration to be paid for it, and which ought to be liberal.

While I was writing the above, M. de Nagell communicated to me a most curious, and I must say unwarrantable note, which he has received from the Prussian Chargé d'Affaires here; he also showed me the *projet* of his answer to it, the observations in which, though perfectly correct, were, from the very nature of the note, necessary to be made, and, if made, likely, as it appeared to me, further to irritate. I therefore requested him to take no notice of the note for a few days, but to give me a copy of it, which I would send to you, and request you frankly to show in confidence to Prince Hardenberg and Count Bernstorf, both of whom, I am sure, will at once perceive that its style is not that which ought to reign in the diplomatic relations of two Powers, whose union, from policy as well as from inclination, ought to be so complete. I should hope means will be taken by them to prevent the recurrence of notes of this sort. If, in such a line of frontier, every drunken squabble between the inhabitants which this Government is— nay, as it appears upon the face of the note itself admitted— ready to punish, threats of reprisal are to be brought forward, it will be impossible long to go on.   The same riots frequently occur upon the French frontier between the subjects of each Crown : but a very different style exists in the communication necessarily made on each side, with respect to these.

M. de Nagell does not appear to me to make any particular complaint against M. Salviati on this occasion, observing that, whether written by the former Minister, M. Brockhausen, by the present Envoy, Prince Hatzfeld, or by the Chargé d'Affaires, the Prussian notes are always in a style either menacing or at least unconciliatory.   I should hope that my troubling you upon this subject will be pardoned in favour of the motive, and am full of expectation that you will converse with Prince Hardenberg and M. de Bernstorf upon it, whose liberal and gentlemanlike feelings will, I am sure, induce them to see the necessity of that free, conciliating, honourable, and confidential communication with this Court, which, I think I may fully answer, will be at all times met with the greatest cordiality and reciprocity.

Adieu, my dear lord.   Ever most affectionately yours.

CLANCARTY.

Mr. C. Bagot to Lord Castlereagh.

Washington, October 31, 1818.

My dear Lord—In my private letter of the 7th of last month, I acquainted your lordship that Mr. Adams was then absent from Washington.   He returned on the 15th, and on the 19th I had an opportunity of communicating to him the papers transmitted to me in your lordship's confidential letter of the 8th of August.   I did not hesitate to permit Mr. Adams to peruse all these papers, and I fully explained to him that, until the receipt of the Duke of San Carlos's Note, inviting the mediation of the Allied Powers upon some specific basis, your lordship had not felt that it was in your power to make to him any communication which would be either useful or satisfactory, but that you had taken the first occasion to make him acquainted with the substance of this correspondence, which would serve to explain to him the general views of the British Government and to show the present state of their negociations upon this important subject.

When Mr. Adams had perused the papers, which he did with great attention, I gave him to understand that the course which the British Government wished to take would necessarily, as he must see, be liable to modification, upon its further discussion with the Allied Powers, and consequently that nothing in the papers could be considered as offering any pledge to the United States, on the part of Great Britain, which might fetter the future proceedings.

He seemed perfectly sensible that the communication was only to be received in this light; but he appeared to attach much interest to it; and he particularly expressed his satisfaction at the full and distinct assurance which was given in your lordship's notes that Great Britain would limit her mediation entirely to the employment of her influence and good offices, and that she was not to be induced to take any measures which might assume a character of force.

Upon my expressing a belief that the sentiments of his Majesty's Government upon this question accorded very much with those of the Government of the United States, Mr. Adams said that he thought that there could be no difference of opinion as to the propriety of the course which the British Government was desirous to pursue; that, with a view, on the one hand, to the present relations of all the Allied Powers with Spain, and, on the other, to the relations in which, by their declarations of neutrality, they were certainly placed, in respect to the South American provinces, the course proposed by Great Britain was undoubtedly the most equitable, just, and noble; and he thought that it was, at the same time, the wisest and the most prudent. But he said that, in his own individual opinion—an opinion which he seemed to intimate that he should be well satisfied to have [made] known to your lordship—he did not think that the proposed measure would be attended with success; and he professed to found his opinion not more upon the Notes given in to your lordship by the Deputies from Buenos Ayres and New Granada than upon the general complexion of all the accounts which were received from South America by the United States' Government.

He then proceeded to say, that if his opinion upon this point should eventually prove to be correct, and if all the efforts of the European Powers to reconcile in any manner the South American provinces to the authority of Old Spain should fail, he thought that then an entirely new state of things must be considered to have arisen, and that the established Governments of the world would, in that case, owe it to the very principle of their present neutrality—to the peace of mankind—and, he conscientiously believed, to the welfare and prosperity of Old Spain—to acknowledge the complete independence of such of the American provinces as had proved themselves competent to self-government. He said that, at this moment some of the provinces were, in point of fact, absolutely independent, but that they were without that responsibility to other nations for their conduct which was so essential to the general peace and security of the world that all independent Governments should have—that this undefined and anomalous state of things was pregnant with evils, of which Great Britain and the United States daily felt the consequences, in the plunder and piracy to which it inevitably led—and that every principle of political morality and public safety required that some responsibility for such atrocities as were now carried on should, if possible, be made to attach somewhere.

·In the course of our conversation, which lasted some time, Mr. Adams expressed himself in very strong terms respecting the manner in which the war was conducted on the part of the Royalists in Caraccas and Venezuela; and said that it would well become the Allied Powers, even in the present stage of the business, to remonstrate earnestly with the Spanish Government against the barbarities which were so unrelentingly and so unwisely exercised by the royal commanders.

Mr. Adams requested to know whether I should have any objection to leaving the papers in his hands, in order that he might take an opportunity of showing them to the President, offering me, at the same time, his assurance that no copies of them should be taken. I felt a good deal embarrassed by this request, with which I did not think that your lordship's letter gave me the liberty to comply; and I evaded the proposal by offering to wait upon him again at any time which he might appoint, and to accompany him, with the papers, to the President. He said that he would certainly make my offer known to the President, but I have not heard from him again upon the subject.

I have the honour to be, &c.,   CHARLES BAGOT.

Mr. Charles Bagot to Lord Castlereagh.

Washington, November 2, 1818.

My dear Lord—In a despatch which I forward to your lordship by this mail, I have transmitted copies of two letters, which I have received from Colonel Barclay, acquainting me that there is every probability that the great fort and the battery which have been erected since the peace, at an enormous expense, by the American Government, upon Lake Champlain, and upon which it is perhaps not too much to say that the command of that Lake absolutely depends, will be found to have been erected upon the British territory.

I have very little doubt that Colonel Barclay is warranted in apprehending some danger to these forts from the rage and disappointment of the people of Vermont, whenever this fact is, as it soon must be, made public; and, though I have not thought it prudent to adopt all the measures which he suggests in his private letter, it has appeared to me advisable, in every point of view, to acquaint Mr. Adams with the apprehensions which were entertained, and to record that I had given him fair warning of their existence.

The only probable interpretation which I can offer of Mr. Adams's very concise note to me is that this Government dare not encounter the unpopularity of taking any steps which might seem, in any degree, to implicate them in the eventual delivery of these works to us. I do not believe that they would suggest or encourage the demolition of them; but they would certainly rather endure any remonstrance which the British Government might make upon such an event taking place than incur the odium of appearing to have protected them for our ultimate benefit : and they perhaps conceive that, as they must belong to them until the final settlement of the whole line by the Commissioners under the 5th Article shall have allotted them to us, they had better take all the chances of that intermediate and probably distant time.

· I am not myself acquainted with the *locale* of these fortifications ; but there is, I believe, no doubt whatever that they are of the utmost importance to either party. I propose to transmit confidentially to the Duke of Richmond a copy of Colonel Barclay's letter of the 23rd of October, taking care, however, distinctly to explain to him that it is only for his private information that I do so, and not with any idea whatever that any measures can be taken on the subject on our part.

I have the honour to be, &c.,

CHARLES BAGOT.

PS. I learn from Mr. Adams that the final instructions of this Government to their Plenipotentiaries in London, upon the subjects of the Slave Trade and impressment, have not yet been sent, but that they will be despatched without delay.

C. B.

Lord Liverpool to Lord Castlereagh.

Walmer Castle, November 4, 1818.

My dear Castlereagh—As you may be pressed for time, and it is, therefore, material that you should be possessed of our sentiments on the paper enclosed in No. 19 as soon as possible, and as Bathurst is in Sussex, I sent the papers, after I had read them, to Canning. I think it best to enclose his note and comments. The general substance, you see, he entirely approves. We both agree that No. 3 would better be dispensed with altogether; but the notes upon that and upon No. 1 are of a *verbal* nature, and can constitute no serious difficulty in the adoption of them or of something analogous to them. The only important criticism is upon that part of No. 2 which affirms an opinion more decided than is necessary, or perhaps prudent, upon the internal state of France. This might *eventually* embarrass us; and I am afraid some circumstances have even recently occurred, which would make such a gratuitous opinion less advisable now than even at the time of signing the Treaty of Evacuation, when it was designedly omitted. The alteration is easily made, and I should think the Allied Ministers would see the propriety of it.

I have marked in Nos. 1 and 3, the verbal suggestions in the copies of the notes which I enclose. Have the goodness to desire Planta to take care of Canning's notes, as I have no copy of them.

The question of Parliament is at length decided, and you may rely on our not meeting before the beginning of January, probably not before the 14th, which would bring the opening for business to the 21st. I leave this place on Friday.

Ever sincerely yours,   LIVERPOOL.

Mr. Edward Cooke to Lord Castlereagh.

Brighton, November 8, 1818.

My dear Lord—I send you a letter from Sir Philip Roche to me. I believe him, as he is very well received and connected in Spain. I have requested him to let me know the particulars, as far as he is informed, of any revolutionary intentions or confederacies. If what he states be true, I think nothing but some kind of revolution can save the Spanish empire ; and my feelings are that nothing short of forming a federative empire can be effectual, on the principles of the old Germanic and present United States' system : and all the provinces should be placed, as to internal government, upon the same footing of independence with Spain herself; and there should be a central body of representatives from each province, to act under and with the King of Spain for imperial purposes.

A constitution of this kind might preserve the Spanish empire, and increase its power and stability. I see the contribution begins to embarrass. Whilst the army contingent remained in France, the extraordinary capital raised for its support producing extraordinary demand for French produce, &c., was an actual temporary benefit. Now, the army being withdrawn, and the demands for its supply having ceased, the extraordinary capital to be raised is to be sent and employed out of France, and becomes to its amount a diminution of active capital, and consequently of demand for the produce of internal industry.

The deduction of ten millions sterling in one or two years from the active capital, with a proportionate decrease of demand, must be felt in a duplicate ratio. Such is my reasoning, true or false.

I do not suppose you can have given much attention to the wild schemes of my nephew, Mr. Way. The Emperor, who knows how to mix piety and self-interest, and is as political as he is chimerical, has been flattering his vanity, and will, I fear, continue to do so. This second instance of suicide by a character of high consideration is very lamentable.

They say here that a paper, signed by 120 names, was presented to Tierney, to induce him to take the lead. Lord Camden and his family are here.

Ever, my dear lord, &c.,   E. COOKE.

The new Kremlin or Alhambra, with all its strange cupolas and minarets, does not create feelings of admiration or approbation.

Pray do not mention Sir P. Roche's name.

[Enclosure.]

Sir Philip Roche to Mr. Edward Cooke.

Madrid, October 22, 1818.

My dear Sir—It has occurred to me that it would not be disagreeable to you to receive a line from this country, and to know the actual state of things here. Believe me that nothing I could say could convey to you an adequate idea of the wretchedness, misery, want of credit, confidence, and trade, which exist from one end of the country to the other.

The King is now more detested than he ever was popular, and all classes of people speak openly of some revolutionary movement being at hand. For two years they have been talking of collecting an army at Cadiz for South America, which is as far distant from sailing as it was the first day. O'Donnel, who was to command it, is removed within these few days; and the new Ministers, who lately succeeded those who were banished, expect nothing less than a similar fate.

Russia is now all the fashion *with the Court;* but beyond the walls of the palace the hearts of all ranks are English. It is utterly impossible things can go on in the present state. Something must happen. The army is naked and unpaid—navy there is none—and the roads are covered with bands of forty or fifty robbers each, so that no escort is equal to them, and nothing but a lucky chance, or travelling in a large caravan, gives security.

If you wish it, I shall be happy to write to you from time to time, and remain always your grateful and obliged humble servant,   P. K. ROCHE.

Bruxelles, November 8, 1818.

My dear Lord—I thank you for yours of the 5th, and the trouble you have taken to infuse a more gentle style into the Prussian notes to this Court, which, I have no doubt, will be attended with advantage. Blessed are the peacemakers. The disapproval by Bernstorf of the menace of reprisal is much. I have communicated this to Nagell, and also your advice, that he should withhold his answer till Hatzfeld's arrival and communication with him : this advice will be followed.

I also, as from myself, suggested to Nagell that some degree of asperity, or, at least an unconciliatory tone, accompanied possibly with some little desire *de chicaner*, the Prussian Government might perhaps reign in their official notes to the agents of and other communications with that Court. He solemnly assured me that this was not the case; that, so far from it, they were more particularly cautious with respect to the terms which they employed in their communications with that Court than with any other ; and this because they were anxious to keep themselves right, where they felt they were treated with wrong; and he could assure me also of the King's practice, wherever feasible, to comply with the wishes of Prussia, and of his wishes (evinced by heavy sacrifices which he had made for this purpose) to conciliate the friendship of that Court.

We had for some days prior to the arrival of your courier of the 5th been aware of the embarrassment which the money market at Paris would present to the making good the payment, under the Convention of the 9th ult. The arrival here on Friday of your decision upon this subject was well-timed ; and I have confidentially communicated to the King the substance of the corrected arrangement, as conveyed by the Protocol, with which his Majesty appears perfectly satisfied. Whether, on your passage home to England, you shall go by

Paris, or at once directly by Calais, still Bruxelles will be your best road; the road to Paris by Namur, though perhaps shorter, is vile, unfrequented, and unsupplied with regular relays. We should hope, therefore, you will come this way, and make as long an abode here as you can.

Ever affectionately yours,   CLANCARTY.

How strange the substance of the papers sent to the Duke by the Dutch courier! with this I was generally made acquainted before his departure. The folly of a plot is no argument against its investigation; and this is properly going on.

Lord Castlereagh to Lord Liverpool.

Aix-la-Chapelle, November 9, 1818.

My dear Liverpool—I received your letter from Walmer of the 3rd, with Canning's notes enclosed, and shall do what I can to profit by your joint suggestions. Some of them have already been, as you will see, attended to. There is no difficulty about the word *solidarité*. They will, I dare say, leave it out. They certainly intend to use it in the fair sense of *solidarité* of the four Powers in their common engagements as against France.

The comments upon the internal affairs of France I managed to avoid in our business proceedings; but when we became composers, and the *redaction* fell into Capodistrias' hands, it was impossible to prevent these episodes, and difficult to displace them when once introduced. Some of them, as *legitime* and *constitutionelle*, you will find, have been admitted by us in some of our joint notes in 1815, at Paris, and are *sacramental* words in the Russian Chancellerie used *as often as possible*. I have, however, endeavoured to reconcile them to reduce, if not to expunge, this species of matter. It is not a point, however, as I hope you will feel, to make a *sine quâ non* upon; especially as the papers, to gain time, have been communicated to the Duke de Richelieu, though confidentially, and have been seen by this time at

Paris. I shall not, therefore, *insist* upon any change of this nature to which he objects: but, in good sense, he ought with us to desire to make the internal affairs of France as little as possible an object of Opposition attack in England. I think he may possibly wish for some expressions of confidence from the Powers towards the King. It was with this view, as strengthening his Government, that the passage Canning has marked was introduced into the note to the Duke de Richelieu. I had much rather it was not there; but, if you examine it, I do not think the two propositions on which it rests would embarrass us much in discussion, even if future events should turn out ill.

We assert that progress has been made in the last three years, and that we rely on the King's wisdom for the *progressive* consolidation of the order of things established in France. The truth of the first cannot well be questioned: it is the basis of our case for evacuating. The second is a hope, advantageous perhaps to the King to have expressed, and in which, if we are disappointed, we cannot incur much reproach. Whilst we preserve our Quadruple Alliance, we essentially prove that we are not defective in vigilance. With this reserve, perhaps, our language may be permitted to take somewhat a tone of hope and confidence without prejudice.

The expressions in allusion to the Holy Alliance, I think Canning, if he reads the Prince Regent's letter to the Sovereigns at Paris, will feel we could not object to; and, if we are to go on with Russia for any time, I fear it is in vain to hope for a pure vocabulary.

I am, &c.,   CASTLEREAGH.

Lord Liverpool to Lord Castlereagh.

Fife House, November 9, 1818.

My dear Castlereagh—I received your despatches of the 2nd of November, just before I left Walmer. You will have received, in my letter of the 3rd, so full a statement of our sentiments upon your former communications, and you appear now to be so entirely apprised of them, by the observations you made to the Emperor of Russia, on Count Capodistrias' Paper, that I have nothing further to say on the subject at present, not doubting that you will be able to reconcile any differences which may continue to exist, and to obviate, in a great measure if not entirely, the objections which we have here felt to some of the passages in the drafts which have been transmitted to us.

The most embarrassing question which you appear now to have to discuss is that relative to the mediation between Spain and her colonies. I should be very glad to think that the Spanish Government had decided not to press the mediation any further; but, from Sir Henry Wellesley's last despatches, I should draw a different conclusion. The new Spanish Minister, however, does not appear to have profited by the errors of his predecessor. He seems even inclined to retrograde; for his last proposition is that the commerce of England and other friendly Powers with the colonies shall only be carried on through Spanish ports. This at once revives the whole colonial system; and, even if it were sufficient to satisfy our interested views, it would reduce the colonies to that state of dependence upon the mother-country, to which it is impossible to presuppose that any of them will in future submit.

There is one distinction upon this question, which I believe I stated before you left England, but to which I doubt whether you have sufficiently adverted—I mean the distinction between those parts of South America which have made *a formal declaration of independence* and those which have not. Now, I confess I do not see how we can expect that the former should ever retract. They may possibly, though not probably, be subdued; but, short of subjugation, I do not see that in honour they have any retreat.

I can contemplate no possible compromise with these provinces but the acknowledging their independence under some younger branch of the Spanish family.

With respect to the provinces which have not yet gone this desperate length, there is room for mediation and negociation ; but, if they are to be undertaken, the Spanish Government should lose no time in bringing forward or authorizing propositions to be made.

The declared independence of Chili was the result of the operations of last year ; and I should think the independence of Peru will very speedily be the result of those of the present.

I saw Count Münster at Canterbury, on my way to town. He had been detained there, in consequence of the Countess being delivered of twins. I was very well satisfied, upon the whole, with the account he gave me of the state of affairs upon the Continent. He speaks in the highest terms of the Duchess of Clarence, whose pregnancy is one of the most important events that could occur, with respect to the situation of this country.

Believe me to be, &c.,   LIVERPOOL.

Lord Liverpool to Lord Castlereagh.

Fife House, November 10, 1818.

My dear Castlereagh—Since I wrote to you yesterday, we have received your despatches of the 5th instant. The Protocol and draft of the declaration contained in them appear now to be as free from objection as we had any right to expect.

The *Protocole reservé*, to which you refer, is not amongst these papers, but I have no doubt you will take care that there shall be nothing in it which will involve us in any difficulties when we come to explain ourselves to Parliament. Bathurst will, I know, write to you upon your other despatches, as well as upon the business of St. Helena.

I think you ought to apprise the Emperor of Russia that

his friend Eugene Beauharnois is certainly conspiring, and will get into a scrape if he is not more guarded in his conduct.

Believe me to be, &c.,   LIVERPOOL.

Lord Bathurst to Lord Castlereagh.

Downing Street, November 10, 1818.

My dear Castlereagh—You have so neutralized the Protocol and declaration, that there cannot be any objection, I imagine, from any quarter against them.

I very much regret Capodistrias' journey to the Ionian Islands, and am much obliged to you for preventing the joint expedition. I will endeavour to prevent a simultaneous residence there. The visit must do mischief; but the best way of treating it is by Sir Thomas covering him with all attentions; and I will write to him to that effect.

Yours very sincerely,   BATHURST.

Lord Clancarty to Lord Castlereagh.

Bruxelles, November 12, 1818.

My dear Lord—Johnson, with your despatches for England and private letter of the 9th, arrived here at a very late hour on Tuesday eve. After detaining him solely for the time requisite for reading the papers under flying seal, he was sent forward.

Certainly, neither the question of guarantee nor the proposal of Hardenberg respecting the Prussian troops, are in a state to be made known here, the latter subject particularly, as coming from Prussia, I hope never will, as the knowledge of it, as proceeding from that quarter, would answer no other purpose than that of irritation and alienation.

If the other Allied Courts shall be absolutely determined to enter into such a Convention of guarantee as is described in Prince Metternich's paper, admitting into it France, the

German League, and the Netherlands, inviting the countenance of Great Britain to the system, and excluding all others
from participation in it, as therein set forth, vague and undefined as I still consider this question of guarantee to be, notwithstanding the more precise form which it has thus assumed,
in my opinion Great Britain should lend herself to the
system by complying with such invitation.   Not to do so
would, in my mind, be to exclude herself from the Continent,
and the more so, as I cannot help thinking that the natural
operation of the projected treaty will be at least the partial, if
not the entire, supersession of that of Quadruple Alliance.   I
am further of opinion that the mode of effecting this should be
by treaty, and not either by note or protocol; as well because
I think this is the most dignified form, as that the matter
should be brought before Parliament, and this directly by
Government, instead of being suffered, as will inevitably be
the case, to be forced forward by Opposition, who, as the invitation will appear in the original Act, will not fail to become
acquainted with it, and unanswerably to press for the production of the answer, in whatever form it may have been given.

What a fortunate circumstance it is that the Queen's state
has enabled you to be at Aix during the whole of this reunion
there ! however much I will allow you are to be pitied for the
struggles you have been involved in by the modern philosophic
rhodomontade, coupled with an eternal *besoin de faire* of one
Court and the pusillanimity of another, while you have, I
believe, found little true assistance from the Minister of the
third, always fluctuating and generally weak and wrong-headed
in his determinations when they are made.   Though I think
Parliament can scarcely find fault with your accession to the
proposed system, the invitation to which is certainly flattering
to Great Britain, and marks the weight attached to her countenance, and this without subjecting her to any onerous stipulation,
yet I wish this subject had not arisen, or could still be avoided
altogether.   Things seem to me to stand well as they were,

and I fear the doing more will produce weakness rather than strength to those who really seek the permanence of peace and the best means of defence in case of war.

In truth, I do not yet well understand the projected measure. What is to be the state of the parties *inter se* under it? It should seem that they cannot go to war with each other, because the principal object is to maintain peace, and because the natural consequence of war between continental powers in the vicinage of each other is invasion, and then the *casus fœderis* arises in favour of the invaded party, whose territories are guaranteed, and this however wrong he may have been in the outset. But, if they cannot vindicate themselves each against the other, must not some mode be assigned for settling disputes between them? None such is stated; and, if means for this purpose were brought forward, would not the association thus raised erect itself into a confederation of States equally with the Germanic body? And what would be the effect of this? Again the parties engage to confine themselves within their actual limits—does the *casus fœderis* arise if they exceed them?—if so, they are equally tied up from making war on others. Would this be wise, or even practicable? If, on the other hand, without impeachment from his confederates, any one of the parties may make war upon other States, then, as conquest is a natural right of war, this part of the engagement becomes a dead letter, or, at most, an honourable undertaking of little value; for it would be absurd to consider a treaty of surrender, or peace, after conquest, as anything like a cession *de gré à gré*, for which an exception is made.

These, and several other equally important considerations on the construction, bearing, and possible effects of such a measure, it would be well for the immediate parties maturely to reflect upon, previously to their entering upon such an engagement. To prevent probable future interferences from some among them, and avoid misunderstandings, loose construction should of all things be avoided. The more simple

and the less multiplied the means by which the great Powers
are kept together for mutual defence and the preservation of
peace, the less likelihood there will be in my view of interruption to their union.

With respect to the second subject on which you have
desired my sentiments, viz., that of Prince Hardenberg's proposal that Prussian troops should be left in the Netherlands, I
have no hesitation in stating it as one to which I conceive it
would be absolutely impossible ever to obtain the assent of this
King; and with this opinion I would close this letter, only I
am desirous of saying a few words on part of Prince Hardenberg's memorandum on the position of Prussia. Much of
what is there said of his difficulties as to the extended line and
division of her territories, the different habits, pursuits, and
religion of her subjects, is certainly true, and renders some
effort by her necessary for the purpose of conciliating the inhabitants of her new dominions to her rule. Alas! none has
been made; but, on the contrary, till a very late period, all,
and, till the present moment, most of the grievous oppressions
of the Provisional Government continue to weigh down the
population of those countries. It is never an easy thing or
the work of a moment to reconcile a people to a new Government placed over them by others. We all know how much
the better part of a century it took to reconcile Scotland to her
union with England; nevertheless it was accomplished; and
with care and attention to their wants, encouragement to their
industry, and mildness of administration, this may and would
be effected, though gradually, in the Prussian transrhenane
provinces. It is admitted that, in the interim, the Government cannot avail itself of their full strength; but, by such
conduct, this strength would daily grow greater in the support
of Government.

Notwithstanding Prince Hardenberg, silent on the great and
even culpable share his Government has had in the promotion
rather than counteraction of this cause of weakness, as appli-

cable to the Prussian State, puts forth the bad spirit of the
people, which he presumes to exist in Belgium, and the impossibility of amalgamating the southern provinces of this
kingdom with Holland, as principal causes of the weakness of
the Belgic bulwark, and accuses the faults of the Constitution
and imbecility of this Government as co-operating therewith,
he would be surprised to find the progress made in the public
mind, within a few months, towards reconciliation with the
present order of things, and the satisfaction which not only the
people but the clergy show, arising from the great prosperity
and encouragement both enjoy under that very Constitution
and Government of which he complains. The vast advance
made in this respect in the short course of twelve months has
exceeded every conception I could have formed.   To say,
however, that the people in the south are enthusiastic in favour
of their Government, or even universally attached to it, would
be going too far: those who could have expected such a result
in so short a period are more sanguine than wise, and are but
little acquainted with the character of this people, but that
they are generally content, and that many thousands among
them will be found ready to fight for their Government, I
verily believe; and this, I am sure, is all that could have been
reasonably looked for within the period.   This part of Prince
Hardenberg's reasoning (and I am happy in feeling myself
able to congratulate him upon it) completely fails; and I
should hope that the good consequences of mild government
and encouragement, so strikingly apparent here, may even
induce him to try the same experiment on the other side of
the Meuse.

With respect to the intrigues of the French emigrants, there
has been no lack of vigour on the part of the Netherlands'
authorities, for more than a year back, in endeavouring to
control them; and to this I partly attribute the better feeling
prevalent in this country; and though very recently a diabolical plot has been discovered among these emigrants, yet

this might have taken place anywhere. It will also, I believe, be found to have existed among the emigrants in other States; while it has not only been discovered here, but the Government have hitherto evinced no want of energy in its investigation. On this score, therefore, I should think Prince Hardenberg may likewise feel himself at rest.

As to the alleged principles which this Court may follow with regard to Prussia, much indeed would it be to be lamented if any could exist on either side of a nature to throw the slightest degree of damp upon the close intercourse which ought to subsist between them. Of the description of these principles, Prince Hardenberg specifies nothing; if he had, it would be my utmost endeavour to have sought to render them such as should tend only to the most sincere harmony and best understanding between the two Governments. While Prince Hardenberg, however, is silent as to their nature, we know that his agents here have passed at least one note, little adapted to the communication between one friendly Government with another, and ill-calculated to inspire confidence, or to render stronger a connexion which, for every reason, ought to be the most entire; and we further know that the Minister of this country has taken the most gentle and conciliatory means to obviate the past and to prevent the future recurrence of such causes of alienation.

I shall say little on the progress of the investigation going on here, as the Duke is regularly made acquainted with all the details. The manner in which I have represented the matter to Government you will find in the duplicate of my despatch on the subject conveyed to you by this messenger. In this I have from misinformation stated that Laborde was the person who went to the King, which is not so; and I am sorry to say this person appears to have escaped, and, as I believe, through the assistance of a German aide-de-camp to the military governor of this town. Cambacérès was under examination last night—I have not yet heard the particulars.

May I trouble you to send me, by the first messenger, a copy of your Protocol, by which the change is made in the terms of payment, as originally arranged under the Convention of the 9th ult.! Nagell has requested me to procure it for him. I have no copy of this, or of any other paper passing through my hands under flying seal. None have been taken, for two reasons: first, for want of permission; and secondly, because such permission should not be sought or granted, as copies could not be taken without the too great detention of the messengers.

Adieu. Pray arrange to pass some days with us in your passage through Bruxelles.

Ever most affectionately yours,   CLANCARTY.

Lord Bathurst to Lord Castlereagh.

Downing Street, November 13, 1818.

My dear Castlereagh—I would not have troubled you with a private letter in addition to the despatch, if I had not thought it desirable to state to you that our Cabinet consisted of only Liverpool, Harrowby, Sidmouth, Vansittart, and myself. In this state we were not prepared to say anything more decidedly than we have done in regard to our accession, as far as good offices go, to the projected treaty, in the event of your not being able to prevail on the Emperor of Russia and the King of Prussia to forego the idea altogether; and yet I thought you would prefer hearing from us immediately to waiting until a Cabinet could be assembled from different parts of the country. There will be a much better chance of our all agreeing on the question when we all meet, if it shall appear that it has not been already concluded. Much, you are aware also, will depend upon the wording. I think all who were present liked the manner in which Prince Metternich stated it; but we are very desirous of getting rid of the business altogether, if you can do so without disappointing the Emperor

of Russia, so as to send him away out of humour.   Liverpool
feels this very much.

Yours very sincerely,   BATHURST.

Lord Clancarty to Lord Castlereagh.

Bruxelles, November 15, 1818.

My dear Lord—The grievances stated in Count Bernstorf's
paper shall be investigated: it is, however, already gratifying
to find it admitted by this paper that, at the respective times
when each of these complaints was officially made known to
this Government, immediate assurances were given of their
redress ; and I am generally assured that, where there has
been ground, the parties transgressing have uniformly been
prosecuted, and, when in the service of this Government, dismissed from their situations.   This seems to be all that can
reasonably be required; to demand that the laws of this
country, upon the statement conveyed in Count Bernstorf's
paper, should be changed, is neither just, nor would compliance
with it be within the King's power.   To prevent the irritation
occasioned by the necessary interference of *douaniers* on both
sides, I am informed that this Government were desirous and
offered to negociate a treaty of commerce with that of Prussia,
but that this was declined.

This Court willingly admits the interest they have in being
upon the most friendly terms with their neighbour, and their
anxiety, strongly shown by substantive acts, to foster good
harmony and confidential relation by every means in their
power, but they state that the tone taken by Prussia (or, possibly, in many cases, by the agents of that Government, unknown to their superiors) is such towards them as to be quite
incompatible with that which should govern the communications of one independent State towards another ; that they
cannot suffer themselves to be considered as the vassals of
Prussia, or allow themselves to be *kicked* by her ; that, if they

were to prepare a recriminating list of grievances, they could easily do so to a far greater extent than that produced, and where no satisfaction, not even that of a civil answer, has been returned. Nay, even such is the contempt with which they have been treated, that where the King, for the very purpose of making a first step towards conciliation, and for the purpose of inviting friendship, had, at my instigation, consented to remit the money due to this country for the subsistence of the Prussian troops in the campaign of 1815, and had personally to his Prussian Majesty, and also officially, made the offer of this sacrifice on his part, that offer was met by the most profound silence, and, up to the present moment, has never even been accepted, far less have any thanks or expressions of gratitude been returned for it. In short, my dear lord, it will require your best offices with Prince Hardenberg and Count Bernstorf, as it will mine with this King and his Ministry, to place things upon the proper footing on which they ought to be between the two Courts.

When I wrote last, I was not aware of the existence of any other Protocol on the money subject than that of the 3rd instant. The receipt of your despatches under flying seal for England made me acquainted with that of the 11th. The necessity of enabling this Government to prepare for their Budget arrangements of the year to be immediately arranged, preparatory to their submission to the States-General, will, I trust, induce your approbation of my having confidentially communicated the substance of these papers to the King, *en attendant* the permission sought by my last for transmitting to him copies of them. The King expressed some dismay at the intelligence, telling me most confidentially that he had reason to be apprehensive that much embarrassment actually existed in the house of Hope at Amsterdam, and that he even apprehended a failure there; that this could scarcely occur without shaking Baring; and, if this took place, all security for the French payments was at an end: however, the embarrassment, which he had strong ground to believe existed, might be got over, and that we should know more of this after the 30th of the present month, when the differences were to be paid. So far his Majesty, who does not seem to me otherwise to care about the postponed payment than as it indicates diminished security.

I shall most heartily congratulate you if, as one of your last despatches expresses the hope, you shall· have succeeded in procuring the adjournment of the Guarantee question.

Shall I procure apartments for you and yours, and to what extent, at the Hôtel de Wellington, close to this hotel, and from what date ? I trust you will stay several days here and live with us, except when engaged to the Court. ·

Yours most affectionately,   CLANCARTY.

November 16, 1818.

· PS. The packet from England not having yet arrived, I am enabled to add that I have this morning had a long conference with M. Six, the Minister of Finance in this country —a very clever man, and well informed on the money transactions of this kingdom. He does not seem the least alarmed or apprehensive of the solvability of the house of Hope at Amsterdam, or otherwise to dislike your late transaction of the 11th instant, the substance of which I stated to him confidentially, than as being less explicit than that of the 3rd, in giving the choice to the several Powers of the places on which the bills for their payment should be respectively made ; and also in being silent as to the payment of interest on the course of the bills of exchange when delivered. I mentioned to him confidentally my conversation with the King, and the fears his Majesty had expressed relative to the house of Hope. He told me that he had daily confidential intelligence from Amsterdam from the very best sources ; and that none of· these in the slightest degree hinted at anything which could give foundation for any apprehension of the nature of that entertained by his Majesty; that it was true, indeed, that the house in question was endeavouring to realize funds, but this was nothing but what, under present circumstances, was to have been expected; neither was there the smallest difficulty in discounting their paper, or consequent suspicion of their credit; that it was also true that the house of Berenbroke, a very considerable one at Amsterdam, had dealt very largely in the late speculations in France, and appeared to be very greatly embarrassed by the course things had taken at Paris, and that by the failure of this house (which he thought not unlikely) it was by no means impossible that some inconvenience might be suffered by that of Hope; but he did not believe that it was at all probable that this could amount to a suspension of payments.

I suspect, therefore, that the state of this house of Berenbroke has operated upon the King's fears, and, in connexion with the fresh postponement of the French liquidations, led his Majesty to apprehend greater evils than the circumstances duly appreciated would warrant, and that this is the whole of the matter.

M. de Nagell has just sent me his answers to the grievances stated by Count Bernstorf. I send a copy of them, opposite to a copy of the grievances, which will enable you to judge how far they are sufficient.

C.

Lord Castlereagh to Lord Melville.

Brussels, November 26, 1818.

My dear Melville—I have not written to you, in reply to your private letter, as I had not an opportunity, till the close of our proceedings, to execute your commission relative to the flags. You will find, by one of our last Protocols, that the several Powers have agreed to instruct their Ministers in London to enter upon this business, and to agree upon one common system of salute, upon a principle of reciprocity.

You will also perceive by my despatches that our delibera-

tions on the Barbaresque question never reached the point
upon which you seemed to doubt: on the contrary, by the
step we have agreed upon, France is obliged to declare herself,
and to execute with us a joint remonstrance in the name of
the other Powers. Without something of this sort, we should
have left Russia in a state of discontent and separation, which
would probably have led to her acceding to the Treaty of
Alcala. The Powers have separated in the greatest possible
good-humour.

I am, dear Melville, &c.,   CASTLEREAGH.

Lord Castlereagh to Lord Liverpool.

Brussels, November 26, 1818.

My dear Liverpool—In reply to your letter on Spanish
affairs, I think it right to mention that we have never been
sufficiently advanced upon details to render it, in my judgment,
prudent to bring forward, at least on our part, any proposition
relative to Buenos Ayres. Our taking the lead would only
have exposed us to additional jealousy; and, as France is
quite decided upon the necessity of treating this case upon its
own grounds, we may safely leave this point to work itself, if
the mediation should ever come to anything, which is now very
doubtful.

I think we have left the whole question in the state which
will give us, as a Government, the least possible trouble.
From the tone of Don Carlos's Note to me, and some language
held by Fernan Nuñez at Paris to the Prussian and French
Ministers, that his Court declined proceeding with the mediation, we consider the whole as at an end, unless Spain should
make some new overture. In this event, we have taken up
our ground upon principles so fair in themselves, yet so repugnant to all the past prejudices of Spain, that either we get rid
of the negociation *in limine*, or we bring Spain to occupy our
ground. In this case, I presume the King will ask the Duke

of Wellington, as a preliminary measure, to go to Madrid, to concert with him a basis of negociation on the part of the mediating Powers. I own I think this a most advantageous part of the arrangement, because it enables us to be sure of our grounds, before we embark, as a Government, in any ostensible proceeding. The Duke of Wellington, going there fully possessed of the views of the Cabinet, would be enabled to bring the Spanish Government much more effectually, and in a much shorter time, to a point, than I could hope to do through San Carlos in London; and, instead of beginning with a negociation in the dark, we should be to decide upon the Duke of Wellington's report, whether there was room to proceed further or not.

It is quite clear that Madrid is the most unfit place of any for negociating with the South Americans, but it is the best to settle the plan in outline. This will be better done by the Duke of Wellington than by a Conference, and his going there would save the Spanish pride, without incurring any inconvenience. The probability is that we shall not again be applied to on this subject; but, if we should, I hope you will concur with me in opinion that we have got the question on good grounds, and that the lead which the mediating Powers are unanimously desirous of giving to the Duke of Wellington in the business will keep the whole in our own hands, without creating jealousy in the other Courts, by withdrawing it absolutely from theirs.

CASTLEREAGH.

PS. We arrived at this place to a late dinner to-day.

Alexander Prince of Solms to Lord Castlereagh.

Paris, le 9 Decembre, 1818.

Milord—Le mot que j'ai osé vous dire hier a donné lieu au travail et à la lettre que j'ai l'honneur de vous confier. La nature est tellement délicate que je ne prétends point savoir si

vous la trouverez digne d'être mise sous les yeux de son
Altesse Royale, ou si vous la jugerez digne d'être détruite.
Restant, Milord, dans cette incertitude, l'indiscretion d'oser
même avoir une opinion sur des matières aussi importantes,
qui me sont aussi étrangères, perd de son poids.   Le bonheur
de son Altesse Royale et celui de votre patrie, Milord, ré-
clamera toujours mes premiers vœux, et la persuasion que l'un
et l'autre sont les vrais soutiens du système auquel l'Europe
devra revenir, et auquel j'ai sacrifié le bonheur de ma vie, mais
avec amertume l'existence de notre maison, me fait redoubler
ces vœux tous les jours.

La position dans laquelle je me suis mis, en me prononçant
si violemment contre la Confédération du Rhin, et en empêchant par la crainte que je leur présentois de l'avenir ceux
de ma famille qui penchoient pour ce système d'en partager les
avantages, m'empêchant d'habiter l'Allemagne, j'achève mon
hiver à Paris, pour aller au printems à Berlin et à Strelitz.
Si mon projet étoit gouté, le bonheur de ma vie seroit de
donner, par mon zèle et ma discrétion à toute épreuve, même
vis-à-vis de ceux qui me sont les plus proches, des preuves de
mes sentimens ; un détour par Turin et Vienne pour me rendre
à Berlin n'étonneroit personne, et des instructions envoyées
ici par un personnage peu marquant ne pourroient être soup-
çonnées par personne.   La mort de Madame la Princesse
Charlotte, et l'opinion du pays qu'elle habite, mettroit bien peu
d'obstacle de la part de la personne qui au premier aperçu
paroit devoir rendre ce projet impossible.   Ma démarche,
comme une preuve de mon entier dévouement et de ma confiance sans bornes, demande votre indulgence et vous dispense
à mon égard de toute réponse, verbale ou écrite, sur une
matière trop délicate pour être abordée sans la plus extrème
discrétion.

J'ai l'honneur d'être, avec les sentimens les plus distingués,
Milord, votre très humble et tres obéissant Serviteur,

ALEXANDRE Prince de Solms.

[Enclosures.]

The Prince of Solms to his Royal Highness the Prince Regent.

Paris, le 9 Decembre, 1818.

Monseigneur—Il faut être pénétré autant que je le suis d'admiration pour votre Altesse Royale, il faut l'être d'autant de reconnoissance pour la bonté avec laquelle elle a daigné me traiter quand j'ai été assez heureux pour lui faire ma cour, pour être emporté par le zèle pour son service au point de vous faire la démarche que je fais aujourd'hui. C'est la circonstance que je puis, par Lord Castlereagh, faire parvenir à ses pieds une idée qui me tourmente depuis long-tems (sans que personne puisse en avoir connoissance) qui me décide à cette témérité.

Il est impossible que la question des Catholiques ne se renouvelle durant le règne de votre Altesse Royale, et il est impossible aussi d'y opposer toujours la même fermeté de laquelle cependant le tableau de la succession au trône montre une si bonne raison. Mon idée favorite seroit qu'au lieu d'un sujet de juste alarme, votre Altesse Royale puisât dans le projet des innovations un affermissement à son autorité Royale : ceux qui auroient remporté le triomphe de l'emancipation des Catholiques auroient mauvaise grace à s'opposer à son mariage avec une Princesse de cette religion, et son choix tombant sur la Princesse de Sardaigne (à laquelle ses deux sœurs ainées devroient céder leurs droits) elle voit mieux que mon foible talent ne pourrait le déduire les avantages de cette position.

Ma démarche sort tellement de toutes les mesures que le respect et la discrétion auroit du m'imposer qu'il n'y a qu'un sentiment aussi vif que l'est celui qui me pénétre pour elle, qui puisse solliciter le pardon duquel j'ai besoin et lui faire agréer les assurances de la profonde soumission, avec laquelle je suis, Monseigneur, de votre Altesse Royale le très humble et très obéissant Serviteur,

ALEXANDRE, Prince de Solms.

[This letter was accompanied by the following genealogical table of the Stuart family, from the time of James I.:—]

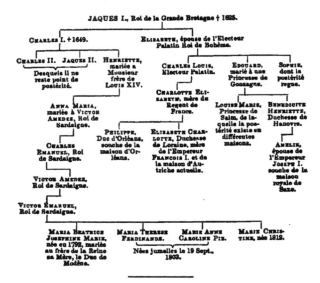

Sir H. Wellesley to Lord Castlereagh.

Madrid, December 21, 1818.

My dear Lord—I beg to offer to your lordship my sincere congratulations upon the very satisfactory termination of your labours at Aix-la-Chapelle, and to repeat my thanks for the perusal of the valuable papers relating to the proceedings there which are returned by the messenger. The arrangements taken at Aix have relieved me from all anxiety as to the alliances which might have been in contemplation here.

I am assured that M. de Tatischeff's influence with the King is greater than ever, and I think we may be certain that, whatever part the Allies may take in the differences between Spain and Portugal and between Spain and her colonies, the Spanish Government will count upon the protection of Russia and of France. There is a strong manifestation of ill-humour towards the British Government, and it is stern towards me, by an effectual reserve upon all questions in which Spain has an interest, and the assumption of a very improper tone upon all commercial questions. The line of conduct which your lordship has presented to me with regard to the mediation between Spain and her colonies is, I think, the most judicious which could be taken under present circumstances, and unless the Marquess of Casa Gonzo [?] chooses to be more communicative on the subject of the Portuguese negociation, I propose to observe the same line of conduct with respect to that question. The question of our commerce and the manner in which our representations are treated, are much more embarrassing, and are a source of perpetual annoyance to me.

Your lordship can form to yourself no idea of the state of this unfortunate country. The only consolation afforded by the present state of affairs is that it cannot last, and all respectable men withdraw themselves as much as possible from observation, and live greatly in the hope and expectation of an explosion which may lead to better times.

I have the honour to be, &c.,   H. WELLESLEY.

The messenger charged with your lordship's despatches arrived in so bad a state of health, and has since been so ill, that he was only able to set out to-day, and I fear that he will be a long time on the road.

Lord Clancarty to Lord Castlereagh.

Frankfort sur Maine, December 24, 1818.

My dear Lord—Nothing has yet arrived from Vienna or Munich to enable us to proceed here. Wessenberg has not hitherto received any notification from his Court relative to your proceedings at Aix; neither has Anstett yet heard from Capodistrias further than you have already been informed.

From the Gazettes we learn of the arrival of M. de Pfeffel at
Vienna on the 14th, but with the precise nature of his mission
thither we are still unacquainted. Two of us, however, are
not, during this pause, idle. Humboldt and Wessenberg are
both engaged in preparing the Articles; those relating to the
Prussian frontier especially must be drawn with care; and the
former is properly employed in this work, which, from time to
time, will be communicated to the rest, for the purpose of previous comparison with the treaties from which their limits are
taken.

Properly speaking, as relating to the territorial arrangements at the disposition of the Allies at Congress, both our
treaty relative to the Seven Islands and that latterly signed
with Spain for the disposal of the Parma reversion ought to
enter into our final act here. Unless, however, I hear from
you to the contrary, I shall say nothing upon either of these
subjects; though, if proposed (which is not likely) by the
others, and authenticated copies of the treaties produced, I
shall feel myself at liberty to assent, on the part of the Prince
Regent, to the annexation of both or either to the act to be
signed here.

There is, however, a subject, upon which I am desirous of
receiving your sentiments, and that immediately. M. de Humboldt acquainted me yesterday that Prince Beauharnois (now
Duke of Leuchtenberg and Prince Eichstädt) was very desirous of having the arrangements under which his establishment in Bavaria has been formed inserted into our final act,
in order that the ratification of the great Powers of Europe to
the whole may afford him an additional security, and possibly
from a degree of vanity that his affairs should, in part, form
an object of sufficient importance to the high Allies to be
thus incorporated with their great territorial arrangements.
Humboldt says that he believes that this desire of his Highness of Leuchtenberg will be supported by Anstett, but that
he (Humboldt) has a positive instruction not to agree thereto;

and he asked me what my opinion was upon the subject. I told him that I had no instruction whatever upon it; that the establishment of M. de Beauharnois did not appear to me to be one of a territorial nature, or one which had necessarily formed part of our functions here; but that he could not expect me to say more, till I should have some intimation of the opinion of my Court upon the subject. For this opinion I now seek: my own is that our final act should have nothing to say either to M. Beauharnois or his concerns, which grew originally out of private assurances given him by one of the Powers, were afterwards treated of at Naples, in a negociation in which we acted as mediators not as parties, and were subsequently terminated at Munich, and, though pressed upon our Protocols here, having no natural concern, direct or indirect, with any part of the motive for establishing this Commission.

   Yours, my dear lord, most affectionately,

         CLANCARTY.

FURTHER NEGOCIATIONS WITH THE UNITED STATES OF
AMERICA—AFFAIRS OF RUSSIA, THE NETHERLANDS,
FRANCE, GERMANY, ETC.

Mr. Rose to Lord Castlereagh.

Berlin, January 1, 1819.

My dear Lord—I thought it better not to mention Prince
Hardenberg's private letter to you in my despatch No. 2: he
read it to me; and I need not express his natural and strong
anxiety on the matter of it. I learn most confidentially from
M. Ancillon, that Count Goltz learns from M. de Cazes that
it was the King of Sweden who obtained, possibly through
the inadvertence of the Prussian Envoy at Stockholm, a copy
of Count Bernstorf's letter, and sent it to the Opposition
French newspapers. In my conversation with Prince Hardenberg, I entirely avoided all mention of General von Clausewitz.
His manner to me was of perfect good-will and friendliness.
He expressed his admiration of the conduct of Government in
the strongest terms.

Learning from Lord Stewart that Count Capodistrias expressed himself to Count Lebzeltern in scarcely fitting terms
respecting our Government, I endeavoured to learn from
M. Ancillon what, according to the information he receives,
are Count Capodistrias' feelings towards it; and he appre-
hends them to be such as would explain his so expressing himself under inadequate notions of its wisdom and vigour. His
present opinions on German matters show the wilful kindness
he is capable of; but I thought it my duty to apprise you thus
privately of what I was told.

The Elector of Hesse consulted M. de Lorenz, either directly or indirectly, on the suggestion that he should withdraw his money from our funds; he wished to know my views of the state of England for his master's information: and, thank God, and next to God, the firmness and wisdom of those, of whom Count Capodistrias seems to think slightingly, the event does not seem likely to belie the decisive representation I gave him in a short private note.

M. Ancillon tells me that, when he apprised Prince Hardenberg that his Royal Highness the Prince Regent had expressed no marked preference for a Prussian officer, as such, as successor to Baron Humboldt, the Prince said repeatedly, " It is singular! Baron Humboldt did not cease to say to me at Aix-la-Chapelle, that the Prince Regent desired him particularly that a military man should be sent."

This Government gives Prince Gustavus of Sweden half a million of francs, 125,000 crowns.

I am, my dear lord, &c.,   G. H. ROSE.

Mr. C. Bagot to Lord Castlereagh.

Washington, January 4, 1819.

My dear Lord—I believe that I have more than once·had occasion to mention to your lordship in my private letters the wish which Mr. Adams has frequently expressed to me that the United States should act in some concert with the British Government in regard to the revolutionary provinces of South America. Soon after it was known here that the Congress at Aix-la-Chapelle had declined to interfere in the questions between them and Spain, Mr. Adams, in adverting to the intelligence, repeated to me, in a more formal manner than he had yet done, his wishes upon this point.

He stated that the American Government had hitherto forborne to acknowledge the independence of any of these provinces, in the hope that an opportunity would be afforded of ascertaining the course which the European Powers might

H 2

adopt in regard to them; but that the refusal of the Congress at Aix to take the matter into their consideration had made it incumbent upon the United States to think seriously of the line of policy which they ought now to pursue. He said that it was the opinion of the Executive Government here that complete independence of the mother country had been virtually effected in nearly all the Spanish South American Colonies—that this independence must inevitably be acknowledged in some way or other in the course of a short time—and that, till it was acknowledged, the evils, and particularly the evils to the commerce of the United States and Great Britain growing out of the present condition of affairs would increase daily, and, he thought, intolerably—that, for this among many other reasons, he wished to act, if possible, in unison with the British Government, and that, with this object, he was prepared, if your lordship should think fit, either to discuss the subject with me, or to instruct Mr. Rush to confer upon it with your lordship.

I of course received *ad referendum* everything which Mr. Adams said, and abstained from expressing any opinion whatever as to the steps which the British Government might be inclined to take; but I promised him that I would report to your lordship, as I had done before, his views of the question.

I do not think it probable that any attempt to procure a direct acknowledgment of the independence of the Spanish Colonies will be made during this session of Congress; but the Government appears to be in constant communication with them, through their deputies or agents, of whom there are not fewer than six or seven now in Washington. There are here Don Lino Clementi, the Minister from Venezuela; El Señor Torres, agent for New Granada; Don Manuel Moreno, from the Democratic or Opposition party of Buenos Ayres, who was exiled by Puyrredon, and was formerly at the head of the foreign affairs in the Democratic period; M. Garros, the Secretary of General Lallemand, who attends all their meetings; a

Frenchman of the name of Ferraut; a M. La Forêt, who is also an agent; and the pirate Laffitte.

I transmit to your lordship, with my despatches by this mail, a copy of Mr. Adams's promised answer to M. Pizarro's note upon the invasion of Florida. Although I was pretty well aware of the intended nature of this answer, I confess to your lordship that I was not prepared for the direct and high-handed defence of General Jackson which Mr. Adams has thought fit to make. There is, however, a key which will explain this, and will always explain every measure of this Government, viz., elections. The Southern and Western States, among which, with the exception perhaps of Kentucky, General Jackson is an idol, must be propitiated before the period of Mr. Monroe's re-election arrives; and Mr. Adams knows perfectly well that there is nothing more likely to secure their favour than a vindication of General Jackson, couched in insulting language to Spain. But, however well this language may be calculated for that quarter, it has certainly not met with universal approbation. Many of the members of Congress, who have spoken upon the subject to me, have expressed their great dissatisfaction both at the reasoning of the answer and at its clumsy *persiflage*; and they seem to think that it will hardly escape without severe animadversion in Europe.

It is true that Mr. Adams has abstained from making any direct charges against Great Britain, but he has not abstained from making insinuations, which, after my communication to him of Lord Bathurst's despatch to Mr. Baker, of the 25th of September, 1815, he was not warranted in making.

I have the honour to be, &c.,   CHARLES BAGOT.

Lord Castlereagh to Lord Clancarty.

Foreign Office, January 22, 1819.

My dear Clancarty—It is quite clear to me that the two Imperial Courts mean to make us their cat's-paw. They are running a race for favour at Munich, and expect us to extricate them finally from their intrigue. Now, my wish is, that you should, very *quietly*, and with good humour, maintain our own ground, till they show us better, but, as to *forcing* the point for them, that you should rather keep back and leave them *in their own trap*.

Great Britain has only a subordinate position, as well as interest, to maintain in this question; and your tone may very well be to throw the onus of settling the matter proportionably upon the three other Courts. I consider this course as the more advisable, as it will force both Austria and Russia, that now shirk, to do their duty.

I entirely approve of your intention of not staying at Frankfort to do nothing, and give you full discretion to use the intimation of absenting yourself as circumstances may suggest.

It occurs to me to point out, in the event of Bavaria's persevering refusal to accept the Aix-la-Chapelle terms, and the Allied Powers ultimately deeming it reasonable to give to Baden her quietus under the Treaty of Frankfort, whether it ought not to be so done as to reserve the several concessions which she is now willing to make in favour of Bavaria so far at the disposal of the Allies, as to admit of making them instrumental to a settlement with Bavaria at some future period, if they should think fit so to employ them.

Upon looking into the Parma Treaty, I think it must be an annex to your final act, and I rather incline to say the same of the Ionian Treaty; but not so of Beauharnois' arrangement.

Mr. Rose to Lord Castlereagh.

Berlin, January 26, 1819.

My dear Lord—When I saw Count Bernstorf yesterday, he had not heard, as I had happened to have done, that the King of Sweden's letter in answer to the King of Prussia's was arrived. No doubt it has reached him to-day. That it will prove to be very unsuitable, I think there can be little doubt: I only know that it is very long.

He desired me to say to you that he is anxious to know what you think will be the best course to be taken in this matter, entertaining a strong wish to have the benefit of your opinions. The confidential friendship which subsists between him and me, gives great facility to an unreserved communication between you and him, on this and all other matters of common interest; and, right and high-minded as he is, he knows how to value it.

        I am, my dear lord, &c.,   G. H. ROSE.

Mr. Rose to Lord Castlereagh.

               Berlin, January 30, 1819.

My dear Lord—This letter is merely as a duplicate of one which I wrote to you six days ago, by a circuitous conveyance. You will see by my despatch of this date, that two days ago the King of Sweden's letter was not then delivered to the King of Prussia, and as his Envoy is still ill, or pretends to be so, which is not likely, and as Count Bernstorf has not given me further information on the subject, I imagine that it has not hitherto reached its destination. There can be no doubt, since that to the Prince Regent is such as it is described to me, that the one destined for the King of Prussia will be unsuitable in no common degree.

Count Bernstorf desired me to say to you that he is anxious to know, and as soon as conveniently can be done, your opinion as to the course that should be adopted in this matter; and he has an anxious wish to act as much as possible in unison with your views, and is entirely disposed to feel the full value of your suggestions. The friendship which subsists between him and me, and of which he gave last summer so unequivocal proof, affords a very natural and easy channel of communication with him; and the value I set on that friendship, long before an idea existed of his occupying his present situation,

rested on my having found him invariably honourable, fair
and liberal, and moderate and just in his views.

I am, my dear lord, &c.,   G. H. ROSE.

Lord Clancarty to Lord Castlereagh.

Frankfort sur Maine, February 2, 1819.

My dear Lord—Many thanks for your kind desire to send
me your fit of the gout, as an enclosure in yours of the
2nd ult. : it would have been very acceptable, and saved me
from a second attack from the flying gout in the head, with
which I was seized some ten days ago, and which, though it
lasted but for a few minutes, was sufficient to create very considerable alarm in my family. I am now quite well again, but
would willingly accept your offer of the *fine vermillion*, to ensure
me against the repetition of attack from my more dangerous
enemy.

My despatches will put you *au fait de nos affaires*, which,
unfortunately, do not much advance. I should scarcely think
the attempt to press Beauharnois' arrangement into our act
will be persevered in. Your messenger arrived here on the
26th, very fortunately just in time to enable me to follow the
line you have chalked out as proper to be pursued by us, under
present circumstances. This has not been adopted without
very considerable disappointment being apparent in Anstett,
who had certainly hoped that from Prussia and us he would
have met with such an opposition to the modifications of the
Aix Protocol (as conveyed in Capodistrias' papers) as would
have enabled him to act under an apparent compulsion in
returning to the Aix decisions. In this, under your directions
he has been foiled ; having opened to them all in conversation
the line of reasoning conveyed in your despatch to Gordon,
bearing, as it does, most convincingly against both the proposed deviations.

I merely stated that, having come here under the orders of
my Government, in consequence of the unanimous determina-

tions taken at Aix, it had now appeared advisable to some of
the Courts to offer fresh suggestions—that though, for the
reasons assigned, these seemed objectionable, yet a doubt was
thus cast, on the part of the proposers, on the policy of the
Aix decision, which it might require time and consideration to
remove, before it might be expedient, or even feasible, to
advance further—that, thus circumstanced, I proposed, till
matters should be brought to a greater state of maturity, so as
to afford hopes of efficient progress, to repair to my Embassy
at Bruxelles, from whence, however, I should return, without
a moment's delay, whenever we could be placed in such a state
as to be enabled in conjunction to proceed forward.

This occasioned a very considerable degree of sensation. All
admitted that, unless despatches with fresh instructions should
be expedited from Vienna, before the Emperor's departure, on
the 10th instant, we might give up all hopes of receiving such
authority from that Court as would enable us to act. Anstett
much lowered his tone on the subject of the divergence in
Capodistrias' papers, and even evaded a suggestion from Humboldt, that he should place such specific proposal thereon as he
might think it requisite to make, upon the Protocol; and all
joined in requesting me to postpone my departure hence till
the 14th instant, under the hope, as expressed by all, that,
before that period, we might be placed in a state to proceed.

Though I am by no means so sanguine on this subject as
they appeared to be, yet I conceived it my duty to acquiesce
in their desire; and I trust you will approve of my having so
done. I shall, therefore, remain here quietly till the 14th
instant, when, if matters shall not be placed in such a train as
to afford some hopes of advance, by the receipt by the Austrian
Minister of adequate instructions, and by the full reconcile-
ment of the Russian with the Aix decision, I shall set out on
my return to Bruxelles.

You will see by the Protocols what has been the result of
my proposal upon the insertion into our final Act of the Parma

reversion. I conceive my colleagues quite wrong upon this subject: nevertheless, it will be necessary, in order to prove this to them, and obtain their assent to our views, to procure instructions for them to this effect from their respective Courts, if you shall persevere in seeking the insertion of the matter. The same may be said of the Ionian treaty; the objections, as stated, being equally applicable to each: and, with respect to both, if copies are to be annexed, certified copies ought to be sent for the purpose, which has not hitherto been the case.

At present, we are far from being in a state of sufficient maturity to think of releasing Baden. Russia will, however, soon probably become desirous of obtaining this release: nevertheless, till we act in unison upon all the terms of the Protocol, I do not think we are called upon to accomplish any part, more especially under the specific terms of your Memorandum, in giving the British decision on this subject at Aix. The holding off with respect to this release will probably furnish us with the best means of leading Russia to do her duty. And when this shall be the case, I will make use of your suggestion, by proposing that the several Baden concessions should be placed in the hands of the Allies, to be hereafter made use of in the manner you mention.

Farewell, my dear lord; I have tried you enough. Pray let me know whether Lord Liverpool would wish me to take my seat and give my proxy. If so, I could run over for a couple of days, when we shall have broken up here, and before settling at Bruxelles.

Ever most affectionately yours,   CLANCARTY.

Count de Ludolf (Neapolitan Ambassador) to Lord Castlereagh.
Gloucester, Fevrier 11, 1819.

Monsieur le Vicomte—Les occupations et la santé de votre Excellence ne permettant pas, à mon très grand regret, que je puisse avoir l'honneur de lui présenter mes respects personnellement, je ne puis tarder à l'entretenir de quelques objets que j'avois l'ordre de ma Cour depuis quelque tems de lui communiquer.

Le Roi mon maître m'ordonne, Monsieur le Vicomte, d'exprimer toute sa reconnoissance et de remercier son Altesse Royale le Prince Régent pour la manière amicale avec laquelle son Altesse Royale a consenti à admettre l'interprétation que sa Majesté a cru devoir donner à l'article de la Convention pour l'abolition des privilèges du pavillon de l'année 1816, et à donner à sa Majesté de nouveaux témoignages de sa précieuse amitié et de son intérêt.

Sa Majesté m'ordonne en outre de remercier son Altesse Royale le Prince Régent de la communication des Actes du Congrès d'Aix-la-Chapelle, que le Chevalier à Court a eu ordre de lui faire, et de manifester sa vive satisfaction pour les expressions amicales dont cette communication étoit accompagnée. Son Altesse Royale le Prince Régent ne doit pas douter un seul instant de l'attachement constant et sincère de mon Souverain, et j'ai ordre de declarer solemnellement à votre Excellence que si, contre toute attente, le système si sage adopté à Aix-la Chapelle, tendant à consolider la paix parmi les Puissances de l'Europe, pouvoit jamais et contre toute attente être altéré, ou si de nouvelles combinaisons avoient lieu, sa Majesté Sicilienne est très fermement décidé à ne jamais se départir du système politique avantageux pour sa Couronne et pour ses États qu'elle a suivie jusqu'à présent, et que, quelques soient les changements imprévus qui pourroient avoir lieu, sa Majesté observera fidèlement les engagements et les liens qui l'attachent si heureusement à ses augustes Alliés, sa Majesté le Roi de la Grande Bretagne et sa Majesté l'Empereur d'Autriche, se flattant en même tems, qu'en donnant cette assurance sincère et loyale, ces Puissances lui continueront leur amitié, leur intérêt, et leur appui.

Je supplie votre Excellence d'agréer ces communications, et de vouloir bien les mettre sous les yeux de son Altesse Royale le Prince Régent ; et je serai très heureux de pouvoir transmettre à ma Cour l'assurance que son Altesse Royale partage les sentiments du Roi mon maître, et lui conservera toujours sa précieuse amitié.

Je saisis avec empressement cette occasion pour votre Excellence d'accepter l'assurance de la haute considération avec laquelle j'ai l'honneur d'être, Monsieur le Vicomte, &c.,

LUDOLF.

The Marquis d'Osmond to Lord Castlereagh.

Dimanche, premier Mars.

Conformément au désir de Lord Castlereagh, le Marquis d'Osmond a l'honneur de lui envoyer ci-joint un extrait de la lettre communiquée hier à son Excellence : elle voudra bien se rappeler et recommander l'importance du sécret, qui seul peut conduire à la découverte des coupables.

Le Marquis d'Osmond prie Lord Castlereagh d'agréer l'hommage de sa haute considération.

[Enclosure.]

Extraits d'une lettre du Duc de Richelieu.

Paris, 23 Fevrier.

Vous savez qu'à la sollicitation du Procureur-Général, Lord Kinnaird s'est rendu de Bruxelles ici, avec le banni Français qui lui avait fait les premières confidences sur le projet d'assassiner le Duc de Wellington : cet homme jusqu'à présent n'a pas encore donné des notions assez positives sur l'auteur de l'attentat pour qu'on puisse le désigner. Il parait cependant par cela qu'on lui a arraché non sans peine que le complot a été formé à Bruxelles, que le chef est un nommé Brice, ancien capitaine dans les chasseurs de l'ex-garde, partisan pendant les cent jours et condamné à mort par contumace. Brifel, ancien maréchal des logis, condamné comme son capitaine sembleroit être l'assassin. Tout cela au reste, n'est qu'une conjecture, probable à la vérité . . . . . Si on peut se flatter de découvrir la vérité, ce n'est que par le plus grand secret et il faut con-

venir qu'il a été bien mal gardé . . . . . Aussi nous ne disons
décidément plus rien : dut le Courier s'étonner encore, comme
il l'a fait, de ce qu'on ne rendait pas compte, jour par jour dans
les journaux de tout ce qu'on pouvait apprendre sur cet évènement. Vous sentez combien nous sommes intéressés à decouvrir
les coupables : l'autorité de M. de Caze y est employée toute
entière, et vous savez qu'il en a beaucoup . . . . . Du reste
nous ne pouvons être qu'infiniment touchés de la manière dont
ce douloureux evènement a été pris en Angleterre.

Palmella est arrivé, &c.

Pour extrait.
OSMOND.

Lord Cathcart to Lord Castlereagh.

St. Petersburgh, March 5, [February 21] 1819.

My dear Lord—I seize the first private opportunity of expressing to your lordship my most sincere thanks for what
you have done and said on the subject of my son Frederick.
The expression that you will have great pleasure in taking
charge of him is duly appreciated, and is most valuable to me,
as it is most honourable and important to him. That expression, and your having so soon submitted his name to his Royal
Highness the Prince Regent for an appointment which has
placed him on the list of his Majesty's diplomatic servants
actively employed, affords to me the kindest and most flattering testimony of the continuance of that friendship and good
opinion with which you have honoured me for so many years.
I trust in that expression, and in his zeal and diligence, that
he may soon arrive at a situation in which he may have more
scope for his industry, and more ample means of rendering his
exertions and the experience and acquirements he has obtained
in the business of foreign affairs useful to the public service.

I am aware that it is a rule (though I thought not without
exception) that candidates for promotion in the diplomatic
profession must begin by the office of Secretary of Legation ;

but I had indulged a hope that the apprenticeship he has passed with me, in the course of a variety of difficult and confidential public business which has passed through his hands on several occasions, during the last fifteen years, might have warranted his passing over the first step of regular progression, especially as he acted, and was seen and known to act, as principal Secretary to the Embassy by *all* the Cabinets of Europe, during the years 1813, 1814, and 1815, while the Emperor was out of his dominions, and during all the business and negociations with which I had any concern in that eventful period.

It would, indeed, afford to him and to me also (for having perhaps too long detained him) matter of painful reflection, if further advancement were regulated by seniority of date of appointment in the several ranks, there being at this moment some Secretaries of Legation who not only began much later than he did, but who actually copied the first documents entrusted to them under his immediate inspection. But I will hope that these advantages, through your lordship's favour, and with a continuance of his exertions, may be of avail to him in the period of his next promotion. Indeed, he has incidentally been placed so high, and is so well known to the diplomatic world here and at the other Courts, that it would appear as if there had been some deficiency on his part, if he were to remain long at the bottom of the list.

I am confident your lordship will pardon my troubling you with these reflections, which, though they flow from a father anxious for the establishment of a son, would be equally due from a person in my situation, in favour of a young man who was no relation, but who had discharged public duties for so many years with such unremitting steadiness and diligence.

It will be a great additional favour if your lordship can give me confidentially any encouragement in these hopes before his departure. No personal consideration would have induced me to detain him from following your lordship's instructions in proceeding to his station, if he could be spared from hence without real inconvenience with reference to the public service, during the absence of the Secretary of the Embassy.

With many apologies for the length of this letter, ever, my dear lord, your lordship's most obliged and faithful servant,

CATHCART.

Mr. C. Bagot to Lord Castlereagh.

Washington, March 6, 1819.

My dear Lord—I have scarcely anything to mention to your lordship by this mail, beyond what is contained in my public despatches. As far as our affairs are concerned, everything here is apparently going on very smoothly ; and, unless the packet which I am daily expecting brings me instructions upon some new points, I shall feel satisfied that there is no particular business left to do, which need prevent my making use of your lordship's leave of absence, and returning to England in the course of next month.

The Congress rose, or rather expired, on the 3rd, after a session in which less has been done than I ever remember since I have been in the country. A great change of Members has taken place in the new Congress, and many. of the most valuable men who sat in the last have been excluded from this.

The treaty with Spain has not yet been published *in extenso ;* but its provisions are very well known to be such as I have reported them. The Spanish Minister now speaks positively of returning to Europe, *viâ* England, by the May or June packet. I believe that he will certainly leave this country, but suspect that he is not much disposed to return to Spain in the present state of things there, if he can possibly avoid it.

No appointment has yet been made by this Government of a new Minister to France, but M. Gallatin is certainly to return home.

I have the honour to be, &c.,   CHARLES BAGOT.

Mr. Joseph Planta to Lord Castlereagh.

Foreign Office, March 12, 1819.

My dear Lord—I send you two papers on the Persian Embassy, by the perusal of which I think you will be made acquainted with the manner in which the question stands, both as to the expenses and to the objects of the Persian Ambassador. By a letter from Paris I learn that his Excellency arrived there on the 7th, so that we shall shortly have him here.

I have had much conversation with Hamilton upon the subject of his expenses and treatment, and we think that we can very well keep him to the payment of his own expenses—certainly at the beginning of his embassy ; and that, if he should afterwards run out, and that your lordship should think fit then to give him some money, (perhaps out of the S. S.) you could do it on the condition of his departure from the country, which is the most desirable object.

We think, however, that, as no money is at first to be given to him, we should treat him with all ceremony in other respects, and that, on every account, both to watch over his proceedings and to check his expenses, and to render him manageable, some person should be appointed to attend him. James Morier has appeared to us to be the most proper person for this object. He is one of the Plenipotentiaries who signed the very treaty on which the Ambassador is coming to negociate. He will therefore be very useful politically ; and, having assisted on the former occasion, under Sir Gore Ouseley, he understands the duties. Willock, who came over with the horses, would not be a man of sufficient weight with the Ambassador ; and Sir Gore Ouseley's appointment, if he would accept the charge, would only make the Ambassador think he was to be treated as before. I hope, therefore, your lordship will approve of this arrangement ; and, if Morier be sent to Dover to meet him, and an extra packet to Calais to receive him, I think that is all we need do at present.

There is a further question about the horses, for which an

expense of near £2,000 has already been incurred, at the suggestion of Sir Robert Liston. I send your lordship extracts of all the despatches which have passed on the subject, and I must ask your lordship's order as to the manner in which you wish this money to be paid.

Your lordship's faithful servant,   J. PLANTA.

[Enclosures.]

Memorandum on the probable Objects of the Persian Embassy.

The objects of the Persian Embassy, according to Mr. Willock's despatch, May 10, 1818, are—

1. To acquire some insight into the general views and policy of Europe at the present period.

2. To procure some pecuniary compensation from Great Britain, in lieu of territorial cession by Russia.

3. To bring an Embassy to Persia, or a mission of a minor rank.

4. To ascertain if Persia will be protected, in case of invasion by Russia.

The language which the Persian Ambassador will most likely hold on his arrival in England will be the same as Mr. Willock mentions to have been used by the Persian Ministers. He will endeavour to resume the discussions which took place during the negociation of the definitive treaty by Messrs. Morier and Ellis; he will state that the Shah resigned the conduct of the negociations with Russia to Sir Gore Ouseley, on the faith of a bond given by that Minister to continue the subsidy of 200,000 tomans annually, in the event of not obtaining the restoration of certain provinces; and that, on the full reliance of the performance of this engagement, his country had concluded a disadvantageous treaty with Russia—that Mr. Ellis afterwards came to Persia on a special mission, and, in conjunction with Mr. Morier, proposed some alterations in the definitive treaty, contracted by Sir Gore Ouseley, and declared that the engagement entered into by that Ambassador was invalid—that, by the tenor of the full powers granted to Sir Gore Ouseley by his Sovereign, the Persian Government looked to the strict observance and performance of every promise which he made in the name of his Government; and that, having always found on former occasions that the engagements of British Ministers were acknowledged and acted upon by their Government, they were much astonished that, on this occasion, it should be otherwise.

The Persian Ambassador will ask why the definitive treaty concluded by Sir Gore Ouseley in 1812, and acted upon until the year 1814, should then be found objectionable—why the engagements of the Ambassador Extraordinary, on the faith of which his King had made such sacrifices, is not binding. He will state that his Government were determined not to sign the new treaty presented by the English Plenipotentiaries, but to lay their grievances before his Royal Highness the Prince Regent, through the medium of an Ambassador—that Mr. Ellis then offered, upon their signing the substituted treaty, to convey to his Government the expression of the King of Persia's expectations, founded on Sir Gore Ouseley's engagement, which his Majesty conceived to be sacred and inviolable—and that then, in firm reliance on the justice and generosity of Great Britain, the Persian Ministers were induced to sign the new treaty, and to accept of Mr. Ellis's agency.

·The Ambassador will then perhaps say that his Government was informed in a general manner by Mr. Morier that the good offices of the British Government would be exerted by the English Ambassador at St. Petersburg in obtaining the fulfilment of the Shah's wishes; but that the Emperor of Russia had come to no determination at St. Petersburg on the question of territorial retrocession—that he, the Persian Ambassador, during his embassy in Russia, had been ordered in that case to proceed to England, but that he was told by his Excellency the Earl of Cathcart that his journey would be unavailing, as the mediation of Great Britain could only be exerted through his Majesty's Ambassador at St. Petersburg ; and that, notwithstanding his persisting in the necessity of obeying the orders of his Sovereign in this respect, he was not permitted to proceed.

In conclusion, the Persian Ambassador will state that his Government had waited the arrival of General Yermolof, the Russian Ambassador, who declared that the Emperor of Russia could not, consistently with his regard to the interests of his empire, make any territorial cession to Persia—that the expectations of Persia having been thus disappointed, he had been charged, on the part of the Shah, to make these representations to his Royal Highness the Prince.

Memorandum on the Expense of the Persian Embassy.

By Mr. Willock's despatch of the 20th April, 1818, it appears that he explicitly declared to the Persian Minister that the whole expense of their embassy to England must be defrayed by the Shah, and his Ambassador be placed on the same footing as diplomatic characters from European Powers.

In his despatch May 10, 1818, it is stated that, at a conference with the Persian Prime Minister, when the ultimate determination of the Shah to order his Ambassador to proceed was announced to him, he again persisted that the Ambassador must be provided with adequate funds to defray his own expenses, as it would not be convenient to the British Government to make him any advance of money. Mr. Willock states that 5,000 tomans, equal to about £3,500 sterling, had been given to the Ambassador by his Government, for the purpose of defraying the expenses of his Embassy, in lieu of 30,000 tomans, which Mr. Willock had mentioned as necessary to that purpose.

Mr. Willock received Lord Castlereagh's despatch of the 27th March, 1818, on the 5th July, at Tabriz, just one day after the departure of the Persian Ambassador from that city. In that despatch, it is expressly stated that the Embassy

must, of course, be on the footing of those from all other
Sovereigns, and be entertained at the charge of its own Court.
The contents of this despatch, as regarding this particular
point, were communicated to the Persian Government, and it
is most likely that the Ambassador was also made acquainted
with them before he had quitted his own territory.

Sir Robert Liston states (9th October, 1818) that the
Persian Ambassador having met on his road a Persian Minister returning from a mission to the Porte, and received from
him exaggerated accounts of the difficulties which he was likely
to encounter on his way to England, waited eight or ten days
at Erivan, the frontier city of Persia, in the expectation that his
Government would countermand his journey ; but he received
peremptory and even angry orders to proceed without delay.

At Sir Robert Liston's first interview, he begged the Persian
Ambassador to consider that our disinclination to receive the·
Embassy was chiefly owing to our doubts of the propriety of
the time chosen ·for it, because of· the umbrage it might possibly give in a certain quarter, but that, instead of having any
objection to him personally, on the contrary, he had never
heard anything of his temper and character but what was
advantageous ; and that, if a Persian Ambassador was to be
employed at the Court of London, the British Government
would be inclined to receive him in preference to any other individual.   He added that, in order perfectly to reconcile us to
the measure, it was necessary that he should defray his own
expenses, and put himself on the footing of a European
Minister.   To this the Persian Ambassador agreed without
hesitation, saying that he was ready to reduce the number of
his servants to any standard that Sir Robert might suggest,
and that he was disposed to regulate his establishment and his
manner of living by that of the members of the Corps Diplomatique where he might be placed.

· With respect to the horses, eighteen in number, which are
intended as a present to the Prince Regent, the Persian Am-

bassador appeared to feel that, if he is to range himself in the
class of European rather than Asiatic Ministers, and is not to
have his charges borne by the country to which he is sent, he
will no longer be expected to make valuable presents; that, at
least, it would not be reasonable that he should lay out upon
the conveyance of those presents the money that may henceforward be required for the current expenses of the mission.
Sir Robert Liston's opinion is that, with a view to decorous
appearances, to conciliation, and to good policy, it would be
proper that he should be empowered to relieve the Persian
Ambassador from the charge of the further transport of the
horses, and conceives that they may be sent by way of Marseilles, without any enormous expense.

The Austrian Court was apprised of the Persian Ambassador having a letter and presents from his Sovereign to the
Emperor of Austria, and had already given instructions to its
Minister at Constantinople, if possible, in friendly and civil
terms to set the mission aside; but that, if the Ambassador
persisted in proceeding through Germany, a positive refusal to
receive him was not to be given, but that he was clearly to
understand that the country through which he was to pass was
not to defray his expenses, or that the Austrian Government
should bear any share of the expenses of his stay. The Ambassador expressed his readiness to continue his progress on
these conditions.

In Sir Robert Liston's despatch, October 24, 1818, in answer
to Lord Castlereagh's of the 2nd September, whereby he is
instructed to take such steps as he may think the most
expedient under the existing circumstances for the conveyance
of the Persian Ambassador's heavy baggage or presents of
horses for his Royal Highness the Prince Regent, his Excellency states that he had freighted a merchant-ship to convey
the horses to Marseilles, and engaged men to aid the Persian
servants in taking care of them during the voyage. It appears
that he has, in consequence, authorised Mr. George Willock,

under whose charge the horses have been placed, to draw for
the expenses incurred in pursuance of that object; for in a
letter from Messrs. Coutts and Co. to Mr. Planta, 9th March,
1819, it is stated that Sir Robert Liston had opened a credit
on them for £1,500 in favour of Mr. Willock, who had alone
drawn bills from Marseilles for £1,470, and from Paris for
£400, and that he had written to say that he will probably
want £100 more.

In a private communication to Mr. Hamilton, Mr. Willock
suggests that, in case the Persian Ambassador's funds should
fall short, advances might be made to him from the pension
which he receives from the East India Company, as there
would be great difficulty in recovering from the Persians any
money advanced by his Majesty's Government.

***

Lord Cathcart to Lord Castlereagh.

St. Petersburgh, March 18-6, 1819.

My dear Lord—In riding with the Emperor the day before
yesterday, his Imperial Majesty said to me, in English, that
he had received a letter from Paris, which contained intelligence by no means pleasant—that the measures adopted by
the Government were not wise, especially in the department
of the Minister of War; and desired me to recollect emphatic
words which he had used to me at Moscow, and since his
return, on the difficulty to be dreaded from the proceedings of
the French Government, however composed.

I ascertained afterwards that this letter could only be of the
18th ult., and that his Imperial Majesty did not learn till
yesterday, by post, the circumstances of M. Barthelemi's
motion in the Chamber of Peers, and that it was supposed a
similar motion will be made in the Chamber of Deputies. I
had not this day an opportunity of renewing the subject with
him. I understood from Count Nesselrode that, by their last
accounts, everything seemed right and in full harmony among
the foreign Ministers at Paris.

General Suchtelen's report of what passed with Count
Engestroem, concerning the Emperor's having refused to receive the King's letter, has not yet arrived. Lord Strangford
had given me an account of this and of the reason of the delay,
which is that the General meant to send by a messenger of his
own, and had despatched the only one at his disposal to
Copenhagen, whose return he waited for. Twenty days have,
however, now elapsed since that conversation took place, and
the messenger is hardly expected. I do not think that any of
the propositions which Count Engestroem told Lord Strangford
he made to General Suchtelen will be attended to.

Your lordship will have heard that the circumstances of
Count Goltz's having made an entry of notes furnished to him
for his private information by mistake in a public Protocol at
Frankfort, has shocked him so much, that he asked his recall,
which was granted forthwith.

I have the honour to remain, &c.,

CATHCART.

I send this by a Prussian courier to Mr. Rose, to whom I
have also sent, but under *cachet volant*, for his information, my
two despatches.

General Count de Ricard is talked of by the French Chargé
d'Affaires as the candidate for the Embassy to this Court
most likely to succeed.

———

The following letter, written by Mr. Planta, evidently to
Lord Castlereagh, is without address or any other signature
than a hieroglyphic, which I take to mean J. P. Jr., (junior)
to distinguish him from his father, who was for many years
Librarian to the British Museum. It is endorsed and dated.

Second Proposition on Persian Embassy.

March 19.

I am sorry to have again to trouble your lordship on the
approach of the Persian Ambassador; but I have had several

conversations with Sir Gore Ouseley and with Mr. Willock, who is arrived with the horses, and who travelled with the Persian to Constantinople; and the impression on my mind now is that it will lead to serious disgust and perhaps to an unpleasant feeling between the two countries, if we do not provide a house and a carriage for him, he feeding himself out of his own funds. Sir Gore Ouseley has several letters from him, mentioning his reception at Vienna, at Paris, and at Constantinople. Everything has been found for him, and at Paris he appears to have been splendidly treated.

I think also that we shall find this mode of furnishing a house and carriage for him cheaper to the public, *in the end*, than if we have to pay up for him a sum of money on his leaving us; and we shall still get no credit with him. He certainly is furnished with money enough for his subsistence, and therefore we should have no other expense. I should think we might get the house and carriage for eight hundred pounds, or less.

Perhaps I may show these papers to Mr. Canning, and consult him on the subject as connected with India; but I should be glad to have your lordship's opinion on the above course, which I conceive to be the best.

J. P. Jr.

Mr. Bagot to Lord Castlereagh.

Washington, April 7, 1819.

My dear Lord—A Mr. Lowndes, who has been for some years one of the representatives in Congress of the State of South Carolina, and who, though a young man, is highly distinguished here for his talents and great knowledge of the commercial and financial interests of the country, embarked at New York for England, on the 10th of last month, in one of the American packets which sail monthly for Liverpool.

Mr. Lowndes professes to have in view no other object than that of making a tour through England during the summer

months, of visiting Paris for a short time, and of returning to
the United States by the opening of the next session of Congress. It is not improbable that he may have been partly
induced to take this journey by a desire to examine England,
and more particularly, perhaps, to obtain information respecting
the Bank : but I think that I have reason to believe that his
journey is in fact taken at the immediate desire of the Government, and that he has instructions to assist in preparing, and
possibly in negociating, a commercial treaty with France. I
think this is the more likely, as M. Gallatin is certainly not in
the confidence of the President. He does not dare to trust
him with his views ; but, at the same time, he desires above
all things to keep him as long as he can at Paris, knowing
very well that, if he returns, (as he constantly threatens to do)
he will infallibly engage in every kind of intrigue against his
administration. I do not know whether this information
is of any interest to your lordship, but I believe it to be
correct.

Although I have known Mr. Lowndes ever since I have
been in the country, he never mentioned to me his intention of
going to England till I spoke to him about it.

I have the honour to be, &c.,   CHARLES BAGOT.

Mr. C. Bagot to Lord Castlereagh.

Washington, April 7, 1819.

My dear Lord—Mr. Adams told me yesterday that he had
received a despatch from Mr. Rush, dated on the 15th of
February, giving him an account of a conversation which he
had had with your lordship on the subject of South America.
He read to me the greater part of Mr. Rush's report of this conversation, having previously read to me the instructions which
he had sent to him in January last.

As I shall probably be in England soon after the arrival of
this letter, I shall reserve for conversation with your lordship

much of what passed at this interview; but it may be important that I should state generally that I rather think that Mr. Rush's report has had the effect of checking in some degree the disposition of Mr. Adams to urge upon this Government the immediate recognition of the independence of any of the insurgent provinces. He stated that he was more than ever confirmed in all the opinions which he had entertained of the inevitable necessity of acknowledging very soon the complete independence of some of the Spanish colonies, and that he thought that this necessity would become every day more apparent to the European Powers; but that he still always wished that the United States should move as much as possible in accord with the other nations of the world in such a question. He said that, the United States having recently adjusted, in a manner satisfactory to both parties, their long and serious differences with Spain, they were not urged by any interested motives to press this matter prematurely, and that he was inclined to think that the President would view the question in the same light as he did; but that, as he was now absent, he could only express his own individual opinion.

This is a very concise account of a conversation which lasted more than an hour; but it is perhaps sufficient to show your lordship the grounds upon which I am disposed to think that this Government will still pause, and that they will not publicly receive a South American agent, even from Buenos Ayres, as soon as they certainly had intended to do. Mr. Adams was véry anxious to know whether I had received any account of this conference between your lordship and Mr. Rush; but I told him that I had not yet received the February mail, and that I had no despatches later than those of the 12th of January.

By a letter which I have received from Sir David Milne, I am led to suppose that the Forth frigate will be in the Chesapeak in a few days. I therefore propose to present Mr. Antrobus in the course of the next week, and then to go to

Annapolis, in order that I may be ready to embark as soon as possible after Sir John Louis's arrival.

I have the honour to be, &c.,   CHARLES BAGOT.

Lord Cathcart to Lord Castlereagh.

St. Petersburgh, May 13-1, 1819.

My dear Lord—I have frequently reminded the Minister of Finance, through the Secretary of State, of his promise to give me some specimens of the new Bank paper, which I applied for last year, in conformity to your lordship's instructions. But I do not expect to receive them till about the beginning of next July, when, as it is announced in the speech of the Minister, (of which I lately sent a printed copy for your lordship's information) the issue of new notes is to take place. I however enclose herewith a specimen of the paper, which I have pro-. cured through a secret and most confidential channel.

The speech states that the appearance of an inconsiderable number of counterfeited notes had attracted the utmost solicitude of the Government; that it was true the construction of the paper currency of the empire in circulation was not such as might be expected from the great perfection to which mechanical arts have attained, and that this circumstance afforded too much facility to forgery and imitation, and that, therefore, the Government had judged it expedient to create a new establishment for this service, which has been for some time at work in full activity.

The history of this preparation is curious. General Bettancourt, a Spaniard, high in military rank as a general officer of engineers in the Emperor's service, and at the head of the whole department of internal communications by land and water throughout the empire, including the establishment for instruction of officers for this service, had a separate commission to prepare and arrange the whole of the new establishment for manufacturing paper currency in all its branches. The General is a very ingenious, well informed, and scientific man.

The plan submitted, and which was at first acted upon, was to give an evident and apparent superiority to the genuine notes by various remarkable perfections, which could only be produced by machinery too expensive for any private concern, and too bulky for concealment. A large house was appropriated in this city, and almost built for the purpose. Very powerful and expensive machinery was procured from England, and placed in this building: to these machines were added several complicated inventions and ingenious contrivances, and a manufactory was formed for the sole purpose of making Bank paper.

A specimen of the paper is before your lordship. It has three different water-marks—one opaque, one half opaque, and one clear. Its toughness will stand any fair experiment. I have seen it pinched up into various shapes, hard rubbed afterwards between hands for many minutes, folded by a strong folder, and smoothed again, without cutting or tearing, or any loss of substance. The notes were to have an ornamented border, and the machinery was contrived to strike off the impression simultaneously on both sides of the paper, so that the impression on both sides was exactly the same, having the same accuracy or the same imperfections on both sides, even to strength or faintness, excess or want of ink in any particular line or hair stroke, without the slightest perceptible difference more than if one were reflected in a mirror—an accuracy which could not be attained by hand, and by which every blot or imperfection gave a fresh security. Not only the border, but the number, and the whole or any part of the inscription, would, in like manner, be struck on both sides at once. I have seen a note so executed, and am promised a specimen, not a note, which, if I obtain, I will send to your lordship. I do not profess to understand the mechanism by which this is done.

The numbers were to be struck by the machine in a continued series, the machine supplying itself with fresh decimals,

so as seldom to interrupt the operation. If any notes were
imperfect, the number could not be changed, but they were to
be destroyed, and the numbers of those notes so destroyed in
the manufactory were to be entered in a book kept for that
purpose.

Suddenly, and during the absence of the Emperor, a stop
was put to the whole proceeding, and the establishment was
taken by the Minister of Finance into his own hands, the
General being relieved from all further concern in it. The
machinery is not used ; the paper could not be carried through
the process for some time, because the men were not perfectly
instructed ; but they have now got tolerably into the way of
making it, but not without calling in the aid of other manufacturers. The number is to be inserted in the old way, and
I understand the notes are to be figured on the back, like
foreign playing-cards, and probably not better executed.

The truth is, all business is carried on through the instru-
mentality of inferior persons in office, who, in fact, do the
business, and are so necessary to the heads of the departments
that they very generally rule everything in their own way.
Great profit is made somewhere by counterfeit notes, and great
quantities of them are and will continue to be in circulation.

The inhabitants of two villages not far from Nigenci Novo-
gorod, where the great fair is held, are generally known to
live by the manufacture of counterfeit notes, and have continued that trade very openly with perfect impunity. I am
credibly assured that quantities of counterfeit notes find their
way into the Treasury, and are reissued in large payments
forwarded with good notes to distant quarters.

I have been tempted to trouble your lordship more in detail
on this subject than I would otherwise have done, as it affords
a striking instance of the difficulty of carrying any improvement to perfection in this country, which was the matter of
part of a former letter. No industry or expense is spared to
discover and transplant new and useful inventions ; but, on

most occasions, as soon as they are in progress, they are abandoned.

This observation, however, does not apply to the numbers and composition of the Army, the arrangement of which continues to improve; it might, perhaps, to the mode of applying that force when in the field, where, I hope and trust, it will not again be employed for many years.

Ever, my dear lord, &c.,   CATHCART.

Lord Cathcart to Lord Castlereagh.

St. Petersburgh, May 20-8, 1819.

My dear Lord—The Emperor lately told me it was his intention that Count Capodistrias should proceed to Paris, to inform himself accurately of the state of affairs on the spot; and that from thence he should go to London, to have a full and confidential communication with your lordship, and with the Ministers of other Powers engaged in conferences there. A frigate is fitting out, to be manned by the other half of the battalion of seamen or marines of the Guard, (not the half which manned the frigate which wintered in England lately) and in that frigate now preparing the Count is to return to St. Petersburgh.

This equipment is also to serve the purpose of practice for the seamen of the Guard, who, during the winter months, do duty in this city as a battalion of foot-guards. The remainder, during the summer, are to man the Emperor's yachts and barges, as usual.

It was in contemplation to equip several ships of the line this year—as far as thirteen or fourteen; but the stores were so much drained in the arsenal, that it could not be effected without delay and difficulty, and great expense; so that the number has been progressively reduced, and will, I believe, not exceed the usual proportion for the annual cruise. Two ships have been ordered to prepare for voyages of discovery, but the commanders were not selected when I last heard of them. I shall know in a few days if any fresh orders have been or are to be given.

I have the honour to remain, &c.,   CATHCART.

PS. I do not hear that the Emperor has any intention of quitting this vicinage before September, when he will probably go towards Warsaw, and may make some excursions in his journey. It is expected that there will be in autumn a grand assembly of the Polish army. The guards are to encamp next month, in succession of brigades, to give time to air and repair their respective barracks; and there is to be, in July, a considerable assembly of cavalry for exercise and manœuvre, which, with business and the improvement of his grounds, will probably afford to his Imperial Majesty full occupation. I think, if any excursions are made before autumn, they will be of short duration.

O.

Lord Strangford to Lord Castlereagh.

Stockholm, May 28, 1819.

My Lord—In the possibility that a letter sent through Hamburgh may reach your lordship sooner than the ordinary mail through Gottenburgh, I hasten to have the honour of informing your lordship that the Swedish Government has this day formally acceded to the propositions for an arrangement with Denmark, which your lordship was pleased to entrust to me.

I have the honour to be, &c.,   STRANGFORD.

Lord Cathcart to Lord Castlereagh.

St. Petersburgh, June 24, 1819.

My dear Lord—Count d'Osery, who is sent with a letter from the King of France, as stated in my despatch, has, I have reason to believe, brought the names of five persons deemed eligible for the post of Envoy from his Most Christian Majesty to this Court, with a request that the Emperor will select one. He is also to represent the present state and policy of the French Government in what is considered by that Court to be its true colours. This will lead to an answer, perhaps Lettre de Cabinet, which, I have no doubt, his Imperial Majesty will communicate, when prepared, to his august Allies.

The language to Count d'Osery is, as far as I am informed, to rejoice in the favourable accounts of which he is the bearer, and to hope their continuance and realization of the expectations derived from them. This General, now Count d'Osery, is General Hulot, brother to Madame Moreau. Your lordship, I think, saw him at Troyes and at Paris, in 1814. He has lost a leg and an eye in the wars. The four for the sweepstakes proposed are Marion, Rutti, Richard, and Ferronaye: my bets would be for the last.

Ever, my dear lord, &c.,   CATHCART.

Count Lieven's courier, with Reports of the Conferences on the Northern question at London, is expected, but not arrived.

Lord Cathcart to Lord Castlereagh.

St. Petersburgh, June 28, 1819.

My dear Lord—The copy of Count Engeström's despatch of acceptance of the proposal furnished by Lord Strangford to General Suchtelen was received here on Saturday morning, the 5th, and, being the morning for diplomatic work, was immediately carried to Zarskoselo by Count Nesselrode. I saw him the next day, and it appears to me that this perspective of amicable termination of this business has given *sincere* and *unqualified* satisfaction to his Imperial Majesty. This I judge from the language of the Count, but not from any express communication, for which there has not been an opportunity. I have not seen the Emperor since. There was probably business done again yesterday, but I have not since that time seen Count Nesselrode.

Lord Strangford sent the same communication to me; but the estafette delivered his despatches thirty-six hours before mine was delivered from the Post-office. I most sincerely congratulate your lordship on this event.

Ever, my dear lord, &c.,　　CATHCART.

Mr. Antrobus[1] to Lord Castlereagh.

Washington, July 1, 1819.

My Lord—I received a few days ago some information on the subject of the expedition preparing by the United States' Government, to proceed to the Yellow Stone River, which, I trust, may not prove uninteresting to your lordship. This expedition is the same as the one mentioned in Mr. Bagot's despatch to your lordship, No. 80, of 1818, which was then fitting out at St. Louis.

It will be in your lordship's recollection that, in the year 1804, an expedition was sent under Captains Lewis and Clarke, to explore the waters of the Missouri, to find a passage across the mountains to the Columbia River, and to proceed down that river to the Pacific. The route taken by these gentlemen was found to be too mountainous to answer the purpose this Government had in view, namely, an inland communication, for commercial purposes, from the Atlantic to the Pacific; and, about five years ago, they employed a person of the name of Hunt, a hunter resident near the mouth of the Columbia, to explore some more practicable route.

In pursuance of this object, Mr. Hunt proceeded up the Multomah River, (I must beg leave to refer your lordship to Mellish's Map of the United States) to its head waters, and, crossing the Stony Ridge in a hilly, but not mountainous, country, endeavoured to find his way to the Missouri, down the River Platte. This river he found was unnavigable from

[1] Successor to Mr. Bagot as Envoy to the United States.

its shallowness, and he was obliged to make his way to St.
Louis through the unreclaimed country on the banks of the
La Platte.

The expedition now preparing, and which has probably
arrived by this time at St. Louis, the place of rendezvous, is
to proceed to the Yellow Stone River, and establish the post
mentioned in Mr. Bagot's despatch to your lordship. A part
of it will then go forward to the junction of that stream with
the Big Horn River, where the merchants of St. Louis already
possess an establishment called Manuel's Fort, proceed up the
Big Horn, which is known to be navigable to its source, and,
crossing the mountains by the track explored by Hunt, descend
the Multomah River, to the Columbia, and thence to the
Pacific. If a favourable report of the practicability of this
route is made by the leaders of the expedition, it is understood
that a federal road will be made through the country lying
between the head waters of the Big Horn and the Multomah.

Such, I am told, is the intention with which this expedition has been fitted out. But I understand from another
quarter that, in all probability, it will not be able to leave St.
Louis this season, owing to an accident, which could not have
been foreseen by this Government. The party consists of 600
United States troops, accompanied by a number of scientific
men. They are to be embarked at St. Louis in six steam-
boats, for the building of which the Government has contracted
with Colonel Johnson, one of the representatives for the State
of Kentucky in the late Congress. These boats were built on
the Ohio, in the neighbourhood of Pittsburgh, and, as they
were descending that river to reach St. Louis, they were
attached by the Sheriff for debts due by Mr. Johnson's house
of business, which had become insolvent.

Mr. Johnson, in his last letters to the War Department,
says he has succeeded in beating off the Sheriff; but advice
has been received at that department that this officer reached
St. Louis before the arrival of the boats, and has there re-

quired of and obtained from the Governor three hundred men to act in aid of the civil authority, as soon as the boats reach that place.

It is reported, but I know not how correctly, that the President, who intended to shorten his tour and not to visit St. Louis, has been sent for express to that place, in the hopes that he may by his presence effect some arrangement, by which the expedition will be enabled to proceed. · But it is much feared that, even should he authorize the purchase of the boats for the United States, the legal delays will detain the party at St. Louis till the season will be too far advanced to allow of its setting out for its destination this summer.

I have the honour to be, &c.,
G. CRAWFURD ANTROBUS.

Sir Robert Liston to Lord Castlereagh.

Constantinople, July 10, 1819.

My Lord—In the conversation with which I was honoured by your lordship a short time before I last left England, you were pleased to inquire how long I meant to remain at Constantinople. I answered—As long as your lordship was of opinion that I could be useful to the public service. But how long, you were kind enough to ask, would you yourself wish to stay? I replied that, if I were at perfect liberty to decide, I should not wish to hold the office for a length of time, merely to do the common *routine* duties of the Embassy; but that I should be happy to see the determination of the matters of a certain difficulty and importance then depending; and then, if nothing interesting occurred, that is, perhaps, at the end of two or three years, to be permitted to return.

Your lordship did not express any disapprobation of the idea. I conceived, on the contrary, that, if the business of the Ionian Islands and of Parga were once settled, and if the differences between Russia and the Porte were amicably adjusted, or the discussion of them referred to an indefinite period, your

K 2

lordship would not then object to my requesting to be recalled : you only desired that, though this arrangement might be confidentially understood to be so agreed to, I should avoid mentioning the matter to any person but your lordship. The affair of Parga and of the Ionian Islands may be said to be finally concluded ; and there is reason to think that the discussions between the Turks and Russians will be ere long adjourned *sine die.* So that it appears to me that, in the space of a year from this time, I may take the liberty of requesting permission to return to England, at least upon another leave of absence, provided that no unforeseen obstacle arise : for I beg respectfully to end as I began, by saying that I will not quit my post as long as your lordship is of opinion that it is proper I should hold it.

But, looking forward to the distance I have mentioned, I am anxious to obtain a favour, which I hope your lordship will obligingly grant me. It is, that you will condescend to lay before the Prince my humble petition to be allowed to spend the most rigorous portion of the ensuing winter on some of the islands, or on some of the coasts of the southern and eastern parts of the Mediterranean.

My wife had so violent and so dangerous a fit of illness during the severity of the last season, that I am very unwilling she should run the hazard of another ; and I cannot help adding that I myself should feel an almost necessary comfort in a temporary relief from the wearing, and I may almost say mortifying, duties of this singular station.

I have, therefore, taken the liberty of sending an official petition for leave of absence, which your lordship may lay before his Royal Highness, if you do not think it unreasonable. The length of time required to ensure the return of an answer from England induces me to trouble you with the application thus early.

       I have the honour to be, &c.,   ROBERT LISTON.

Lord Cathcart to Lord Castlereagh.

St. Petersburgh, 21-9 July, 1819.

My dear Lord—I lately had the honour of mentioning to your lordship, in a private letter forwarded by a Russian courier, six documents sent to Count Lieven, which were intended for your lordship's perusal. The Emperor, in talking over the subject matter of these papers with me, a few days ago, observed that there were two other papers, which did not appear to have been sent to me, but which it had been his intention to have communicated to me at the same time; and, conformably to instructions which his Imperial Majesty was pleased to give to that purport, I have since seen them.

I need not comment upon them, as they have been before your lordship: indeed, the Emperor said he had directed the original of one of these two to be sent to London, on purpose that your lordship might read it in the original; and the answer, of which your lordship has seen a copy, was shown to me in the original draft, as approved by his Imperial Majesty's signature.

Together with these papers, an extract from a despatch from Count Engeström to M. Brandel, Chargé d'Affaires from Sweden at this Court, was communicated in the original, as received from M. Brandel, and I requested a copy, which I have the honour herewith to enclose. Nothing had been received here from Count Lieven on the subject of any communication made to his Excellency by your lordship of Count Engeström's Note to Lord Strangford of the 27th of May; and the words at the beginning of the last paragraph, alluding to an answer stated to have been received from your lordship, made me anxious to send this copy to your lordship without any delay.

General Count Hulot is still here, and I have not heard any day named for his departure. He has had a second audience, and has been twice a spectator of exercises of the troops encamped, at which this Emperor was present, having solicited permission to that effect through Count Nesselrode.

I have the honour to remain, &c.,

CATHCART.

[Enclosure.]

Extrait d'une Dépêche de son Excellence M. le Comte d'Engeström à M. de Brandel, en date de Helsinbourg, le 1 Juillet, 1819.

Vos dépêches du 15 et 18 Juin me sont parvenues avant-hier, et je n'ai pas tardé un moment à les mettre sous les yeux du Roi.

N'ayant jamais rien désiré plus vivement que de voir disparaître le mésentendre désagréable que, durant quelques mois a obscurci les relations des deux Cours de Stockholm et de St. Petersbourg, sa Majesté a reçu avec un plaisir bien sincère la nouvelle que contenaient vos deux dépêches sus mentionnées de la cessation complète de tout ce différend ; et si je vous. parle encore d'une affaire, qui désormais doit être ensevelie dans le plus profond oubli, ce n'est que pour vous exprimer la haute satisfaction du Roi notre Souverain, et de l'issue finale de cette affaire, et de la conduite prudente et régulière à la fois que vous avez observée en cette occasion. Le Roi veut Monsieur que vous ne négligiez aucune occasion pour assurer son Excellence le Comte de Nesselrode de la sincérité et de la constance des sentimens que le Roi n'a cessé de vouer à l'Empereur son auguste ami et allié. Aucune reminiscence, aucun retour sur le passé, ne troublera ces dispositions amicales et sa Majesté a été heureuse de voir que les sentimens de sa Majesté Impériale à cet égard répondent parfaitement aux siens.

Vous exprimerez à cette occasion, au Comte de Nesselrode combien sa Majesté a été sensible aux nouvelles assurances que sa Majesté l'Empereur vous a fait faire par son ministère, de son amitié en général, et plus particulièrement encore par rapport au mariage de la fille du ci-devant Roi avec le Margrave de

Bade. Non que sa Majesté eut eu besoin de ces nouvelles assurances pour rester parfaitement tranquille par rapport aux intentions de l'Empereur relativement à l'ancienne famille royale de Suède. Le Roi connait et apprécie trop bien le caractère personnel de sa Majesté Impériale pour concevoir ou nourrir a cet égard les plus légers soupçons ; mais sa Majesté a aimé de retrouver dans cette ouverture complètement spontanée une preuve manifeste de l'amitié sincère de son auguste Allié ; et plus les éclaircissemens fournis par le Comte de Nesselrode portent l'empreinte d'une complète franchise, plus sa Majesté y a retrouvé un effet des principes et des sentimens personnels de sa Majesté l'Empereur Alexandre—principes et sentimens, que sa Majesté n'a pas tardé à reconnaître d'abord à Abo, et postérieurement dans tous les entretiens qu'elle a eu l'avantage d'avoir avec ce Souverain. C'est sous ce rapport que le Roi considère ces nouvelles protestations comme l'augure d'une intimité qui va renaître plus indissoluble que jamais.

Je suis heureux de pouvoir vous informer que le Gouvernement Britannique, constant dans son amitié pour la Suède, vient de répondre aux dernières ouvertures du Roi d'une manière parfaitement conforme aux vœux de sa Majesté.

Déterminé à mettre autant de facilité possible dans la négociation finale avec le Dannemarc, le Roi croit ainsi pouvoir envisager l'affaire de la liquidation Norvégienne comme presque terminée : et comme sa Majesté Impériale a paru mettre beaucoup d'intérêt à la conclusion de cet arrangement, le Roi ne croit pas devoir hésiter maintenant à vous ordonner, Monsieur, de prévenir M. le Comte de Nesselrode de l'heureux résultat que nous venons d'obtenir. Si sa Majesté n'a pas pu avoir plutôt le plaisir de communiquer à sa Majesté Impériale les espérances fondées qu'elle avait d'obtenir ce même résultat, il ne faut attribuer ce retard qu'aux incidens fâcheux qui se sont élevés, et qui viennent de disparaître d'une manière si satisfaisante pour tous.

Lord Cathcart to Lord Castlereagh.

St. Petersburgh, August 6-18, 1819.

My dear Lord—I have the pleasure to acquaint your lordship that the Marquess of Graham and Mr. Fielding arrived here last Friday, in perfect health, from Stockholm. I have sent letters from them to the Office by this post. In the absence of the Court and of all the principal people, this is rather an unfavourable moment for seeing more than the exterior of this place, but everything will be done for their amusement and information that circumstances will permit.

Your lordship will have seen about this time a circular from this Court to London, Vienna, and Berlin, on French questions, and particularly the answers received from Vienna and Berlin, stating that your lordship had not yet given an answer, owing to pressure of business, which is waiting for final decision. The letter is dated July *generally*. The event of the *succession* is particularly noticed in it.

The Danes wish to include in the Convention an Article to set at rest any remaining question between Norway and Denmark not included in the Treaty of Kiel. This seems to me very improvident, as it holds out a new pretext for delay; and, though no money is to pass upon it, it might equally be regulated by a future Act. They have proposed it here, but cannot have, as yet, any answer at all. Lord Strangford, I have heard, has refused to take any notice of it, as not forming any part of the matter referred to him.

Ever, my dear lord, &c., CATHCART.

Lord Clancarty to Lord Castlereagh.

Bruxelles, August 20, 1819.

My dear Lord—It was in consequence of a communication to me of your wishes to be acquainted as soon as possible with the views of this Government in the Eastern seas that I had a conversation with Nagell, out of which proceeded the order

from the King to Falck to confer with me upon this subject.
I believe myself that all our difficulties with the Dutch in
those parts have originated from Sir Stamford Raffles. His
conduct excited, as it appears, the jealousy of M. Capellen
(who, very happily, is a man of good sense, and fully imbued
with the opinion of the closest connexion with us being requisite for his country). Hence grew several of the establishments made by them, and from these the necessity of making
others on our part appeared to our Government at Calcutta.

M. de Falck, in my conversation with him, seemed to feel
the propriety of not mixing more of Indian knowledge than
was absolutely necessary in the projected negociation, professing himself to deprecate the larger and more essential
interests of the two countries being in any wise influenced by
local considerations: they will probably, therefore, have one
Indian only (not improbably Elort, if he is not drowned) to
join Fagel in the negociation. Nagell tells me that he writes
by this conveyance to Fagel a summary of my conversation
with him of the day before yesterday, with directions, if nothing shall be said to him upon it, to keep it to himself; but,
if spoken to with reference to it, then to show you his version.
Possibly it may be well for you to see this.

In my conversation with Falck, he mentioned the subject of
the island of Billeton, and asked why, as a dependence of
Banca, it had not been delivered to them. I told him that I
was not instructed to enter into explanations and details of
this sort; but, speaking from myself, I supposed it had not
been delivered, because it was not a dependence upon Banca,
and consequently not comprised within the stipulation of
August, 1814. I should hope, but cannot be sure, of bringing
you over somewhat more definite with respect to your projected negociation in London, than I am enabled to convey by
this mail.

Nagell, in gentle terms, but still in those approaching to
complaint, told me that M. Desolles had written him word

that Admiral Fremantle was immediately to meet a squadron of French ships at Marseilles, and thence to proceed in concert to the coast of Barbary. He seemed surprised that an intimation of this kind had not rather reached him from us, and possibly feels that some of the Dutch ships in the Mediterranean might have formed part of this expedition. It may possibly be wise to say a few words to Fagel upon this subject, but without appearing to have derived any hints upon it from me. These little attentions are much appreciated here, most particularly from us.

His Excellency the Director-General of Droits Réunis of this Government, M. Appelius, chose to go the other day to a blackguard Vauxhall at Rotterdam, where his son got into a quarrel, in which he interfered, and was well drubbed. The King, upon hearing this, was afraid, and you will probably hear it so represented, that this was political, and a demonstration of hostility to the Government, but this was not the case.

We propose setting out for England on Wednesday, the 25th, and, as we shall be much too numerous to visit you with all our force, I intend leaving all but Lady Clancarty and myself at Rochester or Dartford, on our way to town, and, with your permission, passing one day with you at Cray. We shall then proceed for, I should hope, a day only, to London, and thence, with what speed we may, to Ireland. Should you propose to be absent from Cray, or your house too full to receive us on Friday, Saturday, or Sunday next, pray let a line be written to us, addressed to the York Hotel, Dover, to acquaint us therewith.

Farewell, my dear lord—*au revoir.* Ever very affectionately yours,   CLANCARTY.

Lord Castlereagh to Sir Charles Stuart.

Foreign Office, August 23, 1819.

Your Excellency's despatch No. 210, of the 5th instant, relative to the claims of the Princess de Montfort, has been

received and laid before his Royal Highness the Prince Regent.
The confidential communication from the Prussian Minister,
enclosed in your despatch, has been attentively considered,
and his Royal Highness cannot but concur in the view which
the Cabinet of Berlin has therein taken upon this subject.
The Prince Regent has invariably considered the Treaty of
Fontainebleau annulled by the subsequent conduct of Buonaparte in 1815; and this opinion of his Royal Highness was
repeatedly stated by Lord Clancarty in the most unequivocal
terms, during the several Conferences that were held at
Vienna in 1815, upon the subject of that treaty as connected
with the disposal of the Italian duchies.

I have therefore to request that your Excellency will not,
without further reference to me, take any step upon this subject, otherwise than that of expressing the above opinion on
the part of his Royal Highness.

I have the honour to be, &c.,   CASTLEREAGH.

Sir H. Wellesley to Lord Castlereagh.

Madrid, August 24, 1819.

My dear Lord—From the tenor of the last despatches
received by the Spanish Government from Paris, some hopes
seem to be entertained of an amicable termination of the negociations between Spain and Portugal, as far, at least, as they
relate to the territory occupied by the Portuguese troops.
From what has fallen from M. Salmon, however, there does
not appear to be any disposition in this Government to treat
at present for the restoration of Olivenza to Portugal. I
should think that a recommendation from the Conference to
his Catholic Majesty's Government of the nature suggested
by M. de Pizarro himself would be attended with a good
effect. But such an overture, to be effectual, should not be
made until after the signature of the other treaty.

I have not yet received an answer to my last note on the

subject of our commerce in the River Plate. I am promised that the answer shall be sent without farther loss of time, and have reason to think that it will be satisfactory.

I am assured that the Duke of San Fernando, who lately married a sister of the Cardinal de Bourbon, and is therefore connected with the royal family of Spain, is to be sent to treat with the Government of the United States. If this information be true, the sending a person of such distinguished rank shows the importance which is attached to the success of the mission.

I have the honour to be, &c.,   H. WELLESLEY.

Count Capodistrias to Lord Castlereagh.

Ce 28 Août, 1819.

Les papiers que je prends la liberté de vous transmettre ci-joint, Mylord, portent quelques notes sur la situation actuelle de ma patrie. Votre Excellence y verra aussi les vœux qu'elle forme. Je n'ose pas accompagner cette communication toute spéciale et confidentielle des documens qui viennent à l'appui des observations qui y sont consignées. Ce sont des actes officiels, publics et imprimés. Mais étant rédigés en Grec et en Italien, ils ne sauroient pour le moment fixer votre attention. Ils doivent d'ailleurs exister en original dans les archives du Ministère.

Que votre Excellence veuille bien se donner la peine de parcourir ces pièces, et de me les faire restituer. Puisque Lord Bathurst a eu la bonté de m'engager à aller chez lui à la campagne, je me propose de l'entretenir de cet object, et de mettre également sous ses yeux sans aucune restriction tous les papiers et documens qui y ont trait.

Ils n'ont aucune forme. Mais ils peuvent recevoir celle que Lord Bathurst jugera à propos de leur faire donner. Je ne demande pas mieux que de suivre ses directions.

Ce qui me tient vivement à cœur c'est de m'acquitter d'un

double devoir—servir ma patrie, justifier la confiance dont vous m'honorez, Mylord, et mériter celle des vos collègues.

Je prie votre Excellence d'agréer mes hommages,

CAPODISTRIAS.

Lord Castlereagh to Lord Bathurst.

Cray Farm, August 28, 1819.

ᶜ My dear Bathurst—I am sorry to find that neither Maitland's prognostics nor my own, with respect to Capodistrias having *left his budget of grievances behind*, have been verified. As I find you have invited Lieven and the Count to Cirencester, I presume and hope they will keep the whole for yourself as a *bonne bouche.*

I had only a very general intimation of his opinions, when Capodistrias delivered to me the enclosed letter from the Emperor; but I found afterwards from the Duke of Wellington that he had been with his Grace the same morning before I saw him, to deliver a letter from the Emperor on the same subject, and had shown him his papers, of the nature of which the Duke told me he should that day send you a report, with the answer with which he had returned the documents.

I did not open the Emperor's letter whilst the Russians staid with me, in order to avoid as much as possible the prolongation of our conversation. I understood, in answer to an observation of mine, " how much had been the general feeling, and of no Sovereign more strongly than the Emperor, that external interference in the affairs of these islands might defeat the beneficent views with which they had been placed under the sole protection of Great Britain"—that what he wished to state was not to be considered in any shape as official; nor were the Emperor's letters to the Duke of Wellington and myself to be regarded in any other light than as the confidential expressions of his Imperial Majesty's personal anxiety for the happiness of these people; that it was his own act as a

native of these islands, in discharge of his conscience, &c., and
to the performance of which he felt himself doubly impelled
by the active share he had taken (which is true) in placing
these islands under British protection.

He adverted in a general way to the complaints he had to
make. I professed ignorance on all these points, and regretted
that your health had deprived you of the opportunity of
receiving him; but that I had no doubt you would receive any
communication which he, as a distinguished citizen of those
islands, might feel it his duty to make to you, provided there
was no reserve imposed upon you, which either might fetter
you in founding upon it the necessary inquiry, or restrain
you from acting upon the whole towards Sir T. Maitland with
the openness which was due to a distinguished officer, placed
in a very arduous and responsible trust—to all of which he
seemed fully to assent. He said the notes he had made were
prepared with a view to a conversation with Maitland himself,
which the General had led him to expect he should hold with
him during his stay in the islands; but that, although he had
overwhelmed him with civilities, he had never allowed him to
execute his purpose, which he was sorry for, as he had no
object but *to do good*.

From what Capo said to me, (and the Duke told me this
appeared in his papers) part of his case rests upon *an alleged
infraction* of the Treaty of Paris. I think it the more material to call your attention to this, without knowing anything of
the merits of his reasoning, because this is a branch of the
question, upon which Russia, as a contracting party, may, if
she thinks fit, clearly take an official proceeding. As any
ostensible cut of this nature would be even more mischievous
within the islands than private and unofficial explanations, and
as the disposition in the House of Commons to look into our
conduct on the coasts of Greece, already inconveniently strong,
would be augmented by an avowed difference with Russia, you
will on this account, I have no doubt, exhaust more than an

ordinary share of patience, philosophy, and management, in order to keep the matter on unofficial grounds.

I think I have now said all I have to say—so farewell.

CASTLEREAGH.

PS. You will see, by the enclosed note from Capodistrias, that I have reckoned without my host, and that I have had his budget sent to me on its way to Cirencester. I have read it over hastily, and, without now examining its details, the *ensemble*, I must say, takes a more serious shape than I had expected, and it is written in a tone of considerable bitterness. These papers, I understand from the Duke of Wellington, had been before the Emperor, when his letters were written. Copies, of course, are in the hands of the Capodistrias family in the islands. We must regard them, therefore, if not intended for publication, as liable to come out at any moment it may suit the Opposition in the islands to bring forward a public appeal. The merits, therefore, cannot be blinked; and we must be prepared with the case on which we mean to rest our conduct, if possible, before Parliament assembles, when, I have no doubt, the residue of the Parganotic question, with any kindred points that can be made inconveniently to bear, will be brought into discussion.

I propose to answer the Emperor generally, stating that the Count, in his visit to you, at Cirencester, will have an opportunity of opening to you his views upon this subject, and that I doubt not your lordship will give to such information as his Excellency may bring before you on Ionian affairs your best attention.

[Enclosure.]

The Emperor Alexander to Lord Castlereagh.

Sarskoë Selo, le 23 Juillet, 1819.

Un motif digne de votre attention et de l'estime que vous inspirez, Mylord, m'engage à vous entretenir un moment.

Il s'agit des Iles Ioniennes. Le Comte de Capodistrias, en vous remettant cette lettre, vous exposera leurs vœux.

J'ai doublement le droit de les recommander à votre sollicitude, et par l'intérêt que j'ai toujours porté à cet État, et par
la confiance même avec laquelle j'ai cru le premier, en 1815,
que son bonheur devait être l'ouvrage du Gouvernement
Britannique.

Veuillez, Mylord, ne point refuser votre appui aux habitans
des Iles.   En contribuant à leur prospérité, vous ferez voir au
monde une nouvelle application des principes que vous avez
dernièrement encore, dans une occasion solennelle, défendu
avec un si beau talent et un si beau succès.

Je me félicite de pouvoir vous réitérer, Mylord, l'assurance
des mes sentimens très distingués.

ALEXANDRE.

Lord Strangford to Lord Castlereagh.

Stockholm, August 31, 1819.

My dear Lord—I have to inform your lordship that to-
morrow is the day fixed for the signature of the Convention
between Sweden and Denmark; and I trust your lordship will
not find any reason to be displeased with the variations from
the precise letter of my instructions, which I was unavoidably
obliged to admit, not only, however, with the consent, but by
the express desire, of the Danish Government.

I shall hope to forward a copy of the Convention by the
Gottenburgh mail of Thursday next.

I have the honour to be, &c,   STRANGFORD.

Lord Bathurst to Lord Castlereagh.

Cirencester, September 3, 1819.

My dear Castlereagh—Capodistrias and Lieven arrived for
dinner on Thursday.   They gave out that they intended to go
the next day, but were easily persuaded to remain over Friday,
and went away early yesterday morning.

Capodistrias opened his business on Friday at some length,
and then left me to read his papers, and returned afterwards,

when we had another long conversation. I cannot attempt to
enter into the whole of what passed. I had proposed to myself
to say little; but I could not help entering into some of the
questions, to which I thought there was an easy reply in
explanation. I thought it right to say, however, that there
was much which required inquiry; and for that purpose I
asked if he would let me have the papers, in order to take
notes, and I would return the papers to him. He said that he
would send me notes of the papers himself; and he seemed
not unwilling to acknowledge that they were written with some
warmth, and made apologies for it, as being written only for
his inspection (you will recollect that they had been submitted
to that of the Emperor). I doubt whether he is much acquainted with the questions. At one time he spoke reasonably, and admitted that the people ought to be essentially
under our influence, but he said what, I am afraid, may be to
a certain degree the truth, that Sir Thomas Maitland's manners are very rough, distant, and unconciliatory; and that he
shows too plainly he thinks ill of the inhabitants. At other
times he held out the prospect of the Emperor's interference,
or of intestine commotions.

We must be prepared with a parliamentary case. The
charge of a breach of the treaty is most material. I think
we can show that the charge is unfounded. With respect to
the Constitution, we can show that the Russian Constitutions
were of the same character; and we have a letter from Capodistrias himself, at that time the Secretary to the Ionian
Republic, in which he remonstrates against too much power
being given to a people so uneducated. We have also the
secret instructions drawn up by the leading people of that time
to their Envoy at Petersburgh, begging the Emperor to give
them any Constitution he pleases, and entreating him to keep
up a large Russian force in the islands, as the only way of
keeping things quiet. These papers may be brought forward,
if necessary. The course which I intend to adopt is, to send

the notes off to Sir Thomas Maitland, directing his attention
to those parts which I think will require particular explanation.   When I have got materials enough, I propose, with
your approbation, to write a letter to Capodistrias explanatory
of what has passed; and should he, in his notes, have omitted
some of the charges to which an easy answer may be given, I
can equally advert to them, having, indeed, taken a note or
two on some of the passages in the papers.   I propose also to
send back to Sir Thomas all his explanations, &c., which he
may in the first instance send to me, with such suggestions as
may be necessary for him to draw up the answers in such a
way as may suit a parliamentary discussion.   One of the inconveniences, to say the least, is this: that, in giving the
answer which I thought I was bound to give, that I would
investigate the statements which I received, I shall enable
Capodistrias to write encouraging letters to his friends.

Yours very sincerely,   BATHURST.

I thought I had better not say much against the Emperor's
interference; but I said that we had *accepted* the protection of
the islands *only on one condition*—for we had never wished for
it—and afterwards, when Capodistrias said that he would
make notes of the papers, which notes Lieven would lend me,
I thought proper to say that I supposed I was to receive them
only as a private communication from Capodistrias, to which
he readily assented.   I think, upon the whole, that it was
better for me to have seen him, though he is probably pretty
well aware that nothing material will be done.   Lieven was in
a fright the whole time.

Lord Castlereagh to the Marquis de Latour-Maubourg.

Cray Farm, September 7, 1819.

Lord Castlereagh presents his compliments to the Marquis
de Latour-Maubourg, and begs to inform him that, on reference to Sir Charles Stuart's despatch of the 2nd instant, it
appears that Admiral Fremantle had arrived at Toulon on the

20th of August, previous to receiving the despatches of his Majesty's Government of the 15th and 29th of June last; and that Admiral Fremantle, conceiving that his departure from Toulon without obtaining pratique might be attended with considerable inconvenience, he had determined to wait at that port for the purpose, and then proceed on to Minorca, where he expected to be about the 25th, to execute the orders which he had received.

Baron Fagel to Lord Castlereagh.

Whitehall Place, Tuesday, September 7, 1819.

My dear Lord—I herewith transmit to you the enclosed, which, although directed to Lord Clancarty, Baron Nagell wishes you to open. It contains the answer to the overtures made by Lord Clancarty on the affairs of India. I make no scruple to communicate to you in perfect confidence M. de Nagell's private letter to me which accompanied the enclosed, requesting you to return it when you have read it.

Ever, my dear lord, &c., R. FAGEL.

Lord Castlereagh to Baron Fagel.

Cray Farm, September 8, 1819.

My dear Sir—I return you, with many thanks, the confidential communication, with the enclosed letter from M. de Nagell. The reply to Lord Clancarty's *note verbale* is, perhaps necessarily, obscure upon the mode of interpreting general principles, as applicable to the relative position of our interests in the Eastern seas; but, as we are agreed in the policy of some clear and friendly understanding, I willingly accept M. de Nagell's assurances as auspicious harbingers of our future hopes, and doubt not the same temper which has carried us successfully through other matters of greater importance will bring us, upon this subject also, to an early and satisfactory settlement.

CASTLEREAGH.

Lord Castlereagh to Lord Bathurst.

Cray Farm, September 8, 1819.

My dear Bathurst—Many thanks for your note. I think your interview with Capodistrias has ended as satisfactorily as could have been expected. You have placed the question upon good grounds in its preliminary stage, and we shall be masters of the course to be pursued, when we have examined and judged our ground. The course you propose to pursue with Maitland appears to me the most fair by him and judicious by ourselves; and I entertain no doubt (troublesome and difficult as the Ionian concern must be in its very nature) that, by neither being afraid of probing the case, nor of holding our own with the Emperor, and by not calling too much mystery to our aid, which I have always found the least imposing with his Imperial Majesty, we shall be enabled to maintain our authority within the islands, without embarrassing our general politics with Russia.

Believe me, &c., CASTLEREAGH.

Rev. Dr. Curtis (Roman Catholic Bishop of Armagh) to Lord Castlereagh.

Dublin, N. Cumberland Street, September 22, 1819.

My Lord—In obedience to the dictates of duty and gratitude, I have the honour of informing your lordship that I have just now received from Rome the authentic advice of my appointment by his Holiness to the Roman Catholic see of Armagh; and that the Papal brief for that purpose will be transmitted to me as soon as it can possibly be expedited. My consecration and instalment to that charge will, in consequence, be then performed in the parish chapel of Drogheda, unless Government should think proper in the mean time to order the contrary, which I have no reason to think will be the case, as I should never have acquiesced in the election made of me by our prelates, had not Government previously vouchsafed to grant its consent and even approbation to that measure, adding, by such condescension, a powerful stimulus to my already fixed resolution to employ every exertion and influence in my power for promoting peace, concord, and a spirit of conciliation rather than controversy, among all classes of people, and to impress on their minds a practical conviction of the impossibility of their being good Christians without having and showing a real love and respect for our august Sovereign and his Government, with a due, efficient obedience to the laws.

Permit me, my lord, to return your lordship my unfeigned thanks for the kind wish you were pleased to express of seeing my promotion sanctioned, and sincerely to assure your lordship I shall be happy to have frequent opportunities of rendering any personal service to your lordship or your friends.

I have the honour to remain, &c.,   P. CURTIS.

Lord Cathcart to Lord Castlereagh.

St. Petersburg, September 22-10, 1819.

My dear Lord—I have only time by this post to acknowledge the great favour of your private letter by Count Capodistrias. The frigate brought him in three days to Copenhagen, and arrived here the fourteenth day from her departure from the English coast, having been at Dantzig to set down Count Capo d'Istrias, who is gone to meet the Emperor at Warsaw. The Emperor has said everything that could be wished on the subject of Mr. B[agot].

Since the departure of his Imperial Majesty, I have learned that the French Chargé d'Affaires has applied for the favourable consideration and for support with other Courts on the subject of their withholding the payment due to Austria, till that Power shall liquidate French claims. Your lordship will understand this without my explaining farther by this post. Count Nesselrode is to give me this day all the details, but I only name it in order to acquaint your lordship that this communication has not yet been submitted to the Emperor, and that nothing has as yet been said or written concerning it from the Foreign Office.

I expect to be on my journey in the first days of October, but it depends upon when we are to take leave. I do not intend to go to Berlin, but to pass through the two Frankforts.

Ever, my dear lord, &c.,   CATHCART.

Mr. Jacob Bosanquet to Lord Castlereagh.

September 29, 1819.

My Lord—Some time ago I wrote to your lordship requesting the favour of an interview. My object was to speak to your lordship respecting the alteration of the tariff at Constantinople, by which the duties of entry into that country are in future to be assessed. I am not aware that I had anything very particular to communicate, but I wished, before final orders were sent to Sir R. Liston upon this subject, (who grows old) that your lordship should be correctly informed upon a subject which, as it bears upon the merchandize of foreign nations at market with ours, might be material in the present restricted state of commerce, and particularly as Turkey is now a very considerable outlet. I consider this matter as now gone by; but I hope that, as your lordship may have more leisure now than you could have during the sitting of Parliament, I may be permitted to bring to your lordship's notice a few matters, two of a public and one of a private nature.

The first is that you will allow me to ask for the appointment of a King's Commissioner for the present Consul-General of the Levant Company and the Agent of the East India Company, Mr. Cartwright, such as was enjoyed by his predecessor, M. Morier, and which was given to him by Mr. Fox. My reasons for making this application, as they might be long, I perhaps need not trouble your lordship with at present: all

I think I need say is, that though this commission may not be indispensably necessary in the present moment, it may be useful, and has been fairly earned by Mr. Cartwright for public services, under the direction of Sir Thomas Maitland, with the Pacha of Janina.

My second business is unreservedly to communicate to your lordship the serious apprehensions which I begin to feel with respect to the country. Standers-by, it is said, (and I believe with truth) often see more of the game than those who are deeply engaged in it. That mischief seems to be coming in, and that very fast, I think that no reflecting man can avoid seeing. Contagion often runs like wildfire, and there requires no prophet to say that, if the flame reaches the military, the country and the Constitution is gone, as was the case in France. No measure appears to me to be so likely to make an early separation of the good from the bad or mistaken part of the community, as some pointed and well drawn-up declaration or address to the Crown. When a separation is once commenced, as Burke well observes, the rent never fails to extend itself. But, to render a thing of this kind thoroughly effectual, it must be done in no common manner; no common hack must be employed in bringing it forward. I have always disapproved of common declarations, and, upon ordinary occasions, they are, in my mind, a mere waste of strength, and only destroy the effect that ought to be reserved for great occasions. I have seen infinitely too many of them during the war.

Your lordship may perhaps recollect the declaration of 1803, in which I officiated as Chairman. I was then head of a great body, and my proper rank was in the front of the battle. I think I may venture, without vanity, to say that the effect produced upon the country was salutary and consequential. I am now completely out of the question for such another attempt; and though in the county in which I reside I am well known, I have never taken such a lead in it at public meetings as to make it wise for me to attempt such a beginning; nor, indeed, do I think that the county of Hertford is exactly the place in which such a beginning should be made: but I really think it would be wise that it should be made somewhere.

There is, in my mind, but one exceedingly weak part, and that is the state of the representation. This cannot be defended by words—the thing is quite impossible; all that could be said would be that good perhaps is the result of it—but, though this may do very well in private argument, it certainly could not be said in public; and the thing must be glossed over as well as it could be done. There would, I think, be no very great difficulty in giving even a good turn to this; but it is, it must be confessed, a very difficult point, because no man can say beforehand what would be the consequences of touching it.

The last point I hope your lordship will allow me to touch is entirely private and respects my son. He is now with me on leave of absence from Paris, where, and at Berlin, he has now passed above four years in the situation of an attaché. His character and conduct will, I persuade myself, bear the strictest inquiry from those under whom he has served. He is twenty-eight years of age, speaks and understands German and French, and being a real good scholar, is (if I am not misled by the partiality of a parent) fit to render himself useful in almost any situation. He has a turn for his present employment, and, if he can form any reasonable hope of advancing in it, I am sure he will not grudge any labour or pains in its pursuit. But if circumstances, of which I do not presume to judge, have closed the door against him, it is better for me at his time of life to endeavour to employ him in some line where he may render himself useful to himself, and, I hope, to the community. He really is too good for a mere clerk's situation, unless it is likely to lead to some better employment.

I am sure your lordship will excuse the freedom with which I write, and that, with the frankness which I have ever considered as part of your lordship's character, if you can say anything to me upon this interesting subject, you will do it.

I have the honour to be, &c.,

JACOB BOSANQUET.

Lord Strangford to Lord Castlereagh.

Stockholm, October 7, 1819.

My dear Lord—I never felt so much difficulty and embarrassment in addressing your lordship as at this moment. I am absolutely destitute of expressions to convey to your lordship the deep and real sentiments of gratitude. which your most flattering and obliging communication of the 18th ult. has excited in my mind. The appointment to which the Prince Regent has been graciously pleased to signify his intention of nominating me had long been my dearest and most favourite wish; and your lordship's kindness in thus enabling me to attain it has given birth to feelings which I trust and hope my heart can never forget.

I entreat your lordship to lay at his Royal Highness's feet the assurance of my humble and grateful acknowledgment of this high and distinguished mark of his Royal Highness's favour, which will stimulate me to make every effort, as long as life shall be granted to me, to prove my zeal and devotion for so good and gracious a sovereign. The only testimony of my respectful attachment to his Royal Highness and of my desire to manifest my obedience to your lordship's wishes, is by remaining at my post during this winter, notwithstanding the seriously impaired state of my health. I have, however, ventured to solicit permission to [return to] England early in the spring, as I have some family affairs of material consequence to me, which I am desirous to arrange before I am sent to my new destination. I beg leave very respectfully to recommend this request to your lordship's favourable consideration.

I have taken the liberty, in a despatch of this date, to call your lordship's attention to the proposal for a new tariff,

which has lately been revived by this Government. I hope
that I shall not appear indiscreet, if I beg to mention my persuasion that, should this matter seem worthy of early notice,
it would be in our power to make an arrangement highly
advantageous to the manufacturing interest of Great Britain.
Nothing would gratify me more than to have the honour and
happiness of receiving and executing your lordship's commands
upon this occasion, should you think [fit] to confide them to
me during my further residence here.   &c.,

I have the honour to be, &c.,   STRANGFORD.

Lord Cathcart to Lord Castlereagh.

St. Petersburg, October 9, (N. S.) 1819.

My dear Lord—I cannot let this messenger go without expressing my best thanks for the private letter with which you
honoured me by Count Capodistrias' frigate, and for all the
marks of confidence and friendly interest by which you have
so liberally and so kindly distinguished me for a series of many
years. Believe me, my dear lord, your esteem, independent
of the distinctions which have followed it, is one of the circumstances of my life on which I have the greatest satisfaction,
and which I shall always most highly prize.

Count Nesselrode has been extremely civil on this as on all
other occasions. I have done everything in my power to lay
a ground for establishing a prepossession in favour of Mr.
Bagot, and I think I have succeeded with the Emperor and
with Count Nesselrode; and I have not neglected Mrs. Bagot's
interest with the reigning Empress.

Travelling with a family, I mean to avoid Courts, unless
your lordship should send me any commands. I go by Riga,
Königsberg, and perhaps Dantzig, to Frankfort on the Oder;
from thence by Torgau, if the roads permit, to Leipzig; from
thence to Frankfort sur Maine, when we shall visit the Prince
and Princess of Hesse-Homburg; from thence by Coblentz and
Cologne to Brussels and Calais, and looking at as many for-

tresses as I can conveniently get at. All this can hardly be
brought within six weeks, allowing a week to the Dwina, a week
for the Vistula, a week for the Oder, and a week for the Rhine,
viz., to Frankfort. My letters from hence will follow me, and
those sent to meet me will probably begin to find me at Leipzig.
I stand at your mercy and indulgence for the most favourable
application of the regulations at your lordship's disposal, in
regard to financial arrangements for the expenses of evacuating
this post, under this consideration of no small importance.

My son Frederick did not recover till very lately; and the
moment the abscesses formed by his fever, and which became
deep wounds, were in a state to enable him to dispense with
professional assistance at least once every day, he took his passage in the first ship, and is now on board the Deniston, Reid,
bound from Cronstadt to the Thames. His health is perfectly
restored, and, if the wind changes, I hope he will soon have
the honour of presenting himself to your lordship.

I think this Court will readily concur with your lordship in
regard to the inexpediency of *Conferences*, except in what
relates to the German constitutions. These are thought useful
by this Cabinet, as proposed to be held at Vienna; but I am
assured the Emperor Alexander does not intend to take any
part, however he may recommend the consideration of the important points which this subject involves to the most serious
attention of those who do take part as a necessary to ensure
the general tranquillity.

I have the honour to remain, &c.,   CATHCART.

I will take means to make your lordship's kind attention to
the Emperor's wish concerning Mr. Porter known to his
Imperial Majesty.

Sir William à Court to Lord Castlereagh.

Naples, October 12, 1819.

My dear Lord—I cannot allow this messenger to return to
England without conveying to your lordship my most sincere

thanks for the very great kindness I have experienced at your lordship's hands on the present occasion. I am fully aware how many and how powerful the competitors were who were ambitious of obtaining this distinction, and that it has been ultimately adjudged me is, I am also aware, less owing to my superior claims than to your lordship's protection. I was before under many obligations to your lordship as Secretary of State: I cannot but feel that I have now a heavy debt of gratitude to Lord Castlereagh.

Repeating my sincere and heartfelt thanks, I have the honour to be, with great respect, &c.,

WILLIAM À COURT.

At the risk of appearing insatiable, as I hear that many changes are in contemplation, I cannot but recall to your lordship how very great a point it is for me to be brought nearer home, if the move be consistent with my rank in the profession. I am now totally separated from my son, who is at school in England, and I have interests at home which, in these days of reform, require much personal attention. Except Constantinople, Naples is the furthest point at which I could be placed in Europe.

Count Münster to Lord Castlereagh.

Hanover, October 17, 1819.

My dear Lord—I have been much gratified by your lordship's obliging letter, and I am perfectly sensible of the honour you do me in thinking that my presence at the meeting at Vienna may be of service. The late proceedings of the King of Wirtemberg prove sufficiently that I judged him right. I confess that his journey to Warsaw at this moment, together with the manner in which that *coryphée* of Liberalism, Capodistrias, has expressed himself at Copenhagen on the subject of the resolutions framed at Carlsbad, make me somewhat uneasy. The French party journals show sufficiently that Prince Metternich has hit the point; and, as I have reason to believe that

Austria and Prussia will persevere in the line they have taken, we may finally succeed.

A letter I received yesterday from Prince Hardenberg proves that he continues firm, although the military faction, who expect great advantage from a dissolution of the Germanic Confederacy, disapprove much of every measure proper to maintain order and tranquillity. It is on the same principle that this party endeavours to promote military measures for the defence of Germany, the expense of which would make the whole odious to the nation. On the whole, the almost general approbation which the Carlsbad resolutions have met with in Germany proves that the great majority of the empire are well disposed. I wish you could give a similar blow to your daily press. I am happy to see that I shall meet Lord Stewart at Vienna.

I have the honour to be, &c.,   MUNSTER.

Mr. Louis Casamajor, Secretary of Legation at St. Petersburg, to Lord Castlereagh.

St. Petersburg, November 13, 1819.

My Lord—Though I have not failed to remind Count Nesselrode, at several interviews, of my anxiety to despatch the messenger with answers to the important matter contained in your lordship's late despatches, his Excellency has requested me still to detain him, under a promise that I shall be put in timely possession of the opinions of this Cabinet upon the Memoir and the Spanish and Portuguese affairs, in which his Imperial Majesty is at present employed.

The decision of this Government will probably (as usual) be sent to Count Lieven in a despatch to be shown to your lordship, which, in fulfilment of the above promise, I shall be invited to read at the Foreign Office.

Count Nesselrode told me, a few days ago, that the Emperor had only twice attended to general political business since his return; that his Imperial Majesty was disposed to employ the utmost attention in replying to the papers I had communicated by your lordship's desire, and that the arguments in the Memoir were in general very analogous to the opinions of this Cabinet. I suspect, this applies more to the existence or not of the Conference, rather than to that part of the Memoir which relates to the provisional instructions to be given to the Ministers at Paris, to provide against particular contingencies.

With regard to the Spanish and Portuguese negociations, there is certainly an opinion that Spain has now placed herself in the wrong, but the moment anything is said about stipulations for a more liberal system in favour of the places to be ceded to Spain, a jealousy of our commerce is apparent, which, as it is constitutional, it is difficult to overrule.

I am to have the honour of being presented to his Imperial Majesty to-morrow, and I hope in the course of the next week to be able to send off the messenger.

I have the honour to be, &c.,
Louis Casamajor.

Sir Robert Liston to Lord Castlereagh.

Constantinople, November 25, 1819.

My Lord—I received with sentiments of cordial gratitude your lordship's letter of the 24th September. The terms in which you are pleased to convey to me the Prince's gracious permission to retire from public service cannot but highly gratify my feelings; and the time mentioned for my leaving this station will perfectly suit my convenience. I have in a former letter acquainted your lordship that I had given up all idea of removing from my post during the approaching winter. It only remains that I should take the liberty of requesting that your lordship will have the goodness to obtain an order that a ship of war may convey me to any port of France or Italy where I may choose to land.

Encouraged by your kind permission, I will venture to take another occasion to speak of further arrangements, avoiding, as

I shall anxiously do at all times, to give your lordship reason to complain either of my indiscretion or my importunity.

I have the honour to be, &c.,   ROBERT LISTON.

Statement of the Arrest of General Gourgaud, and execution of the Order of the Prince Regent for his departing the Kingdom.

B. P. Capper having received the warrant to be executed, he waited on the general on the 14th of November last, accompanied by two messengers to execute the same, early between 7 and 8 o'clock in the morning; he was then in bed. On the production of the King's order and the Secretary of State's warrant, the general endeavoured to seize a brace of loaded pistols, that were within reach of the bed, but was prevented by one of the messengers. After refusing to comply with the warrant for nearly an hour, and whilst he was dressing himself, he seized some loose papers on the chimneypiece underneath which was a dagger; but, it being hid by the papers, he only seized it by the sheath, and the messenger wrested the dagger from his hands.

After two hours' refusing to obey the warrant, and becoming very violent, he was informed no further delay would be suffered; and, having locked up and sealed his papers in a portfolio, which was sent to Lord Sidmouth's office, he then flew to the street window, and beating out the glass with his hands, vociferated "Murder!" and "Thieves!" on which immediately a mob of upwards of a hundred persons collected: when, considering it no longer safe to remain, and apprehensive of a rescue, Capper called in an assistant in waiting outside the house, and ordered him to be conveyed to a coach, in the execution of which he used the greatest violence, calling on the mob to rescue him; during which, one of the messengers was knocked down by a person in the crowd, known to be Cicogne, a countryman of his, who has since absconded.

For safe custody, he was then taken to Mr. Capper's house,

and a reasonable time offered him to remain there, whilst he could settle his affairs and procure his luggage; but on his refusing the same, after a delay of some hours, he was conveyed to Harwich, and, on the road, twice endeavoured to obtain a rescue, and desired to be taken before a magistrate to complain of the illegality of the warrant, and of the persons who had the execution of it not being proper officers, and struck the messenger who accompanied him, who was then obliged to strike him with his fist in his own defence.

At his own desire, he was taken before the Mayor of Harwich, to whom he complained of ill-usage on the road; that he doubted if the papers shown him bore the signature of the Prince Regent and of Lord Sidmouth; and stated that he had Lord Bathurst's permission to remain here when he first arrived : but the Mayor convinced him of the propriety of complying with those authorities. He then asked leave to remain till he could receive such baggage as he wanted. He accordingly sent a written order to one Forbin Janssen, to take from his lodgings the whole of his property, and send him such part thereof as he wanted for his journey; which Capper complied with, and received his baggage from Janssen, and conveyed it sealed up to Gourgaud.

After remaining five days at Harwich, he sailed for Cuxhaven, at his own request, to proceed to Frankfort, as he had learnt that Las Cases had been arrested in Flanders, and a private note was given him to the Post-office agent at Cuxhaven to procure him every facility and the necessary passport to proceed to the interior. It was agreed by himself that when he had ascertained the safety of receiving his private papers, in the portfolio which had been locked and sealed by himself in Capper's presence, he was to send over and to desire them to be forwarded, fearing to have them with him, lest the foreign Governments should deprive him of them.

He accordingly wrote from Cuxhaven, claiming them, and they were immediately forwarded, together with every article that had been detained, viz., two pair of pistols, a dagger, a packet of loose papers, and the portfolio, sealed and fastened as when originally detained, and a receipt was received from the agent at Harwich, the captain of the packet, and the agent at Hamburg, who delivered them personally to Gourgaud, in the same state as when first packed up.

Upon consultation, and looking at his map at Harwich, he fixed upon Cuxhaven as the safest place to go to. Particular orders were given to Capper and Billingsley, the agent at Harwich, to attend to the section of the Act, requiring a due compliance and attention to the causes assigned for delay, &c., in the words of that section.

M. Neumann (Austrian Chargé d'Affaires) to Lord Castlereagh.

Chandos House, December 29, 1819.

Mylord—Dans les dépêches en date de Vienne le 13 Decembre, que j'ai eu l'honneur de transmettre hier à votre Excellence, elle aura vu que l'on désire connaître chez nous le point de vue précis du Cabinet Britannique sur le moyen par lequel la médiation croit pouvoir terminer le differend entre l'Espagne et le Portugal, et la dernière note addressée à ce sujet par le Comte de Palmella aux médiateurs les amène naturellement au point prévu chez nous, et sur lequel on désire, comme en toute autre chose, être d'accord avec le Gouvernement de sa Majesté Britannique.

N'ayant pu avoir l'honneur d'entretenir votre Excellence de cette affaire ce matin, j'ose réclamer de ses bontés de me permettre d'aller encore l'importuner afin qu'Elle veuille bien me mettre à même de répondre à ma cour sur un objet aussi intéressant.

Veuillez bien, Mylord, agréer que je vous réitère l'assurance de ma très haute considération.

NEUMANN.

The Hon. F. Lamb to Mr. Planta.

Frankfort, December 29, 1819.

My dear Planta—I just learn that Russia refers to England before she gives her final answer upon German affairs. In the mean time, her Minister here has orders, in common with all her other agents, to be silent upon them. These are the best orders she can give; all that can be desired is that they should be continued and obeyed.

We have a great fall of snow, but I am well enough to travel, and shall be off to-morrow.

Truly yours,　　F. LAMB.

Prince Hardenberg to Lord Castlereagh.

Berlin, le 30 Decembre, 1819.

Mylord—Permettez que, plein de confiance en votre ancienne amitié dont vous m'avez donné tant de preuves, je me rappelle à votre souvenir et interrompe pour quelques moments les grandes occupations qui pèsent sur vous. Agréez d'abord mes félicitations sincères sur la marche noble, ferme, et énergique que vous avez tenue pour porter remède à la contagion morale qui se manifeste presque partout, et qui, sans des mesures sages et efficaces, précipiteroit les États civilisés dans un abyme de malheur. Vous connoissez celles que nous avons cru devoir prendre de concert avec la Cour de Vienne, moyennant les decrets de Francfort, qui ont suivi les conférences de Carlsbad; vous savez que les Ministres des Membres de la fédération sont maintenant assemblés à Vienne, pour se concerter sur ce qui reste à faire, tant pour opposer une digue aux menées des révolutionnaires que pour s'arranger sur l'exécution des articles de l'acte de la fédération germanique, faisant partie de ceux dont nous sommes convenus durant le Congrès de Vienne.

M. de Capodistrias, dont nous connoissons tous les sophismes, et qui nous à donné tant de fil à retordre à Aix-la-Chapelle, s'est mis dans la tête que nous ne visons à rien moins qu'à changer l'acte de fédération, tel qu'il a été garanti par les Puissances ; que l'Autriche et la Prusse veulent empiéter sur la liberté et la souveraineté des petits ou moindres États de l'Allemagne ; il craint la diminution de l'influence russe, et se plait en puisant ses nouvelles et ses argumens dans les feuilles du parti révolutionnaire en France et dans les Pays Bas, toutes remplies de mensonges ; de tenir un langage d'improbation à l'égard des mesures prises à Carlsbad ; à nourrir par là le germe de mécontentement que l'ambition et les vues de la Bavière et du Wurtemberg n'ont cessé de conserver depuis le Congrès de Vienne ; et à instruire les Ministres de Russie dans l'Étranger dans un sens peu fait pour seconder les vues tout à fait pures et conformes aux traités et aux circonstances que nous partageons avec l'Autriche et la grande majorité des États allemands. Cette marche ne peut qu'opérer d'une manière très nuisible pour le bien général.

Dans la manière de voir du Comte Capodistrias, il croit devoir consulter votre Cour, Mylord, et perdant de vue que les conférences de Vienne et de Carlsbad sont absolument dans la ligne de l'acte de la fédération, et que nos Alliés devroient nous exciter à prendre les mesures dont il est question, si nous pouvions les négliger, il sonneroit la défiance, et serviroit le parti révolutionnaire si le Ministère Anglois étoit moins bien informé, s'il n'étoit à même de se procurer les notions les plus exactes par ces Ministres d'Hannovre actuellement à Vienne. Il faut que j'ajoute que l'Empereur de Russie est lui-même dans de très bons principes, et que ce ne sont que les notions erronées et les opinions du Comte Capodistrias qui l'entraînent à agir, en quelque façon, en opposition avec ses propres sentimens.

Je vais communiquer à Mr. Rose les rapports du Comte de Bernstorl. Il sera à même de se convaincre que les conférences de Vienne ne suivent que le but que je viens d'énoncer ; qu'elles ne donnent lieu à aucune appréhension ; et que même

M 2

cette opposition de la Bavière et du Wurtemberg, que M. de Capodistrias fait sonner si haut, n'existe pas comme il se l'imagine, et qu'au contraire il y a accord sur les objets essentiels.

Je suis entré dans tous ces détails d'une manière franche et *entièrement confidentielle*, persuadé, Mylord, qu'avec votre esprit juste et conciliateur, vous contribuerez à faire disparoître les visions de M. Capodistrias.

Il ne me reste qu'à vous prier de me conserver vos bontés, et de vouloir faire agréer mes respects à Mylady Castlereagh. Faisant toujours les vœux les plus sincères pour votre bonheur, je n'appuye pas sur ceux que je forme à l'occasion du renouvellement de l'année. Comptez sur mon tendre et inviolable attachement.

J'ai l'honneur d'être avec la plus haute considération, de votre Excellence, le très humble, très obéissant, et bien dévoué Serviteur,

HARDENBERG.

1820.

AFFAIRS OF THE CONTINENTAL STATES OF EUROPE IN
GENERAL, AND OF SPAIN AND NAPLES IN PARTICULAR
—CONGRESS OF TROPPAU—ADOPTION OF THE PRIN-
CIPLE OF ARMED INTERVENTION BY THE ALLIED
MONARCHS.

The Hon. F. Lamb to Lord Castlereagh.

Munich, January 4, 1820.

Dear Lord Castlereagh—Since I left Frankfort, I have seen
the circular of Russia to her Ministers.   I can look upon this
paper as nothing else than a manifesto to the German Courts
to assure them that they will be supported in their opposition
to the measures of Austria.   She is indifferent what answer
she may receive from England, and expects her purposes to be
answered by the circulation of this paper.

This opinion has been confirmed by my conversation of this
morning with M. de Rechberg, who went so far as to say that
the object of Russia was *de tout embrouiller,* and that it was
impossible to feel assured of the tranquillity of Europe as long
as she maintained such a vast army, organized in corps, and
ready to be put in movement by a single signature.   The
phrase in the Russian memoir relative to the dictatorial power
to be given to the Diet he allowed to be written in so evidently
mischievous an intention as to be likely to defeat its own
object : at the same time, he said that the Emperor, in conversation with M. de Bray, had decidedly approved of the
measures taken with respect to the newspapers and the universities.

This I believe to establish the real distinction as to the sentiments of the Emperor. He wishes the revolutionary spirit to be put down, but is an enemy to the German Confederation, and regards it as an arm to be used against himself. I cannot but regard it as an extreme weakness ever to have asked the opinion of Russia upon the measures under consideration at Vienna. Every article of the Federative Act requires a development which is necessarily to be given by the German Powers themselves. Among all the articles under consideration at Vienna there are only two with which any foreign Power has, in fact, any concern; these are the fortresses, the funds for which are given by a Protocol signed by the four Powers; and the question of peace and war—and it is upon this that Anstett has tried (and probably with success) to excite the jealousy of his Court. In the preparatory report of the Committee on the subject will be found, about the 4th or 7th paragraph, (for I have not the paper with me) a proposition that the Confederacy shall not march its troops beyond its own frontiers, in case of a war existing, in which it shall take part with a Power partly federative and partly European, unless in case of the existence of particular treaties. This has been represented by Anstett as clearly indicating treaties to be made by Austria and Prussia with the Confederation for the defence of their extra-German possessions against Russia. This is a misfortune attendant upon the nature of the Diet with all its reports and papers; they express too clearly what had better be unsaid till it is acted upon.

I am assured in confidence by Wessenberg that Golowkin is only kept at Vienna for show, and has not the confidence of his Court, which trusts entirely to the reports of secret agents. It has long surprised me that Wessenberg should be retained at Frankfort, with nothing to do; and many things have lately concurred to make me think that he has a secret correspondence, if not with Metternich, with some of the other Ministers, and perhaps with the Emperor himself. This induces me to mention to you that he insists, in his confidential conversations, that Metternich is the only Austrian Minister who is anxious for the consolidation of the Confederation; while Stadion, Schwarzenberg, and Saurau, and the Emperor himself, look upon it as a means of embarrassing Austria with the decisions of an assembly which she never will be able to direct. I mention this chiefly as an evidence that it is not of vital importance that all the questions in agitation at Vienna should be carried in the Austrian sense. But that which is really so is the question on the establishment of constitutions. The necessity of establishing a uniform system in Germany is a fair ground for modifying what is established in some of its States; and if this is not now done, the evil will not fail to spread, and to produce much embarrassment.

Rechberg holds out hopes that some good will be done upon this head at Vienna; but the best evidence of this would be a disposition in Bavaria herself to allow a revision of the sense-less Constitution which she has given. Rechberg and one other Minister are ready to agree to it, but are in a minority in the Council, the three other Ministers being determined to support what exists. The King shifts and wavers, and starts at the shadow of anything which can be thought to attack his sovereignty. Montgelas and Wrede separately look on, and are ready to adopt anything in order to gain power, which the first, if he had it, would make use of to overthrow the Constitution, and the second would not know how to make any use of at all.

Rechberg is decidedly well disposed. I am to see him again to-morrow, and have my audience of the King the day after; I shall try to make use of this opportunity to do good, but I have little hope of being able to render a service which Mr. Hervey has been unable to effect. It is pleasing to find any person so universally beloved and respected as he is here.

I have to beg a thousand pardons for this long, incorrect,

and rambling letter. It is written in the greatest hurry, not to detain Lord Stewart's courier, and with an anxious wish to give your lordship every information which can have any bearing upon the important questions before you. On a separate paper I shall put some conversations with the Russian Minister at Frankfort.

I am, dear Lord Castlereagh, &c.,   F. LAMB.

[Enclosure.]

Conversations with Anstett.

Anstett called upon me with the answer which had been made at Petersburg to M. de Lebzeltern's representations upon his conduct. These had been founded on a report of his having said publicly, at a great dinner to the Minister of Wirtemberg, that the Emperor had guaranteed the constitution given by the King. The answer, as he read it to me, was, that whoever had spread such a report *avoit menti*. He was very triumphant, and repeated what he had once before said, that he was *diablement ancré*, and could not be shaken. In these affairs he is identified with Capo d'Istrias.

Some days afterwards, he informed me of the papers which had just passed to the Court of London, and then told me that it was wished he should go to Spain, from whence Tatischeff was to be removed, but expressed his unwillingness to go there. Upon considering what other Russian Minister might probably be sent, he said that Pahlen would not, because he had broken his neck at Munich, in the affair of the Austrian treaty about Salzburg; that if he, Anstett, had been there, that treaty would never have been concluded; but that Pahlen had not understood the instructions of his Court, and that he was a fellow without courage.

Upon this I represented the advantage of his going himself to Spain. " Non," he said ; " on ne parvient pas à détruire l'influence d'une Cour, qui est aussi enracinée que celle de la votre, et puis vous savez comment cela va : c'est toujours

l'Angleterre, la Prusse, et l'Autriche—et la Russie seule."—
" Mais tenez, mon cher !" I answered : " vous pourriez y faire
bien mieux que de détruire notre influence si vous y alliez, pour
faire revenir votre Cour sur cette idée là.   Qu'a-t-elle à faire
de détruire ce qui ne la gêne en rien, et ce qui n'a jamais été
exercée que pour le bien !"

This put a stop to our conversation, and I only repeat it as
a specimen of what I observe to be Anstett's constant feeling,
that the merit of all Russian agents is in proportion to the success of their efforts to thwart the views and to destroy the
influence of Austria and England, and to establish that of
Russia in their place.

I beg not to be understood as giving the language of an
inferior agent as the measure of the feelings of his Court ; but
these small facts may help to make up the great mass of
information upon which your lordship's judgment must be
formed.

If I am asked the reason of his holding to me so unguarded
a language, I refer it in the first place to his extreme vanity ;
next, to his idea that he can direct my opinions ; and to his
contempt for me as a novice, at which I cannot feel hurt, as
he equally ranks Clancarty in the number of his scholars ;
and lastly, to a great habit of my society and some liking
for it.

Pozzo di Borgo's letters anxiously anticipate the fall of
M. de Cazes, which, Rechberg says, will have the very worst
effect, in raising the hopes of the Liberal party in Germany,
whom he looks upon as put down for the present, but requiring a long continuance of the present measures entirely to
suppress.

He says that the King of Wirtemberg's visit started the
hare with the Emperor of Russia ; but that deputies have since
gone to him from the Liberal party in various States.   I never
heard this before, and do not know how far to believe it.

Sir H. Wellesley to Lord Castlereagh.

Madrid, January 6, 1820.

My dear Lord—I have heard through various channels of instructions having been sent to the Duke of San Carlos of the nature stated in my despatches of this day's date; but I have heard nothing from the Duke of San Fernando upon the subject, excepting what relates to the mission of General Vives. I understand that the principal object of his journey to Paris will be to endeavour to obtain from the French Government the same declaration as to the boundaries of Louisiana as was made by Bonaparte, when that territory was ceded by him to the Government of the United States; but that declaration was made at a time when Bonaparte was desirous of confining the territory to be occupied by the Americans within as narrow limits as possible; and, from what I can learn from the French Embassy at this Court, the actual Government of France will not be much inclined to incur the risk of involving themselves in a dispute with the Government of the United States, which might happen, if they were to make a similar declaration. General Vives is still at Madrid, and I heard last night that his journey was likely to be deferred until intelligence had been received from the United States of the measures likely to be adopted by Congress, after the President's message had been taken into consideration.

The American Minister here (Mr. Forsyth) has given great offence to the Government by the violence of his notes, and by abstaining for the last four months from his attendance with the other foreign Ministers at the King's levées, which are held twice a week. General Vives has been desired not to have any communication with him; and the footing he is upon with the Government must make his situation very uncomfortable.

The negociations at Paris are seldom talked of and appear to have lost all interest here. Nothing has been heard of relative to these negociations since the extraordinary answer given by this Government to the proposal for sending a Spanish Prince to the Rio de la Plata.

Your lordship will see by my despatches that the Duke of San Fernando complains of the frequency of my representations upon commercial subjects. In other respects, we are upon very good terms; but he is evidently apprehensive of the effect which my complaints may produce upon the Prince Regent's Government; and I believe that upon this account he has been less communicative to me than he would otherwise have been. He is really desirous of doing everything in his power to give us satisfaction; and it must be admitted that, upon the whole, things have gone on better since he has been in power than before.

I beg to offer to your lordship my cordial congratulations upon the complete success of your labours in this arduous session of Parliament. It was impossible not to feel some anxiety at the accounts received here of the state of England, but I trust that the energetic measures adopted by the Prince Regent's Government will have all the effect which they are calculated to produce.

I have the honour to be, &c.,   H. WELLESLEY.

Sir H. Wellesley to Lord Castlereagh.

Madrid, January 9, 1820.

My dear Lord—There is nothing so difficult as to obtain accurate information in this country relative to passing events; but I have every reason to believe that the intelligence contained in my despatch No. 9, relative to the conspiracy said to have broken out in the expeditionary army, is correct. It is impossible to say what may be its effect, if the troops are faithful to their officers; for the same spirit prevails generally among the officers of the army. One of the consequences must be the abandonment of the expedition; and it seems probable that this must be given up even in the event of the conspiracy being crushed.

It cannot escape observation that the King has lost much of his popularity. Even upon the occasion of his marriage, when he appeared in public, with the Queen, there were none of those demonstrations of loyalty and attachment to his person which used to be so manifest upon all public occasions. At Madrid, a general apathy and indifference as to public events seems to pervade all classes of society; and in the provinces the system of government is execrated, and the conduct of the King and of his Ministers spoken of in terms of great disrespect.

I shall lose no time in forwarding to your lordship any further intelligence which may reach me from Andalusia; and I have the honour to be, with great truth and respect, &c.

H. WELLESLEY.

Sir H. Wellesley to Lord Castlereagh.

Madrid, January 11, 11 A.M. [1820].

My dear Lord—I scarcely know, even now, what to say of this insurrection. I have just been informed, from what I consider to be good authority, that no intelligence had been received from Cadiz at a late hour last night, and that the insurgents were in possession of the towns of the Isla de Leon, Port St. Mary's, Jeres, Lebrija, Arcos, and Bornos. If this be the case, their numbers must be much greater than they are stated to be in my despatches. They are likewise stated to have money sufficient to pay the troops for some time. It seems that the account of General Ferras having attacked them with the cavalry is correct, and that he was repulsed, and did not renew the attack. I should detain the courier for further intelligence, were I not apprehensive of his being again stopped by the Government.

I remain, my dear lord, &c.,   H. WELLESLEY.

Lord Castlereagh to Prince Hardenberg.

Hockeril, January 15, 1820.

Mon Prince—I have charged Mr. Rose to communicate to your Highness the reply which the Prince Regent has returned to the Emperor of Russia's overtures, and it will be a high personal gratification to me to learn that it meets your approbation. I hope it preserves his Royal Highness in an advantageous position to smooth difficulties, should they hereafter arise; whilst, at the same time, it aims at protecting your deliberations now in progress against unseasonable interruption. The accounts we receive from Vienna promise an early and satisfactory termination of your labours, and it cannot but add to the glory of the two great German Cabinets, should they succeed in carrying the Germanic Diet through the arduous details which now occupy their attention. I need not say how fervently our good wishes attend you in this as in all your undertakings.

The position of things at Paris is still full of anxiety. The illness of the Chiefs of the two Chambers is a fatality at such a moment. I understand, however, that M. de Cazes holds a confident language as to his means of fulfilling the hopes announced in the speech from the throne, and declares that he is irrevocably determined to bring the *projet* forward for modifying the Election Law, and in the precise form the measure was first agreed upon previous to the meeting of the Chambers.

Mr. Rose will put into your Highness's hands a despatch addressed to our Ambassador at Vienna, in reference to French affairs, and the late interchange of sentiments between the Allied Courts with regard to them. The despatch itself will explain why our wishes upon these matters have been directed at the present moment towards the Cabinet of Vienna; but, in truth, the explanation is equally intended for the Courts of Berlin and St. Petersburgh, and copies will be sent to each for their confidential information. I have given the communication the shape of an instruction to our own Minister, as favouring the termination of the discussion, a result which, for the reasons therein submitted, I recommend very earnestly to your Highness's favourable consideration and protection.

I am so far on my way to a shooting party in Norfolk. I hope to have a fortnight's relaxation, which, after our short but active session, I in some measure *require.* As far as we can judge, our measures have operated very favourably on the internal state of the country. Radical stock is very low indeed at the present moment, and the loyal have resumed their superiority and confidence. The provisions of the laws which have been enacted will, no doubt, do a great deal to repress the mischief; but your Highness may rest assured that, whatever our reformers may choose to say, the voice of Parliament is in itself still all-powerful in this country, when clearly pronounced: and, as it never spoke on any former occasion in a more manly and determined tone, to this is chiefly ascribable the great moral change that has been wrought in so short a time.

Lady Castlereagh is now sitting by me, and enjoins me to offer to your Highness her kindest remembrances. It has been a source of a thousand gratifying recollections to have been honoured with a private letter from your Highness, for whose person and eminent services I shall ever retain the most lively and affectionate respect.

With the highest consideration, &c.,

CASTLEREAGH.

Lord Castlereagh to Mr. George Rose.

Hockeril, January 15, 1820.

My dear Sir—I trouble you with a reply to Prince Hardenberg's private letter, which I shall be obliged to you to deliver to him, if convenient, in person, as it will enable you to go through with him the instruction both on German and French affairs, and thereby to ascertain his Highness's impressions more correctly on both. I have earnestly recommended to his protection my request to Prince Metternich that the discussion which has been so long pending may not be revived. Our Allies must recollect that we have a Parliament to manage, and it is essential to their interest not to have angry discussions on continental politics provoked, where they lead to no substantial result. I have no doubt the good sense and accommodating temper of the Allies will conform on this subject to our views.

Have you ever seen a Prussian Memoir on this subject? It was sent to St. Petersburgh in reply to the Emperor's first paper: it is referred to in his Imperial Majesty's second Memoir, and forms one of the enclosures. I have seen the paper, but, as it never was communicated to us, as all ours have been to them, it is not in my office. I ask the question, not in complaint, being satisfied it arose from accident, and not from any disposition to withhold their views on this or any other important question from a Government so sincerely attached as ours is to Prussian interests.

To save time, I have desired my brother to communicate to Count Bernstorf at Vienna the papers which you now receive in duplicate.

Believe me, &c.,   CASTLEREAGH.

Lord Clancarty to Lord Castlereagh.

The Hague, January 25, 1820.

My dear Lord—I abundantly thank you for your few lines of the 17th, from Attleborough. The communications to the King and Nagell, of Nesselrode's despatch to Lieven, and your answer of the 14th instant, were graciously received. These friendly intimations do much good, as serving to increase and strengthen confidence. I wish you had caused to be sent to me the Russian circular instructions and the supplement to them, spoken of in the despatch to Lieven.

You will see they are desirous here of postponing your Eastern negociation till April. I believe the real reason of this to proceed from no diminution of their desire to come as soon as may be to a final arrangement upon this matter, but that they feel somewhat the want of Falck, now absent at Vienna, and would, upon the whole, rather that he was present than absent, during the negociation. I do not believe you will be inclined to thwart them in this view, conceiving rather that some little relaxation will be of use to you ; but, if you should wish otherwise, the mere expression of your wish will send M. Elout over to you directly.

Adieu ! I shall interrupt your pleasures as little as possible ; and fortunately foresee nothing at present likely to induce my interference with them for some time.

      Ever yours most affectionately,   CLANCARTY.

Baron Fagel to Lord Castlereagh.

Whitehall Place, Wednesday, January 26, 1820.

My dear Lord—It has happened rather unfortunately, owing chiefly to the late severe weather, that my letter to the Baron de Nagell, in which I informed him of your lordship's proposal of the first week in February for our Conferences on our Eastern business, only reached him on the 20th. You will see by the enclosed (which I have this moment received) that they are not quite prepared, on the other side of the water, for so early a beginnning of these deliberations. M. Falck's absence is certainly very inconvenient. I have a letter from M. Elout to the same effect. They would wish the Conferences to be put off till the first week in April. I shall be anxious to communicate your answer on this subject as soon as possible to Baron Nagell. May I request you to return me the enclosed ?

    I have the honour to be, &c.,   R. FAGEL.

[Enclosures.]

M. le Baron de Nagell à Son Excellence M. le Baron Fagel,
Amb. Ex. et Plen. près de la Cour de Londres.

La Haye, ce 21 Janvier, 1820.

Votre lettre particulière, mon cher Monsieur, du 7 instant,
ne m'est parvenue qu'hier, le 20.   Le retard de 13 jours rend
absolument impossible de répondre à l'invitation de Lord
Castlereagh, et de vous faire assister par votre co-Commissaire
pour les affaires de l'Inde : vers le commencement de Fevrier
époque si prochaine, différer de quelques jours se seroit, d'un
autre côté, rencontrer le moment où les affaires parlementaires
reprennent leur cours.   Je vous prierais donc, mon cher Monsieur, de proposer à Lord Castlereagh de fixer l'époque des
négociations à entamer aux premiers jours du mois d'Avril, ou
à tel autre que son Excellence trouvera bon de déterminer.

Le retour du Ministre Falck de Vienne est une autre circonstance intéressante pour faciliter la marche de la négociation,
qui pourroit difficilement se terminer sans la participation du
Ministre qui dirige les affaires des Colonies.   Je me flatte
que Lord Castlereagh voudra bien admettre la justesse de ces
réflexions, et adopter le bref retard que les circonstances me
forcent à lui demander.

Recevez l'assurance renouvellée de tous mes sentiments,

A. W. C. de NAGELL.

Extrait d'une Dépêche de M. le Prince de Metternich à
M. de Neumann.

Vienne, le 26 Janvier, 1820.

La déclaration demandée par le plénipotentiaire portugais
pourroit être rédigée de manière à ne rien compromettre dans
les rapports présents et futurs des Puissances envers l'Espagne.
Il ne seroit point nécessaire d'énoncer dans cet acte la suspension ou la continuation de la médiation.   La cour de Rio
Janeiro n'a besoin, pour sa satisfaction et pour sa sûreté, que
d'une pièce officielle qui constateroit qu'elle s'est prêtée dans le

cours de la négociation à tout ce que les Puissances média-
trices ont exigé d'elle pour arriver au but, et que, par conséquent, elle se trouve aujourd'hui parfaitement en règle envers
ces Puissances. Toutes les autres questions resteroient in-
tactes, et les explications à donner ou les mesures à prendre
par la Cour de Madrid n'en seroient nullement affectées.

Count Lieven to Lord Castlereagh.

Harley Street, le 26 Janvier, 1820.

Mylord—Ayant accompagné les deux pièces que vous
m'avez fait l'honneur de me communiquer des traductions en
les transmettant à ma cour, je crois de mon devoir de vous en
soumettre des copies ci-joint afin de vous mettre à même de
juger si j'ai réussi à rendre fidèlement vos idées en Français.

Veuillez, Mylord, agréer l'assurance renouvellée de ma haute
considération, et de mon sincère dévouement avec lesquels j'ai
l'honneur d'être de votre Excellence le très humble et très
obéissant serviteur,

LIEVEN.

[Enclosure.]

TRADUCTION.

Lettre du Vicomte de Castlereagh au Comte de Lieven.

Londres, le 14 Janvier, 1820.

Monsieur le Comte—Je me suis empressé de porter à la
connoissance de M. le Prince Régent la dépêche confidentielle
de Petersbourg et ses annexes en date du 22 Novembre (4 Decembre) dont vous avez bien voulu, d'ordre de votre Cour, me
faire la communication pour l'information particulière de son
Altesse Royale.

Quoique les notions que le Ministère du Prince Régent
possède actuellement sur l'objet auquel se rapportent les pièces
précitées soient encore tellement insuffisantes qu'il lui seroit
impossible de prononcer une opinion positive sur les matières
graves et intéressantes vers lesquelles sa Majesté l'Empereur
de Russie a bien voulu appeler son attention, toutefois M. le

Prince Régent a été désireux de répondre sans le moindre
délai à une ouverture que son Altesse Royale reconnoit, avec
un sensible plaisir, être une nouvelle preuve des sentimens
d'amitié et de confiance réciproques qui ne cessent de carac-
tériser tous les rapports des Monarques Alliés entre eux : j'ai
reçu en conséquence l'ordre d'adresser sans retard la présente
lettre à votre Excellence sur ce sujet.

Je dois avant tout, Monsieur le Comte, assurer votre Excellence que c'est avec la satisfaction la plus vive que son Altesse
Royale M. le Prince Régent a vu dans les opinions émises par
sa Majesté l'Empereur de Russie avec tant de franchise et
d'abandon, que la ligne de conduite que les Cours de Londres
et de St. Petersbourg se sont tracée jusqu'ici relativement aux
affaires d'Allemagne, quoiqu'adoptée sans aucun concert pré-
alable entre les deux Cabinets, se trouve néanmoins dans cette
occasion, ainsi qu'elle l'a été dans d'autres non moins importantes, fondée sur une stricte conformité de vues et de principes.   Les deux Cours apportent le même soin de s'interdire
toute intervention dans les affaires d'Allemagne—intervention
qui pourroit être considérée comme une violation des droits et
de l'indépendance de la Confédération Germanique. . Elles
expriment, l'une comme l'autre, le vœu de voir les conseils de
cette Confédération signaler leurs délibérations ultérieures à
Vienne par l'esprit de concorde et d'unanimité qui ont si
éminemment distingué les Conférences préliminaires à Carlsbad ; enfin les Cabinets de St. Petersbourg et de Londres
professant, avec une sincérité et une ardeur égales, le même
désir, celui de voir les efforts des Puissances Germaniques, tant
pour arrêter les progrès de la tendance révolutionnaire, que
pour consolider les liens de leur Confédération, dirigés de
manière à pourvoir à la tranquillité générale de l'Allemagne,
dont celle de l'Europe est inséparable, et à remplir en même
tems ces grandes vues politiques, qui, lors de la tenue du
Congrès de 1815, ont présidé à la formation de l'Acte fédératif.

N 2

Ces principes ont déterminé la conduite que le Cabinet de St. James a tenue dans une circonstance récente, lorsque les Cours de Vienne et de Berlin lui ont fait connoître la substance des mesures adoptées à Carlsbad et à Francfort. Quoique ces communications semblassent de nature à justifier, et peut-être même à provoquer, une énonciation spéciale et publique des sentimens du Prince Régent à cet égard, néanmoins son Altesse Royale n'a pas jugé qu'il fût convenable d'exprimer, soit dans les pièces par lesquelles elle répondit à ces explications confidentielles, soit dans les instructions transmises à ses agens diplomatiques dans l'étranger, aucune opinion sur les arrêtés de la Diète Germanique. Elle les a considérés (et dans toute la rigueur du terme) comme des Actes passés par des Gouvernemens étrangers et indépendans dans la vue unique de régler leurs affaires particulières et l'administration intérieure de leurs États. Son Altesse Royale a d'autant moins hésité à adopter cette marche qu'elle est intimément persuadée que les motifs de sa réserve ne pouvoient être méconnus, et que le silence gardé par elle en cette occasion ne sauroit faire mettre en doute le grand et vif intérêt que lui inspirent et la situation des Puissances Allemandes et leurs efforts pour garantir leur sûreté et leur bien-être à venir.

Tout en rapellant ainsi les principes généraux qui ont réglé à cet égard la politique du Prince Régent, et que l'Empereur votre Maître, j'ose le croire, saura, dans sa justice, apprécier et approuver, tout en confessant l'extrème regret que feroit éprouver à son Altesse Royale la nécessité d'une intrusion quelconque dans les affaires intérieures de la Confédération Germanique, je dois néanmoins prier votre Excellence de ne pas me supposer l'opinion que les mesures actuellement agitées en Allemagne ne puissent un jour, et malgré les soins qu'on apporteroit pour l'éviter, amener des résultats qui seront de nature à autoriser ou même à appeler l'intervention des Puissances non-Allemandes.

L'assemblée des Ministres réunis à Vienne, doit s'occuper,

non seulement à délibérer sur le mode d'application des mesures
arrêtées par la Diète, concernant les objets inhérens au repos
intérieur de l'Allemagne, mais encore à donner au corps même
de la Confédération ces loix organiques dont la formation a
été expressément déférée à la Diète par une clause du Recès de
1815.   Les pouvoirs dont, par les stipulations du traité
général, la Diète a été investie à cet effet sont sans contredit
de la plus grande étendue : il n'est pas impossible que l'usage
qu'on en fera donne lieu à quelque sérieuse infraction des
articles de ce même traité, auquel toutes les grandes Puissances Européennes ont pris part ; il est également possible que
des scissions parmi les États dont se compose la Confédération
venant à éclater prennent un caractère tellement menaçant
pour leur propre tranquillité, et par conséquent pour celle de
l'Europe, qu'il deviendra légitime aux Puissances amies et
Alliées (surtout si elles y sont invitées par l'opinion dominante
en Allemagne) de faire avec prudence, et dans des vues de
conciliation, quelques démarches, soit pour obtenir des explications concernant les transgressions signalées des traités
existants, soit pour appaiser les dissensions qui se seroient
élevées, et pour ramener par leurs bons offices tous les États
Germaniques à l'exécution unanime des devoirs que leur impose l'Acte fédératif.   Mais aucun de ces cas n'existe encore,
en ce moment, et si nous venons à considérer combien de fois
l'attente seule d'une intervention étrangère a suffi pour retarder
la marche des négociations les plus importantes, ou même pour
empêcher la conclusion des transactions définitives, votre
Excellence me permettra de lui représenter l'extrême importance que ma Cour attache, dans l'état actuel des affaires, à ce
qu'il soit tenu un langage tel qui fasse disparoître en Allemagne
jusqu'au soupçon qu'une pareille intervention soit agitée.   Cette
réserve semble d'autant plus convenable à présent, que nous
avons peu de notions sur ce qui s'est passé jusqu'ici à Vienne,
et que les Ministres qui y sont rassemblés n'ont encore, à ce
que je crois, statué rien de décisif sur aucune des nombreuses

questions commises à leurs délibérations par leurs Cours respectives. On a fait, il est vrai, courir le bruit que des symptomes de divergence se sont montrés, et ces bruits (ainsi qu'il est judicieusement observé dans la dépêche que votre Excellence m'a communiquée) ont acquis, par les exagérations communes de la diplomatie et les malignes interprétations des révolutionnaires, un caractère alarmant. Mais la connoissance que nous avons du caractère des Souverains les plus intéressés dans ces transactions, la confiance que nous sommes autorisés à placer dans la prudence et l'esprit de conciliation qu'ils ne manqueront pas sans doute de faire porter aux importantes délibérations qui les occupent nous permettent-ils de concevoir la moindre inquiétude ?

Au surplus, il est assez naturel que les dispositions faites à Carlsbad, et ensuite sanctionnées avec plus de solemnité à Francfort, aient pu dans le premier moment, lors même de la forte sensation que des mesures de cette importance devoient nécessairement produire, et avant que les moyens de les mettre en exécution fussent suffisamment examinés et préparés—il est naturel, disons-nous, qu'elles aient pu produire quelques divergences d'opinions entre quelques uns des États de l'Allemagne.

Ces mêmes considérations expliquent l'agitation et l'inquiétude qui se manifestoient généralement à l'époque où fut écrite la dépêche que votre Excellence a reçue ; mais depuis, si nous devons en croire les rapports successivement parvenus à notre Gouvernement, ces alarmes se sont en grande partie calmées, et surtout depuis la réunion à Vienne des Plénipotentiaires, dont tous les discussions ont, selon ce qu'on nous mande, porté jusqu'ici les caractères de la sagesse et de l'unanimité : on est autorisé, sous ces auspices favorables, à concevoir l'espérance que les questions nombreuses et difficiles, qu'en vertu des stipulations de l'Acte fédératif la Diète peut être appelée à discuter et à décider, seront abordées par toutes les parties avec bonne foi et modération ; que les intérêts et les vœux des

divers Gouvernemens seront consultés, examinés avec patience,
jugés avec équité et sagesse ; enfin, que les États les plus puis-
sans se prêteront s'il est nécessaire à renoncer à une partie de
l'influence que les Actes précédemment passés par la Confédération parvenoient leur attribuer ; qu'ils agiront ainsi dans la
vue de remplir tous les devoirs de convenance et de délicatesse,
de calmer toutes les inquiétudes, de s'accommoder, pour ainsi
dire, à la situation des Puissances moins considérables, sur le
principe prudent, que, dans une ligue comme celle de l'Allemagne, le meilleur moyen d'établir et d'assurer pour une longue
suite d'années de la consistance, de la stabilité, et une force
réelle, c'est de rendre cette union non-seulement protectrice des
intérêts des plus foibles États, mais encore en harmonie avec
leurs sentimens.

Ces observations, que je viens de soumettre brièvement à
votre Excellence, convaincront, je l'espère, parfaitement votre
Cabinet que, du moins à l'époque actuelle, il seroit encore
impossible de se former une opinion juste des affaires d'Allemagne ; que nous devons attendre la fin des délibérations de
Vienne, et peut-être même le moment où les résultats de ces
délibérations seront soumis à la Diète de Francfort avant de
hasarder un jugement quelconque sur leur nature et leur tendance.   Ce retard est d'autant moins à regretter qu'il peut, et
que selon toute apparence il doit amener des changes qui
affranchiront les Puissances non-Allemandes de la tâche toujours embarrassante d'énoncer formellement une opinion sur
les transactions des États fédérés.   La scrupuleuse délicatesse
que sa Majesté l'Empereur de Russie a apportée dans ses
relations avec l'Allemagne, et qui ne lui a jamais permis d'intervenir dans les affaires de la Confédération, les vues nobles et
grandes qui ont motivé la déclaration que sa Majesté Impériale
vient de faire, et par laquelle elle annonce que, dans cette conjoncture aussi grave que délicate, elle est déterminée à n'agir
que de concert avec ses Alliés, et spécialement après l'échange
des plus franches communications avec son auguste ami le

Prince Régent, tout nous donne l'assurance que sa Majesté Impériale accueillera avec plaisir l'espérance de n'avoir pas à remplir, à l'égard de la Confédération, un devoir qui ne saurait être que pénible.

En rendant hommage à la conduite éclairée que sa Majesté l'Empereur a tenue dans cette occasion, et en recevant avec reconnoissance les flatteuses marques de la confiance que sa Majesté Impériale place dans la pureté et l'impartialité qui, sans nul doute, présideront aux Conseils de M. le Prince Régent, si son Altesse Royale est appellée à délibérer sur ces importans objets, je dois, M. le Comte, remplir encore un autre devoir bien agréable—c'est de prier votre Excellence d'exprimer à sa Majesté l'Empereur, au nom de M. le Prince Régent, combien son Altesse Royale est profondément sensible et reconnoissante des formes franches et amicales, par lesquelles votre Excellence, a d'ordre de son Cour, communiqué à son Altesse Royale les vues et les sentimens de son auguste maître sur un objet d'un si haut intérêt.

J'ai l'honneur d'être, &c.

TRADUCTION.

Dépêche de Lord Castlereagh à Lord Stewart, Ambassadeur Britannique à Vienne.

14 Janvier, 1820.

Mylord—Vous recevez ci-joint un Mémoire du Cabinet de Russie, que le Comte Lieven m'a communiqué et qui sert de réponse aux mémoires confidentiels des Cours de Vienne et de Londres du 24 et 30 Septembre de l'année passée.

Je présume que le Ministère Autrichien se trouve déjà en possession de la pièce sus-mentionnée et je la transmets à votre Excellence dans le but unique de vous faire connoître en même tems, que dans les observations et les raisonnemens qui y sont consignés, nous n'avons trouvé aucun motif d'altérer les impressions d'après lesquelles notre mémoire du 30 Septembre a été rédigé, et qui nous ont porté à le soumettre à l'attention des Souverains Alliés.

Votre Excellence observera que dans le mémoire du Cabinet de St. Petersbourg, après avoir succinctement rappellé les sentimens que l'Empereur a exprimé à des époques antécédentes, on signale les différences d'opinion qui paroissent, à l'égard de l'objet dont il est question, exister parmi les autres Cours Alliées, et que sa Majesté Impériale semble abandonner à ces Cours la discussion ultérieure d'un objet auquel une insinuation du Cabinet de Vienne auroit la première donné lieu.

En conséquence je crois devoir inviter votre Excellence à représenter au Prince de Metternich combien, d'après l'intime conviction du Prince Régent, il seroit utile de ne point laisser cette discussion se prolonger dans les circonstances actuelles. Les vues générales des divers Cabinets ont déjà été suffisamment développés. Si des dangers viennent à se manifester, nous ne ferons point de difficulté à les prendre alors dans la plus mûre et la plus ample considération. En attendant, le point de contact moral entre les Cours Alliées existe suffisamment, nous n'avons jamais trouvé de difficulté à nous confier réciproquement nos observations et nos plans les plus intimes; on peut même dire que ces sortes de communications sont d'un usage constant et presque journalier. D'un autre côté il me seroit aisé de démontrer que chercher à établir cet échange d'informations et d'idées dans un point central et unique, ce seroit le restreindre au lieu de la faciliter, et donner naissance à des conjectures erronées et à des vaines alarmes. Pourquoi donc abandonner un système dont l'expérience a jusqu'ici constaté la bonté?

Mais le Ministère Autrichien paroit attacher de l'importance à une autre partie de la question, c'est à dire aux instructions éventuelles qui pourroient être données aux représentans des Puissances Alliées à Paris, pour le cas du décès de Louis XVIII. À cet égard vous direz au Prince de Metternich que la réflexion n'a servi qu'à confirmer le Ministère du Prince Régent dans l'opinion que toute démarche officielle à ce sujet, et à l'époque actuelle surtout, ne pourroit être qu'imprudente et préjudiciable aux intérêts de l'héritier du trône de France.   Le Ministère de l'Empereur d'Autriche ne peut ignorer que le Gouvernement Britannique, malgré la sincérité de ses vœux et de ses sentimens en faveur de ces intérêts, ne sauroit cependant se permettre de contracter *à priori* l'engagement de suivre une ligne de conduite déterminée pour le cas calamiteux où l'ordre de la succession légitime en France viendroit à être renversé : d'ailleurs, en continuant à délibérer sur cette question pour l'insignifiant objet que l'envoi des instructions éventuelles peut faire atteindre, le Ministère du Prince Régent s'expose de se voir forcé de donner des éclaircissemens, qui en aiguisant la publicité ne peuvent que compromettre la cause que nous sommes tous également désireux de favoriser. Le Prince de Metternich saura, je suis convaincu, apprécier ces considérations avec sa pénétration et son esprit de conciliation habituels ; nous avons donc lieu d'espérer que le retour de ce courier nous apportera, de votre part, Mylord, l'assurance de ne plus nous voir appellés à revenir encore sur une discussion dans le cours de laquelle nous n'avons pas pu nous plier aux vues de nos Alliés, par la nature même de notre Gouvernement.   Il est tel que ses moyens de préférence décroitroient à mesure que le Ministère se compromettroit ou même seroit seulement soupçonné de se compromettre, en traitant d'une semblable question.

Il faut en conséquence que, pour conserver intacts entre nos mains les moyens de délibérer et d'agir avec succès au moment de la crise, s'il venoit malheureusement à avoir lieu, il faut, disons nous, que nos Alliés nous laissent persister dans l'attitude que nous avons prise, et qui nous permettra d'apprécier et de juger cet évènement avec pleine liberté, non plus comme ayant trait uniquement à l'ordre de succession établi en France (dont nos traités ne parlent point) mais comme un objet d'un intérêt général pour la politique Européenne.   Sous ce rapport, sa véritable importance ne sauroit être sentie d'avance, car

elle ne peut se déterminer que par les circonstances qui auront
accompagné cet évènement funeste.

J'ai cru m'appercevoir quelquefois que la circonspection
extrême qui règle notre politique, et dont nous devons ne
jamais nous écarter en traitant des objets de cette nature, avoit
induit quelquesunes des Cours Alliées à prendre le change sur
notre véritable situation et à interpréter faussement les sentimens du Gouvernement Britannique à l'égard de la France.
Votre Excellence saisira, en conséquence, l'occasion de s'expliquer itérativement avec le Prince de Metternich sur ce sujet,
et de l'assurer que le Ministère du Prince Régent n'est jamais
entré dans aucune relation exclusive et confidentielle avec le
Gouvernement Français, ni même dans aucun autre rapport
que ceux qui résultent naturellement de l'état d'amitié existante entre les deux pays, et des liens que les traités publics de
paix et d'alliance ont fait contracter.

Nous n'avons jamais cherché même momentanément à
exercer une influence suivie et systématique dans les Conseils
de la France ; et notre Ambassadeur à Paris ne s'est jamais,
du moins à ce que nous savons et croyons, entendu d'une
manière isolée avec le Ministère Français sur aucun objet
politique.   En se séparant ainsi des Conseils de ses Collègues,
les Ministres des Puissances Alliées, il se seroit placé dans
l'opposition la plus directe avec les ordres précis et réitérés qu'il
a reçu de notre Gouvernement.   Les Ministres du Prince
Régent ne se sont point aveuglés sur les fautes des Adminis-
trations successives en France, ni sur les dangers qui pourront,
tôt ou tard, résulter pour l'Europe des dissensions intérieures
dans ce pays, que des projets hostiles que peuvent nourrir
quelques uns des partis qui l'agitent ; mais le Cabinet Anglois
a toujours élevé le doute, et le fait encore, si une intervention
de la part des Alliés peut servir à prévenir le péril, ou à diminuer le nombre des chances qui semblent devoir l'amener: cette
question, pour les raisons détaillées dans notre Mémoire pré-
cité, nous a toujours paru devoir être résolu négativement.

Si le Roi de France, ou les Ministres qui composent son Conseil, au milieu des complications et des difficultés contre lesquelles ils ont presque sans cesse à lutter, pouvoient à leur gré diriger la marche des affaires, alors le Cabinet de Londres auroit pensé, avec celui de St. Pétersbourg, qu'un énoncé grave et solennel des sérieuses allarmes que les Cours Alliées ont conçues seroit de quelque utilité : mais il nous a toujours semblé que les obstacles qui s'opposent en France à l'établissement d'une Administration sage et stable proviennent d'autres causes, et non de manque de bonnes intentions ou des dispositions particulières des Ministres du Roi.

Ces obstacles le Gouvernement Britannique les voit plutôt dans les effets prolongés de la Révolution, dans la composition actuelle de la Législature, dans la nouveauté pour la France du régime représentatif, sous lequel elle se trouve placée en ce moment pour la première fois.   La difficulté de conduire ces affaires par un Ministre, un parti quelconque, ou un amalgame de partis auquel le Ministère pourroit avoir recours, n'est pas assez généralement reconnue et appréciée ; enfin, ces obstacles se trouvent (et en grande partie) dans les effets des loix sur les élections et le recrutement—mesures de concession faites aux vœux de l'armée et du peuple—mesures adoptées, nul doute, dans les intentions les plus pures, et prises avant la réunion des Souverains à Aix-la-Chapelle—mais mesures qui n'ont cessé depuis d'affoiblir visiblement l'autorité Royale, et qui sont malheureusement de nature à pouvoir être plus aisément adoptées que modifiées, ou rapportées définitivement.

Telle étant l'opinion des Ministres du Prince Régent, ils ne sauroient se persuader qu'une intervention étrangère dans les affaires de France puisse produire d'autre effet qu'aggraver les dangers qu'on s'efforce de conjurer.   Si le Gouvernement Britannique s'est prononcé moins hautement que ses Alliés contre quelques uns des actes du Ministère François ; s'il s'est moins fréquemment permis d'exprimer le pressentiment des dangers auxquels peut conduire le système suivi en France ; soyez convaincu qu'il n'en a pas moins observé les évènemens qui ont lieu dans ce pays de l'œil le plus attentif. Une réserve portée jusqu'a un certain degré, c'est la conduite qu'il convient le mieux pour les Cours Alliées de tenir à l'égard du Gouvernement François, dans l'état indécis où se trouvent actuellement ses affaires. Mais cette réserve doit, selon nous, avoir le caractère d'une sage déférence pour le sentiment national et les institutions existantes. Nous ne cessons pas de penser que toute démarche comminatoire et toute intrusion dans les querelles qui divisent le public François ne feroit qu'irriter au lieu de concilier. Nous sommes loin, sans doute, de nous flatter qu'une conduite quelconque de la part des Alliés puisse les garantir suffisamment contre tout désastre à l'avenir : nous croyons seulement, et avec un sentiment de conviction intime, que la politique circonspecte, dont nous avons développé et recommandé les principes dans notre Mémoire du 30 Septembre, est encore celle qui offre le plus d'avantages, en ce qu'elle sert à maintenir la grande Alliance dans l'attitude à la fois la plus imposante et la plus sûre à l'égard du Gouvernement François, qui, quelles que soient ses erreurs et ses fautes dans son Administration intérieure, s'est toute fois depuis la retraite de l'armée d'occupation montré inoffensif et irréprochable dans ses relations avec les autres Puissances.

En terminant, je n'ai plus, Mylord, qu'à exprimer ma conviction que les opinions des quatre Cabinets Alliés bien entendues sont essentiellement identiques, et ne diffèrent entre elles que par des nuances sur les moyens de parvenir au but commun qu'on se propose. La forme de notre Gouvernement doit nécessairement nous rendre plus circonspects que les autres États dans nos transactions avec les puissances étrangères, mais spécialement à l'égard de la France, nation long tems rivale et ennemie de la Grande Bretagne, et par conséquent plus susceptible de s'irriter de ses procédés que de ceux d'un autre État ; mais, dans sa fidélité et son attachement à la Grande Alliance, jamais le Prince Régent ne cédera à aucun

de ses augustes Alliés; et votre Excellence peut, sur ce point
essentiel, s'exprimer dans toutes les occasions de la manière la
plus positive comme la plus forte.

J'ai l'honneur, &c.

Lord Castlereagh to Count Capodistrias.

Colonial Department, January, 1820.

Sir—In conformity with the assurance which I have already
given to your Excellency, in my letter of the 11th ult., I have
now the honour of submitting to you in detail the explanations
upon the several points adverted to in the Memorial which
you communicated to me confidentially in your letter of the
— October last.   In doing so, my only anxiety is to give your
Excellency a clear insight into the actual state of affairs in the
Ionian Islands, and into the true character of the representations which have been made to your Excellency.   I trust that
in expressing my opinions without reserve, I shall be considered by your Excellency as best fulfilling the object for which
the Memorial was brought under my consideration.   After the
statement which I took occasion to submit to your Excellency
in my former letter with respect to the interpretation of the
4th Article of the Treaty of 1815, and the views and intentions of the negociators as regarded the Constitution of 1803,
I feel it unnecessary again to press upon your Excellency's
attention the grounds upon which I must protest against the
construction contended for by the Memorialists.   I will only
add, that the further consideration which I have given to that
construction, as compared with the stipulations of the Treaty
of 1815, convinces me that the charge of a violation of the
Treaty of 1815 cannot be supported without either misquoting
the terms or perverting the obvious meaning of the articles to
which reference is made.   With regard to the other complaints
of the memorialists, it appears to me that they may be divided
into two classes, the one applicable to the mode in which the
Constitution has been formed, and the other to the manner in

which the Government has been administered under that Constitution. To these two heads of complaint I propose to address myself separately.

In the first place, your Excellency, I am sure, must be aware that the memorialists have entirely misstated the treaty, when they contend that it prescribed to the Lord High Commissioner the manner in which the Legislative Assembly for the purpose of drawing up a new Constitutional charter was to be convoked, and that it prohibits his directing the new elections for that Assembly, except by virtue of the ancient laws of election. Whether by the ancient laws of election they mean those which were established in 1803, or at any other time, it is quite clear that no such injunction was prescribed by the treaty, which left it, on the contrary, to the Lord High Commissioner to regulate the form in which this Legislative Assembly was to be convoked. For if ever there was a general latitude left to an individual as to the means by which a given object was to be attained, it is to be found in those words of the treaty which distinctly provide that it shall be the Lord High Commissioner of the protecting Power " who shall regulate the forms of convocation of a Legislative Assembly, of which he shall direct the proceedings, in order to draw up a new Constitutional charter."

Your Excellency must at once see that neither the ancient laws of election, nor the existing Constitutions, nor the Constitution of 1803, have anything to do, under the treaty, with the form by which the convocation of that Assembly is to be regulated. It is true indeed that, for the purpose of carrying on the provisional Government until the charter should be settled, the existing Constitutions in the different islands were stipulated to continue in force, and to retain their authority subject to the pleasure of the Prince Regent in council. But the regulation of the forms by which the Constituent Assembly was to be convoked, and the direction of its proceedings when convoked, is left absolutely to the Lord High Commissioner.

It is limited in no respect, except in so far that the result of those proceedings should be a Constitutional charter, which should give effect to the stipulations contained in the 1st, 2nd, and 3rd Articles of the treaty, and should found the political organization of the States upon that which was then actually in force.

The only point therefore for consideration is, whether the Constitution of 1817 has fulfilled this important object. I am confident that I may safely appeal to your Excellency for a confirmation of this truth, that, in order to secure to any Constitution the necessary *consistency and action*, (which is the first point that the treaty requires) it is indispensably requisite that the Constitution should be formed with a due regard to the state, habits, and education of the people to whom it is to be applied. It became, therefore, the bounden duty of the Lord High Commissioner to direct his attention to this important object. I am ready to admit that, if a longer time had been allowed between his arrival at Corfu and the convocation of the Constituent Assembly, he might by personal observations have become more intimately acquainted with the dispositions and character of the inhabitants of the Septinsular States, and I must also admit that for this there was ample time given to the protecting Power under the treaty. While it left absolutely to the Lord High Commissioner the form in which this Constituent Assembly was to be convoked, it prescribed no definite period, and indeed implied none, within which this convocation should take place. It provided also that no Constitutional charter should have effect, unless duly ratified by his Majesty, and, up to the time when his Majesty should duly ratify such charter, it gave to his Majesty in Council the power of altering the existing provisional Constitutions in the different islands.

Under this treaty, therefore, his Majesty had in fact the power of legislation for an indefinite period over the Ionian Islands; and if a Constituent Assembly were convoked, and a

Constitutional charter ratified before the Lord High Commissioner had acquired all the information which might have been desirable, it could only have proceeded from the Prince Regent's anxious desire to divest himself as soon as possible of the unlimited power with which the confiding spirit of his allies had thus liberally entrusted him.   Called upon by the provisions of the treaty to direct the proceedings of the Constituent Assembly, it became the duty of the Lord High Commissioner to examine whether there was any form of Constitution to which the Ionian people were from long habit peculiarly attached.   But in this particular he soon found that he could derive no assistance.   They had for a long period undergone so many changes, that they could not be expected to have any prevailing attachment to any particular form of government. He found this strongly demonstrated in the Instruction given by the Ionian Government to the Chargé d'Affaires of the Seven Islands at St. Petersburg in 1802, in which it is distinctly stated "that the primary cause of the late calamities of the Ionian Islands was to be ascribed to the Constitutional code, subject by circumstances to disputes adapted to keep the passions in a constant state of ferment, and which being suspended by some and inflamed by others, generally irritated and exasperated the hopes of all; and that the whole of the people were disposed to receive any Constitution that may be offered to them with blind resignation, and to carry the same into execution, without any other condition being annexed than what may proceed from the adored hand of Alexander, and not be susceptible of valid objections, and that his will shall be inviolable law to us, as forming the supreme guarantee of the infallible validity of the Constitution."

With respect to the Constitution of 1803, your Excellency knows that the people could not have formed any particular attachments to it, as it was not in activity long enough for them to have experienced any of its beneficial results; but your Excellency's sagacity appears to have convinced you at

an early period of some of its defects; for, in your letter to the
same Chargé d'Affaires,[1] you state " That you cannot conceal
from him the circumstance of the Constitution containing some
imperfections, it being a fact of which you are now perfectly
convinced, and that it requires revision and amendment; because, by an enthusiastic admiration of abstract principles,
with a disregard of facts, a work had been completed, beautiful
perhaps in the eye of a solitary philosopher, but not adapted to
answer the wise views of a father of a numerous but indocile
and uneducated family."

I need not remind your Excellency that the many changes
to which the islands were exposed between the date of that
letter and the signature of the Treaty of 1815 were not peculiarly propitious either to the education or to the habits of the
inhabitants. It is, however, the Constitution of 1803 which
your Excellency will observe has been in a great measure the
basis of that which has been now established; and, after what
I have stated, you will, I am sure, have too much candour not
to admit that a departure in some instances from the Constitution of 1803 is not sufficient of itself to condemn the
Constitution of 1817.

With respect to the statement made as to the mode of
election of members for the Legislative Body, that the greater
number were the candidates on whom the minority of votes
had been bestowed, I can only assure your Excellency that,
from every inquiry I have made, I believe it to be positively
false. I can readily understand that those who had been
accustomed to the mode of election resorted to under the Constitution of 1803, might object to the alterations introduced in
the elections of 1817. The electors, who had been reconciled
to vote by ballot, to see the officers in the employment of
Government take possession of the boxes, to carry them away
and on some future day declare whom they considered to have
been elected, might feel some surprise at the novelty of being

[1] Count Capodistrias was at this time Secretary to the Ionian States.

called upon to vote personally, to see the number of votes cast up publicly, and to hear the result immediately announced. Whether their rights are more likely to be benefitted or injured by the change is a question which I will leave to your Excellency to decide; but I confess that I cannot understand how any prejudice in favour of the former mode of election could appear to the Memorialists to call for or to justify an assertion which now appears to be inconsistent with truth.

With regard to the powers granted by the charter to the Lord High Commissioner—and it is to these powers that the Memorialists mainly object—the chief difference in this particular between the two Constitutions, if they are carefully compared together, will be found to consist in this: that the present charter has distinctly defined the power of interference, and so far has materially benefitted the people, by guarding against the existence of those elements of abuse which always lurk in undefined power, in whatever Constitution it may be found.

I might, as a proof of this, refer to some transactions in the Ionian States, during the time that they were under the protection of his Imperial Majesty, if I were not satisfied that the instances of it must still be fresh in your Excellency's recollection. The Memorialists complain, however, that the Lord High Commissioner is altogether freed from all responsibility.

The Memorialists do not understand the British Constitution. The Lord High Commissioner is a public servant of the Crown, duly appointed by the Crown, and we will never admit that a public servant of the Crown is not responsible to Parliament for the manner in which the power with which he is entrusted is discharged. If that power be not, as I am sure it is not, beyond what experience has proved to be necessary for preserving the existence of the States, any control over it by the States themselves, as it could only act in derogation of the authority which it is presumed the Lord High Commissioner ought to possess, could only be injurious to the ends for which the power was conferred.   But the Memorialists assert "that every advantage given to the islands by the treaty has been done away by the Constitution;" and this is attempted to be established by showing that no convention has been entered into with the States relative to the maintenance of the British troops.   In reply, I would simply refer your Excellency to the 12th article of the 2nd section of the 7th chapter, by which the number of British troops for which the Ionian States shall be alone chargeable is distinctly limited to three thousand, and I would ask your Excellency whether any conventional instrument can be more solemn than the insertion of the necessary stipulation in a charter signed on the one hand by the leading inhabitants of the States on behalf of their fellow citizens, and ratified on the other by the Prince Regent on behalf of the protecting Power.   The Memorialists also complain that the number of British troops stationed in the islands is excessive; and they charge the protecting Power with an avidity to seize upon and apply the revenues of the Ionian States to their support, instead of allowing the military establishment of the islands mainly to consist, as they contend it ought to consist, of Ionian troops.   The fact is, the number of British troops generally maintained in the islands does not exceed that of the Russian troops which the States required in 1803; and the whole pay of those British troops has up to the present moment been defrayed, not from the revenue of the Ionian States, but from the resources of Great Britain.

If any jealousy had been shown by the Ionian States in 1803, with regard to the number of Russian troops stationed in the islands, I should have been prepared to expect the same jealousy on the same establishment of British troops.   But your Excellency knows that, so far from any dissatisfaction of this kind having been felt, the subject of one whole chapter of the instructions from the Government of the Seven Islands to their Chargé d'Affaires at St. Petersburgh (of which a copy is given in the Appendix) was to prove to him, and through him to impress upon the Emperor, that the whole military force of the islands must of necessity consist of foreigners—" that the nation themselves were unfit, from their known habits of insubordination and violence, to be loyal and obedient republican soldiers; and that, if the troops could not be Russian, they must be foreigners of some other description."

They further state, " that the Russian soldiery were the life and soul of the State; that it was to them that they were indebted for security of person and property; that they were solicited and longed for as a gift from Heaven; and that if they were to depart, it would involve their complete destruction, and leave no other alternative than that of drowning themselves in the surrounding seas."

After this, I need not observe to your Excellency, that when the Memorialists contend that the treaty stipulates that the garrisons should consist jointly of British and Ionian troops, it is a direct misstatement of the article which relates to this subject. Your Excellency would never have encouraged a stipulation inconsistent with the opinion you formerly entertained; and the fact is that the 5th Article distinctly provides that it shall be his Majesty who shall have the right to occupy the fortresses. The only mention of the military force of the Ionian States is in the concluding sentence, for the purpose of placing that force absolutely under the command of his Majesty's Commander of the forces. It is true, that the Commander of the forces may, under that stipulation, order the Ionian troops to occupy the fortresses; but he may also order them to withdraw whenever he may judge it expedient.

Having said so much with respect to the first series of complaints, I will now trouble your Excellency with a few observations upon what the Memorialists call the result of the system established in the islands by the charter of 1817; and here I think I shall have no difficulty in convincing your Excellency that an attempt has been made to deceive you by a strange perversion or utter misstatement of the facts which it is professed to bring forward.

The Memorial begins by asking " whether the inhabitants are contented with their actual situation." To this I can have no difficulty in replying, (what is admitted in another part of the Memorial) that a large portion of the inhabitants are contented, and have expressed their satisfaction in terms not to be misunderstood. Not, indeed, that I am ignorant that there are now, as there always have been, persons averse to the existing order of things, and willing both to encourage dissatisfaction and to speculate on the possibility of a change. That there existed persons of this description in 1803, (though I do not pretend to say they were the same individuals) is sufficiently evident from the official records of the Government, of which some are to be found in the Appendix ; and, without imputing any particular blame to the parties who have furnished your Excellency with this Memorial, I would generally state that where changes of Government and system have been so rapid and so frequent, there must always be some dissatisfied persons anxious to undervalue and depreciate the existing order of things, in the hopes of securing in its overthrow a greater share of political power or individual advantage. That this party is at present more numerous, or (notwithstanding the very intelligible threat of insurrection held out in the Memorial) more formidable than their predecessors in their opposition to the then existing Government, I have no reason to believe, and I have therefore but little doubt that they will become either more reconciled or more harmless, as the permanency of the present system becomes confirmed and established. But I own I am surprised to find any disposition to hold up the Venetian administration of the islands as a system favourable to general liberty, or as in other respects deserving of approbation. That the Venetian system was one of " corruption, vice, and imbecility," is justly stated in the instructions to which I have so frequently referred. Your Excellency, too, is perfectly aware that the leading principle of that Government was the elevation of the order of nobility, and the sacrifice to the interests of that privileged order of every other class of the community, making the whole subservient to the wealth and grandeur of Venice itself. To this, as a principle of government, I am sure your Excellency would feel insurmountable objections. There may, under the present Constitution, be some who deeply feel the loss of an oppressive authority, but that the people generally have been benefitted in every mode in which benefits can be conferred by an improved system of judicature, by a more effectual collection of the revenue, by a regular and impartial administration of the Government, will the more appear as the system is in its details the more examined.

But, to come to particular evils, it is stated—

1st. "That the taxes are double what were paid before."

From the manner in which this statement is made, it is natural that your Excellency should imagine that heavy additional burdens have been imposed upon the people. But I must, in the first place, assure your Excellency that, with the exception of three-quarters of a dollar on every barrel of oil, (which, considering the present increased value of that commodity, does not press so heavily upon it as the lower rate did formerly) no new taxes have been imposed; and secondly, that the great increase of the revenue (and I gladly appeal to it as a solid proof of the benefits derived from the present administration of the Government) results principally from the reform of abuses which heretofore prevailed in its collection. This improvement is principally attributable to the abolition of the system of farming the different branches of revenue to particular individuals, who made large profits at the expense of the public. The ill effects of such a system have been so long recognized in this country, and the prejudices against it are besides so strong, that its abolition could not but be a necessary consequence of the connexion of the islands with Great Britain.

While, however, I feel all the evil of the farming system, I have no difficulty in acknowledging that, as a considerable portion of the Ionian nobility directly or indirectly derived large emoluments from the farms, I should have been disposed to condemn their abolition, if it had not been gradually introduced. I should have felt that its immediate overthrow, by interfering so materially with the pecuniary interests of so many leading individuals, could not but indispose them to the administration of the protecting Power, while the people at large, by habit probably reconciled to what they had long endured, would not at first be alive to the beneficial effects of the reform. But I have the satisfaction of knowing that the farms have in all instances been resumed with the utmost consideration for the holders, to an extent perhaps more calculated to reconcile them to their loss than justifiable to the public interest.

I do not know how I can better prove to your Excellency the forbearance which has been exercised than by referring you to the case of Signor Mastraca, as developed in the annexed extract of the resolution of the Senate, as that gentleman was the farmer of the principal branch of the revenue, from the resumption of which the greatest profit has resulted. Your Excellency will observe that, although the irregularity and want of punctuality on the part of the Signor Mastraca had given the Government a right of resuming the contract, and enforcing a penalty of 15 per cent. against the contractor, yet that they acceded to his own proposal of accepting 12,000 dollars in satisfaction of an actual debt from him to the Government of 14,630, and further remitted to him a sum of near 3,500 dollars, being one-fourth of the valuation of a house which the Government having accepted in part of payment had a perfect right to retain. Moreover, by releasing him from his contract six months previous to its expiration, at a time of year when the whole of the oil had been already made, it is evident that a further profit was secured to M. Mastraca, which may fairly be calculated at 4,000 dollars a month, the whole of which must have been lost to him, if he had continued to hold the contract till the end of the year. It results from this statement, that the whole sum allowed to M. Mastraca, on the resumption of his contract, is not less than 30,000 dollars or tallari, and exactly five times that sum of 6,000 tallari, which the Memorialists consider as too great a remuneration even of the highest public servant of the Ionian States. Whether in this arrangement a due regard has been paid to the public interest may be questionable, but the individual at least has had no cause to complain ; and if what I understand be true, that your Excellency has been unfortunately impressed, during your residence at Corfu, with a belief that, in the prosecution of the measures of Government, due attention has not been shown to those who have the honour of being more immediately connected with your Excellency's family, and that the resumption of the farms, or the manner of executing it, has been adduced as a proof of it, the instance which I have brought forward will, I hope, be sufficient to remove so erroneous an impression.

2ndly. It is stated—" That the greater number of employments are conferred on British, Maltese, and Sicilians, and that the few Ionians who are employed are not persons of consideration."

I cannot better answer this charge than by referring your Excellency to the accompanying list of appointments in the Ionian States, and of the persons by whom they are held : whether the proportion of British officers employed is more than circumstances require, I will leave to your Excellency to decide. With respect to natives of Malta, there is not, as far as I have been able to discover, any native of that island in any public situation. In regard to Sicilians, it is most true that there are a few employed, either as seamen, or in the Sanità, or in the Customs ; but I am ignorant of any Sicilian holding a place of importance. With respect to those in the inferior offices of the Sanità and the Customs, your Excellency will permit me to observe that it has ever been thought expedient in the Mediterranean and in other places, when the danger of infection from plague is imminent, that all the Sanità officers and guardians, and some of those in the Customs, should be utterly disconnected with the population of the country; but, after all, if an instance could be produced of any of these foreigners holding a high official situation, I am sure that his Imperial Majesty has had too much experience of the advantage which he has derived from the services of eminent men not natives of Russia, to entertain any apprehension that the employment of a foreigner in a public situation is necessarily calculated to prejudice the interests, or can be regarded as derogatory to the honour, of an independent State.

With respect to the rank and consideration of the Ionians employed, I would only beg your Excellency to read over their names, and to bear in mind how many of the present Senate held offices of high trust under the Constitution of 1803, and I would then leave it to your Excellency to decide how far the objection of the Memorialists applies.

On the subject of the revenue and expenditure of the islands, of which the Memorial states that the inhabitants are now for the first time kept in perfect ignorance, I would request your Excellency's attention to the annexed statement, promulgated by the direction of the Lord High Commissioner, under the sanction of the Legislative Body, about the period when your Excellency was in the islands, as it is remarkable for being the first public statement of the receipt and expenditure of the Ionian revenue which was ever made to the people under any of their numerous Constitutions; and I must here take the opportunity of expressing my regret that your Excellency did not condescend to avail yourself of the offer made by the Lord High Commissioner to give every explanation which you might desire with regard to any of the proceedings of the Ionian Government. It is true, I find upon inquiry, that he made the offer only once, but his apology is that he was not encouraged to repeat it, by your Excellency observing that you had never read the Constitution; from whence he not very unnaturally concluded that either, as his Imperial Majesty's Minister, you abstained from all possible interference with the internal proceedings of the islands, in rigid conformity with the 2nd Article of the Treaty, or that, for some other reason, you had decided to have no communication with him on the subject.

In reply to that part of the Memorial which refers to the comparative expense of the present Government, and those which preceded it, I will just take leave to point out to your Excellency one great fallacy, which at once overthrows the argument which the calculation is intended to establish. It is simply this, that the expenditure of 1817, as stated in the Memorial, includes what that of 1803 excludes, the whole expenses of collecting the revenue. If your Excellency will only add to the statement of 1803 the profit made by the farmers of the revenue, which was, in truth, the expense of its collection, and which may in a great measure be estimated by a comparison of the revenue actually received then, with that received now upon the same articles, I should not only not shrink from the comparison, but shall confidently claim credit from your Excellency for a real reduction of expenditure. I must further observe that in this comparison I do not take into account that, according to the existing establishment, all those fees of office are abolished, with the payment of which the people were formerly charged, and which, arbitrary in their extent, and in practice not unfrequently corrupt, formed the principal emolument in those establishments with which the present have been compared.

But, even were the case otherwise, I am sure your Excellency is too enlightened to consider the nominal expense of a Government without reference to the mode in which the

Government is conducted, as any test either of economy or efficiency. Adequate salaries ultimately both diminish expenditure and increase the revenues of a State, and the observation of what has taken place in the Ionian States confirms in the strongest manner the truth of this general position.

It is next made a subject of complaint that "the trade in corn was free, and that it is now subjected to a monopoly." Like many other facts in the Memorial, the statement is only to a certain extent true. It is true that from May, 1816, to September, 1818, the corn trade was free, and it was so because Sir T. Maitland had, at a former period, put an end to the monopoly which previously existed, and recorded the opinions upon its general effect. In adducing, therefore, the present monopoly as a grievance, it would have been more candid in the Memorialists to have put your Excellency in possession of this fact, and of the circumstances in which the renewal of the monopoly originated, and not to have permitted your Excellency to infer that it was a new and gratuitous evil, unattended by corresponding benefits. The enclosed memorandum will make your Excellency master of the real circumstances of the case.

You will observe, in the first place, the measure has never been applied, except to Corfu, and that wheat alone, which, your Excellency knows, forms but a part of the subsistence of the inhabitants of the villages, has ever been the subject of its provisions. You will observe further that it originated in a moment of the most pressing necessity, when only three days' corn remained in the island, and no person was disposed to undertake the supply on private account. In considering, therefore, whether the monopoly is an evil, the evil of famine against which it was intended to guard, and which its institution at the moment prevented, cannot be overlooked. Its continuance or abandonment must of course depend upon circumstances, but I can never consider the administration of the corn laws at Corfu to be a grievance, which supplies the inhabitants with bread notoriously superior to that consumed in the other islands, and at a price not disproportioned to its superior quality.

Another head of accusation is, "that the administrator of the Customs is authorized to possess himself of all merchandize on paying the proprietor 15 per cent."

If I had yet to seek an instance of the industry which has been exercised to mislead your Excellency, I could scarcely find one more characteristic than this perversion of an ordinary process for the protection of the revenue into a measure for the destruction of the Ionian commerce. Your Excellency knows full well that, in order to levy an *ad valorem* duty, (a duty in itself the least liable to objection of any which affect commerce) it is necessary to establish the true value of the article on which the duty is to be laid. With a view to check on the one hand any fraud on the part of the importer, and on the other any extortion on the part of the revenue officer, the practice in this country has always been to call upon the importer to fix himself the value of his own commodity, leaving to the officer an option of purchasing it on payment of an additional 10 per cent. above the value so fixed. This principle, it appears, has been extended to the Ionian States, but with this additional advantage to the trader that, instead of 10 per cent., the Ionian trader is entitled to 15 per cent. in all cases in which the justice of his valuation may be doubted. It is further not a little remarkable that, up to the date of the last advices from the Ionian States, not a single instance has occurred in which the officer of the Customs had had occasion to resort to the alternative of taking the goods of the importer on payment of 15 per cent. above his own valuation. And yet this commercial regulation, so essential for the protection of the honest trader, as well as of the public, of which the alternative complained of has never yet been exercised, and which, when called into action, has the peculiar benefit of not being susceptible of abuse to the prejudice of the importer, is

nevertheless spoken of as a crying grievance, and charged as
an evil consequence resulting from the Constitution, and requiring a return to that of 1803.

Having now explained, I trust to your Excellency's satisfaction, the real state of the transactions which the Memorialists have made the foundation of their complaints, I
cannot conclude without referring to other complaints which
have been advanced since your Excellency's departure from
Corfu.

By a paper which I have seen, I find that intelligence has
been received at St. Petersburgh of the Senate having recently
imposed in the Ionian States new and oppressive taxes on
wine, on animals, and on wells and fountains. I beg to assure
your Excellency that this intelligence is false, and is a gross
imposition on the sensibility entertained at St. Petersburgh
towards the inhabitants of the Ionian States. With respect
to the local and temporary tax on those articles levied in lieu
of others on the inhabitants of Santa Maura for the construction of a mole, which, on their own immediate application, has
been undertaken, the manner in which the peasants were
encouraged to acts of insubordination by the grossest mis-
representations will already have been' explained to your
Excellency; and, if those local and temporary taxes are the
taxes to which the paper has so generally referred, the statement made with respect to them is a most artful and most
unwarrantable perversion of the truth.

As the falsehood of such a report so generally stated must
have been known in the States, it has not, so far as I can
learn, been circulated there, but there have been other reports
industriously disseminated throughout the islands, which are
equally without foundation. One is, that it is the intention of
the Prince Regent, as soon as the Ionian militia is organized,
to order them to the British colonies in the West Indies.
Another, that Sir T. Maitland had, during the time he was at
Paris, privately received money which was due from the

French Government to the Ionian States. I do not advert to these reports for the purpose of refuting them, or of proving their malignity, but as a pregnant evidence that there can be no real causes of complaint where they, who are acting in decided hostility to the existing Government, find themselves under the necessity of having recourse to falsehood to excite the people to discontent.

I have thus briefly adverted to the leading subjects of complaint contained in the memoranda, and to those which have been since promulgated. Your Excellency will, I trust, pardon me, if I altogether decline entering into any examination of the means by which the Memorialists propose to improve the existing Constitution. It is sufficiently evident that what is meant by improvement is the utter subversion of all that has been done under the Treaty of 1815. Your Excellency cannot but feel that the great evil with which the Ionian States have had to contend has been the rapid succession of different systems of Government, and the belief thence induced that no Government was ever to be permanent.

Hence the unsettled habits of the people, the perpetual recurrence of cabal and intrigue, and their defective knowledge of what Government ought to be, which your Excellency may remember were not less deplored when under Russian protection than by all those who have at any other time administered the Government of the islands. Whatever defects, therefore, the present system may possess, (and that there may be defects I am by no means disposed to deny) it is not the less requisite to inculcate the necessity of adhering to the charter, which has wisely made provision for the gradual improvement of the Constitution. For it is not by perpetual succession of new Constitutions that order, and security, and content, the result of good Government, can ever be acquired. Still less is it to be expected in the Ionian States that the public mind should ever be settled while countenance is given to the idea of fresh changes, and the people are taught to believe that the existing authorities may therefore be insulted with impunity.

I cannot adduce a stronger proof of the mischief which has grown out of the reports which, since your Excellency's departure from Corfu, had been, with no common measure of industry and confidence, generally propagated, that all that had been done under the Treaty of 1815 was to be subverted, than to inform your Excellency that the primates of some of the villages in the neighbourhood of Corfu had been wrought upon to present an address to the Lord High Commissioner, calling upon him to refund the sums which they stated him to have received at Paris and to have appropriated to his own use. Your Excellency must feel that no Government thus publicly insulted could avoid adopting some decisive measures by which it might vindicate its authority and assert its own stability. And his Royal Highness, being convinced that the machinations of those who from the beginning have been active in the opposition to British protection have left him no alternative but that of abandoning his authority as protecting Power, or evincing his unalterable determination firmly to assert it, has commanded me to convey to the Lord High Commissioner his entire approbation of the measures which he had, under such circumstances, been imperiously called upon to adopt.

I cannot conclude this letter without expressing my confidence that your Excellency has too much candour to complain of the time which has elapsed between the receipt of the Memorial and the reply which I now do myself the honour of forwarding to your Excellency. Upon so grave a subject, your Excellency could not have expected that I should proceed without inquiry on the spot, more especially as the documents in my office at once convinced me that, with respect to many particulars, great imposition had been practised on your Excellency. If, when you first showed me the Memorial, in August, you had complied with my wish of leaving with me a copy of it, the inquiry would have been long since completed.

I am far indeed from complaining that more than three months afterwards elapsed before the Memorial reached my office, because I believe it has undergone some material alteration, and I am aware that a shorter period would not have enabled your Excellency to communicate with Corfu. But I take the liberty of reminding your Excellency of these circumstances, in order to convince you that there has been no want of readiness on my part either to make the necessary inquiry, or to communicate to you the result.

I beg your Excellency to accept the assurances of my high consideration.

I have the honour to be, &c.

Lord Castlereagh to Sir Charles Stuart.

London, February 4, 1820.

My dear Sir—I think you judged quite right to confine the communication of my note to Count Lieven, the Russian Minister, from whose Court the overture proceeded, if the contents were not confidentially communicated to the *French*, as well as to the Austrian and Prussian Ministers. In limiting the communication to the Powers represented at Aix-la-Chapelle, I certainly meant to *include France*.

The circumstance that suggested the propriety of sending you a copy of this document was your previous intimation that the Russian note had been sent to General Pozzo, and having also learnt at the same time that it had been communicated to several of the German Courts. If the subject is quiet at Paris, perhaps the better way may be to leave it there; but if you have reason to suppose that the Russian Minister has opened himself to the French Government on this subject, or that they have received any false impression, you will, in that case, avail yourself of some occasion of apprising them of the real facts of the case.

I recollect, when Count Capodistrias was here, there was an uneasiness on the part of the French Government at our being

supposed to have conferences on German affairs to their exclusion. You know the truth was, our conferences were on
Swedish and not German affairs. In the present instance,
nothing has passed but a consultation between two of the
Allied Powers, *not German*, whether there is any ground for
the Allies (which would include France) to interfere in
German affairs. This Government has discouraged such interference; and I have only to hope that this sentiment may
correspond with the dispositions of the French Government,
and I think they cannot justly take umbrage at anything that
has passed, or suppose that it evinces any disposition, either
in the Russian or British Government, to act in such matters
to the exclusion of France.

Lord Castlereagh to Lord Stewart.

St. James's Square, February 13, 1820.

My dear Charles—My official letter of this date will convey
to you the whole of the King's commands, such as they were
given me in charge. Similar orders are transmitted by Baron
Best to Count Münster. His Majesty's only observations to
me were that Count Münster's return could not be *too much
expedited*—that his desire was that *your* arrival might be
accelerated as much as possible, but that he did not, however,
thereby mean that you should travel night and day. You
will make the best temporary arrangement in your power for
the business of the Embassy, and I will endeavour to despatch
Gordon in a few days to resume his functions as Minister
Plenipotentiary in your absence.

To enable you to understand the curious posture of affairs
at home, which has given rise to your sudden recall, it will be
enough to put you in possession of a very short outline, as we
are so soon likely to meet. So long as the King lived, the
question of the Princess was one with regard to which you
might or might not advise the Prince Regent to institute a
proceeding in Parliament; but, upon the King's demise, the

matter forced itself upon the Crown and the Government in more shapes than one—in the Litany, in the Coronation, in the future pecuniary maintenance to be assigned to the Princess. Thus, exclusive of the measure of divorce, the question inevitably and immediately called for a decision, and especially as the very first act of the new reign required that the prayers for the royal family should be adapted to the new circumstances of the case.

You already know the position in which the whole of this business rested before the Cabinet when this event occurred. The Government had just received the supplementary information which had been collected in the last four or five months, and were upon the point of taking the whole case into their mature consideration. The celerity of the King's illness, (which has had a most providential termination, entirely owing to Sir M. Tierney's intrepid conduct in bleeding his Majesty almost to death) precluded our access to him; whilst the horror of having the Queen made an object of the prayers of his people haunted his imagination and distracted his rest. His servants had no hesitation with respect to the advice they should offer him upon the single point of the Litany; but they did not feel that they should act honestly by his Majesty or by themselves, if, in tendering their opinion upon this insulated question, they did not submit it in connexion with their view upon the whole of the case. They accordingly employed their utmost diligence for nine or ten days successively to weigh with the most anxious solicitude the whole of this most arduous, perplexing, and most painful subject. The result of their unanimous judgment was submitted to the King on Friday, in a long, reasoned Minute; and they had the following day the regret to receive from his Majesty, (though not unforeseen) also in a written Minute, the disapproval of that advice, with a distinct intimation that, if they were not prepared to advise his Majesty to proceed by way of divorce, his determination was taken, namely, to change his Government; and if he could not form a Government which would relieve him *to that extent*, his Majesty's intention was to retire to Hanover.

I may here mention that the advice of the Cabinet did not go that length, at least, not as a *first measure*. In advising that the measure of divorce should not be originated by Government, they did not preclude themselves from proposing that measure, in the event of the Queen and her advisers provoking a Parliamentary inquiry, and the production of evidence becoming thereby necessary; but they deemed it advisable, in the first instance, to bend their course to such a proceeding as it might be competent for Parliament to *take up on the public notoriety of the Queen's conduct*, and the established separation long subsisting. This, in their judgment, would include omitting her name in the Litany, avowedly denying her the honour of coronation, and making her pecuniary provision wholly contingent upon her perpetual residence abroad, in the mode and in the scale of granting which they conceived terms might be made with the Queen, by which she might agree to lay aside the title of Queen of England, and to abstain from the exercise of such of the few legal privileges belonging to a Queen Consort which could by possibility give umbrage (even during her exclusion) to the King. In short, their object was substantially to deliver the King from all personal annoyance from this infamous woman, to stamp upon her conduct the stain which the voice of Europe affixes to it, but to avoid volunteering, on the part of the King, the scandal and the dangers of a public trial in these factious times. If forced upon them, the reproach would rest with their adversaries; and it would be for them to draw, for the King, from the calamity of an hostile inquiry, whatever further measures of relief the temper of Parliament and of the country would afford a prospect of their being enabled to attain.

Such was the outline of our views, which the many past conversations we have had will enable you to appreciate. The King's feelings that nothing but divorce would satisfy his

honour, you will also well understand.   In this position matters now stand; and, although we have to submit such observations as occur to us upon the King's note, I consider the
Government as virtually dissolved, and that the existing
Ministers only hold their situations till their successors are
named.

I need not say how deeply I have felt for the King's anxiety
upon this occasion, and how much I deplore the view his Majesty has taken of what is due to his own honour, in contrast
with what his servants have felt to be prudentially due to his
interests and those of the monarchy; but, having done our
duty, we must leave the rest to Providence, and hope, on this
as on so many other occasions, it will vouchsafe to us its
protection.

I am afraid, amongst other distressing considerations, the
inconvenience of an unexpected and *hurried* journey to Lady
Stewart may press upon you.   I forgot to mention, at the
outset of my letter, that the King said that he looked to your
return to Vienna, but that your presence here was *now* essential
to his service.   You have now the whole before you, to arrange
for the best, and I earnestly trust your wife's health will be
fully considered, and may be saved from serious hazard.

This, of course, puts an end to the pleasure I should have
had in officially talking over in this country with Prince Metternich all our future plans for settling and keeping the world
at peace.   I should have had very peculiar pleasure in seeing
him in England, not only to endeavour to return all the personal attentions which I have received from him when on the
Continent, but I should have proposed to myself the utmost
possible advantage from endeavouring to explain to him, *on
the spot*, the many peculiarities which in this country must be
attended to, in the management of certain points of foreign
politics.   I am satisfied that, in a few days of personal intercourse here, we should so thoroughly have understood each
other, that our correspondence, for some time at least, would

be nothing more than a detail of events. Although it will not belong to me to convey to his Highness a repetition of the pleasure with which the King would undoubtedly see him visit England, yet I shall still indulge the hope that, as a *Kentish farmer*, I may have the gratification of receiving him, and of talking over with him those past concerns in which we have both felt so deep an interest. Remember me in the kindest manner to the Prince, and assure him of the satisfaction with which I learn that he is about to close the transactions at Vienna in a spirit of concord, which will in it itself do much to avert mischief and to create strength. These once closed, he may possibly find time to be the bearer in person of the Emperor's congratulations to the King on his accession.

Lord Clancarty to Lord Castlereagh.

The Hague, February 25, 1820.

My dear Lord—I am greatly obliged to you for your letter of the 20th; it relieved me from much anxiety. Rumours, supported by late editions of some of the English newspapers of the 15th, have been afloat here since Sunday last, proclaiming changes of Administration; these I was the more inclined to credit, from knowing the probability of the very questions arising on which the changes were made to rest; and the consequent anxiety was only dissipated by the arrival of yours which reached me yesterday morning.

Whether the late political position to which your letter refers extended to the contemplation of a total change, or only of one in which you were immediately concerned, I am to this moment ignorant: some of the accounts might be said more to support the former, others the latter of these conclusions. Neither does your letter otherwise throw light upon this matter than by seeming to strengthen the second alternative. However this may be, or however desirous I may feel, as a point of history, to be acquainted with the fact, I hope you cannot imagine that any part of the anxiety experienced by me during the interval alluded to, could have arisen from the slightest doubt or hesitation as to what would be the course of my own conduct in either case; or that, after having (how unprofitably to you, although sensibly felt, need not be stated) derived every political advantage which I enjoy immediately from your friendship, with the addition thereto of some and no very mean degree of public consideration, I should now, at an advanced time of life, be guilty of the folly of absolutely sacrificing this last by separating my political interests from those *of my Chief*, and this for the miserable and precarious gratification of perhaps a few months' longer enjoyment of an office, deprived as it then would be, in the case supposed, of its principal attraction.

I have been led into this rhapsody, if you will, by an expression in your letter which I would fain wish to think unguarded, viz, that, during the late crisis, you considered yourself only *as my Chief ad interim* ; as if you would not still have continued *my Chief* equally out of as in power ; or, as if, after having gone through now somewhat a long course of political life under *your Chieftainship*, reaping every possible benefit, far, very far, beyond expectation, from a connexion, the advantages of which, moreover, were all on one side, I could now consent, except, indeed, *ad interim*, to act under any other Chief. But enough of this.

Thanks for the early dissolution of Parliament—this is well done. Martin has some time since written to ask from me my support in Galway, and, conceiving that, as *your right-hand man*, he had merited it, I wrote to assure him of it, unless Daly's interests should be attacked thereby, or some immediate connexion of my own should propose himself. I hope and believe there will be no contest in that county, the disturbed state of which, I am sorry to say, is dreadful. Something you must do for us immediately on the assembly of the new Parliament, in order that Ireland may at length have a Government, and the lives and properties of his Majesty's subjects there be protected.   I conceive the first step must be the re-enactment of the Insurrection Act.

I read to Nagell the last paragraph of your letter concerning the special message, and the King's *éloge* on Baron Fagel: he chuckled much at finding his opinions confirmed by yours and by the practice of our Court, and was much pleased at his Majesty's condescending expressions in favour of Fagel.

Adieu.   Yours ever most affectionately,

CLANCARTY.

Mr. Rose to Lord Castlereagh.

Berlin, March 4, 1820.

My dear Lord—Immediately on the receipt of your letter, I proceeded to act on the directions it contained respecting a mission of compliment, and I hope you will not disapprove the course I followed.   Had my situation been that which is usually the relation of a foreign Minister towards the Minister for Foreign Affairs, I should have probably been able first to ascertain whether it was the spontaneous intention of this Court to send a mission of compliment to his Majesty on his accession, from the Minister himself; but here, whilst the intercourse of the Foreign Ministers is now with M. Ancillon, all determinations as to missions and as to persons to fill them remain with Prince Hardenberg.   Now, the previous knowledge I wished to gain could have here been only obtained by demanding a formal conference, with every probability of his hearing me indistinctly and remembering what I said inaccurately.

I therefore thought it best, as I can depend upon M. Ancillon's honour and perfect good-will, to tell him precisely how the matter stands, and I used precisely the words of your letter, than which none can be used more impossible to be understood incorrectly; and I repeated them twice, so that he knows distinctly that, as it is not the practice of the Court of St. James's to send missions of compliment, it neither claims nor, indeed, expects that any should be sent to it. He entirely entered into my situation with respect to Prince Hardenberg in this matter, understanding it completely. We agreed, therefore, that he should see the Prince, and learn of him whether it is his intention to recommend to the King to send a mission of compliment, apprising him at the same time, as if of his own knowledge, of the practice of our Court. He thought that the Prince, in this state of things, would certainly determine that no such mission should be sent, and then he was to drop the subject; but if, contrary to his expectation, he learnt that the Prince, knowing our practice, did mean to advise such a mission, he was then to intimate the particular satisfaction his Majesty would have in seeing General Count Tauenzien charged with it. He told me he knew the King of Prussia had said he was aware it was not the usage of our Court to send complimentary missions. I impressed strongly upon his mind the necessity of his following most precisely the line agreed upon between us.

I received this morning from M. Ancillon a note, of which the enclosed is a copy: as I was answering it, I received from Prince Hardenberg a private letter of which I enclose an extract, which is the only part of it referring to the matter in question; and this afternoon Count Tauenzien called upon me, having been summoned to dine with the Prince, who then informed him of his Sovereign's intentions. I took care to apprise him of his Majesty's feelings towards him, and his views in his favour in this matter. He is gratified and delighted beyond measure, and flattered, as he ought to be, by so strong a proof his Majesty's good-will. I find from Count Tauenzien that this Court is aware that Prince Philip of Hesse-Homburg will be sent to compliment his Majesty by the Emperor of Austria.

One word as to the leave of absence you have kindly procured for me, that I may not seem capricious or inconsistent in not using it now. Essential law business and arrangements in

my affairs made it very important for me to be in England for
a short time this year ; but, on the demise of his late Majesty,
I thought I could have arrived at the end of the session, so as
to be sworn in anew as Clerk of the Parliament, (which is indispensable) and then have gone down to stand at Christchurch at the dissolution.   But, not getting my leave till the
1st, the proposed day of the dissolution, I cannot be sworn in
until the end of April, when Parliament will first begin to sit.
Setting off now, I should scarcely have reached Christchurch
in time ; but had I, I could not in conscience have remained
several weeks in England, until sworn in in the House of
Lords : and, if I do not get sworn in then, an object of vital
importance is lost.   I therefore propose, with your leave, to
quit Berlin about the middle of April, so as to reach London
when Parliament meets.

I find that, when Prince Hardenberg proposed to his Sovereign that a mission should be sent to compliment his Majesty,
he assented to it instantly, saying that he had already thought
of it ; and the moment Prince Hardenberg suggested the
appointment of Count Tauenzien, he agreed to it with the
utmost readiness.

I am, my dear Lord, &c.,   G. H. ROSE.

[Enclosures.]
Copy of a private Letter from M. Ancillon to Mr. Rose.
Berlin, le 3 Mars, 1820.

Je m'empresse, Monsieur, à vous annoncer qu'à la suite de
la conversation que j'ai eu l'honneur d'avoir hier avec le Prince
de Hardenberg, sa Majesté a résolu d'envoyer un personnage
de distinction pour porter des complimens au Roi votre maître,
et que son choix est tombé sur le Comte Tauenzien. Le Prince
se fait fête de vous l'annoncer lui-même ; ainsi je vous prie de
me garder le secret. Si j'ai pu contribuer à faire prendre à
cette affaire la tournure desirée je m'en félicite pour la Prusse
et la Grande Bretagne ; car tout ce qui tend à resserrer et à

constater l'union de nos Souverains ne peut que contribuer au
bonheur reciproque des deux États et des deux Princes.

Agréez l'assurance, &c.,　　ANCILLON.

*Extract of a private Letter from Prince Hardenberg to Mr.
Rose, dated March 3, 1820.*

Je me fais un plaisir de vous prévenir, Monsieur, que le Roi
va envoyer en Angleterre, M. le Général Comte de Tauenzien,
pour complimenter sa Majesté, votre auguste Souverain, sur
son avènement au trône. Ce Général aura l'honneur de s'annoncer chez vous, pour faire toutes les commissions dont vous
voudrez bien le charger.

Prince Metternich to Lord Castlereagh.

Vienne, ce 7 Mars, 1820.

Je profite de l'envoye d'un courrier de Mylord Stewart,
mon cher Lord, pour faire passer à M. le Prince Esterhazy
une dépêche de laquelle il reçoit l'ordre de ne faire qu'un usage
confidentiel vis-à-vis de vous. J'y ai consigné une partie de
nos vœux dans un moment de crise très imminent. Ne croyez
pas, Mylord, que nous voyons plus en noir que les circonstances ne l'exigent impérieusement; ne croyez surtout pas
que nous admettions la possibilité qu'il pourroit exister un
moyen matériel quelconque d'influence de la part de l'étranger
sur la France, qui ne seroit pas condamné par nous comme
positivement dangereux. Mais il ne faut pas se cacher que le
sort de ce pays est placé hors de la possibilité d'être calculé;
et c'est ce fait que nous regardons comme le pire de tous. Les
maladies aigues sont préférables, en politique comme pour les
individus, aux maladies de langueur enracinées.

Ce que je vous demande est ce qui de tous tems eut du
exister—l'uniformité la plus entière de la marche de nos représentans à Paris. Voulez-vous qu'ils parlent? Eh bien, que
ce soit d'une manière uniforme : voulez-vous qu'ils se taisent?
Que tous se taisent.

Il est peu de points sur lesquels il soit plus facile de juger

des dangers dont est menacé la dynastie royale en France que
tout juste du point de Vienne. Le Bonapartisme se couvre
vis à vis de nous d'un voile infiniment plus léger que vis à vis
de tout autre. Le fait est simple, mais plus il est tel, plus il
est dans le cours des choses naturel que nous devons être les
plus directement appelés à avertir nos amis.

Le but de ma dépêche, mon cher Lord, n'est au reste autre
que de nous orienter sur ce qui est possible et sur ce qui ne
l'est pas. Croyez que nous connoissons assez les positions
pour savoir que tout ce qui est désirable n'est pas toujours
possible. Ce qui toutefois l'est toujours c'est de voir clair, afin
de pouvoir calculer et les chances de danger et les mesures
de précaution qu'il est dans le devoir de tout grand État de
prendre pour son propre salut.

Je charge le Prince Esterhazy de ne communiquer à votre
Cabinet que mes dépêches à Paris.

Lord Stewart a bien voulu m'informer du bonheur que j'ai
eu de voir considérer le Roi l'opinion que je vous avois énoncé
à Aix-la-Chapelle et à Bruxelles, sur l'un de ses intérêts les
plus directs et les plus chers, comme venant de la part d'un
homme sincèrement dévoué à sa personne et à sa gloire. J'ai
le sentiment du mal qu'auroit fait à tous les trônes le scanda-
leux procès en divorce à un point qui me fait un devoir de vous
féliciter sincèrement sur le succès que vous avez remporté.
Vous êtes demeuré ferme sur une thèse indubitable, et que
l'expérience n'eut pas manqué de prouver telle. Dans un État
bien organisé, les grandes vérités finissent toujours par rem-
porter le triomphe.

Je vous prie au reste, mon cher Lord, de croire que la seule
récompense que j'ambitionne pour ma vie très laborieuse est de
pouvoir marquer les époques qui prouvent que les principes
que je me fais gloire et honneur de défendre ne sont point
perdus pour le bien général.

Veuillez agréer les assurances de ma sincère amitié et de ma
plus véritable et haute considération.

                                        METTERNICH.

————————

Sir Henry Wellesley to Lord Castlereagh.

Madrid, March 13, 1820.

My dear Lord—As no event that happens in this capital is ever truly represented, it is not impossible that exaggerated reports may be sent to England relative to the threat of the populace to search my house, for the purpose of ascertaining whether or not the Duke of Wellington was concealed in it. I have, therefore, thought it advisable to inform your lordship of what passed in a private letter.

I believe that the circumstance which gave rise to this most absurd report was my having, on the 6th instant, received a letter from Barcelona by the general post, addressed to " Sir Henry Wellesley, Duque de Ciudad Rodrigo." This was stated on the following evening in a coffee-house, when the public mind was considerably agitated; and the reporter added, that he knew to a positive certainty that the Duke of Wellington was at that moment in my house, and that 30,000 British troops were upon the Portuguese frontier, ready to enter Spain at a moment's warning, and to take part with the King against the Constitution. A motion was immediately made for proceeding with the mob to my house, and they were actually on the way to it, when one or two persons, who knew me and were aware of the absurdity of the report, turned the attention of the mob to the prisoners in the Inquisition, and succeeded in leading them to that prison. Several other attempts were made on the following days to excite the mob to assemble before my house, but without effect, but the Duke of San Fernando has since informed me that he had so much reason to believe that my house was to be attacked, that he had had thoughts of sending a guard to protect it. I am extremely glad that he did not take this step, being convinced that, if the mob had been excited to assemble in the street where I live, they would have dispersed without committing any outrage. I am the more confirmed in this conviction, because, during the prevalence of these reports, I walked about the town as usual, without having experienced the slightest insult from the mob.

With respect to public affairs, I have nothing to add to my despatches of this day's date. The city is now tranquil, and, if its tranquillity is not disturbed before the meeting of the Cortes, I trust that assembly will make the necessary alterations in the Constitution. This appears to be the general wish; and I trust that nothing will happen to prevent its accomplishment.

I have the honour to be, &c.,   H. WELLESLEY.

Sir Henry Wellesley to Lord Castlereagh.

Madrid, March 20, 1820.

My dear Lord—I am extremely sorry for the recall of the Duke of San Carlos from London; but he was so much concerned in advising the King, upon his restoration, to decline accepting the Constitution, that any application on my part, with a view to his being allowed to continue in England in a public capacity would be useless, if not injurious to him. The Duke de Frias was appointed last night, and called upon me this morning to announce his appointment. He informed me that he had been introduced to your lordship at Paris.

I am, with great truth and respect, &c.,

H. WELLESLEY.

Sir Charles Stuart to Lord Castlereagh.

Paris, March 30, 1820.

My dear Lord—Your lordship's private note of the 18th of March renders it necessary for me to explain the grounds of the allusion contained in Monsieur de Talleyrand's message shortly after the late change of Ministry.

Your lordship will probably recollect the Duke de Richelieu was named to compliment his Majesty upon his accession to the throne, some time before the assassination of the Duke de

Berri, at a time the state of his Majesty's health would not have permitted the reception of that Minister as could be wished. I therefore received directions to express the satisfaction with which his Majesty had learned the selection of M. de Richelieu to execute such a service, and at the same time to hint the expediency of delaying his journey, until the King's recovery should be sufficiently advanced to enable his Majesty to hold a Court.

Having no reason to conceal the nature of this communication, the cause for delaying the Duke de Richelieu's departure was generally known at the time when the assassination of the Duke de Berri gave rise to the movement in the Cabinet, which terminated in the change of Ministry; and, as Monsieur de Cazes informed me, it was some time doubtful whether Prince Talleyrand or the Duke de Richelieu would be placed at the head of the new Administration.

The message contained in my private letter shows that the former attributed this disappointment and failure of his endeavours to regain his old seat in the Cabinet to my interference, which, by preventing the departure of the Duke de Richelieu upon the day he proposed, may have been the cause of that Minister's nomination to the Presidency of the Council.

Believe me, my dear lord, &c.,

CHARLES STUART.

Prince Hardenberg to Lord Castlereagh.

Berlin, le 31 Mars, 1820.

Mylord—Accoutumé par vos bontés à une confiance illimitée et sachant par de nombreuses expériences que vous rendez justice à la pureté de mes intentions, qui ne visent qu'à notre but commun de cimenter de plus en plus, pour le bonheur de l'Europe, l'union entre les puissances Alliées, et particulièrement entre l'Angleterre et la Prusse; bien persuadé que vous ne m'accuserez pas, Mylord, de la présomption de vouloir vous donner des conseils, je n'hésite pas de vous com-

muniquer une dépêche du Comte Golz à Paris, concernant le
Ministre de votre Cour, en vous abandonnant le prix que vous
voudrez y attacher.

Les évenemens arrivés en Espagne peuvent amener de
grands dangers pour le repos de l'Europe. L'exemple d'une
armée faisant une révolution est infiniment funeste. La Cour
de Pétersbourg, quoiqu'ignorant, encore l'effet de l'insurrection,
a cru nécessaire qu'on se concertât sur les mesures qui pourroient être prises d'un commun accord, en y faisant concourir
la France, qui, sans doute, y est doublement intéressée. Elle
propose de faire servir à cet effet les conférences subsistant
toujours à Paris, pour la médiation entre l'Espagne et le Portugal. Je crois cette idée fort sage. Nous serons prêts à
nous concerter sur toute mesure utile. En attendant je crois
que le Roi s'empressera de renvoyer son Ministre le Baron
de Werther à Madrid. Il n'a été jusqu'ici qu'absent par
congé.

Nous avons toujours l'espoir de voir les affaires de France
prendre une bonne tournure, pourvu que l'exemple de l'Espagne
n'y influe pas en mal. Louis XIV. disoit, il n'y a plus des
Pyrénées. Il seroit à desirer qu'elles fussent maintenant une
barrière impassable.

Agréez vous, Mylord et Mylady Castlereagh, tous mes
hommages, et ne doutez jamais de mon attachement et de
la haute considération avec laquelle je ne cesserai d'être de
votre Excellence le très humble, très obéissant, et très devoué
Serviteur,

HARDENBERG.

Berlin, le 31 Mars, 1820.

Dans cet instant, Mylord, je reçois des dépêches de Paris
du 25 qui me portent à faire un PS. à ma lettre. Si je pouvois
avoir moins de confiance dans votre façon de penser, Mylord,
je devrois m'en abstenir; mais la haute estime que j'ai pour
vous me décide sans hésiter. L'on a cru à Madrid que Sir

Henry Wellesley n'avoit pas été étranger à la révolution : on s'est permis même en accuser le Cabinet Britannique à Paris, où on a eu des inquiétudes à cet égard, que les propos de Sir Charles Stuart ont beaucoup augmenté,· surtout la mesure qu'il a pris d'envoyer avec la plus grande hâte un courrier à son collegue à Madrid, afin de l'avertir de l'envoi résolu de M. de la Tour du Pin, contre lequel il s'étoit déclaré. On en inféroit des doutes sur la politique de la Cour de Londres ; et craignoit un changement de système contraire à l'étroite union des Alliés. On étoit alarmé. Je suis loin de partager cette opinion, Mylord ; tout ce que nous savons s'y oppose. En attendant la mission de M. de la Tour du Pin a été suspendue.

Veuillez agréer l'assurance renouvellée de tout mon attachement.

HARDENBERG.

La fermentation étoit très grande à Paris.

[Enclosure.]

Copie d'une Dépêche du Comte de Goltz, en date de Paris le 18 Mars, 1820.

J'ai eu l'honneur de recevoir le rescrit No. 10, que le Ministère de votre Majesté m'a adressé en date du 11 de ce mois.

Les malheureux évènemens en Espagne ont fait ici une très grande sensation. Votre Majesté daignera voir, par les journaux soi-disant libéraux d'hier et d'aujourd'hui, avec quelle avidité ils exploitent cette nouvelle mine féconde, pour exciter les méfiances et les alarmes, et pour regagner par cette tactique révolutionnaire ce qu'ils ont perdu déjà et ce qu'ils sont menacés de perdre encore par les décisions des deux chambres. Les Ministres François éprouvoient naturellement déjà de grandes inquiétudes à l'arrivée des nouvelles dont j'ai eu l'honneur de faire mention dans mon rapport No.14, mais ils étoient, comme tout le monde, loin de s'attendre au funeste parti que le Roi

d'Espagne a cru devoir prendre, de se laisser imposer de force
la constitution des Cortès de 1812. Le Baron Pasquier pré-
suma, ainsi que le Duc de Richelieu, qu'une convocation des
anciens Cortès du royaume pourroit bien avoir lieu et il con-
sidéra cette mesure déjà comme très dangereuse. Dans une
conversation qu'il eut dimanche passé avec moi sur cet objet il
me dit entre autre, que le Roi d'Espagne, aveuglé sur les conséquences d'un mécontentement de l'armée et du désordre
excessif dans les finances, avoit perdu son tems et laissé ac-
croître le mal jusqu'au plus haut degré, sans songer seulement
à y apporter aucune espèce de remède ; qu'aucun souverain de
l'Europe n'auroit pu trouver dans les mœurs et les habitudes
de ses sujets et dans la division territoriale de son royaume
autant de facilités que lui à établir une Constitution d'États
provinciaux, qui eut pu suffire aux besoins du Gouvernement et
de la nation Espagnole sans pouvoir devenir dangereuse pour
le trône ; mais que croyant toujours, comme il me l'avoit dit
l'année passée déjà relativement à la Prusse, que toute grande
assemblée, réunie sur un seul point pour délibérer sur les
intérêts d'une nation entière, pouvoit se dénaturer pour le
choc des opinions et des passions et produire souvent, contre
toute attente même, les résultats les plus funestes, il craignoit
même que les anciens Cortès quoique composés des trois ordres,
ne dégénérassent, s'ils étoient convoqués dans les circonstances
présentes en nouveaux Cortès ou du moins en une Assemblée
Constituante, qui ne laisseroit plus l'initiative au Roi, et qu'il
étoit au reste d'avis qu'un Souverain qui avoit des motifs
suffisans pour devoir admettre la possibilité d'être forcé par
un commencement de révolution *d'accepter* une Constitution
démocratique devoit se garder de perdre le moment d'en
donner une monarchique. Celle des Cortès de 1812, dont je
joins, dans la supposition qu'elle pourroit ne pas être sous
les yeux de votre Majesté un exemplaire à ce rapport, est
non-seulement plus démocratique qu'aucune de toutes celles
qui ont existées jusqu'ici, même dans les républiques, mais

aussi tellement incohérente et contraire à tous les principes
d'ordre et de stabilité, qu'on ne conçoit pas même comment
elle seroit à mettre, pendant un court espace de tems seulement, à exécution.

Il est malheureux de ne pouvoir nier que cet épouvantable
état des choses auroit pu être prévenu en Espagne bien plus
facilement que dans aucun autre pays, si sa Majesté Catho-
lique, toujours mal-conseillée, n'avoit pas fait pendant six ans
fautes sur fautes, tant dans l'administration intérieure de son
royaume, que dans toutes ses négociations.   Mais il me paroit
que ce souverain n'a pas prévu même toutes les conséquences
de la plus grande des fautes qu'il vient de faire à mon avis.   Je
crois qu'il valoit mieux s'exposer à tout que de se soumettre,
sans restriction et sans exiger même aucune délibération pré-
alable, à l'acceptation d'une Constitution aussi contraire à la
liberté et au bonheur du peuple qu'à l'intérêt et à la dignité
du trône.   Une abdication motivée et conditionelle, pour le
cas qu'un appel à la nation fut resté sans effet, m'auroit même
paru devoir être préféré à un acte, qui ne ressemble que trop
d'ailleurs à une déchéance formelle.   En voici les résultats
probables, suivant mon opinion.

La lutte entre les intérêts des différentes classes de la nation
va s'établir en Espagne, comme elle l'est malheureusement en
France, par suite de la révolution.   Le Roi se trouvera dans la
situation de devoir non-seulement pardonner, mais même ré-
compenser ceux qui l'ont trahi.   En attendant les élections et
la réunion des nouveaux Cortès, le Souverain se verra gou-
verné complètement par les chefs militaires de la révolte.
L'armée, sous ces chefs, élevant ses prétentions en proportion
des grands services qu'elle prétendra avoir rendus à la patrie,
ne sera pas plus satisfaite de ce que les Cortès pourront ou
voudront faire pour elle que de son existence antérieure.   Elle
se prononcera bientôt alors contre les Cortès, qui, portant dans
leur sein déjà tous les germes de la discorde, livreront enfin
l'Espagne à l'anarchie et au despotisme militaire.

Si l'on ne pouvoit pas craindre l'effet d'un aussi funeste exemple sur un pays comme la France, j'aurois maintenant plus d'espoir que je n'en avois depuis plus d'un an que le repos pourroit enfin se rétablir et la Constitution se consolider dans ce pays.   Le Gouvernement a pris une attitude plus forte, une majorité qui ne peut devenir envahissante des pouvoirs constitutées s'est formée dans les deux Chambres, pour le soutenir.   Les Ministres sont unis et marchent dans le même sens.   Le Duc de Richelieu se livre avec zèle et sans faire paroître de l'inquiétude à ses importantes fonctions.   Je sais que le Baron Pasquier a dit ces jours derniers de lui, qu'il ne le reconnoissoit pas ; qu'il n'étoit plus le même homme ; qu'il remplissoit ses devoirs avec autant de courage que d'activité ; qu'il alloit d'un de ses collègues chez l'autre pour s'entretenir avec eux de tout ce qui lui paroissoit être de quelque importance et qu'il s'occupoit particulièrement avec le Ministre de la guerre des moyens de donner un bon esprit à l'armée et d'empêcher surtout qu'il ne devienne plus mauvais qu'il n'est. Sous ce rapport, on n'est pas également content de tous les régimens, et la cause doit en être attribuée à la loi de recrutement et à la grande quantité d'officiers à demi-solde que le Maréchal Gouvion St. Cyr, signant de confiance la plupart des dispositions que lui présentèrent ses chefs de bureau, y a fait entrer dans les derniers tems.   Mais on est assez satisfait en général, et toute la garde royale, en particulier, continue à se montrer parfaitement bien, peut-être même un peu trop animée contre les prétendus libéraux.

La loi sur les journaux sera adoptée, selon toutes les apparences, par une plus forte majorité que ne l'étoit celle sur la liberté individuelle.   Le Sieur Froc de la Boulaye a fait, dans la séance du 16, au nom de la commission, nommée pour l'examen de la première de ces lois, un rapport très favorable, par lequel son adoption sans amendemens a été proposée.   Cette même séance a été remarquable par les explications loyales et satisfaisantes que le Général Foy a données sur la sortie

violente qu'il sembloit avoir faite, dans la séance du 13, contre
tous les ci-devant émigrés François et à laquelle M. de Corday,
oncle de la fameuse Charlotte Corday, n'avoit pu s'empêcher de
répondre par une insulte personnelle. Le duel qui a précédé
cette explication n'avoit eu d'ailleurs aucun résultât fâcheux,
puisque, le sort ayant donnée au Général Foy l'avantage de
tirer le premier, il a tiré en l'air, et son adversaire alors a
renoncé au droit de faire feu à son tour. Le Général Foy
n'avoit été excité que par les astucieuses observations que le
Sieur B. Constant, véritable serpent dans la Chambre des
Députés, avoit cru devoir faire. Ce Général est très vif et
facilement emporté, mais comme il n'est pas d'un méchant
caractère et qu'il a des moyens, le Ministère avoit même
espéré de le détacher des hommes du côté gauche qui se sont
emparés de lui. C'étoit probablement un motif de plus aux
yeux du Sieur Constant pour tâcher de le compromettre avec
le côté droit. Quoiqu'on puisse se féliciter du bon dénoue-
ment de cette affaire, on ne sauroit toutefois assez déplorer le
ton de fureur par lequel les orateurs du côté gauche enveniment
en général déjà les discussions d'une assemblée délibérative.
Les meneurs de ce parti, voyant que leurs efforts pour le rejet
des lois proposées sont inutiles, paroissent, en s'exprimant
ainsi, n'avoir d'autre but que de produire un fâcheux effet en
dehors de la chambre, et de traîner les discussions en longueur
pour profiter aussi longtems que possible de la licence de la
presse. Celle-ci a fait malheureusement déjà, depuis la promulgation de la loi encore existante un mal inoui ; mais il faut
arrêter au moins ce mal et voir si l'on pourra empêcher encore que le venin déjà répandu ne produise un trop funeste
effet.

Il n'y a guère que le Vicomte de Chateaubriand et deux ou
trois autres écrivains royalistes qui ont assez d'amour propre
pour croire que leurs écrits, quoiqu'ils aient fourni évidemment
à leurs adversaires tant de prétextes et de motifs pour attribuer
aux royalistes de mauvaises arrière-pensées, ont produit un

bien infini. L'état des choses devroit, dans ce cas au moins, ne pas être vingt fois pire qu'il n'étoit avant la liberté de la presse. Mais l'auteur sus nommé est tellement aveuglé sur ce point, qu'il a même cru devoir voter dans la Chambre des Pairs contre la nouvelle loi sur les journaux, tandis qu'un républicain, M. Gallatin, Ministre des Etats Unis d'Amérique, qui passe avec raison ici pour une des meilleurs têtes politiques, n'hésite pas de dire qu'il croit l'établissement d'un gouvernement absolu ou représentatif, légitime ou illégitime, en France, incompatible avec la liberté illimitée de la presse. La discussion sur le projet de loi y relatif commencera Mardi prochain dans la Chambre des Députés. Une très bonne proposition du Sieur Maine de Biran a été développée et prise en considération dans la séance du 16, qui tend à régulariser le droit de petition. Ces développemens vont être examinées préalablement, comme de coutume dans les bureaux. Le Sieur Benoist a fait hier la lecture d'un des deux rapports de la commission chargée de l'examen des comptes antérieurs à 1819. Ses conclusions tendent à l'adoption pure et simple de la loi. Mais le second de ces rapports ne sera entendu que Lundi prochain et c'est dans cette séance aussi que la Chambre entendra un rapport sur la proposition du Sieur B. Constant relative à un nouveau mode du scrutin. Le Ministre de l'intérieur a présenté hier à la Chambre des Pairs le projet de loi, adopté par la Chambre des Députés, sur la liberté individuelle.

J'ai cru devoir me rendre, quelques jours après l'arrivée du rescrit No. 9, du 4 de ce mois, chez le Duc de Richelieu pour lui dire, tout ce que ce rescrit renferme d'agréable pour lui. Il a été extrèmement sensible, et, après m'avoir prié d'en témoigner sa profonde reconnoissance à votre Majesté, il fit la remarque qu'il désiroit que les cours étrangères voulussent cependant bien avoir en considération des grandes difficultés qu'elles ne pouvoient méconnoître, quelque indulgence pour lui. Il m'a montré au reste de nouveau à cette occasion le courage d'esprit si necessaire à un homme d'état dans les graves circonstances actuelles, en me disant entr'autre que la lutte étoit établie entre le génie du bien et le génie du mal ; qu'elle étoit trop grande et trop importante pour qu'il n'ait du renoncer à l'idée et au désir de mener une vie tranquille ; qu'il ne pouvoit prévoir le résultat de ses efforts, mais qu'il se croiroit le plus heureux des hommes s'il pouvoit attacher son nom au rétablissement du repos et du bonheur de sa patrie, et qu'il étoit fermement résolu de rester au poste où le Roi et de malheureuses conjonctures l'avoient placé, jusqu'à ce que le vaisseau de l'état seroit à flot ou qu'il seroit submergé avec lui.

Au sujet des plénipotentiaires des cours étrangères il me dit encore, que nous ne pourrions mieux aider le Gouvernement François qu'en n'en ayant pas l'air, parceque, la nation Françoise étant la plus vaniteuse du monde, tout prétexte trouvé pour faire croire à une influence étrangère ne pourroit que nuire à la marche du Ministère. Je lui répondis que je n'avois eu que trop d'occasion de remarquer le mal que l'on a su faire, en attribuant une grande influence personnelle à l'un ou l'autre des Ministres étrangers, et que toute ma conduite depuis six ans devoit lui avoir montré combien je partageois son opinion sous ce rapport. Il répliqua bien vîte, que ce qu'il me disoit ne m'étoit aussi nullement applicable, et que personne ne savoit mieux apprécier que lui la sagesse et la prudence avec lesquelles le Baron de Vincent et moi nous étions constamment conduits. J'ai vu dans cet entretien, qui rouloit encore sur des objets moins intéressans, que le Duc de Richelieu, sans supposer que le Duc de Cazes puisse un jour rentrer dans le Ministère, le regarde cependant toujours comme un obstacle à une marche plus assurée et à une attitude égale du Gouvernement François, particulièrement vis-à-vis des quatre Cours Alliées. Il m'a dit qu'il avoit vu la lettre que le Roi actuel d'Angleterre a écrite de main propre au Roi de France, pour l'assurer de tout le plaisir qu'il éprouvoit de le

recevoir comme Ambassadeur à sa Cour, et que cette lettre
contenoit entre autre même la phrase extraordinaire, "qu'il le
recevroit non-seulement avec bienveillance mais même avec
cordialité."

Je me suis aperçu malheureusement aussi que j'ai eu trop
bonne opinion des réflexions que Sir Charles Stuart sembloit
avoir faites sur sa position relative aux circonstances présentes.
J'ai appris de plusieurs côtés qu'il se prononce de nouveau, ne
fut-ce même quelque fois qu'en haussant les épaules, contre le
Ministère et le système qu'il a adopté ; et me trouvant, avant
hier au soir, lorsque les dernières mauvaises nouvelles d'Espagne
venoient d'arriver, chez le Duc de Richelieu, ce Ministre me prit
par le bras et, en s'eloignant avec moi de la société, il me dit,
"Pouvez vous vous faire une idée de l'inconcevable conduite de
Sir Charles Stuart ! Il semble non-seulement apprendre avec
un certain plaisir les plus malheureux évènemens, mais il vient
de l'air le plus indifférent me dire même tout à l'heure, à moi,
Ministre d'un Roi de la famille des Bourbons, qu'il étoit déjà
question à Madrid d'un changement de Gouvernement, et que
l'Archiduc Charles devoit être appelé au trône d'Espagne."
Le Duc de Richelieu ajouta que la nouvelle étoit évidemment
fausse, puisque les lettres de l'Ambassadeur d'Angleterre
n'étoient aussi que du 8 et qu'il auroit été impossible de
penser à Madrid le jour même où l'acceptation de la Constitution fût publiée, à un changement de Gouvernement ; qu'il
devoit par conséquent supposer que l'Ambassadeur n'avoit
voulu que jouir du plaisir de lui causer du chagrin. J'ai
tâché de calmer le Duc de Richelieu sur son sujet ; mais
j'avoue que si j'ai toujours considéré la présence de Sir Charles
Stuart à Paris, depuis le changement de Ministère de la fin de
1818 comme un très grand inconvénient, je la considère maintenant comme un véritable malheur. Un Ambassadeur qui
tient plus ou moins à l'opposition en Angleterre, et qui se
jette encore, de quelque manière que ce soit, dans une opposition qui menace l'existence même du Gouvernement auprès

duquel il est accrédité, ne peut que nuire à ce Gouvernement et à l'intérêt général. Le Général Pozzo nous avoit déjà parlé plusieurs fois dans ce sens, mais j'ai cru jusqu'ici qu'il exagéroit un peu, et que d'ailleurs, pour pouvoir continuer d'être modérateur entre lui et Sir Charles Stuart, il failloit ne pas donner trop d'importance à ce qu'il me disoit. Je crois cependant les circonstances présentes trop graves pour ne pas soumettre respectueusement l'opinion à votre Majesté que les liens de la Quadruple Alliance me paroissent un peu relâchés ; que les sentimens sur lesquels elle a été fondée sont bien les mêmes encore, mais que la direction uniforme qui lui donnoit tant de force a commencé a manquer déjà depuis 1818, et qu'il seroit nécessaire d'employer tous les moyens pour revenir aux principes de cette alliance et surtout à celui de sacrifier toutes les convenances particulières à l'intérêt général.

Pour ce qui concerne l'influence du Général Pozzo di Borgo sur les affaires intérieures de ce pays, elle est différente de celle qu'il exerçoit jusqu'à la fin de 1818. Ce n'est qu'une influence d'opinion sur le système et la marche du Gouvernement en général, que nous avons tous jusqu'à un certain point, suivant notre position personnelle et le degré de confiance que nous avons inspiré. Or, comme il est bien avec les royalistes depuis l'époque précitée, et qu'il tâche de contribuer à l'affermissement du trône légitime, cette influence, pourvu qu'il continue de la faire remarquer aussi peu que possible, ne pourra qu'être utile à la bonne cause. Consolider tous les Gouvernemens et maintenir la tranquillité publique, voilà à mon avis les grandes questions du moment. Celles-ci une fois résolues à la satisfaction de tout le monde, on aura assez de tems encore pour empêcher que des relations particulières entre cour et cour ne dérangent l'équilibre politique de l'Europe.

La Cour de France prendra Mardi prochain un deuil de 8 jours pour son Altesse Royale feu Madame la Princesse Ferdinand de Prusse.

Je suis, &c.

Mr. Ross to Lord Castlereagh.

Berlin, March 31, 1820.

My dear Lord—I had occasion to write not long since to
Count Bernstorf a private letter for a paper belonging to me.
In his answer of the 13th inst., after replying to the object, he
says, " Il me tarde de plus en plus, de vous revoir et de causer
avec vous. Je voudrais surtout pouvoir vous dire à quel point
j'apprécie les *renseignemens* que Lord Castlereagh nous a
rendus. Malgré la sagesse, malgré la délicatesse, malgré la
force de la logique, qu'il a mise dans sa réponse au Comte
Lieven, il n'a pu lui-même se douter de tout l'effet qu'aurait
cette excellente pièce pour le bien de notre cause. Je bénis la
Providence d'avoir détourné de lui le coup affreux, dont il a
été menacé de si près et dont la seule idée fait frémir."

When I saw Prince Hardenberg on the 25th inst., he put
into my hand General Count Goltz's despatch, containing
Spanish and French intelligence, referred to in my No. 32.
The Count states that the Duke of Richelieu had expressed to
him his anxious wish that the foreign Ministers should abstain
from expressing any opinions on French politics, whether
favourable or unfavourable to the Ministers. Count Goltz
assured him that he had always striven anxiously to avoid all
expression of opinions on these matters in public, and in any
manner that can attract attention. The Duke interrupted him
quickly to say that he knew that he and Baron Vincent had
uniformly abstained from so expressing themselves, and that
he did full justice to the prudence of their conduct in this
respect.

After this, and in a separate paragraph, the Count proceeds
to complain strongly of Sir Charles Stuart's conduct in marking his slight opinion of the King of France's Ministers, and
doing so publicly, shrugging up his shoulders when there is
mention made of measures of theirs; and he states an earnest
complaint made to him by the Duke of Richelieu of the matter

and manner of Sir Charles's observations on Spanish affairs, and of intelligence respecting them communicated by him, and which the Duke denies he can have received in a particular instance. The Count expresses his regret that the British Ambassador should be a man in opposition to his own Government.

When I had read this despatch, the Prince said he was much inclined to write to you a private letter on this matter, sending you an extract in it of Count Goltz's despatch, and that he wished to know whether I approved this idea. I said I did entirely—that Sir Charles Stuart is an old and valued friend of mine, of whose honour and understanding I have a high opinion—that his political connexions in England are with the Government mainly—that I could not speak positively to his present feelings on French affairs, nor could I answer for what might possibly be the effect of manner in the eyes of others—but that I could nowise take upon myself to discourage a communication to you, such as the Prince·was inclined to make—that the present system and state of Europe render it highly important that nothing in the conduct of any foreign Minister of any of the great Courts should tend to lead to the idea of a divergency of opinion on the part of his Court, or to division between him and his colleagues, or between him and the Ministers of the Court he is accredited to—and that, if this is generally true, it is more especially so at Paris—that, moreover, it is but justice to Sir Charles, and what is expedient for a useful discharge of his important functions, that he shall have the means of vindicating himself from this imputation.

I imagine the Prince will send you his letter by the opportunity by which I write, and which I announce to him, as he expressed his desire, in which I fully concurred, that this communication should be as secret as possible.

I was struck by the commendation given by the Duke of Richelieu to Count Goltz of his conduct, and Baron Vincent's, as implying that, if his Grace disapproves of Sir Charles Stuart's, on one hand, he is perceptibly inconvenienced by M. Pozzo di Borgo's on the other.

I am, &c.,   G. H. ROSE.

PS. Since writing this letter, I have received Prince Hardenberg's, which I add.

G. H. R.

And since a second.

G. H. R.

Mr. Ross to Lord Castlereagh.

Berlin, April 1, 1820.

My Lord—My despatches of this date are sent by a confidential person to the agent for his Majesty's packets at Cuxhaven.

Monsieur d'Alopeus has made communications to this Court on the affairs of Spain, by order of his Government, the same as those which, no doubt, Count Lieven will have to make to your lordship. M. d'Alopeus said to me that they are not applicable to the present state of that country, and that he has suggested here the expediency of a Conference being formed at Paris between the English Ambassador, the Russian, Prussian, and Austrian Envoys, and the French Ministers, to determine what conduct the great Powers should hold respecting those affairs.

Monsieur de Lobo has suggested to this Government that, with respect to Portugal, there are three dangers: that it may revolutionize itself, excited by the example of Spain and by Spanish emissaries; or that it may accept an invitation which Spain will be ready to make to it to attach itself to her as a separate kingdom, and of these two dangers he deems this far the greatest; or that Spain will attempt the conquest of Portugal; and he urges that the Allies shall call upon the Spanish Government to desist from all attempts that may compromise the independence or tranquillity of that kingdom.

The Marquis de Bonnay has apprised this Government that the King of France has sent M. de la Tour du Pin to Madrid to urge his nephew, the King of Spain, to obtain in the new Constitution amendments, such as are indispensable for carrying it into effect and for the honour and safety of his Crown. The Marquis observed that such representations will come more fitly and usefully from the King of France than from any other Sovereign; but that it will be highly desirable that his Ambassador, in his communications with the Spanish Government, of which the object will be to render the late revolution as little noxious as may be to the Crown and to the European system, shall be supported by the Ministers of the four Powers at Madrid.

I had a full conversation with M. Ancillon on these matters two days since. I found him decidedly of opinion that, whatever right in theory there may exist in other Powers to object to a Constitution fraught with revolutionary principles, like that adopted in Spain, it is perfectly impracticable to take such objections with any useful effect; neither France nor England, though for different reasons, can do so, and they are the only Powers that can come in contact with Spain; and I observed we could the less object to this Constitution, as it was formed during the time our armies were in Spain and expelling the French from her territory. With respect to the advice to be given to the King of Spain, he tells me that this Court thinks, as France has taken the lead, it may be fitly left with her, in consideration of the consanguinity of the Royal families and of the contiguity of the kingdoms; and that the Ministers of the Allies may usefully support the French Ambassador in such matters as their Courts approve their so acting in: but he expressed a natural doubt how far the King of Spain will be able to act upon such advice.

As to M. de Lobo's suggestion, he observed that, if high language is used abruptly to the new Spanish Government

respecting Portugal, it would probably irritate it and provoke
a reply that it will not be dictated to by other Powers as to its
differences with another State; but that, at a proper time, it
will be fit to express in conciliatory terms to Spain the decided
interest the Allies feel in maintaining the independence and
peace of Portugal. I observed to him that the delicacy in this
matter is the greater as the persons to be dealt with are new
men, heated with revolution and success, and in whom the
peculiar features of the Spanish character—overweening confidence and a distrust of strangers—are to be expected in a
high degree; that, however, they may possibly be made to
feel the advantage of acting fairly and frankly in the present
European system, ensuring thereby respect to their new institutions; and that the mediation between Spain and Portugal,
to which the Powers were called, gives them a right to inter-
pose their good offices. I observed also that the change of
men and measures, likely to take place rapidly at Madrid for
some time, will probably render it extremely difficult to devise
any fixed plan to be followed exactly by the Allies respecting
Spanish affairs.

M. Ancillon then told me it is the opinion of this Court
that it will be better for the Allies, in the first instance, to
confine themselves to insinuations of their opinions to the
Court of Spain, avoiding any formal declaration to it; and
that it is desirable that the Allied Courts should instruct their
Ministers at Paris to communicate with the French Ministers
as to what passes in Spain, and as to the measures to be
adopted by the Allies, without establishing any formal Conference for that purpose; that, in such a Conference, M. Pozzo
di Borgo is sure to have an ascendency, which renders Russia
very desirous that it should take place, and gives a strong
reason to the other Courts to object to its being set on foot.
He said that the preference to Paris for this purpose arises
from the relationship between the two Royal families, the
comparative vicinity of the two Courts, and the line

which has already been taken by that of the Tuileries in this matter.

I have, &c.,   G. ROSE.

Cardinal Consalvi to Lord Castlereagh.

Rome, ce 7 Avril, 1820.

Mylord—Le courier Anglais étant revenu de Naples deux jours plus tôt qu'on me l'avait annoncé, et ne s'arrêtant à Rome qu'un instant, je me trouve avec regret dans l'impossibilité de faire dans le moment ma réponse à la lettre de votre Excellence relative au changement proposé sur Malte. Je transmettrai donc par la poste la lettre que j'aurois voulu donner au courier, et votre Excellence me pardonnera ce retard involontaire de neuf ou dix jours. Je me fais un devoir de l'en prévenir, et je réitère à la hâte à votre Excellence l'assurance de la haute considération avec laquelle j'ai l'honneur d'être de votre Excellence le très dévoué et très obéissant serviteur,

H. Card. CONSALVI.

Je prie votre Excellence de tourner la feuille.

PS. L'illustre personne qui se trouve à Rome va nous quitter dans deux jours pour s'en aller à Pesaro. Elle dit qu'après une courte demeure à Pesaro, on partira pour l'Angleterre. Plusieurs personnes disent qu'elle le dit pour en tirer profit, mais qu'elle ne le fera pas. Elle est *furieuse* contre moi, parceque je suis resté ferme dans le parti pris, et je n'ai voulu céder même à de menaces de vengeance.

Lord Castlereagh to the Duke de Richelieu.

St. James's Square, April 10, 1820.

Monsieur le Duc—I have the honour to enclose to your Excellency copies of two letters which were received by me when in Ireland. They appear to me to be the production of some very wild individual, if, in truth, they shall prove to have any real existence whatever. I nevertheless think it right that they should be submitted to your Excellency's inspection, however absurd in conception and design. To the original letters a name, real or fictitious, I know not which, is annexed.

If you consider this production deserving of any attention, and desire to have the name, I shall feel it my duty to communicate it, only begging, in that case, that your Excellency will use it for purposes of *precaution* and *surveillance*, and not of *punishment*.

Allow me to take this occasion of offering to your Excellency my congratulations upon your return to the administration of public affairs in France. I am conscious how great a sacrifice you have made of private comfort to a sense of public duty and devotion to the interests of the King and of his august family. I sincerely hope your Excellency may succeed in carrying the vessel of the State through the arduous difficulties with which you have to contend, but from which, in these days, it may be truly said that no European Government is wholly exempt.

I have the honour to be, &c.,

CASTLEREAGH.

PS. There being a name referred to in the second letter of a person resident at No. 54, Poland Street, Golden Square, in this metropolis, I have requested Lord Sidmouth to have inquiries made whether such a person resides at the address given, and what his character is. I shall not fail, if the result should lead to any intelligence of sufficient importance, to impart it to your Excellency.

The Duke de Richelieu to Lord Castlereagh.

Paris, ce 17 Avril, 1820.

Milord—J'ai reçu la lettre que votre Excellence m'a fait l'honneur de m'écrire, ainsi que les papiers qui y étoient joints. Je vous prie, milord, de recevoir mes plus sincères remercîmens pour cette communication : elle me prouve de plus en plus l'intérêt que vous nous portez et la confiance que vous avez en nous, dont je suis fort touché. S'il y avoit quelque manière d'obtenir de l'homme qui vous écrit la connoissance des moyens dont il croit pouvoir se servir pour amener l'évasion du prisonnier de Ste. Hélène, sans qu'on put en accuser votre Gouvernement, ce seroit une chose extrèmement utile, et qui tranquilliseroit sur toutes les tentatives dont les bruits se renouvellent de temps en temps. J'ignore si votre Excellence auroit quelque moyen pour amener cet homme à s'ouvrir plus complètement. En supposant son existence et la réalité de son projet, il seroit inquiétant qu'un homme crût pouvoir, avec 20 mille livres sterling, faire évader Buonaparte. J'abandonne à votre prudence, milord, le parti qu'on pouvoit tirer de cette ouverture, bien sûr que vous ferez tout ce qui sera nécessaire pour prévenir tout ce qu'on pourroit essayer en faveur de votre prisonnier.

Nous vous serions fort obligés de nous envoyer les originaux des lettres que vous avez reçues, afin que, si nous parvenions par l'écriture à connoître l'individu qui les a écrites, vous puissiez nous mettre en garde contre ses projets ultérieurs. Quant à exercer contre lui quelque poursuite, je vous promets, milord, que nous nous en abstiendrons, ainsi que vous le désirez, et que tout se bornera à la surveillance.

Je suis très sensible à tout ce que vous avez la bonté de me dire sur ma rentrée dans les affaires. Mon dévouement à mon Roi et à mon pays m'impose le pénible devoir. Je ne me suis pas dissimulé les difficultés que j'aurai à surmonter ; mais il s'agit de la cause la plus sainte, de celle de l'ordre social et de l'humanité, et cette grande considération est bien faite pour donner du courage. Nous sommes tous plus ou moins sur la brèche, milord ; et je ne vois plus pour les nations comme pour les Gouvernemens qu'un grand intérêt, qui leur est commun à tous, celui de s'opposer à l'invasion de l'anarchie, qui s'avance pour détruire la civilisation. Si, comme je l'espère, les grandes puissances restent étroitement unies entre elles, il y a encore des ressources, et j'espère que nous ne succomberons dans la lutte que nous soutenons.

J'ai l'honneur d'être de votre Excellence le très humble et très obéissant Serviteur,

RICHELIEU.

Lord Castlereagh to the King.

Foreign Office, April 17, 1820.

Lord Castlereagh has the honour to submit for your Majesty's signature a letter to the King of Spain in answer to a letter which his Catholic Majesty has lately addressed to your Majesty, and which your Majesty's servants deem it expedient that your Majesty should reply to in general terms of civility, without employing any expressions which either indicate opinion, or which pledge your Majesty to anything beyond the mere courtesy of not leaving the King's intimation unacknowledged; an omission which, in the present critical state of affairs in Spain, (as reported in Sir H. Wellesley's despatch of the 6th April) might give rise to inferences most prejudicial to the King's interests and possibly to his personal safety.

Sir Daniel Bayley to Joseph Planta, Jun., Esq.

St. Petersburg, April 17-29, 1820.

Dear Sir—I begin to be extremely anxious to hear from you, for I find by the packets received by the post last night, of the 7th instant, from your office, that the death of poor Casamajor was known there, though I have not a line. The packets being simply addressed to his Britannic Majesty's Chargé d'Affaires was enough to show this almost to a blind man.

In addition to the advantages I mentioned to you in my last letter, and to Lord Castlereagh in my despatch No. 14, of the 6-18 April, granted to certain manufacturers in this country an ukase is just printed, though not published, granting a drawback of the whole of the duties on white cottons imported and used by the proprietors of works for printing cottons. Certain regulations and restrictions are imposed, to prevent frauds, and the advantages are limited to the port of St. Petersburg, and, for the present, to one year.

This will give a very important, *fair* advantage to the printers, and open a field for *advantages not contemplated by Government.* It will also be highly prejudicial to their own manufacturers of white calicoes, which are extensive and flourishing, and be injurious to the regular importer both of them and of cotton twist from Great Britain. These evils, and those I set forth in the letter alluded to, are not small; but I conceive the merchants and manufacturers must, for the present, be left to work out their own salvation.

The ice has totally disappeared in the river, but the navigation with Cronstadt is still closed by it; and, indeed, we must yet expect a quantity of floating ice from the Ladoga Lake, and there is not a green leaf or blade of grass to be seen.

I am, with the greatest respect, &c.,

DANIEL BAYLEY.

Mr. Hamilton to Lord Castlereagh.

Paris, April 20, 1820.

My dear Lord—Your lordship will best see, by Sir Charles Stuart's letter of this date, how far I have duly executed your instructions in reference to the communication I was to make to him on the subject of the relations in which he stood towards this Court and those of the Allied Powers, and on the expediency contemplated at home of making an arrangement more congenial to the views of the ruling party in this country for the transaction of his Majesty's affairs here. In getting over the difficulty which I anticipated of breaking to him the views of the Government upon this subject with respect to his conduct, without hurting his feelings too strongly, I was most gratified to find that he received the communication quite in the same spirit in which I was instructed to make it; and he contented himself with lamenting the very difficult and awkward circumstances in which he had been placed from the beginning, and more especially since he had ceased to act under the Duke of Wellington's advice. He was aware of the enemies he had, of the activity with which stories are fabricated and exaggerated in this city of all the corps diplomatique generally and particularly of himself.

I ought perhaps to apologize, under the circumstances, of having given him the use of my pen in copying out his private letter to your lordship, in reference to my communications; but I thought that secrecy for the present was of so much importance that I could not help proffering my services. With regard to Stuart's conduct and language here, from the little I have seen of him, I can still see that there is every probability that they have been on several occasions incautious, not to say imprudent; but I think I can say this is more owing to indolence in acting up to his right notions than to any wrong notions which he entertains, either of his duty or of the views of his Government; and to this indolence is to be added an excess of good-nature, which prevents him from expressing what he feels of other individuals, when he sees that they are going wrong, and that he himself may be the victim. In saying this, however, it is well that I should add that I have very explicitly stated to him that your decision with respect to him is made, and that his Embassy is to close this ensuing summer: but I felt that this was perfectly compatible with his endeavouring to set himself right in your opinion, and to make out his own case in the best colours it would admit of. I could also plainly see that, had I been authorized to encourage any hopes of a *change of Embassy* or of early future employment, he would contemplate a removal from Paris, not perhaps as a favour, but certainly as a relief from great cares and great responsibilities to which he is neither equal nor partial: and I should think he would willingly accept any one of the other Christian

Embassies rather than, as he expresses himself, " *aller planter ses choux à quarante ans*."

I cannot conclude without repeating to your lordship the expression of my regrets that I am running away from my duties at a time when you must be most in want of labourers in the vineyard; but I hope ere long to return more equal to those duties than I have been for some time past. My general health sensibly improves under this delightful sun. I can say nothing of my leg for some time. They tell me several weeks must elapse before Barèges is dug out of the snows. I beg my respectful compliments to Lady Castlereagh, and am your Lordship's very obedient, humble Servant,

WILLIAM HAMILTON.

Sir Charles Stuart to Lord Castlereagh.

Paris, April 20, 1820.

My dear Lord—Mr. Hamilton having made known to me the substance of a conversation which he had with your lordship shortly before he left London, detailing the sentiments of his Majesty's Ministers respecting the conduct of this Embassy during the two last years, the desire I entertain not to forfeit your Lordship's good opinion of the zeal and discretion with which I have hitherto conducted his Majesty's affairs at this Court, as well as a feeling of what is due to my own character, induce me to lose no time in submitting to your lordship a few observations upon the points to which that gentleman alluded.

The evident impossibility of carrying into effect the main object of the great European confederacy, unless unanimity prevails among their diplomatic agents, who have been specially chosen to watch over the progress of affairs in that country whose political aberrations would most seriously affect the tranquillity of Europe, has been so often pressed upon my attention in your lordship's instructions, and I have so frequently observed the jealous apprehensions mutually entertained by my colleagues, accredited from the other Courts

engaged in the alliance, that I have been particularly careful
to avoid even the appearance, much more the reality, of any
difference of opinion amongst us.

My despatches will have shown that the late President of
the Council did, in conversation with me, and very frequently,
indulge in the expression of ill-humour against one or other of
my three colleagues, and particularly against the Prussian and
Russian Envoys, with whom he had involved himself in a personal quarrel.   But I invariably reminded his Excellency that
my situation did not permit me to participate in his feelings;
and more than once I prevented an open rupture : and I have
every reason to believe that the maintenance of tranquillity
between the French and the Allied Courts is in some measure
owing to my friendly interference.   With the same view, I
have uniformly abstained from making any allusion whatever
to such conversations, both in my daily communications
with the parties concerned, as well as in my habitual correspondence with his Majesty's Ministers accredited at the other
Courts. ·

. It is indeed to this line of conduct which I had adopted, in
the true spirit of my instructions, that I attribute the re-
establishment of a far more cordial intercourse with my Russian
colleague from the commencement of last year until the present
time than had existed at any former period of our residence in
Paris.   This cordiality, indeed, has not passed unnoticed by
the Austrian and Prussian Ministers, though it appears to
have been considered by them with less umbrage than my
confidential habits during the same period with M. de Cazes.

After I received your lordship's despatch No. 14, of the
23rd March, 1819, the expression of our several opinions in
the meetings which took place was not accompanied by any
real difference of feeling which I might have thought worthy
to be reported to my Court; for I had never thought it necessary to trouble your lordship with the detail of our daily discussions respecting the means by which the objects of the

common alliance were effected, although they occasionally left for a time M. de Vincent and myself, or M. Pozzo di Borgo and myself, in an opinion opposed to our other colleagues.

I must further observe that, never having been in the habit of expressing any dissatisfaction at many proofs I witnessed in former times of the ascendency obtained by the Russian Minister over the French councils during his intimacy with M. de Richelieu, I had no reason to expect that habits of friendship between myself and M. de Cazes at a subsequent period, which in no instance can be alleged to have been directed to the attainment of an undue influence on the part of my Court, (for I was well aware that my duty was to support and not to guide) should have now become a subject of severe reprehension on the part of Russia; and I am particularly mortified that such animadversion, which can only relate to a state of things now no more, should make such a forcible impression upon his Majesty's Government at a time when, I am convinced, the four Ministers are drawing more cordially together, and more thoroughly united in their opinions upon every question connected with the interior administration of this country, than in any former crisis.

My correspondence with your lordship during the last two years will, I think, further prove that my intimacy with the late Minister, which has been the subject of such severe comment, was not sought for by me; but that the circumstances in which M. de Cazes was placed at the formation of his Administration made him believe it expedient for the success of his Government to convince the nation that he stood high in the good opinion of his Majesty's Government: and, in this feeling (as M. de Talleyrand had done three years before), I fear he promoted the circulation of reports and correspondence to this effect, which, whether true or false, offered the most effectual mode of attaining his object, though at my expense.

It is a satisfaction to me, however, to think that, among persons whose opinions have changed in every direction, (I

allude to my Russian colleague among others) and in a country
where nothing is stable, I have considered myself as a mere
spectator of their public affairs, and that, without committing
my Government, by attaching myself to any set of men or
pleading for any particular set of measures, I have invariably
expressed my conviction that the best hope of tranquillity for
France, and the line of conduct most congenial to the wishes
of my Government, would be secured by avoiding the exagge-
rations of both extremes, and by the maintenance of a system
which would admit of the conciliation of the old and the new
interests which divide France. If I have not predicted so distinctly as his Majesty's Government may have expected the
consequences which are likely to result from an abandonment
of this system, should it ever be attempted, your lordship must
attribute the omission to the difficulty of forming a decided
judgment upon reports in different senses which daily reach
me, and which do not allow me to look forward to future
contingencies with any degree of certainty during a week
together.

The necessity of proving my desire at all times to support
the existing Government, in whosesoever hands the King to
whom I am accredited may think fit to place it, is so strongly
impressed on my mind that, on the very day I learned M. de
Cazes' resignation, I requested him to communicate this my
conviction to the Duke de Richelieu, and begged him to assure
that Minister of my anxious desire to maintain with him the
same habits of cordiality, from which M. de Cazes often assured
me that the interests of the French Government had derived
advantage: and, though your lordship's conversation with
Mr. Hamilton shows that the illness and sudden departure of
M. de Cazes from Paris prevented him from delivering this
message to his successor, yet all the intercourse which has
hitherto taken place between the Duke de Richelieu, M. Pasquier, and myself, since the former came into office, has been
in every respect, both of form and substance, so perfectly

satisfactory, that I am at a loss to account for any complaint he can have brought forward, unless my language and conduct respecting the late changes which have taken place in Spain have been much misrepresented.

With respect to the point mentioned in my despatch No. —, I certainly did answer M. de Richelieu's inquiries respecting the intelligence which I might have received by my last advices from Spain, by apprising his Excellency of a report which, I was assured, prevailed at Madrid respecting the possible invitation of a foreign Prince to the throne of that country, and I at the same time urged the Duke to take some effectual steps for contradicting a report of such fatal tendency; and, in respect to the intended mission of M. de la Tour du Pin, I was careful to take no steps which might in any manner commit my Government (in a case, the urgency of which precluded me from asking for instructions from home) without previous communication with the Count de Fernan-Nuñez. His Excellency made no objection to the measure which I adopted upon full consideration, and he profited by the conveyance to forward a private letter of his own to Madrid. Could I have secured the object with less exertion on my part, I should certainly have preferred to gain it by convincing M. de Pasquier of the imprudence of the advice which had been given to his Sovereign. As it was, I contented myself with sending by my Secretary, who conveyed to Madrid the despatches from England, which were already in my office waiting an opportunity, extracts of my letters upon this subject to your lordship. The enclosed reply from Sir Henry Wellesley will best show the light in which his Excellency considered the service which was so done; and I have only to add that the Spanish Ambassador here, who had before received his letters of recall, and who has since been instructed to give up the affairs of his embassy, at times attributes this instruction to this measure of mine, and at times assumes to himself the merit of preventing La Tour du Pin's mission.

His recall is, however, well known to be the result of a correspondence with his Government respecting the employment of Swiss troops in Spain.

In placing before your lordship this plain statement of facts, I do not think myself at liberty to indulge in the expression of my own feelings. The repeated and signal proofs of justice and friendship which I have received from your lordship will induce me to submit without repining to the alternative which your lordship may think the public service requires me to adopt.

Believe me, &c.,   CHARLES STUART.

PS. Being aware of your lordship's wish that the purport of this letter should be kept perfectly secret, I have accepted Mr. Hamilton's obliging offer to write it out, in preference to the gentlemen of the embassy.

· C. S.

[Enclosure.]

Sir H. Wellesley to Sir Charles Stuart.

Madrid, April 6, 1820.

My dear Sir Charles—I have received your ciphered letter, and you certainly have rendered a great service in preventing the departure of M. de la Tour du Pin; for, in the present temper of men's minds, there is no saying what might have been the consequences of his appearance here. I hear that the Government (that is to say the Provisional Junta) are very angry with Fernan-Nuñez. I did not mention his name to Jabat, nor did I make any allusion to him; but I have heard that he wrote a private letter to the Duke de San Fernando, mentioning the intention of the French Government. It is said that he has been ordered to give up the affairs of the embassy, and the Duke of San Carlos likewise.

I have nothing to add to my despatches.

Ever, &c.,   H. WELLESLEY.

Lord Castlereagh to the Duke de Richelieu.

Foreign Office, April 24, 1820.

Monsieur le Duc—The assurance your Excellency has given me is perfectly satisfactory, and I have no difficulty in confiding to your Excellency the original letters, copies of which were before transmitted. I have not yet been able to obtain any satisfactory information respecting the individual in Poland Street to whom I am referred, and I am unwilling to push my inquiries so far as to open any communication with the individual, until I hear again from your Excellency.

You will no doubt be enabled to ascertain whether the writer of the letters really resides at Dunkirk, and who he is. This may possibly suggest some expedient, by which the means of the parties to undertake such a project may be estimated or put to the test, or by which their scheme, most probably framed for swindling purposes, may be detected. Your Excellency may rest assured of the best assistance I can afford you in dissipating all anxiety which might result from the supposed ability of these parties to effectuate such an object. Our parliamentary campaign opens on Thursday. I have every reason to hope that the new Parliament will be found to be as firmly attached to the good cause as the last; more they cannot be. Your Excellency will observe with satisfaction that our State trials have been very successfully conducted. The proceedings of our juries in every part of the empire have been most exemplary. In the multitude of trials to which our disturbances have given birth both in Great Britain and Ireland, I do not recollect a single instance of a verdict of which we had any right to complain; and, what is singularly satisfactory and contrary to all experience, our prosecutions for libels have been not less successful than those for the more atrocious crimes.

I shall watch with the utmost possible interest the progress of your new election law; and trust the moment may arrive when we may feel a mutual and undivided confidence in our respective Parliaments on opposite sides of the Channel.

CASTLEREAGH.

Sir Charles Stuart to Lord Castlereagh.

Paris, April 24, 1820.

My dear Lord—I availed myself of an opportunity two days since, to ascertain from the Duke de Richelieu that his Excellency had not received the communication from me which M. de Cazes undertook to deliver, at the period he quitted Paris, and to which I referred in the private letter I had the honour to address to your lordship by the last messenger. I must, in justice, say that the marked expression of his Excellency's surprise, upon hearing the details of the conversation which passed with M. de Cazes, proves the sincerity of the assurances to which this communication was calculated to give rise.

. The Duke de Richelieu was pleased to tell me that he learned my personal desire to support his administration with the more satisfaction, because former observation had shown, even although circumstances should place me upon distant terms with the French Government, that I was not likely to disguise my real feelings upon the subject of what is passing around me—that he regretted the pressure of other matter should not have enabled him to receive the avowal of my opinions and intentions sooner—that, under the present circumstances, however, he could promise me that his confidential language would, in future, give me the same satisfaction he hoped, in his turn, to derive from my communications, and that he flatters himself that many evils will be prevented by the colour which our intercourse and mutual good understanding may enable me to give to the transactions it is my duty to report.

I merely thanked his Excellency for the justice he was pleased to render to my private opinions, telling him that, as

long as I continue to act under the instructions I have
received, it is impossible that I can discredit the measures of
his Government—that, placed as I am, I can have no separate
interest from my colleagues, all of whom concur with me in
the wish, as far as it is within the sphere of our duty, to
uphold the Administration the King has established—and
that, whenever he may be of opinion that our impulse, jointly
or separately applied, can contribute to the attainment of
that object, future circumstances will show that it shall not be
withheld.

The manner and tone of the Duke de Richelieu so little
resembled the reserve I have witnessed upon former occasions,
that I have great reason to augur every favourable consequence
from what passed between us; and your lordship may be
assured I shall lose no opportunity of cultivating a direct and
frequent intercourse, which, if I had not unfortunately trusted
in M. de Cazes, I am sure, would have been established six
weeks ago.

Believe me, my dear lord, &c.,   CHARLES STUART.

Sir Charles Stuart to Lord Castlereagh.

Paris, April 27, 1820.

My dear Lord—I return to your lordship the copies of the
papers which the four Courts have interchanged during the
year 1819, upon the subject of French affairs, and which were
delivered to me by Mr. Hamilton, when he passed through
Paris. My recollection of many hints and expressions which
have fallen from the French Ministers in the course of the
year convinces me that they have long been acquainted with
the contents of several among these Papers. I therefore feel
that the considerations which have induced your lordship to
delay the communication of what has passed to his Majesty's
Embassy at Paris until the present moment have relieved me
from much embarrassment.

The unanswerable arguments contained in your lordship's

Memorandum of the 24th of September, 1819, remove all doubt respecting the principle upon which the conduct of the Confederation towards France ought to be guided; and, as these arguments are followed by the expression of your lordship's conviction that it is expedient to check any difference of opinion among the Agents of the four Powers, which may weaken the effect of the Alliance, I cannot but think that the known loyalty and good faith of his Majesty's Government would have entitled the repetition of opinions precisely analogous to your lordship's sentiments to due and favourable consideration on the part of the other Courts; for the language his Majesty's agents have founded upon these papers cannot be interpreted to manifest a reluctance to cultivate the intimacy upon which the attainment of all the objects of our union must in great measure depend, more justly than your lordship's observations upon the reasoning of the other Cabinets respecting certain parts of the system to be pursued at Paris can be deemed a proof of divisions unfavourable to the general interests of the Alliance.

My conviction that, whenever the opinions of my colleagues lead the four Courts to attempt an interference in the affairs of France, which they are not all equally able or even willing to carry through, they risk the loss of the great advantage which may be derived from their present position, has rendered me particularly desirous to avoid both measures and language which may commit the four Powers, or my own Court in particular, to adopt the system of any party.

I therefore profess to abstain from acting, in every case, without an instruction *ad hoc;* and I merely consider myself a spectator, bound to report everything which passes before me, leaving my Government perfectly unshackled and at liberty to take the course which circumstances shall render the most expedient.

I have never concealed from your lordship my own opinions, when I thought a bad position was likely to be aban-

doned by the French Ministers, for the purpose of giving a
tendency to their measures which is congenial to the feelings
of the nation, and *vice versa:* but, in expressing my sentiments, it has been my fixed principle to leave them to be duly
weighed at home; and, as I have avoided committing my
Government or myself by the language I hold to the French
Ministers upon such subjects, I have not placed myself in a
situation here which has rendered it difficult to follow the
course my Court may choose to adopt.

  I have the honour to be, &c., CHARLES STUART.

Lord Castlereagh to the King.

St. James's Square, April 30, 1820.

  Lord Castlereagh, not being as yet sufficiently recovered to
request permission to attend your Majesty in person, begs
leave humbly to submit, for your Majesty's gracious consideration, a memorandum approved by your Majesty's servants
in Cabinet, in which they have endeavoured to bring before
your Majesty, in a connected point of view, those reflections
to which the present seriously important state of continental
affairs has given rise.

  Should your Majesty be graciously pleased to approve of
the course of policy therein submitted, they would humbly
propose that the substance of the reasoning contained in this
minute should be thrown into the form of a circular despatch,
which your Majesty's Ministers should be directed to communicate confidentially to the Allied Courts, as a full and candid
exposition of your Majesty's views and sentiments at the present conjuncture.

  They humbly conceive that an exposition of this nature
may be desirable to be made to your Allies, on the part of your
Majesty, at the present moment.

  1st. In order, without condescending to a justification, by
an explicit avowal of your Majesty's sentiments on the late
events in Spain, to repel the calumnies which have been

recently circulated with respect to the course of your Majesty's policy in Spain—calumnies, against which the uniform tenour of your Majesty's policy in all countries, but more especially in Spain, ought to have been more than a protection—as well as to lay down that course which, in your Majesty's judgment, it is most expedient the Allies should pursue, in the actual and very critical state of affairs in that country.

2ndly. To furnish, on the part of your Majesty, a reasoned reply to the several propositions brought forward by the Russian Government in the despatch to Count Lieven of the 3rd of March;—as well as to the still more objectionable overture received from Berlin, and which has been most properly, as appears by Lord Stewart's despatches, already disapproved by the Austrian Government.

3rdly. Once more to recall the attention of the Allied Cabinets to the true and correct principles of the Alliance, and to the necessity of not generalizing them so as to render the concert an embarrasment, especially to a Government constituted like that of your-Majesty.

4thly. To decline, in the manner the least likely to give umbrage to the Emperor of Russia's personal sentiments, the renewed overture contained in the Russian despatch of the 4th of February to M. Alopeus, for reducing the Treaty of the Holy Alliance into the form of a treaty of general guarantee between all the European Powers.

5thly. To endeavour in some degree to dispel the alarm at present prevailing throughout Germany, by pointing, with some degree of precision, the attention of the principal Cabinets to the means of security most within their reach, and to the improvement of which, especially against the danger of *military revolt*, their immediate efforts should be chiefly directed, instead of occupying themselves with distant considerations of policy, over which they can, in point of fact, exercise no effectual control whatever.

So soon as Lord Castlereagh shall have been honoured with

your Majesty's commands upon the matter now submitted, he
proposes, with your Majesty's approbation, to communicate to
the several Allied Courts the steps already adopted by your
Majesty with respect to the affairs of Spain, as given in
instructions to Sir Henry Wellesley, in the despatches, official
and secret, already laid before your Majesty.

Your Majesty will appreciate the anxiety which your Allies
naturally feel to be informed of your Majesty's decision, as
early as possible, upon this important subject.

The Duke de Richelieu to Lord Castlereagh.

Paris, May 1, 1820.

Milord—Je vous prie de recevoir mes plus sincères remercimens pour la marque de confiance que vous avez bien voulu
me donner en m'envoyant les originaux des lettres dont vous
m'aviez déjà transmis les copies. Je vous assure que nous
n'abuserons pas de cette complaisance, et que nous nous
bornerons à une surveillance de prévention sans inquiéter ni
poursuivre en aucune manière l'auteur de ces lettres.

Je fais des vœux bien sincères, Milord, pour que votre campagne parlementaire s'écoule sans orages, et d'une manière plus
calme que la notre. Vous êtes nos modèles dans cette carrière,
et je voudrois que nous fissions en sorte de vous mieux imiter.
Tout ce qui sert au reste à raffermir l'ordre social dans un
pays est utile aux autres, et c'est sous ce point de vue que j'ai
remarqué avec une véritable satisfaction l'unanimité des juge-
mens rendus par les différents tribunaux contre les perturba-
teurs de toute espèce qui ont été traduits devant eux. Cela
prouve le bon esprit de la classe d'hommes dont sont tirés les
jurés, et tant que cette classe intermédiaire reste attachée à
l'ordre social, et qu'elle est convaincue de la nécessité de ré-
primer les factieux, l'État n'est pas sérieusement menacé.

Nous allons incessamment discuter la nouvelle loi d'élections ;
c'est le moment critique, vu nos ennemis qui, craignant de se
voir arracher le pouvoir, mettront tout en œuvre pour conserver

l'instrument dont ils se servent pour renverser l'ordre de choses
établi. J'espère qu'ils n'y réussiront pas, et je puis vous
assurer, Milord, que dans le grand combat, nous ne manque-
rons pas à ce que nous nous devons à nous mêmes, à notre
Roi, à notre pays, et je dirai à la civilisation Européenne. Je
me flatte que vous ferez des vœux pour nos succès : les intérêts
de tous les gens de bien sont les mêmes aujourd'hui d'un bout
du monde à l'autre.

Agréez l'assurances de la haute considération avec laquelle
j'ai l'honneur d'être, Milord, de votre Excellence le très
humble et très obéissant serviteur,

RICHELIEU.

Lord Castlereagh to Prince Metternich.

May 6, 1820.

It has been a subject of some grief to me, mon cher Prince,
to have been so long in possession of your private letter of the
7th March, without offering you my cordial acknowledgments
for this renewed mark of your regard and friendship. The
fact is, I wished immediately to answer it, but I wished still
more to answer it fully, and with the frankness which we have
long promised to each other. To do this, I could not touch a
single string without calling many into vibration, and I really
felt the gravity of the occasion so deeply that I could not
bring myself to send you the result merely of my own
reflections.

It was one which not only warranted but demanded the
anxious reflection of every individual member of the Government ; and I have the consolation of hoping that, if I have
been somewhat slow, I have, by the delay, procured the
fullest and most deliberate examination of the subject in the
largest sense, and that I can now refer you to the exposition
which my brother will convey to you, as the unanimous opinion
of the British Cabinet, formally submitted to and approved by
the King. We cannot give to others a more decisive proof of

our sincerity and our attachment than in the endeavour we have upon this occasion made to open ourselves to them without reserve.

Your Highness will observe that, although we have made an immense progress against Radicalism, the monster still lives, and shows himself in new shapes; but we do not despair of crushing him by time and perseverance. The laws have been reinforced, the juries do their duty, and wherever the mischief in its labyrinth breaks forth, it presents little real danger, whilst it furnishes the means of making those salutary examples which are so difficult whilst treason works in secrecy, and does not disclose itself in overt acts.

Our session is likely to be a troublesome one, and to me it begins inauspiciously, having been seized by the gout two days before the battle was to commence. I am, however, getting better, and expect to be in my place in the course of next week. Much will depend on the course her Majesty shall think fit to pursue. If she is wise enough to accept the *pont d'or* which we have tendered her, the calamities and scandal of a public investigation will be avoided. If she is mad enough or so ill-advised as to put her foot upon English ground, I shall, from that moment, regard Pandora's box as opened. I cannot sufficiently express how much I feel your Highness's conduct upon this question. You have given us in the most handsome and honourable manner the full weight of your authority; and I have no doubt your individual opinion has had its due weight in reconciling our royal master to the advice which his Ministers felt it their bounden duty to give to his Majesty.[1]

PS. I wished to have addressed this letter to you, mon Prince, in my own hand, but as it is painful to me to write in bed at this moment, I have availed myself of my friend Planta's pen for the purpose.

---

[1] So far this brouillon is in Lord Castlereagh's own handwriting; the postscript is in Mr. Planta's.

Lord Clancarty to Lord Castlereagh.

The Hague, May 9, 1820.

My dear Lord—I wish the newspaper accounts from you, the only ones brought us by the last mail, were as good as those I am enabled to give you of this King. His Majesty is quite recovered, and those who have seen him say, has been much cleared and benefited in appearance by his late illness. This change from extreme cold to mild spring weather will probably send him to the Loo early in the next week. He has sent to tell me by Nagell that he would by no means wish me to postpone my journey on account of the short adjournment which has taken place in his, and has fixed on Thursday next to see me positively, for the purpose of taking leave. I shall therefore continue my intention of embarking on Saturday next at Helvoetsluys. Mr. Eliot will remain here to take care of the passport branch of our business during my few days' absence : the rest of my young men will take that opportunity of paying a short visit to their friends, and will therefore embark with me.

I have fortunately nothing to write on Netherland politics. Adieu, *au revoir.*

Yours most sincerely,   CLANCARTY.

Lord Castlereagh to Sir Charles Stuart.

Foreign Office, May 12, 1820.

Dear Sir—So few foreigners understand the constitutional principles by which our political system is regulated, and they are so liable to misinterpret the caution with which we act for indifference, that I have some fears lest the explanations we have given to our Allies on some of the points to which our Minute applies, might, if they should leak out of the Foreign Office at Paris, and especially in a garbled or imperfect sense, do mischief to a cause, the support of which we have so deeply and sincerely at heart.

You·will therefore make the Duke de Richelieu distinctly understand that the attachment we feel to the King's interest and that of his family alone suggests the caution which is enjoined in the despatch I have addressed to you on this subject. The Duke may possibly wish to communicate these papers to the King and to the Minister for Foreign Affairs, but not to make them official, or he may wish to retain the Minute for his own information : to neither of which courses we can have any objection. Our wish *bonâ fide* is to give him all the advantage of the information ; at the same time, to save him as far as we can from any of those possible inconveniences or risks to which false inferences of our views and intentions might expose the legitimate Government and succession.

M. Caraman, by desire of M. Pasquier, has asked me for a confidential explanation of our views with respect to Spain. I have told him that we should take steps fully to explain ourselves at Paris on this subject, and that we had every desire to cultivate a good understanding with his Government upon this as upon all other subjects ; but that our general views were strongly against taking any measures whatever of interference, under present circumstances, in the affairs of that country.

If the Duke de Richelieu should express a wish that the King should be made acquainted with the tenour of our instructions to our Ministers in Spain and Portugal, you will offer to attend his Majesty, and to read them to him ; but it is not deemed proper that you should part with these instructions or give copies.

　　　　　　　I am, &c.,　　　CASTLEREAGH.

Lord Castlereagh to Prince Hardenberg.

. Foreign Office, May 12, 1820.

Mon Prince—Accept my best thanks for your private letter of the 31st March, with its enclosures. Your Highness may be assured that I shall always receive with the greatest interest any communication with which you may honour me; and that the frankness with which you may apprise me of any reports (however strange and incredible they may be) that might prejudice the politics of this Court in the eyes of other Governments, or which might affect the interests of the Alliance, will always be regarded by me as so many additional and valuable pledges of your Highness's confidence and regard.

I have delayed replying to your Highness's letter, deeming the most satisfactory answer I could give would be to send you a full exposition of our views of the transactions out of which those mystifications have proceeded; and I flatter myself that the reasons which are stated in the several documents which Mr. Douglas has been directed, in Mr. Rose's absence, to lay before your Highness, will satisfy you that the British Government has invariably pursued a correct course in what regards Spain; that the views which they have taken of late events are consistent with their uniform principles; and that the *projet* of sending M. de la Tour du Pin was most unadvised.

As I have inflicted a severe budget of official papers upon your Highness by the present courier, which I know you will read with the attention and good-will which animate all your feelings towards this country, I will not longer trespass than to assure you, &c.,

CASTLEREAGH.

I did intend to have addressed this letter to your Highness in my own hand, but hope you will accept my apologies for not having done so, as I am not yet recovered from my indisposition.

Sir Henry Wellesley to Lord Castlereagh.

Madrid, May 15, 1820.

My dear Lord—I was very much surprised to learn, by your lordship's private letter of the 25th ult., that his Majesty's Government have been supposed to be at the bottom of the late revolution in Spain. A very different opinion prevailed here during the first days of the revolution; but I think that there is now a disposition to do us more justice, and I am persuaded that we shall find the good effects of an adherence to the line of conduct pointed out in your lordship's instructions. The French Ambassador is taking great pains to ingratiate himself with the persons now in power here; it is possible that he may be instructed to do so, with a view to removing the impression made here by the intended mission of M. de la Tour du Pin.

It is reported that the Americans are so angry at the refusal of the Government to increase the number of supplementary deputies, that they have it in contemplation not to elect any deputies to Cortes. Such a resolution would, I think, be advantageous to the affairs of the Peninsula, but would probably create a bad impression in America.

I am extremely sensible of your lordship's kindness relative to my leave of absence. Your lordship may be assured that, as long as my presence is necessary here, I shall not make any application of the kind. Lady Georgiana leaves Madrid on the 17th, and I propose to accompany her as far as Vittoria; but I shall not be absent more than a week.

I have the honour to be, &c.,   H. WELLESLEY.

The Hon. F. Lamb to Lord Castlereagh.

Frankfort, May 28, 1820.

Dear Lord Castlereagh—After reading these letters, you will not wonder that I should not have written to you. Till the death of Sand, there has not been a circumstance upon which to hitch a despatch. It would be idle in me to write upon what is doing at Vienna, which you know much better than I do, and this country is the picture of tranquillity: to the eye it presents nothing but ease, abundance, and peaceful, orderly enjoyment.

In a despatch of December last, I stated the great change for the better which had taken place in the habits of the people.

This change has since been confirmed and extended. It can only be described by negatives. There is no eager inquiry after political events, no discussion upon public measures, no murmurs, no curiosity, no discontent; and the groundwork of all this is that there is no want.

Does this statement appear to be in contradiction with my account of the execution of Sand? I do not think it is. Even before that event, in the midst of this tranquillity, I never supposed that the feelings and opinions which had been so enthusiastically adopted could in so short a time have been rooted out, and especially not among the very classes where they had taken the strongest hold. But the extension of these opinions is stopped; their exaggeration is become an object of ridicule rather than of admiration; and the quiet and orderly disposition of the people, and their enjoyment of the great goods which they possess, are every day gaining ground and confirming the tranquillity of the country. These are not only my own opinions, they are those of every enlightened man with whom I have had an opportunity of conversing on the subject.

Two questions seem to me to arise from the above statement. From whence does this tranquillity proceed? Is it likely to be permanent? I will try to answer them. The present tranquillity of Germany, compared with the measures which have been taken to produce it, seems to me to prove that the really dangerous part of the community consisted in some thirty periodical writers, and in the large proportion of the professors in the schools and universities. Since the establishment of the censure, the former have become comparatively harmless: their spirit is still the same; but they labour with such a true German perseverance to veil the obnoxious part of their articles, that they render them unintelligible, except to a very small proportion of their readers.

The account of the death of Sand is one of the worst articles I have seen, and this is the fault of the Government which

allows it to pass; for it is to be observed that neither the existence of the censure, nor its exercise, has as yet created a
murmur or the expression of a wish for its removal. This
primary element of mischief seems, therefore, to be entirely
within the power of the Government; and I repeat the opinion
of better judges than myself when I say that, under no circumstances could the tranquillity of this country be compatible
with the existence of such a press as was allowed to agitate it
for a period of years.

The state of the universities is less immediately dangerous,
and less easily altered. It is, however, much improved, and
might be much more so. The universities of the grand-duchy
of Baden, and particularly Heidelberg, are in a worse state
than most others, which does not contribute to give me a high
idea of the administration of our friend Berstett. The students
there still wear the absurd dress which is the rallying sign of
their party. Those of Göttingen have within the last three
days filled the town of Cassel in the same costume, and their
appearance in it in numbers is always attended by a feeling of
their strength, and by their proportionate insolence and ob-
noxiousness. But I cannot hear that the inhabitants of these
towns or of their neighbourhood show any signs of fellow-
feeling with the students: on the contrary, in passing through
them, one hears general complaints of their license, which is
left unchecked merely by the supineness of the Government,
and by their non-execution of their own engagements.

The measures of compression have, however, succeeded so
perfectly, as far as they have been tried, and what remains to
be done by them is so clear, that I cannot doubt of its being
gradually carried into effect in this slow country. The changing
the spirit of the instruction must be a work of greater time,
but it is one for which time can be afforded: and, in looking
to the probability of its ultimate success, it should not be forgotten that almost all the obnoxious professors, almost all the
periodical writers, were, in their origin, the tools of the same

statesmen who are still in power, nursed with hopes, fed with promises, urged on in their career, and used as instruments for the raising a spirit in Germany, to which they gave a direction, the ultimate danger of which was at the time overlooked in favour of its actual utility. I recall this fact, which no man will contravene, because I infer from it that the race of agitators is less likely to have recruits and successors than if it had arisen under less extraordinary circumstances and with less unnatural encouragement.

The above statement is intended to apply to the South of Germany in general: of the North I know nothing, and even in the South I must make one or two exceptions. The left bank of the Rhine is represented to me as partaking, though in a less degree, of the general tranquillity. I shall take an early opportunity of acquiring some more positive knowledge upon its situation. It has lost too much by its separation from France to be so soon reconciled to its lot. Another exception applies to the Tyrol, where the population is much alienated from the Austrian Government. The causes of this have nothing in common with the agitations of Germany. They are three: the continuance of the conscription, which was first introduced by the French; the want of a provision for the families of those Tyroleans who fell in their various struggles in favour of the House of Austria, amounting, I am assured, to about four thousand, whose destitute state contrasts too strongly with the pensions which are received by such Tyrolese as have been wounded in our foreign regiments; and thirdly, and above all, the introduction of the Austrian prohibitive system, and the establishment of her custom-houses. I do not mean that these causes are likely to lead to disturbances in the country; but they have totally destroyed that ancient and romantic attachment which existed to the House of Austria. Instead of having the whole population at her devotion, it is highly probable that not a single man would take arms in her behalf. Having witnessed the former enthusiasm of the country, I have felt pain from seeing the present alteration in its feeling. The want of a market for the surplus produce is more severely felt in the Italian Tyrol than in the German, and, whether justly or not, is attributed entirely to the restrictive system.

I can answer for the same feeling existing in the eastern provinces of France and in Lombardy, where the prohibitions have extended the system of smuggling into so formidable a shape that it can only be checked by a large military force upon the frontier, which, however, fortunately for the country, has hitherto been inadequate to its suppression. The general opinion has become so hostile to the restrictive system that I think its downfall may already be predicted. I hope I may be excused for mentioning to your lordship that the tax imposed upon wool last year has contributed to increase the unpopularity which attaches to our commercial regulations. The growers of wool in Bohemia have suffered greatly from the depression of its price; and I have not found any one of them who could be induced to admit that this might have arisen from any other circumstance than the imposition of the tax in England.

I am aware that the latter part of this letter relates to circumstances with which I have nothing to do; and that the beginning is merely a most lengthy mode of stating that the country is perfectly tranquil, with the exception of some few absurdities which only exist by sufferance; and that it is likely to continue so. But my object is that, by opening my whole budget, you should see how very little I have had to write; and I sincerely hope that the same justification of silence may continue to exist. The business is expected to begin here early in June. I shall then probably trouble you with a *few unnecessary observations.*

Wessenberg is still going, but never gone; and I am, dear Lord Castlereagh, ever faithfully and devotedly yours,

F. LAMB.

The Hon. F. Lamb to Lord Castlereagh.

Frankfort, May 29, 1820.

Dear Lord Castlereagh—Since my letter of the 28th, I have been over to Darmstadt, to learn what turn the States are likely to take there, which assemble in the middle of June. There is a notion that the deputies from the left bank of the Rhine are likely to be intractable, which made me curious upon the subject, and I am glad to say that there is every prospect of their passing with the greatest harmony. The Grand Duke is reducing his army to the limit required by the Confederation. He has contented the *médiatisés*, and will be able, instead of requiring additional supplies, to diminish four or five hundred thousand florins of the present taxes. Such, at least, are the representations which have been made to me, and which I have no reason to doubt. It must be an odd Chamber which will not be contented with such measures as these; nor is it indifferent that these assemblies should get a habit of passing off quietly. Nassau and Wirtemberg have set the example. Carlsruhe is the only one I am afraid of. Berstett is better in words than in action. There are a great many difficulties in their finances, and, I am afraid, no Minister who is equal to facing them, or capable of leading the State. The German has lived so lately under absolute Governments, that he still requires to be ruled: the only difference in him is that he now insists upon its being done with justice, and this may be conceded to him.

I am, dear Lord Castlereagh, &c., F. LAMB.

Lord Castlereagh to Sir H. Wellesley.

London, June 2, 1820.

My dear Sir—In the present critical state of affairs in Spain, I have thought it might be both satisfactory to yourself and useful to the public service that you should have an opportunity of perusing such communications as have lately passed between this Government and the principal Continental Powers, in order that you may collect from them the spirit in which your Court wishes to conduct its foreign policy. As these papers are of a strictly confidential character, I wish you to consider them as intended only for your own perusal, and to be returned by the first messenger. You may, however, take such notes as you may deem necessary for your own personal use, keeping them, however, sealed up, and among your own private papers.

You will find among these papers a report of yours on the then state of Spain. I hope you will not disapprove of my having communicated this document confidentially to our Allies. Your despatch, coupled with that of Commodore Bowles, addressed to Sir T. Hardy, appeared to me to give so comprehensive and so advantageous a view of our policy, both in the Peninsula and in South America, that I deemed it of the utmost importance to communicate both, in order to repel (without condescending to an explanation) the calumnies which had been circulated, both with respect to your conduct and our views.

You will also see that the instructions given to you by the last Messenger have been sent to the Brasils, with a suitable injunction to that Government to respect Spanish interests in the present embarrassed state to which the King is reduced. In order that there may be no clashing of views, Sir C. Stuart has been authorized to read to the Duke de Richelieu the Minute of Cabinet founded on the Duke of Wellington's Report, together with his Grace's Paper, as also my instructions to your Excellency and Mr. Thornton, including your and Commodore Bowles' despatches; and I have received from Sir Charles an assurance that the French Government entirely concur in the policy laid down in these papers, and that the instructions sent to the Duke de Laval entirely correspond with those of your Excellency.

When you next write, I should be glad to know your

opinion of the Danish Minister at Madrid, M. Dernath. I
think it right you should be informed that his reports have
not been of *the most friendly character*. You will profit by
this hint, but not evince to that Minister any consciousness of
this fact.

Being returned late from the House of Commons, I have
only time to write these few lines. I have nothing special to
add to my former instructions, and, with respect to our general
views, I send you ample materials.

CASTLEREAGH.

PS. The despatches addressed to Sir C. Stuart, Nos. 28
and 37, are copies, *mutatis mutandis*, of the despatches to our
Ministers at Vienna, St. Petersburgh, and Berlin: but as I
thought there was some risk in the exposition of our views
being deposited in the Foreign Office at Paris, it was left to
the Duke de Richelieu's option to receive the communication
personally, or to have it officially communicated through the
Secretary of State for Foreign Affairs. His Excellency, with
great prudence, preferred the former mode, returning the
papers when read. They were, however, seen also by the
King and M. Pasquier.

Lord Clancarty to Lord Castlereagh.

The Hague, June 6, 1820.

My dear Lord—Immediately on the arrival here of this
King, on Sunday last, he sent to desire to see me, for the purpose of receiving the communication of the papers confided to
me, on the next day (yesterday) at two o'clock. We read
through the whole of these papers together, interrupted only
by his expressions of approbation and entire coincidence; and,
when they were finished, he desired me to report the same to
my King, together with sincere assurances of his gratitude to
his Majesty for the marked confidence reposed in him by this
interesting communication. He desired me also to express
his personal obligations to you on the same subject.

I cannot enough recommend that frequent communications of our proceedings with our Allies should continue to be made in confidence to this King and his Minister. These tend to keep up our influence here, and please the more, because our policy is exactly that which the King of the Netherlands would, for his own sake, most wish it to be.

Nagell was not long in finding out that our line of non-interference, abstracted from its other merits, had necessarily placed us in the situation of directors of the Grand Alliance. I should fear that the answer given by the Emperor of Russia to the notification from Spain of the late revolution there may tend to expose our leading position in the Alliance more than might be wished.

I took advantage of my private interview with the King to communicate confidentially to him the intelligence received by you, through Vienna, from Paris, on the subject of General Savary's intimations to M. de Vincent. His Majesty has desired me to acquaint you in equal confidence that, if such a conspiracy does still actually exist as that referred to, he is totally ignorant of it, and firmly believes that the Prince is equally so—that he is quite satisfied with the late conduct of his Royal Highness, whose laudable object now appears to be to conciliate as much as possible the affections of the Dutch— that the Prince has lately visited Amsterdam, and has other northern tours in contemplation; and such has been the state of things between his Royal Highness and his father of late, that the King thinks the Prince would on no account receive or entertain any correspondence which could, however remotely, implicate him in an affair of this nature, without immediately communicating the same to his Majesty. I therefore conceive the existence of any matter of the nature of that referred to, at Paris or elsewhere, with the knowledge or participation of the Prince, may be safely denied as at least highly improbable. Should further proof be required, I know of no other than what can be furnished by my speaking to the Prince upon the subject, which, if you should wish it, I will do. The King did not offer (neither do I wonder at his refraining from doing so) to speak to his son himself on this subject; and I did not think it right to ask him. My own opinion of the Prince, as I believe you already know, is that he is weak in the extreme, vain to excess, and that he has been led into great absurdities by those who surround him; but I nevertheless think he possesses at bottom a good heart and an honourable disposition.

I return the box of papers confided to me by this conveyance, having only (under your permission, signified by Planta) retained a copy of your excellent Cabinet Minute. I could have wished also to have kept a copy of the Duke of Wellington's Memorandum; but, no permission having reached me for this purpose, it is returned without even a note of its contents being reserved in writing.

Yours, my dear lord, &c.,   CLANCARTY.

The Hon. F. Lamb to Lord Castlereagh.

Frankfort, June 26, 1820.

Dear Lord Castlereagh—I enclose communications which I have received on German affairs, and which may be fully relied upon. The authority they come from shall be mentioned whenever an English courier passes; in the mean time, allow me to suggest that it had better not be known at Vienna that any such communications have been received through me. In many instances, these reports are a mere repetition of what has already been advanced; but there is this difference, that they state from positive information what has hitherto been matter of inference and opinion.

Ever faithfully yours,   F. LAMB.

From the same source I learn that the Emperor of Russia has tried to be invited to the camp at Pesth, and that, although no invitation has yet been given, still it is not certain that he may not arrive there. As my first information upon this came through the King of Wirtemberg, I conclude that the present intention of the Emperor is to go there.

F. L.

Communications.

Austria is convinced that the project of fortifying Ulm has been withstood, not from military but from political reasons. She has even positive evidence of it from a secret Memoir drawn up by order of the King of Wirtemburg, upon the fortification of Rastadt, in which it is stated that the independence of Wirtemberg is incompatible with the existence of an Austrian garrison at Ulm. The knowledge of this must make Austria cautious that no fortress shall be constructed which may be liable to be used against herself.[1] For this reason, she cannot agree to the fortification of Rastadt, though she might to that of Manheim or Germersheim.[2]

The latter is the point to which there exist the fewest obstacles. The chief one arises out of the insufficiency of the funds. An adequate sum can only be provided by the union of the fifteen millions given to Bavaria, with the twenty destined for the construction of a fortress upon the Upper Rhine. Austria has already applied to Bavaria upon this subject, and has found her willing to consent, but upon the condition of a right of garrison, to which Austria can never agree, for the reasons above stated. The wish of Austria is, that Germersheim should receive a real federal garrison, to which each Power should contribute, according to their respective contingents. Austria, giving in consequence one-third of the garrison, would be stronger than any other single Power, and might expect, in case of a rupture, to remain mistress of the place.

The intention of Austria is, whenever the question shall be

[1] Observation 1. Both sides reason with equal correctness, but their arguments give the measure of the value of the Confederation for military measures or external relations.

[2] Observation 2. See the enclosure A.

revived, to press the fortification of Ulm with her utmost weight. She thinks herself sure of carrying this point by a large majority in the Diet, and hopes that Bavaria may be so far alarmed thereby, as to become more tractable upon the arrangements at Germersheim.[1]

Besides this motive for continuing to press the fortifications of Ulm, Austria still retains the *arrière-pensée* of the possibility of carrying the point, in consequence of the jealousy felt by Wirtemberg at the supposed increasing intimacy between Austria and Bavaria. If this should lead Wirtemberg to concede, Ulm would then be fortified in spite of the opposition of Bavaria.[2]

The difficulty would be to find the requisite funds, as Prussia would be unable to contribute. Austria, however, would be disposed to make every possible sacrifice for such an object as this.

With respect to more general views, it is stated that the

---

[1] Observation 3. The success of this finesse must depend upon its secrecy, of which my being acquainted with it already is but a bad omen. Before receiving this communication, I had perceived, from a conversation with the Bavarian Minister here, what were the projects of his Court upon this subject. Nor do I know any Power less likely to be induced to recede from them, particularly as the only real alternative of the non-construction of a federal fortress is, that Bavaria will retain a portion of the funds in her own hands. The fear of an Austrian garrison at Ulm is the only motive which can act upon her.

[2] Observation 4. This is highly improbable, and perhaps as little desirable. Surrounded as Bavaria is on two sides by the Austrian dominions, the addition of an Austrian garrison on her chief western line of communication would reduce her to the state of an Austrian province. She is so sensible of this, that there is no combination she would not attempt to avert it. As it would require five years to complete the fortifications, it is difficult to say what opportunity for trying the chances of a war might arise in the course of them. If I may judge from what has dropped from the Russian Minister, his Court feels considerable interest upon the subject, and might perhaps be expected to make an immediate reference to England, whether a fortress at Ulm could be considered as defending the Upper Rhine, and consequently as fulfilling the conditions of the Protocol.

conferences at Vienna were only kept together in order to show that a conclusion could be arrived at, and to disprove the reports which had been made, and, in fact, truly made, by Anstett, to the contrary. In a few months, Russia will understand that the Act contains nothing; but, in the mean time, she has doubted herself to be misled by Anstett, and has imposed silence upon him.[1]

With regard to the Act itself, Austria is well aware that there is very little in it, and even feels that the Articles on the Constitutional question had better been omitted altogether. But it was well known to Metternich that the King of Wirtemberg had virtually received an assurance of support from the Emperor Alexander, which made it necessary to conciliate him upon the subject, in order to take from him the part which he would otherwise have been capable of playing, by separating himself from the Confederation, and figuring as the head of the Constitutional party in Germany.

The 25th and 26th Articles are felt to be good, particularly that part of the 26th, which gives to the Diet the power of deciding on the necessity of suppressing troubles in any State of the Confederation, without a previous application from its Government. No positive reliance, however, can be placed upon decisions to be taken by an assembly so composed as the Diet. Two cases may be foreseen, either of which will show with what practical advantage it may be employed. The one may arise from the bad disposition of the King of Wirtemberg; the other from the bad situation of Prussia. In either of these cases, a great facility would be afforded if the Confederation would assist; if, however, it should hesitate, it would be equally necessary for Austria to suppress the danger; in the

---

[1] Observation 5. Metternich is much deceived if he thinks Russia can have mistaken for a moment the real value of what has been doing at Vienna. It is only since her point was carried that she has imposed silence upon her Ministers. Anstett has evidently received positive orders upon the subject, and he obeys them; but this does not affect his reports.

first case, by bringing the King of Wirtemberg to reason; in
the second, by assisting the Prussian Government; and, in
either of these events, the Confederation would be dissolved.

In the mean time, it is probably true that, up to this period,
Austria would have possessed greater influence in Germany if
no Confederation had existed; as, in that case, the jealousy
which has been felt of her would not have been excited; and
several of the smaller States, finding themselves unsupported,
would have attached themselves to her, and made common
cause with her.   Much harm has also arisen from the incapa-
city of the Austrian and Prussian Ministers, which Metternich has neglected to remedy, from a persuasion that it is
indifferent what agents he employs, as he can conduct all
affairs himself.   This may be true at a Court, but it is false in
an assembly where there is a necessity for answering at the
moment.   Prussia has felt this, and it was with a view of
employing M. de Plessen at the Diet, that she proposed to him
to enter her service and quit that of Mecklenburg.   At present the object of M. de Metternich is to let the Diet sink
into a state of inactivity;[1] and it was with this view that he
proposed that the vacation should last eight months in the
year and the sittings four.   This proposition was opposed by
the members of the Diet, who feel that it would destroy their
own importance.

It must not be supposed that Metternich is entirely master
in the affairs of the Confederation; the whole military party
in Austria are decidedly hostile to its existence.[2]   They contend that experience and probabilities equally point out that
all serious shocks to Austria must be expected from the East,
and they ask what assistance is to be expected from the Con-

---

[1] Observation 6.   I have long been convinced that the best policy
Austria can pursue with the Confederation is to let it hang as loosely
together as it may, for the chance of making use of it on an emergency.

[2] Observation 7.   This confirms the statement in my private letter of
the 4th of January last.

federation in Gallicia. Their idea is that, if no such union existed, separate alliances might be formed with several of the German States, which would provide a much more efficient assistance than is to be expected under the present plan. Metternich persists in supporting the Confederation, first, because it exists; secondly, because the change of system might lead to war, which, to speak the truth, it is not the object of the military party to avoid.

Military Communications.

A.

The reasons which would induce Austria to prefer Germersheim to Rastadt are the following:—Germersheim would give a bridge over the Rhine, which is much wanted, as Germany possesses none to the south of Mayence. It would be an offensive point and a support to Landau.

In case of its being given up, it could be of no prejudice to Germany. Austria, in its construction, would take care that the *tête de pont* on the left bank should form the strongest part of the fortress, and, whenever this could no longer be defended, it would be the duty of the officer commanding to blow up the works on the right bank.

Rastadt would offer none of these advantages; it would be besieged by the French with the guns of Strasburg and the other fortresses on the Rhine, while Austria, if it were ever lost, must bring her guns to retake it from Comorn and Peterwardein: so that it may be safely said that it might more easily be taken six times by the French than once by the Austrians.

The additional works and repairs at Mayence will cost about five millions. There remain of the fund destined for this object between two and three millions. The repairs of Luxemburg will require two millions, leaving about fifteen millions disposable for the construction of a new fortress.[1] If to this

[1] Observation 1. It may be a question whether the Confederation is justified in such an application of a portion of a fund, the destination of

can be added the fifteen millions which will remain in the hands
of Bavaria, exclusive of the sums expended upon Landau, it
may be calculated that, with the interest, thirty-two millions
may be applied to Germersheim, during the five years in which
it is proposed to complete the works; and this sum will be
sufficient.

Extract of a Despatch from Sir William à Court.

Naples, July 5, 1820.

Your lordship will undoubtedly remark that there is not a
shadow of blame attempted to be thrown on the existing
Government in the enclosed proclamation. A diminution of
one-half of the duty on salt is the only advantage held out to
the people. In fact, it would be difficult to fix blame where
none exists. So paternal and so liberal a Government was
never before known in these kingdoms. With more severity
and more distrust, a different result might have been obtained;
but it was fated that an excess of liberality here should lead
exactly to the same end as an excess of an opposite nature in
Spain. The spirit of sectarism and the unheard-of defection
of an army well paid and clothed and wanting for nothing, has
caused the ruin of a Government popular (notwithstanding
these late events) with the great mass of the people, and
which will hereafter be long and deeply regretted; and it is
not unworthy of remark that these sects owe their origin to
the very Government they have now so much contributed to
overthrow. They were imagined and encouraged as an engine
the most likely to sap the power of the French, then in possession of the country. The scheme took root more deeply
than its inventors intended, who have lived to reap the bitter
fruits of their short-sighted policy.

---

which is fixed by a public Act. When the three federal fortresses are
delivered over to the Confederation, which is shortly to take place, it
will be important that an efficient and adequate fund should be provided
for their repair: even this, however, will encounter many difficulties.

Sir William à Court to Lord Castlereagh.

Naples, July 6, 1820.

My dear Lord—The revolution it is my painful duty to detail to your lordship in my despatches of this date is one of the most singular in the annals of history. A kingdom in the highest degree flourishing and happy, under the mildest of Governments, and by no means oppressed by the weight of taxation, crumbles before a handful of insurgents that half a battalion of good soldiers would have crushed in an instant!

Such is the force of bad example and of a watchword which half of those who use it do not understand. Every officer now would be a Quiroga, and "a Constitution" is the rallying word, which acts like a charm on all.

I cannot foresee what is to become of this unhappy country, or the effect that this revolution will produce on the rest of Italy. I fear it will lead to bloodshed and confusion everywhere. We must not deceive ourselves. "Constitution," indeed, is the watchword used, but what has happened is nothing less than the triumph of Jacobinism—it is the war of poverty against property. The lower classes have been taught to know their own power, and that the armed force (which unfortunately is not incorruptible) is the only counterpoise on the side of the rich, which prevents their will from becoming law. They have proved it here—may the example never be followed!

I write in the greatest haste, as I am desirous my despatches should reach your lordship as soon as possible. I shall write more at length in a few days.

I have the honour to be, &c.,   WILLIAM À COURT.

Prince Castelcicala to Prince [no address].

Paris, ce 17 Juillet, 1820.

Cher Prince—Vous aurez appris avant celle-ci les évènemens désastreux, qui ont eu lieu à Naples ; mais voici dans la

feuille ci-jointe, et que Sir Charles Stuart m'a communiqué,
ainsi qu'au Ministère Français, ni celui-ci ni moi nous n'avons
aucun courier ni nouvelle.   J'avois bien raison de dire qu'il
falloit, sans perte de tems, que votre Cour et la mienne se
concourassent pour empêcher les mauvais effets de l'exemple
qui s'est fait en Espagne. Si ce qui s'est passé à Naples se
consolide, à-part des malheurs que cela entraînera sur l'Italie,
qui sera bouleversée, tout le monde y passera, et l'état actuel
de la société en Europe périra et sera remplacé par un
despotisme militaire : car les militaires qui font les Constitutions, les déferont tout aussi bien, et n'y manqueront.

L'exemple de l'Espagne n'étoit donc pas un danger imagi-
naire mais bien réel.   Les conspirateurs de toutes les couleurs
ont sçu en profiter, et ils n'ont pas perdu du tems.   Le Ministère François est désolé de tout ce qui s'est passé.   Le Duc
de Richelieu et M. Pasquier sont venus hier me faire visite
pour me le témoigner, ainsi que beaucoup d'intérêt.   Vous
avez vu que la cocarde tricolore entre dans toute cette affaire.

J'ai reçu à présent mon cher Prince, la confirmation de tout
ceci par des dépêches de Naples du 6.   Tout me fait une peine
infinie.   Je vous embrasse du fond de mon cœur,

CASTELCICALA.

Sir Charles Bagot to Lord Castlereagh.
St. Petersburgh, July 19-31 [1820].

My dear Lord—I am at length enabled to send away the
messenger Latchford, having received from Count Nesselrode
the communication of the papers which he had promised me,
and which you will find in my despatch of to-day.   Count
Nesselrode brought these papers to me himself on Friday last,
having heard that I was confined to my house by a slight
illness, of which I have now got entirely rid.   I had proceeded
to read them, when he told me that, if I wished it, I was
at liberty to keep them for a few hours.   I gladly availed
myself of this offer, in order that I might take copies; and

thus it happened that I had hardly any conversation with Count Nesselrode on the subject of them. I ought, perhaps, to add that the communication of the despatch to Baron Tuyll is considered as confidential, because I know that Count Nesselrode, although he has read it to M. de Lassa, the Portuguese Minister, has not given him a copy of it.

Baron Lebzeltern has read to me confidentially the despatches with which he has transmitted these papers to his Court. He is but little satisfied with either of them, and has entered, in his despatch to Prince Metternich, into a very minute examination of the despatch to Count Golowkin, which he considers as little else than verbiage, and in which he thinks that nothing is apparent but the constant desire of this Government to shake off the inconvenience of the Quadruple Alliance by extending and generalizing it as much as possible. Your lordship will judge how far this view of the paper is correct; but there are certainly several expressions in both the papers which seem to warrant these observations.

With the despatch to Baron Tuyll, Baron Lebzeltern finds more serious fault. He thinks that the declaration there made by the Russian Government, that they coincide entirely with that of Portugal upon the subject of general and mutual guarantee, and that, two years ago, they had submitted to Austria, France, England, and Prussia, a proposition for such "*garantie explicite, universelle, et réciproque*," to which proposition no answer had ever been returned, is calculated to give a very unfavourable idea of the unanimity and accord subsisting amongst the Powers composing the Alliance, and likely, on that account, to have very injurious effects. Baron Lebzeltern has not confined these remarks to Prince Metternich. He tells me that he has equally, though privately, made them to Count Nesselrode, with whom he lives upon terms of great intimacy, and also to Count Capodistrias.

I have the honour to be, &c.,   CHARLES BAGOT.

Sir Henry Wellesley to Lord Castlereagh.

Madrid, July 24, 1820.

My dear Lord—I have now the honour to return the box of papers which your lordship had the goodness to transmit for my perusal. I have not much to add to my despatches relative to the state of public affairs in this country. There is said to be a formidable body of insurgents near Burgos, who have taken up arms against the Constitution, and a similar spirit has manifested itself in other provinces. The country is certainly in a most critical state; but I believe the intentions of the Ministers and of their friends in the Cortes to be honest; and I see no hope of salvation for the country or for the King, but by his uniting cordially with these men, and discouraging every attempt at a counter-revolution. The clubs are making rapid advances in Jacobinism. There is one society, to become a member of which, an oath is taken nearly as atrocious as that of the Illuminés in Germany; and all the maxims of this society are subversive of monarchy. In short, there is much to apprehend here; but I am unwilling to relinquish the hopes I have formed from the talents and disposition of the moderate party, at the head of which, in the Cortes, are the Conde de Toreno and M. Martinez de la Rosa, who are by far the ablest and best speakers in that assembly.

Your lordship has expressed a desire to know my opinion of Count Dernath, the Danish Minister at this Court. Count Dernath is nearly sixty years of age, and, I understand, has always been remarkable for affecting a singularity of opinion upon all subjects. This leads him to differ with his colleagues on most points connected with the actual state of this country; and I have often pitied his Court at having to wade through the mass of absurdities, false information, and false reasoning, with which, to judge of his correspondence by his conversation, his letters must be filled. When I heard of the conduct attributed to this embassy, I had no difficulty in deciding from whence the information came. Count Dernath, upon his arrival here, formed an intimacy with M. de Tatistcheff; and, I believe, is inclined to support the policy of Russia with respect to this country.

I have not said anything to your lordship relative to the supposed project of placing the Prince of Lucca at the head of the Government of Buenos Ayres, being convinced that no such project was ever entertained here, or would have been listened to for one moment. In fact, such a proposal would have met with a worse reception than that of Count Palmella, for placing one of the King's brothers at the head of the vice-royalty of Buenos Ayres.

I have reason to know that M. Pardo, the Spanish Chargé d'Affaires at Lisbon, is in constant correspondence with the clubs here, and has made a favourable report of the success of his intrigues with the officers of the army, &c. M. Saldanha, the new Portuguese Minister at this Court, entreated me to mention this to your lordship, in the hope that his Majesty's Chargé d'Affaires at Lisbon might be instructed to watch M. Pardo, and to counteract his intrigues.

I have taken the liberty to apply for a discretionary leave of absence, but your lordship may be assured of my not making use of it as long as my presence can be necessary here.

I have the honour to be, &c.,   H. WELLESLEY.

I do not think that the King's journey will do him any mischief, if, on his return, he gives his full confidence to his Ministers.

A courier is arrived from Rome, with an account of a revolution having taken place at Naples; yet this intelligence has not produced any great effect here, and some doubt appears to be entertained of its authenticity.   H. W.

Lieut.-Colonel Browne to Lord Castlereagh.

Milan, July 29, 1820.

My dear Lord—Sir William à Court and Lord Burghersh having sent the despatches which I now forward to your lordship under flying seal to me, for the purpose, no doubt, of enabling me to make the Austrian authorities here aware generally of the scenes which are passing round them, without the delay of going first to Vienna, I felt it my duty to make copies of them, and to send them by courier to Lord Stewart.

I trust that existing circumstances will plead my excuse with your lordship for the irregularity, and that, if I have done wrong, you will view my conduct with indulgence, as proceeding from the best of my judgment, for the good of the service. The infection from Naples has reached Milan, and reports of all sorts are in circulation: the coffee-rooms are more crowded than usual, and the subjects of conversation more assuming and desperate—Constitution and insurrection are in every one's mouth. The Liberales here are loud in their celebration of the Spaniards and Neapolitans. They are ripe for anything; but the fine garrison of Hungarian grenadiers in this city, who are the most anti-constitutional characters possible, keep everything quiet; and the report which is prevalent here, and encouraged by the authorities, that Austria has already ordered an increase to her force in Lombardy, has the effect of maintaining public tranquillity, for the interruption of which there is not the slightest apprehension, so long as a single Austrian battalion shall remain here.

General Bubna told me in confidence this morning, that he had received a positive order to march upon Parma, should any insurrection take place there, and that he had recommended to his Government the provisionary fortification of Plaisance, and other measures of precaution. He also mentioned to me that a trustworthy person, who had just returned from Turin, where he had been sent, and had remained during the last fortnight, to make himself intimately acquainted with the spirit and sentiments of the Piedmontese army, had returned with satisfactory accounts; that the army was not ill-affected to the existing order of things, but were in want of an active and decisive chief; that they appear satisfied, and not desirous of any change.

I cannot, perhaps, give your lordship a better idea of the extent to which the question of the Queen is mixed up with politics here than by mentioning that a leader of the democrat party said in society, a few evenings since, " The Queen of England *shall* triumph; and two or three questions of a similar nature are all that are now wanting to restore the rights of man, and to rid us of all our tyrants at once."

I have only again to entreat your lordship to receive this letter with indulgence, and to believe me, &c.,

T. H. BROWNE.

Count Lieven to Lord Castlereagh.

Harley Street, le 21 Août, 1820.

Le Comte de Lieven présente ses complimens à Mylord Castlereagh, et a l'honneur de faire tenir ci-près à son Excellence les copies de cinq dépêches, avec leurs annexes, qu'elle avoit désiré posséder.

[Enclosures.]

Copie d'une Dépêche de M. le Comte de Nesselrode à l'Ambassadeur Comte de Lieven.

St. Petersbourg, du 15 Juillet, 1820.

Monsieur le Comte—Le Ministère Impérial est chargé de transmettre à votre Excellence la copie d'une dépêche qu'il vient à addresser par ordre de l'Empereur à M. le Général Baron de Tuyll.

Alarmés des projets qu'ils ont cru pouvoir supposer au nouveau Gouvernement Espagnol, les Ministres et agens de sa Majesté Très Fidèle en Europe ont exprimé le désir de voir le Portugal placé sous la garantie des principales Puissances Européennes. Cette garantie étoit, d'après l'opinion qu'ils ont émise, un résultat implicite des Traités de Vienne et de l'Acte du 14-26 Septembre, 1815.

Vous devez, M. le Comte, connoître les principes que le

Cabinet de Russie professe à cet égard. Nous les avons développés à Aix-la-Chapelle, dans un Mémoire et dans une Note Verbale, dont vous avez pris lecture. La première de ces pièces définissoit la nature et l'objet des engagemens contractés par les Puissances qui avoient signé ou sanctionné le Recès de Vienne et l'Acte du 14-26 Septembre, 1815, notamment par celles qui, placées au centre de l'Alliance générale, devoient préserver de toute atteinte ce système conservateur. La seconde avoit pour but l'application immédiate et pratique d'une doctrine si salutaire.

Notre Note se trouvoit encore jointe aux communications qu'ont reçues de notre part, sous la date du 4 Fevrier de l'année courante, les Cabinets de Vienne, de Londres, et de Berlin, et elle est également annexée à la dépêche que nous addressons à M. de Tuyll.

Quelques sincères que soient nos vœux pour la sécurité de sa Majesté Très Fidèle, il nous est impossible de déférer à sa demande. Le silence des autres Cabinets au sujet de nos propositions relatives à un Traité général de garantie réciproque, ne nous permet pas d'articuler *seuls* une réponse positive. Mais la conjoncture qui a donné lieu aux démarches des Ministres Portugais prouve évidemment l'utilité de notre idée.

Veuillez donc, M. le Comte, profiter de cette circonstance pour en entretenir encore une fois le Cabinet de St. James. L'Empereur vous autorise à mettre sous les yeux du Ministère Britannique la présente dépêche, ainsi que les deux pièces qui y sont jointes, et désire que vous nous rendiez compte de l'opinion qu'il aura exprimée sur leur contenu.

Agréez, &c.

Copie d'une Dépêche de M. le Comte de Nesselrode à l'Ambassadeur Comte de Lieven.

St. Petersbourg, le 15 Juillet, 1820.

Votre Excellence a déjà plusieurs fois été appellée à faire valoir auprès de la Cour de Londres la sollicitude que l'Empereur se plait à vouer aux intérêts de Madame la Princesse de Montfort.

J'ai l'honneur de lui communiquer aujourd'hui la dépêche ci-jointe motivée par les délais que le Gouvernement de sa Majesté Très Chrétienne apporte à faire droit aux réclamations de cette Princesse.   La tâche qui nous est réservée dans cette occasion, M. le Comte, consiste à faire connoître la pièce susmentionnée au Ministère Britannique, et à lui proposer de munir son Ministre à Paris d'instructions conformes à celles que reçoit le Général Pozzo di Borgo.   Nous aurions à croire que le Cabinet de St. James, après avoir accordé sa bienveillante intercession à Madame la Princesse de Montfort, ne se refusera pas à poursuivre et à remplir la tâche qu'il s'est si généreusement imposée.

Recevez, &c.,   NESSELRODE.

Copie d'une Dépéche au Général Pozzo di Borgo.

St. Petersbourg, le 15 Juillet, 1820.

Votre Excellence nous a rendu compte, par sa dépêche sub No. 910, de la démarche faite auprès du Ministère François, relativement au douaire dont Madame la Princesse Catherine de Montfort réclame la restitution.   Plus de cinq mois se sont écoulés depuis, sans que le Gouvernement de sa Majesté Très Chrétienne paroisse s'être expliqué d'une manière quelconque sur la Note collective des Plénipotentiares Alliés.

Cependant l'Empereur a voué une trop juste sollicitude à la pénible position de Madame la Princesse de Montfort pour ne pas désirer sincèrement que les vœux de son Altesse Royale obtiennent un prompt et entier accomplissement.

Sa Majesté invite donc votre Excellence à s'entendre avec ses Collègues afin de renouveller conjointement avec eux, et d'une manière plus pressante encore, la demande adressée à cet égard au Baron de Pasquier.

L'unanimité qui a présidée à la première démarche des quatre Ministres, la justice de la cause qu'ils sont appelés à

plaider, les talens qui les distinguent, enfin, l'équité du Cabinet
François, ne nous permettent pas de douter d'une issue favorable. L'Empereur vous saura gré, M. le Général, de tout ce
que vous aurez fait de votre part, dans la vue d'accélérer ce
résultat.

Recevez, &c.

Copie d'une Dépêche au Baron d'Alopéus.

St. Petersbourg, le 15 Juillet, 1820.

Le Ministère accuse à votre Excellence la réception de ses
rapports jusqu'au No. 64 inclusivement. Nous avons aussi
reçu des communications directes de la part du Ministère Prussien en réponse à nos propositions du 20 Avril, concernant les
changemens survenus en Espagne, et les moyens d'armer l'Alliance générale d'un pouvoir d'action plus sensible et plus réel.

Comme d'un côté nous attendons encore des explications au
sujet de nos dépêches du 20 Avril, de la part des Cours d'Angleterre et de France, et que de l'autre le Cabinet de Vienne
a développé sur ces matières inquiétantes une doctrine et des
opinions entièrement semblables à celles que nous a fait connoître le Cabinet de Berlin, nous croyons devoir adresser à
votre Excellence la copie ci-jointe d'une dépêche que reçoit
d'ordre de l'Empereur M. le Comte de Golowkin.

Vous voudrez bien, M. le Baron, en donner connoissance au
Ministère Prussien. Elle ne renferme que des réflexions
générales et préliminaires ; mais nous nous réservons de lui
adresser une réponse circonstanciée dès que les observations
que doivent nous transmettre les Cours de Londres et de Paris
nous seront parvenues.

Recevez, &c.

Copie d'une Dépêche au Comte Golowkin.

St. Petersbourg, le 15 Juillet, 1820.

Le Ministère a reçu vos rapports jusqu'au No. 96, inclusivement, et les a mis sous les yeux de l'Empereur. Notre

dernier courier, en nous apportant une réponse sommaire du Cabinet de Vienne à nos dépêches du 20 Avril, nous prévenoit que le Ministère Autrichien alloit incessamment nous adresser des explications directes et circonstanciées.

Ces explications nous sont en effet parvenues par la voie de M. le Baron de Lebzeltern, qui nous a communiqué deux dépêches de M. le Prince de Metternich, en date du 5 Juin, où ce Ministre discute avec son talent ordinaire les graves questions sur lesquelles nous avions appellé l'attention des · Cabinets Alliés. L'Empereur a lu et médité l'opinion du Ministère de sa Majesté Impériale et Royale Autrichienne, et vous voudrez, M. le Comte, lui exprimer toute la gratitude que nous inspirent les nouveaux témoignages de confiance qu'il nous donne. Nous ne serons pas moins sincères, mais nous ne nous voyons point encore à même de répondre en détail à ses observations.

Les propositions que renferment nos Mémoires et notre dépêche du 20 Avril avoient été soumis à l'examen des quatre Cours qui se trouvent placées, comme la Russie, au centre de l'Alliance générale. Le Cabinet de Berlin nous a déjà fait connoître la pensée toute entière du Roi sur les communications dont nous venons de citer la· date. Mais le Cabinet de St. James n'a discuté que nos ouvertures du 3 Mars. La réponse qu'amèneront de sa part nos dépêches postérieures nous est inconnue jusqu'à présent ; et, ainsi que le Ministère Britannique, le Ministère François médite encore la sienne.

Nous nous trouvons donc dans la nécessité d'attendre que les Cours d'Angleterre et de France aient énoncé leur opinion, avant que nous puissions adopter et articuler l'avis qui consacrera et l'autorité d'un suffrage plus général et celle des principes conservateurs, qui constituent la règle de conduite de toutes les Puissances Européennes. Nous pouvons, en attendant, nous féliciter d'un premier résultat. Le Ministère de sa Majesté l'Empereur d'Autriche partage nos sentimens sur le dangereux mode d'innovation que le 8 Mars avoit signalé en Espagne. Il approuve la doctrine que nous avons développée à cet égard ; et si notre langage n'a pu devenir le sien, nous avons eu, d'un autre côté, le plaisir d'apprendre que les intentions et les vœux de l'Autriche ne différoient pas des intentions de la Russie.

Plus nous sommes convaincus de l'identité des maximes qui dirigent les Cabinets Alliés, plus est irréfragable et imposante la preuve que les Actes d'Aix-la-Chapelle offrent de cette unanimité de vues et d'actions, plus ces Actes démontrent que les Monarques dont ils émanent se considèrent comme uni par un lien de fraternité générale à toutes les Puissances qui ont signé le Recès de Vienne et les transactions subséquentes, ou qui y ont accédé ; enfin, plus il est incontestable qu'à moins que la France ne sorte de ses limites, ou qu'une nouvelle révolution ne vienne l'agiter, son Gouvernement doit participer à l'association formée par les Cours d'Autriche, de la Grande Bretagne, de Prusse, et de Russie, pour assurer l'inviolabilité de ce système de paix et de concorde, et plus nous devons regretter que des conjonctures particulières rendent quelquefois divergente la marche que les Cours Alliées sont, pour ainsi dire, forcées de suivre, quand il s'agit de mettre en pratique la théorie de l'union universelle.

Nous nous estimerons donc toujours heureux de rencontrer des circonstances où règne un complet accord entre le désir et la possibilité, entre les principes et les faits. L'Empereur a trouvé ce motif de satisfaction dans la dépêche de M. le Prince de Metternich relative aux instructions éventuelles que recevroient les Ministres des Cours Alliées en France, pour le cas de la succession au trône, et sa Majesté s'empresse de déclarer ici que les ordres qui seront expédiés sous ce rapport à M. le Général Pozzo di Borgo ne différeront en rien de ceux que l'Autriche se propose de transmettre à M. le Baron de Vincent.

Le Cabinet d'Autriche a bien voulu nous communiquer une traduction Françoise de l'Acte final des Conférences à Vienne.

L'Empereur lira cet Acte avec toute l'attention qu'il mérite. Mais sa Majesté vous charge de répéter dès à présent au Premier Ministre d'Autriche qu'elle se félicite de voir qu'une harmonie inaltérable ait présidé aux délibérations des Plénipotentiaires Germaniques.

Quoiqu' étrangère à la fédération, que l'Acte final paroit devoir cimenter, sa Majesté ne cessera de faire des vœux pour qu'il assure à tous les États d'Allemagne le bienfait de l'union et d'une prospérité toujours croissante.

Nous engageons votre Excellence de donner lecture de la présente à M. le Prince de Metternich, et nous en adressons copie à M. le Baron de Lebzeltern.

Recevez, &c.

Copie d'une Dépêche au Baron de Tuyll.

St. Petersbourg, ce 18 Juillet, 1820.

Les Ministres et agens de la Cour de Rio Janeiro en Europe ont, à la suite des derniers évènemens d'Espagne, manifesté de vives appréhensions sur le sort que pourroit éprouver le Portugal. Leurs inquiétudes provenoient, d'après ce qu'ils ont témoigné, des projets qu'annonçoient à Madrid quelques hommes, qui, cherchant à usurper une influence illégitime dans les affaires publiques, vouloient communiquer au Portugal la commotion révolutionnaire que venoit d'essuyer l'Espagne, reculer les limites de ce dernier pays, et réunir la Péninsule toute entière sous un même Gouvernement. En exprimant ces alarmes, les agens Portugais ont énoncé le désir d'opposer dès à-présent à toute violation des droits de sa Majesté Très Fidèle, l'intention que proclameroient les principales Puissances de lui garantir l'intégrité de son territoire en Europe.

Ce vœu a été articulé sous diverses formes par les Ministres de la Cour de Rio Janeiro. M. le Marquis de Marialva a cru devoir adresser une Note officielle au Ministère François. M. le Vicomte de Lassa s'est contenté de nous faire connoître, de vive voix dans une conférence, ses craintes, leurs motifs, et la demande qu'elles lui avoient suggérée.   Pour plus de précision, nous rapporterons ici la substance et des propositions du Représentant de sa Majesté Très Fidèle et de la réponse qu'il a reçue de notre part.

M. de Lassa souhaitoit que les Cours signataires des Traités de Vienne et de l'Acte du 14-26 Septembre, 1815, déclarassent solennellement :

1°. Que les dits Traités et Actes contiennent implicitement une garantie générale et réciproque de leurs territoires respectifs, ainsi que de la légitimité et de l'indépendance de leurs Gouvernemens.

2°. Que les Puissances se considèrent comme obligées de soutenir, de toutes leurs forces, la garantie résultante des traités en question.

À l'appui de ces propositions M. de Lassa a cité un Traité d'Alliance et de garantie conclu en 1799 entre la Russie et le Portugal.

Voulant témoigner au Ministre de sa Majesté Très Fidèle une juste réciprocité de confiance, nous n'avons pas pu lui dissimuler que l'Empereur ne sauroit reconnoître l'existence de la garantie de territoire statuée par le Traité de 1799 ; et que d'un autre côté, il ne dépendoit pas exclusivement de sa Majesté Impériale de déduire cette même garantie des Traités de Vienne et de l'Acte du 14-26 Septembre, 1815.

Le Traité de 1799 doit, sans doute se trouver aux archives de votre Légation, et il sera facile de vous convaincre que les engagemens contractés par cet Acte entre la Russie et le Portugal n'étoient que temporaires, et que le terme en est expiré depuis l'année 1808.   Nous devons, en conséquence, regarder ce Traité comme non avenu.

Quant à l'Acte du Congrès de Vienne, et à celui du 14-26 Septembre, 1815, vous connoissez, M. le Baron, la valeur que nous avons toujours attachée aux stipulations qu'ils renferment, et à la signature collective, à la sanction générale, dont ils sont revêtus.

Nous n'avons cessé d'y voir la double garantie et de l'état
de possession actuel de toutes les Puissances signataires ou
accédantes, et de la légitimité des Gouvernemens rétablis en
Europe.

Lors de votre séjour à Aix-la-Chapelle vous avez eu occasion de lire les Mémoires dans lesquels nous avons développé
cette doctrine conservatrice, et vous avez été, si l'on peut
s'exprimer ainsi, témoin de l'intérêt que l'Empereur mettoit à
la faire unanimement adopter. À la clôture même des Conférences, pour rendre plus sensible, pour convertir en un fait
matériel et incontestable l'esprit des transactions qui constituent le droit public Européen, nous avons remis aux Plénipotentiaires des Cours d'Autriche, de France, d'Angleterre, et
de Prusse, la Note Verbale ci-jointe en copie, renfermant la
proposition d'une garantie explicite, universelle, et réciproque.

Nos vœux sont donc les mêmes que ceux de la Cour de Rio
Janeiro. Cependant comme nos ouvertures à l'égard d'une
traité général de garantie mutuelle restent jusqu'à présent
sans réponse définitive, sa Majesté Impériale ne peut offrir au
Gouvernement Portugais que l'expression du désir de voir le
principe qu'il invoque consacré par l'assentiment formel de
toutes les Puissances Européennes. Cependant si, dans l'inter-
valle des négociations auxquelles pourra donner lieu l'opinion
que nous avons si souvent énoncé sous ce rapport, le Portugal
devenoit l'objet d'une aggression illégitime de la part de
l'Espagne, la Cour de Rio Janeiro trouveroit la conduite de
l'Empereur indiquée d'avance par celle qu'il a tenue envers la
Cour de Madrid, lorsque celle-ci réclama son intervention dans
le différend qu'avoit provoquée l'occupation de la rive orientale
du Rio de la Plata. Les sentimens que l'Empereur a témoigné
dans cette circonstance au Gouvernement Espagnol il est prêt
à les témoigner au Gouvernement Portugais, si l'Espagne diri-
geoit une attaque injuste contre le territoire de sa Majesté Très
Fidèle. C'est ainsi que nous nous sommes expliqués verbalement avec M. de Lassa. Pour qu'il ait une idée plus précise

de notre manière d'envisager cette question, nous lui ferons lecture de la présente dépêche. Vous pourrez, de votre côté, en donner connoissance au Ministère Portugais s'il vous exprime les mêmes appréhensions. La présente sera communiquée circulairement aux Cours de Vienne, de Paris, de Londres, et de Berlin.

Recevez, &c.

Copie d'une Dépêche de M. le Comte de Nesselrode à l'Ambassadeur le Comte de Lieven.

St. Petersbourg, le 18 Juillet, 1820.

La dépêche principale que vous porte notre courier était déjà approuvée par l'Empereur lorsque nous reçûmes les rapports que votre Excellence nous a transmis par M. le Chambellan de Krivtzoff.

Nous y avons vu que dans son dernier entretien avec votre Excellence, Lord Castlereagh, pour toute réponse à nos communications du 20 Avril, s'était référé au mémorandum dans lequel il avait développé l'opinion du Gouvernement Britannique sur nos propositions du 3 Mars.

Nous croyons donc, M. le Comte, que, pour remplir les instructions que vous recevez aujourd'hui, il vous suffira de donner lecture à Lord Castlereagh de la dépêche qui les renferme, et de lui demander si nous devons voir dans le mémorandum cité plus haut une réponse implicite et fait d'avance à notre mémoire du 20 Avril.

Votre Excellence voudra bien nous informer des résultats des nouveaux entretiens qu'elle aura à ce sujet avec M. le Vicomte de Castlereagh.

Recevez, &c.,   NESSELRODE.

Copie d'une Dépêche de M. le Comte de Nesselrode à l'Ambassadeur le Comte de Lieven.

St. Petersbourg, 18 Juillet, 1820.

L'Empereur s'est empressé d'accorder à M. le Chevalier de

Bagot, l'audience de réception, où cet ambassadeur a présenté ses lettres de créance à sa Majesté Impériale.

Elle ne peut que se féliciter du choix que sa Majesté Britannique a fait de son nouveau représentatif, et l'Empereur a trouvé que M. de Bagot justifiait pleinement les témoignages honorables que le Ministère Anglais s'était plu à lui rendre.

En expédiant ce courier à votre Excellence nous n'avons en vue que de lui fournir une voye sûre pour nous transmettre ses rapports.

La plus importante des dépêches dont il est porteur est relative à la demande présentée par le Ministre de la Cour de Rio Janeiro. Mais comme nous nous croyons être suffisamment expliqués tant dans notre dépêche au Général Tuyll, dont vous recevez copie, que dans la circulaire qui l'accompagne, nous ne reviendrons ici sur cette matière.

Nous avons reçu des Cours de Vienne et de Berlin des réponses à nos propositions du 20 Avril, concernant les affaires d'Espagne et les questions de politique générale.

Mais comme nous attendons encore sur ces sujets importans des explications de la part des Cours de Londres et de Paris, nous n'avons pu adresser à nos Ministres près celles de l'Autriche et de Prusse que les dépêches dont copie ci-jointe.

Veuillez, Monsieur le Comte, en donner lecture au Vicomte de Castlereagh, et rappeler à l'attention du Ministère Britannique nos communications du 20 Avril. L'importance que l'Empereur attache à l'opinion du Gouvernement Anglais, nous fait vivement désirer une réponse.

Recevez, Monsieur le Comte, l'assurance, &c.,

NESSELRODE.

Lord Castlereagh to Sir William à Court.

Foreign Office, August 26, 1820.

Sir—In the present unsettled state of affairs in the kingdom of the Two Sicilies, and until the King shall be enabled to form a more correct judgment of the nature and result of the late revolution, his Majesty does not deem it proper that I should send you any official instructions.

You will receive in due time the King's approbation of the prudent and firm course of conduct which you have pursued throughout the late trying scenes; and you will continue to abstain from giving any opinion which can in the slightest degree commit the opinion of your Government, with regard to the events which have already taken place, or which are in progress.

I beg to express my particular thanks for the very valuable and interesting reports of these extraordinary transactions which you have furnished for the information of your Government. I attach the utmost importance, at such a moment, to the presence at Naples of a British Minister of your tried judgment and experience; and I therefore cannot, in the existing state of things, encourage you to expect that your services at the post you so usefully occupy can be dispensed with.

CASTLEREAGH.

Sir Charles Bagot to Lord Castlereagh.

St. Petersburgh, August 26 (September 7), 1820.

My dear Lord—Having two messengers here, I have thought it worth while to send home one of them, with my despatches of this date. I have little to add, either in the way of fact or commentary, to my despatch No. 18, reporting my interview with Count Nesselrode, and my communication to him of your lordship's despatch to Lord Stewart of the 29th of July. If, as I at one moment imagined, there was something like a feeling of jealousy which crossed Count Nesselrode's mind, at finding that we had, in the first instance, declared ourselves to the Court of Austria, I am satisfied that I succeeded in removing it, and that he is now quite sensible that it was the natural and obvious course for us to take. He was very anxious to ascertain whether we only desired to avoid Ministerial conferences at Paris (in which he thought us most judicious) or whether we inclined to avoid conference altogether.

I reminded him that your lordship's despatch was written at the moment of the first arrival of the intelligence from Italy, and that it was not to be supposed that his Majesty's Government could have come to any settled opinion upon this, or on any other questions, till it was further known what was the course which affairs might take in Italy, and till the sentiments of the Court most immediately endangered by the late events should be better ascertained.

Since closing my despatch I have received a private note from Count Nesselrode, in which he tells me that he has just received a courier from Warsaw, that " les nouvelles sont du 17-29 Août. On attendoit la réponse de Vienne, pour savoir définitivement à quoi s'en tenir relativement à l'entrevue des Souverains."

I should think that, from Count Nesselrode's manner of speaking of him, Prince Carietate will meet with but a cool reception whenever he presents himself here; but I imagine that, after what took place at Vienna, he will take care that there is no want of formality in his credential.

I have felt rather embarrassed to know how to make my report upon what passed between Count Nesselrode and me upon the subject of the Buenos Ayres affair. I felt that, if Count Lieven's communication of last year had escaped his or your lordship's recollection, or if it had been imperfectly made, some inconvenience might grow out of a public despatch, detailing all which Count Nesselrode said to me, if it should ever be necessary to lay it before Parliament. I have, therefore, thought it might be useful to give the fuller report in a separate despatch.

A courier arrived from Paris, two nights ago, to M. de la Ferronays, with accounts of the detection of the conspiracy against the Royal Family. Count Nesselrode has just sent me the Moniteur of the 20th, containing the report of it. It is remarkable that M. de la Ferronays has never said one syllable to me upon this or any other public matter, since my arrival in the country ; he has never mentioned to me, much less shown to me, the Memoir of the French Government, which he received more than three weeks ago, in answer to the Russian Memoir respecting Spain ; and the only communication which he has ever had with me on matters of business was to convey to me, very indirectly and circuitously, a positive denial of M. de Caze's intrigue, and the authenticity of the Buenos Ayres papers. Nothing can be more civil than he is to me personally, and his society is always agreeable. But I think that I see in his course here a secret but constant endeavour to sow distrust, and jealousy, and want of confidence amongst the Allied Powers.

Our latest accounts from England are to the 15th of August.

I have the honour to be, &c.,   CHARLES BAGOT.

The Hon. F. Lamb to Lord Castlereagh.

Frankfort, August 27, 1820.

Dear Castlereagh—I enclose an extract of a report to a German Court from an agent who sometimes is well informed.

Ever faithfully yours,   F. LAMB.

[Enclosure.]

Extrait d'une Lettre de Naples sur la Révolution qui y a eu lieu.

1. Que l'association connu sous le nom de Carbonari, malgré les efforts des Gouvernemens pour la dissoudre et la détruire, est très nombreuse et très répandue dans toutes les parties de l'Italie, et dans toutes les classes de la société, surtout dans les armées.

2. Que, dans les provinces du Royaume de Naples, les chefs de cette association sècrete ont convoqué dans les mois de Mars et d'Avril, sur différens points, les Carbonari, et que ceux-ci ont exactement répondu à l'appel.

3. Que l'impulsion paroissant donnée par la haute Italie, il

en résulteroit que les troupes qui seroient envoyées par Autriche au secours du Roi de Naples pourroient bien se trouver placées entre deux soulèvemens.

4. Que les troupes réunies au camp de Sessa ont eu une occasion facile de se concerter, et qu'en effet elles ont arrêté là leur plan, dont, chose extraordinaire, rien n'a transpiré jusqu'au moment de l'explosion.

5. Que le mouvement devoit éclater le 31 Mai, et qu'il a été différé pour une cause que j'ignore.

6. Que le Prêtre Minichino, qui dirige la Révolution depuis son origine a du risquer d'agir avant d'avoir reçu les derniers ordres du dehors, parceque le Gouvernement avoit reçu des avis de ce qui se tramoit en secret. Ce Minichino, après avoir fait de longs voyages en Italie, en France, en Allemagne, en Angleterre, et en Amérique, est revenu l'année passée à Naples, et s'est retiré à Nola, qui est devenu ainsi le centre des mouvemens révolutionnaires.

Lieutenant-Colonel Browne to Lord Castlereagh.

Milan, August 29, 1820.

My dear Lord—In the uncertainty in which I am as to the latest accounts your lordship can have received from Sicily, I think it my duty to copy from a letter which has been this day received here the following extract. It is from a most respectable mercantile house in Palermo to one in Genoa.

" Palermo, August 18, 1820.

" A large armed force has set out into the interior, to subdue Trapani, Girgenti, Catanisetta, Catanea, and Messina. The three first joined the cause of independence. Catanisetta, however, rose again, and the inhabitants have nearly been put to the sword, the city sacked, burned, and almost levelled to the ground. It is supposed the force will amount to 50,000 men ere it reaches Catanea. We are in suspense as to what Naples will do. The refusal of the Prince to receive the

deputation has only served to add fuel to the flame, and
thousands, that before were lookers-on, have since joined the
standard of independence. The English have not been molested,
but their pockets have suffered from forced contributions."

The Government here has received accounts this day in a
great measure confirmatory of the above intelligence. The
names of the leading men who joined the cause of the Inde-
pendents in Sicily are: Prince Villafranca, Prince Trahia,
Prince Paterno, Duke Monteleone, Duke Panteharia, Cardinal
Gravina.

Believe me, &c.,   T. H. BROWNE.

The Hon. F. Lamb to Lord Castlereagh.

Frankfort, September 1, 1820.

My dear Lord—The real difficulty about the fortresses is
the unwillingness of certain Powers of the Confederation to
contribute to the support of fortresses which, in fact, instead
of being in the hands of the Confederation at large, are in
those of three of its members. The objection which is put
forward about Landau cannot be got over, and this place may,
perhaps, in consequence, cease to be considered as a federal
fortress, which will suit the views of Austria well enough.
The difficulties put forward about Mayence and Luxemburg
are capable of arrangement; but, to come to one, it will be
necessary that Austria should retract her original proposition,
and allow the conditions to be settled previously to the adoption of the principle.

I have no idea what her determination will be. In the
mean time, Mayence is rapidly decaying. Of the two millions
and a half which have been spent there, not above 30,000
francs have been laid out on the fortress; the rest has been
absorbed, as money is liable to be, over which many have a
right and nobody a check. I should not state this unless upon
undoubted authority. It is to be hoped that this state of

things may soon be put a stop to in a place of such great importance as Mayence. It has been remedied in part by an order to lay out no more money on any account whatever; but the consequence of this is an accelerated decay of the place for want of the most necessary repairs.

I am, &c.,   F. LAMB.

Sir Charles Bagot to Lord Castlereagh.

St. Petersburgh, September 4-16, 1820.

My dear Lord—Monsieur de Lassa, the Portuguese Minister, called upon me four days ago, and read to me the translation of a despatch which he had received from M. Saldanha at Madrid, dated the 2nd of last month, acquainting him that he had obtained possession of the "*statuts*" of the secret societies in Spain, and particularly those of the club which had given to M. Pardo, the Spanish Chargé d'Affaires at Lisbon, the instructions mentioned in my despatch No. 15, and also, as M. Saldanha now states, instructions to M. de Onis at Naples.

M. Saldanha informs M. de Lassa that it appears by these *statuts* that the object of these societies is to establish republics in every country in Europe; and that, for this end, they have agents in every quarter, but that the principal central societies are established at Paris, Venice, Genoa, Leghorn, in Prussia, and in Poland. M. Saldanha proceeds to state that, if necessary, he will furnish M. de Lassa with copies of all the documents which have fallen into his hands. In the mean time, he insists that the affair is so serious that it requires the immediate interference of the Powers of Europe, and he declares the state of Spain to be such that an explosion must take place there before the expiration of two months.

It appears, by M. Saldanha's despatch, that he had communicated all these documents and this information to M. Bulgacy, the Russian Chargé d'Affaires at Madrid, who had immediately despatched a courier to the Emperor at Warsaw.

It was by this courier that M. de Lassa received M. Saldanha's letters, which were forwarded to him through Count Nesselrode.

I have nothing to add to my public despatch of this date, excepting perhaps that, in the conversation which I had a few days ago with the young Duke of Serracapriola, I found him very uneasy at the reception he had met with in Vienna. He told me that he had remained there eight days in vain endeavouring to be permitted to deliver to the Emperor the letter of which he was the bearer from the King of Naples; and that, at last, the Austrian Government had desired to have his passports, in order that they might be *viséd*—a measure certainly very little short of ordering him to leave Vienna. I believe that he is a man of very loyal principles towards the King; but he thinks that the affairs of Naples are in such a state that any external attempt to control them will only be fatal to whatever popularity or influence the King may yet have left. He told me that he had distinctly stated to Prince Metternich that the first Austrian soldier who passed into the south of Italy would destroy the Neapolitan monarchy.

Count Nesselrode's last letters from Count Lieven are of the 22nd. He read to me yesterday Count Lieven's despatch, reporting the questions put by Lord Holland and Lord John Russell, respecting the Russian note to M. Zea Bermudez, and the answers given by Lord Liverpool and your lordship. He expressed himself greatly pleased with the language of the Government upon that occasion.

I have the honour to be, &c.,   CHARLES BAGOT.

Sir Henry Wellesley to Lord Castlereagh.

Madrid, September 7, 1820.

My dear Lord—I have very little to add to my despatches of this day's date. Affairs certainly wear a more favourable appearance here, and the disturbance of last night will contribute to strengthen the hands of Government, and will justify even stronger measures than those in contemplation for keeping the clubs in order, and for preserving the tranquillity of the city. The Government, and their friends in the Cortes, have, I think, fairly got the upper hand in that assembly. Much praise is due to the spirited conduct of the Conde de Toreno, M. Martinez de la Rosa, and M. Calatrava, who may be considered as the leaders of the party supporting the Government.

Although I am convinced that M. Pardo has not had any instructions from the Government to promote the revolution in Portugal, yet I have all along had reason to believe that he has been in correspondence with the clubs at Madrid; and it is probable that he has acted under their instructions in his proceedings with the insurgents, if his influence has really contributed in any great degree to bring about the events which have taken place in the north of Portugal. It is M. de Saldanha's intention to demand his recall, and I have promised to assist him in this object. It is difficult to meet with a Spaniard who will talk reasonably upon the subject of Portugal; for there is hardly one of them who would not think any measures justifiable which had for their object the annexation of that country to Spain.

I have the honour to be, &c.,   H. WELLESLEY.

Lieutenant-Colonel Browne to Lord Castlereagh.

Milan, September 10, 1820.

My dear Lord—The Neapolitan Consul and Vice-Consul here were sent for to the police on the 7th instant, and, their passports being delivered to them, they were ordered to leave the place as soon as possible. They went off to Naples last night. The march of troops from the Tyrol and Austria continues in every direction. A second battalion of Tyrolese chasseurs passed through this place on the 6th instant, on their road to Pavia.

Everything here is as tranquil as possible; nor are there any rumours of an unpleasant nature from the surrounding countries.

Believe me, my dear lord, &c.,   T. H. BROWNE.

Lieutenant-Colonel Browne to Lord Castlereagh.

Milan, September 10, 1820.

My dear Lord—Let me hope that your lordship will be induced to accede to Lord Stewart's request that I should be the military reporter attached to the Austrian head-quarters, in the event of such an appointment being determined on by the Government.

It is needless for me to detail what has been my situation here for some time past; and I am sure your lordship's feeling towards me will induce you to consent to an arrangement, which would bear me honourably through the part by finishing in a soldierlike manner. I do not think there is any chance of Austria moving forward in right earnest before I could be conveniently spared from here. I will not add more, but trust to your lordship's goodness for the appointment.

There is a tremendous fire here, and the whole Milanese is together by the ears on this question of the Queen.

Believe me, my dear lord, &c.,   T. H. BROWNE.

Extrait d'une Dépéche de M. le Duc de Laval.

Madrid, le 11 Septembre, 1820.

L'aspect de la Capitale est tout-à-fait changé depuis la journée du 7 où les mesures énergiques du Gouvernement et l'appareil militaire déployé dans les places publiques ont tellement imposé aux factieux qu'en aucun lieu l'autorité ne rencontre de résistance.

Une soumission si complète, qui a succédé à la licence portée à son comblé, est une démonstration de la foiblesse du parti des agitateurs, et est également une preuve bien rassurante pour l'avenir du bon esprit des habitans et des troupes, qui ont fait leur devoir avec une modération qui a mérité les justes éloges du Corps législatif.

Il y eut quelques arrestations qui ne troublèrent point le calme dans lequel on peut assurer que la ville est plongée depuis quatre jours. Ces succès ont encore cimenté l'union du Gouvernement et des Cortes. Les questions où les passions pouvaient être en jeu, dans les dernières séances se sont toutes résolues comme on le verra à l'avantage, des bonnes doctrines et du Gouvernement, et n'ont été combattues que par une faible opposition de cinq ou six voix.

M. Calatrava a défendu la plus précieuse prérogative de la Couronne, en fesant observer à l'assemblée le danger d'établir entre les lois et des décrets une distinction, qui tendrait à soustraire ceux-ci à l'obligation de la sanction royale. Le Ministère et le Congrès sont remplis de satisfaction et d'un juste orgueil en considérant cette amélioration de choses, et avec quel admirable discernement ce peuple, averti par l'autorité a su se maintenir et temoigner son éloignement et son mépris pour les factieux qui prétendaient l'entrainer dans le désordre. Aussi M. Arguelles, dans son beau discours du 8, a-t-il fait remarquer que l'Europe attentive savait établir des distinctions entre la révolution de Naples et l'état de l'Espagne.

On est à la recherche des auteurs des mouvements en sens divers, qui ont eu lieu sur la place, dans les cours, et sous les voûtes du palais en présence du Roi. Les malins qui mêlaient aux cris de *Vive la Constitution!* le cri de Riégo et de son rappel se composaient de quelques centaines d'ouvriers, de femmes publiques, et d'enfans payés et dirigés par les clubistes que l'on distinguait à leur habillement plus décent.

Il ne tenait qu'au Gouvernement de faire suspendre les séances des sociétés patriotiques jusqu'à ce qu'elles fussent soumises aux règlemens dont une Commission des Cortes est chargée de présenter le rapport. Il a cru inutile cette précaution, qui n'aurait point été contrariée par le Congrès. Mais il n'entre pas dans la politique du Gouvernement de

s'opposer à l'exercice de l'esprit public dans ces réunions patriotiques.   La pensée est que la nation plus monarchique que
ses institutions nouvelles, a besoin d'être instruite et d'être
excitée aux jouissances de la liberté.   On ne prétend que
modérer l'ardeur de ces sociétés; et on ne redoute rien de
l'esprit national plutôt apathique que séditieux.

Les Ministres disent avoir en main des pièces qui pourraient
au moins faire conduire Riégo dans une forteresse; mais ils ont
voulu épargner un jugement à ce général, que la jeunesse et
l'enivrement rendent excusable.

Les mouvemens des *Serviles*, ceux qui ont crié Vive le Roi
seul!—à bas la Constitution!—partent d'une source plus inconnue, sont plus compliqués, et éveillent de nouveau sur le Roi, les
Infans, et la composition du vieux Palais, la sollicitude du
Ministère.   Il aurait souhaité que le Roi dans la soirée du
6 parût au balcon, et tint au peuple et aux troupes sous les
armes un langage constitutionnel, qui aurait rappelé au devoir
les deux partis en présence, mais ce prince a jusqu'à présent
gardé le silence.

Le Ministère, peu satisfait, veut éclairer ses doutes: on a
cru découvrir des subalternes du Palais dans les groupes; on
croit être informé qu'on a distribué de l'argent, et que 6,000
piastres de la caisse de la grande maîtrise ont été répandues: on
a cru remarquer que dans cette nuit on fesait déjà des paquets,
qu'on rassemblait des bijoux.   L'Infant Don Carlos entre
toujours dans les soupçons plus avant que les autres Princes.

La confiance entre le Roi et son Ministère (qui, à mon sens,
est son unique ancre de salut) ne se rétablira solidement,
qu'après que celui-ci aura obtenu de sa Majesté le renvoi de
quelques anciens officiers et serviteurs, que le parti constitutionnel accuse d'opinions serviles et d'influence sur l'esprit
irrésolu et dissimulé du Souverain.

Telles sont selon toute probabilité les préventions du Ministère: il croit avoir donné au Roi dans ces dernières circonstances preuves de courage, de dévouement, et de force, par

son union avec leurs anciens collègues des Cortès.   On s'est
expliqué sérieusement ; on aurait encore parlé de démission,
qui laisserait le Roi dans un abandon affreux et à découvert
devant ses ennemis.

Des couriers ont été expédié dans les provinces, pour prévenir du triomphe sur les anarchistes, et le faire servir d'exemple aux agitateurs.   Les lettres de Cadix et de l'Isle de
Léon du 5 rapportent que les troupes, dans la même position,
se flattaient encore de ne point sortir d'Andalousie.

Les nouvelles de Lisbonne vont jusqu'au 3.   Il paraîtrait
par les rapports de ce Gouvernement que la Régence a peu
d'espoir de maintenir les troupes dans leur fidélité.   Le provinces de Tra-los-Montes, d'Alentejo, et de Beyra, à l'exception
de Coimbra, étaient dans le devoir.

· Voici à ce qu'il paraît la conduite que ce Cabinet a déclaré
au Ministre Portugais et à l'Ambassadeur d'Angleterre vouloir observer relativement à l'insurrection de Portugal—se
maintenir dans une stricte neutralité, ne prêter aucun appui
aux mécontens, désavouer toutes les démarches du Chargé
d'Affaires d'Espagne, si cet agent, en contravention à ses
instructions, avait commis des imprudences et excité à la
révolte ; le rappeler même, si c'est jugé utile à la tranquillité
de la Régence ; ne s'inquiéter en aucune manière d'un dé-
barquement de troupes que le Gouvernement Britannique en-
verrait pour appuyer la garantie du Portugal.

Sir Charles Bagot to Lord Castlereagh.

St. Petersburgh, September 13-25, 1820.

My dear Lord—Count Nesselrode will leave St. Petersburgh
for Troppau about the 25th of this month (O.S.).   There is a
ruumor that the portefeuille is to be left in the hands of Count
Potocki, a young man with whom I have not any acquaintance ;
but I believe that nothing certain is yet known upon this subject.   Count Nesselrode speaks loudly against Prince Metternich's idea of Ministerial conferences, and considers the questions

growing out of the Naples affairs as much too grave to be discussed by anything less than the assemblage of Allied Powers in the persons of their Sovereigns, or their most confidential Ministers.   He goes further, and seems to say that no accredited Ministers dare take upon themselves to pledge their Courts to a concurrence in such measures as it may possibly be necessary to suggest.   He seems to be very anxious to learn who is to be appointed to assist at the conferences on the part of Great Britain.   He tells me that there is some doubt whether the King of Prussia will be able to attend in person; but that Count Bernstorf will certainly be there.

The Duke of Serracapriola holds his post here, and he tells me that, though he is urged on many sides to abandon it, he is resolved not to do so.   The crisis has been too much for him, and I think that his understanding is evidently shaken. He has received a letter from the Duc de Calabre, which he has shown to me, instructing him " so to act with this Government as to induce the Emperor to prevent the Neapolitan dominions from being *oppressed* so long as things go on well;" which the Duc de Calabre contends that they now do.   A Secretary of Legation, of the name of Micheroux, has been appointed to the Neapolitan mission here, and is expected immediately at St. Petersburgh.

Count Nesselrode showed to me, a few days ago, the despatches from Count Lieven, dated on the 22nd July, (3rd August) 1819, respecting the mission of General Hulot, and what had passed upon the subject of the Buenos Ayres' monarchy.   The Emperor had sent this despatch back from Warsaw, with directions that it should be shown to me.

There are accounts from England, by the way of Holland, to the 1st instant, but there are three English mails due, and I have nothing later than the 25th of last month.

I have the honour to be, &c.,

CHARLES BAGOT.

Lieutenant-Colonel Browne to Lord Castlereagh.

Milan, September 16, 1820.

My dear Lord—Two battalions of the Bohemian regiment " Vogelsang" arrived this day in Milan, on their route to Pavia. They are not strong, in consequence of their sudden march, which did not admit of time to call in the men on furlough, who are to follow.

A letter has been received here from the Marquis Campo Chiaro to M. Palembo, the Neapolitan Vice-Consul, who has remained here a few days after the departure of the Consul Simonetti. It is dated Naples, the 8th inst. The Vice-Consul is instructed to spare no pains nor expense in transmitting to his Government the most accurate accounts of the march of the Austrians, their numbers, cantonments, &c., and entreating him to communicate frequently and by safe means.

· M. Palembo leaves Milan to-morrow, having only been permitted, as a favour, to remain a few days after the departure of the Consul Simonetti. Some merchants have yesterday received accounts of a Constitution' having been proclaimed in Portugal. It remains to be seen how far they will prove correct.

I have thought it right to send to Lord Stewart the copies of Sir W. à Court's despatches taken by this courier, and which reached me under flying seal, and I trust your lordship will excuse my having made the communication respecting M. Palembo direct to you, as I dare not say anything about it by the post to Lord Stewart, in consequence of its having been an interception of *this* Government, (with which I am on very confidential terms) communicated to me, which would be read by the police at Vienna, and might be the means of preventing every access to similar information for the future.

Believe me, my dear lord, &c.,   T. H. BROWNE.

Several letters have been received here, mentioning that a violent ferment existed, and open rebellion was preparing in Manchester and Birmingham.

The Hon. F. Lamb to Lord Castlereagh.

Frankfort, September 16, 1820.

Dear Lord Castlereagh—Shortly after my confidential letter of 12th August last, I learnt from Anstett that he had sent the Prince Gallitzin to Warsaw, to await the arrival of the Emperor there, with despatches containing his views upon Naples. He subsequently read to me his principal despatch, which contained only a development of what I have already written to you. He has to-day informed me that the Russian courier who passed through this place, on his way to London, brought the Emperor's thanks and acknowledgments to M. Anstett, and a full approbation of his views. If this be true, as I judge from his manner that it must be in the main, a judgment may be formed of the line which Russia is likely to take, in case her proposition for a Congress should be accepted.

It is unfortunate that Anstett has given me a rendezvous for to-morrow, at which he promises to read to me all the papers he has received, some of which, as he says, have not been communicated to my Government. I cannot put faith enough in this sort of assertion to delay the courier; and if I learn anything, it must be delayed for another opportunity. The part of his argument which appears to me to be intended to have a practical application is this—

That if, in any case, it is justifiable for a Power to take upon itself a character which does not rest upon treaties, such as the protectorship of the tranquillity of Italy, it can only be in a case where no ambitious views can be attributed to that Power, not in one where the result of the principle put forward would be to place in its grasp the object which, of all others, it may be the most suspected of coveting.

With regard to Sicily, his doctrine is that, between a revolted province and the Power which held it in subjection no third party is authorized to interfere, and that the subjugation of that island, if it is to be attempted by force, must be effected by Naples alone. This doctrine, I think, has not yet been transmitted to Warsaw, but it is probably on the road, and its adoption, of recent date, proves to me that he speaks truth about the favourable reception of his previous despatches.

I see I have omitted to mention that the corollary from the reasoning upon Naples is, that not an Austrian but an Allied army should be employed in Italy, of which a Russian corps is of course to form a part.

The Emperor of Russia has many difficulties in Poland. The Poles are discontented; those of the provinces first annexed to Russia more so than any others. The Emperor had thought fit to give the government of the provinces of the kingdom of Poland exclusively to Poles; and there is not one of these Governors against whom there are not complaints to the Diet. The taking all the Polish officers out of the Russian army, to concentrate them in that of Poland, has deprived the Emperor of the only partisans in that country upon whom he could really count. These statements have been confirmed to me from more than one source.

I shall do all I can to learn more distinctly what are the views of Russia, not without a hope of talking to you in person upon the subject, on your passage through this town; for, if the interval from the affairs of our gracious Queen gives you time, never was a determination more important to be taken than that of the line now to be pursued; nor were there ever affairs in which your presence was likely to be more beneficial.

Adieu, dear Lord Castlereagh, ever faithfully yours,

F. LAMB.

Lord Castlereagh to Lord Stewart.

Foreign Office, September 16, 1820.

My dear Charles—In addition to my official despatches, which will put you in possession of the measures which we have adopted under the present exigency, chiefly upon the recommendation of Sir William à Court, sanctioned by the concurrence of his Russian and French colleagues; and which will further convey to you the restrictions under which you are authorized to confer with the other Allied Ministers upon the present affairs, I think it may be useful and acceptable. to you to receive some general observations from myself altogether for your private information. With all the respect and attachment which I feel for the system of the Alliance, as regulated by the transactions of Aix-la-Chapelle, I should much question the prudence, or, in truth, the efficacy, of any formal exercise of its forms and provisions on the present occasion.

If the existing danger arose from any obvious infraction of the stipulations of our treaties, an extraordinary reunion of Sovereigns and of their Cabinets would be a measure of obvious policy; but when the danger springs from the internal convulsions of independent States, the policy of hazarding such a step is much more questionable: and when we recollect to what prejudicial misconceptions and popular irritation the conferences at Pilnitz and the declaration of the Duke of Brunswick, at the commencement of the late revolutionary war, gave occasion, it may well suggest the expediency that whatever ought or can be done for the general safety against the insurrectionary movements of conspiring and rebellious troops should be undertaken, after full deliberation, in the manner which will afford the least handle for misrepresentation and excitement, and which may give the effort to be made the fullest justification of a local and specific necessity arising out of the particular case.

I therefore hope that the Emperor of Russia will be content to confine the interview at Troppau within the prudent limits proposed by his Ally the Emperor of Austria, that whatever Ministerial conferences may be held may be regarded as only adding to our other means of confidential explanation, and that whatever is done shall be upon the particular case, without hazarding general declarations, containing universal pledges that cannot be redeemed, and which, from the first, will be seen through and despised. Dissertations on abstract principles will do nothing in the present day, unless supported.

. It is highly satisfactory to observe that, in all other respects
than the form of proceeding, the Emperor of Russia seems to
concur fully in the general sentiments, and looks to the Court
of Vienna as the Power, from its exposed position, on which
necessarily devolves the task of proposing for the consideration
of its Allies the course to be taken on the present occasion.
As far as I have been able to examine the Memoir which, in
furtherance of this purpose, the Austrian Minister has prepared for consideration, it appears to me that it hardly touches
the real question.   It assumes a fact, viz., the duress of the
King, and proposes to found upon it a blind engagement, which
no responsible Government can possibly contract; but it leaves
all the essence and difficulties of the business, namely, the end
and object of the league, in obscurity.   The substance of the
Paper is to be found in the series of propositions, five in number, with which it closes.   Coupling these propositions with
the avowed preparations of one of the Powers, namely, Austria,
and her understood purpose to march an army into the kingdom
of Naples for the liberation of the King and for the destruction
of the existing order of things, no doubt can exist that these
propositions, if agreed to, would substantially amount to the
formation of a hostile league, on the part of the five Powers,
against the *de facto* Government of Naples.   If all are pledged
not to recognize but with common consent the order of things
now subsisting, that force, if requisite, is to be employed for
its overthrow, all are principals, not only morally but *de jure*
in the war, though all may not bear arms in the execution of
the common purpose.   Now, this is a concert which the British
Government cannnot enter into.

1st. Because it binds them to engagements which they could
not be justified in taking without laying the whole before Parliament.

2ndly. It creates a league which at any moment may involve them in the necessity of using force: for it is clear the
de facto Government of Naples, upon such an act being agreed

to by us, might, according to the ordinary laws of nations, without further notice, sequester all British property at Naples, and at once shut their ports against British commerce; and it further makes the continuance of that league dependent upon the common deliberation of all the Powers composing it.

3rdly. It is further inconsistent with the principles of the neutrality which this Government, with a view to the security of the royal family of Naples, has been induced to authorize Sir William à Court to declare and to act upon.

4thly. Such a league would render the British Government, both morally and in a parliamentary sense, responsible for all the future acts of the league; and, consequently, if Austria should move forward her army into the Neapolitan territory; for the acts of a Power, over whose councils in the execution of her intended measures they could not and ought not to have that species of detailed control which would justify such a responsibility.

5thly. Before such a power could in reason be delegated by the Alliance to Austria, the whole course of measures must previously be settled by common consent, which is, from the very nature of the case, impracticable, or the Austrian Commander, in the execution of the service, must be saddled with and act under the direction of a Council of Regency of the Allied Ministers residing at head-quarters, which is equally impracticable and inexpedient.

6thly. Such a league would most certainly be disapproved by our Parliament; and even could it be sustained, it is obvious that, from that moment, every act of the Austrian army in the kingdom of Naples would fall as much under the immediate cognizance and jurisdiction of the British Parliament, and be canvassed as freely and fully, as if it was the act of a British army and Commander-in-Chief.

The objections to such a system in a Government such as ours are inseparable; and I presume the consequences of it, as above stated, would be no less alarming to Prince Metternich;

you will not, therefore, give his Highness any expectation of
the possibility of our concurrence. I shall endeavour, however, to point out the more natural course into which this
business, as it appears to me, may practically fall.

The revolution at Naples does not, in strictness, come within
any of the stipulations or provisions of the Alliance. It is,
nevertheless, an event of such importance in itself, and of such
probable moral influence upon the social and political system
of Europe, that, in the fortunate intimacy of counsel which
prevails between the five principal Powers of Europe, it necessarily occupies their most anxious attention.

The result of their first explanations has sufficiently established that they concur in regarding the change as pregnant
with danger and of evil example, as having been the work of
rebellious troops and of a secret sect, the known and avowed
object of whose institution is to subvert all the existing Governments in Italy, and to consolidate the whole into one
Italian State. This danger, however, bears upon the different
Allied States so very unequally as to vary essentially the
course which each may feel disposed or enabled, or even justified, to adopt, with respect to it. To apply this remark to
two of the principal Powers, viz., Great Britain and Austria,
the latter Power may feel that it cannot hesitate in the adoption of immediate and active measures against this danger—the
former State may, on the other hand, conceive that it is not so
directly or immediately menaced as, according to the doctrines
on which an armed interference in the internal affairs of another
State has hitherto been sustained in the British Parliament,
would justify it in becoming a party to such an interference.

If this is the actual position of these two Powers, they
cannot become joint parties to a league leading to measures of
force, and which involves a common and equal responsibility;
whilst the exclusive power of execution necessarily belongs to
the State principally exposed. The same reasoning will more
or less apply to all the other Allied States.

The natural result of this seems to be, that Austria must, at least as far as we are concerned, make the measure, whatever it is, her own; that she may, by previous and confidential intercourse, collect the sentiments of her Allies, and thereby satisfy herself that she is not likely to incur their disapprobation, or be disavowed by them in what she proposes to attempt; but she must adopt it upon her own responsibility, and in her own name, and not in that of the five Powers, and she must be satisfied to justify it upon the grounds that decide her to act, receiving such an acquiescence or such an approbation from the other Powers as they may be prepared to afford to her.

Before such acquiescence or approbation can be expected, Austria must, however, be prepared to satisfy her Allies that she engages in this undertaking with no views of aggrandizement; that she aims at no supremacy in Italy incompatible with existing treaties; in short, that she has no interested views; that her plans are limited to objects of self defence; and that she claims no more from the country she proposes to enter, than having her army sustained in the usual manner, whilst necessarily stationed beyond her own frontier.

Prince Metternich, I have no doubt, really means so to limit his views; but, to inspire the confidence necessary to his own purpose, and to protect himself against the jealousy of other States, he must explain himself more explicitly than he has done in the Memoir in question. This being done, whatever hesitation particular Powers may have with respect to their own line of policy, none, I apprehend, will feel themselves disposed or entitled to impede or embarrass Austria in the course she may feel it necessary to pursue for her own security and that of her Italian States.

But, although Austria may not expect or wish other States to charge themselves with any part of the exertion which she conceives their safety as well as her own requires, yet she may wish to be publicly countenanced in what she may undertake,

by their moral *appui*.   This *appui* she will in a great measure
carry with her, if, after a full explanation of her general views,
they acquiesce in her measures, if they abstain, under existing
circumstances, from re-establishing the usual diplomatic relations with the present Government of Naples.   Their concurrence in her measures may be marked more or less de-
cisively, according to their particular circumstances, but it
seems too much to expect that the other Powers should wholly
identify themselves in a proceeding which must mainly be conducted by Austria alone.

For these reasons you will see that engagements of such a
nature, at least on our part, are out of the question.   We
desire to leave Austria unembarrassed in her course; but we
must claim for ourselves the same freedom of action.   It is for
the interest of Austria that such should be our position.   It
enables us, in our Parliament, to consider, and consequently to
respect her measures as the acts of an independent State—a
doctrine which we could not maintain, if we had rendered ourselves, by a previous concert, parties to those acts; and it
places us in a situation to do justice in argument to the considerations which may influence her counsels, without, in doing
so, being thrown upon the defence of our own conduct.   Austria must, as I conceive, be contented to find in these Conferences the facilities for pursuing what she feels to be her own
necessary policy; but she must not look to the involving by
this expedient other Powers in a completely common interest
and a common responsibility.   The consequence of so doing
would be to fetter her own freedom of action.   She must preserve to herself the power of pursuing with rapidity and effect
her immediate views of security; and the other Allied States
must reserve to themselves the faculty of interposing, if they
see cause for doing so.

I have thus endeavoured to state for your information, in
some detail, the chain of reasoning which brings us to the conclusion, which has already been stated to you in my despatch

of the 29th of July, as well as in others of this date, namely,
that the King's Government cannot attempt, by force of arms,
to deal with this particular case; and that, however they may
understand the considerations which may bring the Austrian
Government to a different conclusion, and however they may
respect that determination, they must distinctly decline the
responsibility of advising or being in any wise parties to that
decision; and, so far from embarrassing the Court of Vienna
by the part they are now taking, I am confident Prince Metternich must feel that, by the step we have adopted for the
protection of the royal family, we have essentially contributed
to relieve his Court from one of its most anxious embarrassments, and that his course is thereby infinitely more facilitated
than it could possibly be, were we to consent to incorporate
ourselves with the other Allied States, as a passive member of
the projected League, the formation of which, I am satisfied,
is not essential to his object, and which, I am confident, can
never be reduced, for any efficient purpose, into practice.

Ever, dear Charles, &c., CASTLEREAGH.

Sir Charles Bagot to Lord Castlereagh.

St. Petersburgh, September 17-29, 1820.

My dear Lord—One of the first steps taken by Baron
Lebzeltern, upon receiving from Prince Metternich the intelligence of the revolution in Naples, and his orders to proceed to
Vienna, was to communicate with the Sardinian Minister here,
to whom he spoke very openly of the possibility of its being
necessary to march an army into the south of Italy, and of the
force which the King of Sardinia might be able to furnish for
such an object.

The effect of this conversation with Baron Lebzeltern has
been to fill M. Brusasco's mind with real or pretended alarms
respecting the views of Austria against the whole of Italy;
and, being without instructions from his Court, and on the eve
of setting out upon his temporary mission to Constantinople,

he took upon himself to desire an interview with Count Nesselrode, to whom he has spoken very earnestly upon the whole
subject. He has shown to me confidentially the despatch
which he has written to his Government, reporting this conference, in which he appears to have recalled to Count Nesselrode's mind the uniform policy of Austria, as it has respected
Italy, the views of conquest which she has always had in that
quarter, and the danger of her availing herself of the present
favourable occasion to carry those views into effect. He contended that, if it should be necessary to move an army into
Italy, it ought to be any army rather than that of Austria, as
the universal hatred which prevailed against the Austrian
troops throughout all Italy would infallibly arm against them
those upon whose assistance the forces of any other country
might perhaps rely ; and he seems to have concluded by saying
pretty broadly that, partly through fear of sharing in this
hatred, and partly through apprehension of the moral infection
to which Sardinian troops might be exposed by any contact
with the Neapolitan States, the King of Sardinia would not
consent to furnish any contingent which Austria might require
on the present occasion.

Count Brusasco reports that Count Nesselrode listened with
great attention to everything which he had urged, and has
said that hitherto the Austrian Government had not manifested any fixed determination to march an army into the
south of Italy, much less to do so with any view to its conquest, nor had they, as far as he knew, made any overtures to
the King of Sardinia, or to any of the Italian States, to furnish
troops for any purpose.

Count Brusasco sought this conference with Count Nesselrode, and gave these opinions, as he assures me, without any
instruction whatever from his Court; but, as he thought it
worth while to acquaint me with the step which he had taken,
I have thought it might be worth while to report his proceeding to your lordship, even at the expense of troubling you

with so long a letter. Count Brusasco is an accomplished man, and a man of ability, but he is a violent anti-Austrian, and has visions of Italy becoming an independent kingdom, &c.

Three days ago I received by the captain of a merchant ship, which arrived in eight days from Hull, the intelligence of what was reported to be a complete revolution in Portugal. I immediately communicated the news to the Portuguese Minister here, and to Count Nesselrode, who had heard nothing of it. A Hamburgh newspaper of the 16th instant has been since received, by which we learn that the mischief had first broke out at Oporto, and that it had not then spread to the capital. This is all that we yet know.

I am assured that M. de la Ferronays, the French Minister here, is to attend the conferences at Troppau, but not as first Plenipotentiary of France. I have learnt this, however, very indirectly, as he has never spoken to me upon the subject.

Count Nesselrode's departure is now fixed for the 26th.

I have the honour to be, &c.,   CHARLES BAGOT.

The Hon. F. Lamb to Lord Castlereagh.

Frankfort, September 21, 1820.

Dear Lord Castlereagh—Anstett kept his word. The papers which he read to me were seven:

1. The Emperor of Austria's invitation.
2. The Emperor of Russia's answer.
3. A private letter to Lieven.
4. A despatch common to Lieven and Alopeus.
5. A despatch to Pozzo di Borgo.
6. A despatch to Golowkin.
7. A private letter to Anstett.

The private letter to Lieven was merely to express a doubt whether the invitation to the Emperor of Russia had been communicated by the Austrian Government to that of England, and to direct him, therefore, not to show it to you unless you should ask for it. The despatch was to be communicated: it is therefore unnecessary for me to say any more upon the four first papers. The despatch to Pozzo di Borgo is perhaps unknown to you; I therefore put an account of it upon a separate sheet, that you may read it or not as you please. The despatch to Golowkin was the only one which he did not read to me entire: what I recollect of it is not worth repeating.

The private letter to Anstett begins by conveying the warmest acknowledgments on the part of the Emperor, "*pour ses beaux et utiles rapports.*" It says that the impossibility of the Emperor's going to a distance from Warsaw has served as a pretext for declining the proposed meeting, and adds that Great Britain has recognized that a partial reunion cannot be adequate to the present circumstances. Two remarkable phrases in the letter seem to me to mark the real sentiments of the Russian Court. The first is in speaking of the Spanish and Neapolitan Governments—" Pourquoi n'ont ils pas donné des institutions capables d'assurer la tranquillité de leurs peuples?" The second relates to Austria: " L'Autriche a demandé un blanc seing des autres Puissances, pour faire la loi à Naples et pour dominer l'Italie au nom de ses Alliés— voilà le fond de sa pensée." All these letters are from Capodistrias.

Anstett assures me that Russia will be found as favourable to the existence of Constitutions as she is hostile to the forcible manner in which they have been introduced. He adds, as a certain fact, that Austria is determined to begin her operations in Italy, whatever may be their nature, by giving a Constitution to her own provinces there, but he refuses to tell me the source of his information. Perhaps you will forgive me if I state my opinion that there is no longer any permanent safety except in Constitutional systems. At the same time, the establishment of one, even in Lombardy, draws necessarily and rapidly after it the establishment of one in Prussia, which will be a most hazardous task; it is one, however, which is not likely to be facilitated by delay. The hatred to her in her provinces on the Rhine is stronger than ever; and I am assured that the feeling in Saxony is the same. Fortunately, the rest of Germany is tranquil, and there is every probability of its remaining so.

Believe me, &c.,   F. LAMB.

Sir Charles Bagot to Lord Castlereagh.

St. Petersburgh, September 25, (October 7) 1820.

My dear Lord—The Portuguese Minister here put into my hands last night the translation of the two despatches which he had just received—one from the Marquis de Marialva, at Paris, the other from the Chevalier de Brito, at the Hague. The former despatch contains nothing which will not have been known to you long ago; but the latter may be interesting, and I therefore enclose it to you.

I have the honour to be, &c.,

CHARLES BAGOT.

Traduction d'une Dépêche du Marquis de Marialva, datée 14 Septembre, 1820.

Les dépêches que dans ce moment je viens de recevoir du Gouvernement de Portugal confirment la triste nouvelle de l'insurrection de la ville de Porto le 14 du mois passé, et me font savoir que la révolte s'étoit propagée jusqu'à Coimbra et Abrantes, tandis que les provinces de Tras os Montes, Alentejo, Beira Alta, et Algarves persistoient dans leur fidélité.

Les mêmes dépêches me donnent l'assurance que le Comte d'Amarante, Gouverneur militaire de Tras os Montes, avoit réuni quelques troupes avec lesquelles il vouloit marcher sur Porto, en défense des droits sacrés de notre Souverain.

On mande aussi que le Lieutenant-Général Antonio Marcellino da Vitoria, chargé du Gouvernement militaire de Beira, et le Lieutenant-Général Joaõ Lobo Brandaõ de Almeida, Gouverneur d'Elvas, avoit pris des mesures énergiques et convenables pour maintenir la tranquillité publique dans les districts de son commandement.

Les Gouverneurs du Royaume ont pris, comme on devoit s'attendre toutes les mesures que l'urgence des circonstances exigeoit, mais telle a été leur angoisse qu'ils ont pris la résolution de convoquer un conseil des personnes les plus distinguées de Lisbonne, et après avoir entendu leurs avis, ils ont décidé de convoquer les Cortes, et on publia à cet effet une proclamation le 1r du mois courant.

Le Gouvernement prétend par ce moyen parvenir à frustrer les machinations des factieux et arrêter le progrès du mal.

Extrait d'une Lettre du Chevalier de Brito, datée de la Haye, le 18 Septembre, 1820.

La révolution de Naples qui ressemble à une parodie de celle de l'Espagne, est en effet méditée pour que l'anarchique constitution des Cortes de Cadix serve comme de transition pour le régime républicain. La conspiration militaire de Paris avoit le même but, de substituer à la Charte la Constitution de 1791. Mais comme dans la Péninsule on ne pourroit pas exécuter ce plan ténébreux pendant que le Portugal seroit monarchique, des émissaires y sont accourus afin de fomenter l'idée d'une alliance fédérative, en divisant la Péninsule en trois Républiques, et en réunissant à celle de Portugal la Galicie et l'Estremadure jusqu'à la Sierra Morena. C'est pourquoi votre Excellence remarquera l'aheurtement avec lequel les feuilles publiques Espagnoles et les nouvelles des confrères répandent que la constitution a été adoptée à Porto. Le refus de Riégo et sa résistance aux ordres du Roi, qui l'envoyoit pour prendre le commandement en Galicie, et le partage de l'armée de l'Isle de Léon en différentes garnisons, sont d'accord avec le plan sus-dit.

NB. Dans cette lettre on parle encore des intrigues du Chargé d'Affaires d'Espagne à Lisbonne, M. Pardo, et on y dit, chose assez remarquable, que M. de Saldanha avoit découvert que le plan de la conspiration générale avoit pour but de détrôner tous les Bourbons, ce qu'ayant été communiqué au Marquis de Marialva, celui-ci en avait donné connaissance au Gouvernement Français.

Mr. Stratford Canning to Lord Castlereagh.

Washington, October 9, 1820.

My dear Lord—I have detained the packet for several days, in the hope of hearing again from Mr. Adams on the subject of the President's return to town, and my presentation to him. But, being informed from good authority that his absence is likely to be prolonged till the end of the week, I do not feel myself justified in detaining the packet beyond this evening; at the same time that I think it best to abstain from making any fresh application to Mr. Adams, as it is not probable that the return of the President would be accelerated by it, and the delay of a few days is of little consequence.

Mr. Antrobus has handed the mission over to me under such quiet circumstances, that I feel as if I shall be peculiarly responsible for any of a less *peaceful* nature that may arise in future; and therefore I venture to recommend myself thus early to a more than usual share of your lordship's indulgence. The question of the tariff, respecting which your lordship received a despatch from Mr. Baker the day I left London, is one of the most important likely to come before Congress during the next session : of the probable issue of it I am as yet but little qualified to offer an opinion, as Washington is quite empty at this season, and I have no opportunity of seeing a single individual, except the gentlemen of the mission, with whom I can converse on any subject of politics.

I am almost as much at a loss to know what to augur of the intentions of this Government on the subject of the Slave Trade. In the conversation which I had with Mr. Adams, all his objections were positive and circumstantial, while his favourable expressions were vague and general. From the manner in which he dwelt upon the inconveniences to be appre-

hended from admitting a mutual right of search, I should not
be greatly surprised if he had it in view to attempt the settlement of the old question in dispute on terms favourable to the
United States, as a condition of their acceding to that part of
the system now in force for the repression of the illicit Slave
Trade. But this surmise is grounded on the very doubtful
supposition of their being inclined to enter into some sort of
formal engagement on the subject with Great Britain. The
most promising symptom of such an inclination, is a resolution
which passed the House of Representatives at the close of last
session, but which was prevented, I believe, by some informality, from passing the Senate also, to the effect "that the
President be requested to consult and negociate with foreign
Governments on the means of effecting an entire and immediate abolition of the African Slave Trade."

In the course of our conversation, Mr. Adams quoted the
French Government as coinciding with the United States in
their sentiments on the measure of searching for slaves at sea;
assuring me, at the same time, that this coincidence of opinion
was not the result of any agreement or consultation between
them, and that the United States had received no overture on
the subject from any Court but that of England.

Mr. Adams seems to attach considerable importance to the
idea of a free communication of the proceedings and discoveries
on both sides respecting the Slave Trade, and it was perhaps
to illustrate his meaning that he informed me of a strong
suspicion resting on the island of St. Thomas, as being concerned in the illicit trade. It appears that this Government
has two cruisers on the African coast. Several prizes have been
sent in, one of which is claimed by the Spanish Minister.

I have the honour to be, &c.,   STRATFORD CANNING.

———

Sir Henry Wellesley to Lord Castlereagh.

Madrid, October 9, 1820.

My dear Lord—There is a circumstance connected with the
Duc de Cadaval's pretensions in Portugal, which I think it

right to mention to your lordship, particularly as I know it to be the intention of the Austrian and Russian Chargés des Affaires at this Court to call the particular attention of their Courts to it. I have no other information upon the subject, however, excepting what has been derived from the Portuguese Minister.

The Duchess de Cadaval is cousin and sister-in-law to the Duc de Laval, and I understand that he has been apprised by her of the Duc de Cadaval's pretensions to the throne, as being related to the royal family, and that he has been induced to promise her his support. The Duc de Laval has been more than usually eager upon the subject of the affairs of Portugal; has expatiated, as I understand, with a little too much complacency, upon the probability of the English having lost their influence in Portugal, and upon the injury which their commerce would be likely to sustain in consequence of the new order of things, and has expressed it to be his opinion that the King of Portugal cannot leave the Brazils without exposing his territories in that quarter to serious danger; but, in all conversations upon the subject of the affairs of Portugal since the revolution has broken out there, with me, or with my colleagues, he has carefully abstained from any mention of the name of the Duc de Cadaval.

The important question for consideration is, whether the pretensions of the Duc de Cadaval are likely to be supported by the French Government; and whether the Duc de Laval in promising his support is acting with the authority of his Court. If not, his individual support can be of little importance, either one way or the other. And although I have thought it right to mention the subject to your lordship, yet I should be extremely sorry that any report of mine should injure the Duc de Laval with his Court.

I have the honour to be, &c.,

H. WELLESLEY.

The Hon. F. Lamb to Lord Castlereagh.

Frankfort, October 17, [1820].

Dear Lord Castlereagh—By to-day's courier from Warsaw, we learn that the King of Prussia sends the Prince Royal and Hardenberg to Troppau on the 20th, and goes there himself ten days after. The character given of the state of feeling at Warsaw is "qu'on y est plus inquiet qu'incertain"—more resolved upon the course to pursue, than sure of the good that will come of it.

About France I get contradictory accounts. Berstett says that he has the best information about Alsace from persons appointed by M. de Richelieu to communicate with him, and he affirms the state of opinion to be much improved of late. I must own I place little confidence in anything that comes from Berstett: he is always exaggerated. Langenau speaks from the intercepted letters; and he says they all concur in anticipating danger during the winter. I asked him if there were any which he thought entitled to confidence. He said that perhaps no one was particularly so; it was only their concurrence which persuades him of their exactness. He says the birth of the Duke of Bordeaux has only served to prove the persevering hatred of the Anti-Bourbon party to the present dynasty. Some of the letters, however, I perceive, upon which he counts the most, are from foreign Ministers accredited at Paris; perhaps these are what you will judge best worthy of attention. When he recommended secrecy to me, I said he might be sure that Metternich communicated to you every information which was worth it. He said he did not know; that Metternich had a great trick of reading no reports which contained what he did not wish to hear. If you think these interceptions worth knowing, a few civil words, said as from you to Langenau, will perhaps induce him to communicate them regularly and more particularly.

Faithfully yours,   F. LAMB.

I must add, that he says there is every appearance of correspondence with Eugene; that he has received of late many couriers, and that the letters to him by post from France are evidently written in cipher; that they speak of colonies and transactions with which the writers have no concern, and which must convey conventional meanings. I am far from meaning to give any opinion upon the truth of this myself.

F. L.

Sir Charles Bagot to Lord Castlereagh.

St. Petersburgh, November 7-19, 1820.

My dear Lord—The enclosed is the copy of a despatch which has been addressed by the new Government of Portugal to the Portuguese Minister here, and which he received a few days ago by the post. As it is in itself rather remarkable, and as it may perhaps differ from the first communications made to other Portuguese Ministers in Europe, I have thought that you may be glad to see it. M. de Lassa has determined to take no notice of it, and he has privately transmitted a copy of it to Count Nesselrode at Troppau, telling him at the same time of the course which he intended to observe, at least for the present.

Your lordship will be so well aware that, in the absence of the Emperor and both the Secretaries of State for Foreign Affairs, I can have but little of public interest to report from hence, that I need hardly offer any excuse for not sending any public despatches by the present opportunity. Everything here is perfectly quiet, and has continued so ever since the date of my last despatches.

I do not learn that any answer has yet been received from the Emperor, since he was made acquainted with the proceeding of the Semenoffsky regiment of Guards; but I am happy to say that that proceeding has not been followed by any further disturbance of any kind.

I received your lordship's letter respecting Mr. Chamberlain, and I hope that I need not add that I shall do everything in

my power to assist him here. I think, from what I have
already observed, that I can undertake to say the same on
behalf of Sir Daniel Bayley. He has been very attentive to
him, and seems anxious to assist and encourage him in all ways.

I have the honour to be, &c.,   CHARLES BAGOT.

[Enclosure.]

*Traduction d'une Lettre d'Hermano Jose Bramcamp de Sobral,
datée Lisbonne le 3 Octobre, 1820.*

Très Illustre et très Excellent Seigneur—J'ai l'honneur de
vous communiquer que le premier du mois courant on a effectué
l'union désirée du Gouvernement établi *ad interim* à Lisbonne
avec la Junte Provisoire du Gouvernement Suprème du Royaume de Portugal, conformément à la lettre et à l'ordre
(*portaria*) ci-joint par copie.

La Junte Provisoire du Gouvernement Suprème du Royaume
désire que votre Excellence lui communique toutes les nouvelles qui puissent intéresser à la sûreté et prospérité de cette
portion des États de sa Majesté très Fidèle le Roi notre Maître.

Je profite, &c.

Sir Charles Stuart to Lord Castlereagh.

Paris, November 9, 1820.

My dear Lord—The King having repeatedly complained
that the dulness of his Court and the want of society since the
dismissal of the Duke de Cazes had rendered his life extremely
irksome, it has long been evident that his Majesty would take
advantage of the first opportunity to establish a confidential
intercourse with some person whose manners and conversation
might offer some amusement to his leisure moments.

There is no longer any doubt respecting the individual who
is honoured with this distinction. The Vicomtesse du Cayla,
daughter-in-law of Lieutenant-General the Comte du Cayla,
who superintended the household of the late Prince de Condé,
being involved in a lawsuit with her husband, found it neces-

sary, some months since, to apply in person to his Majesty for protection. Her conversation having pleased the King, his Majesty expressed his hope that she would repeat her visit; and so great an intimacy has ensued, that she not only passes much of her time in his Majesty's apartments, but an epistolary correspondence occupies the hours she is absent from the Tuileries.

In justice to Madame du Cayla, I must add that his Majesty could not have admitted to his society a person more eminently distinguished by her mental and personal qualifications.

Believe me, &c.,
CHARLES STUART.

Circulaire.

Troppau, Decembre 8, 1820.

Informé des bruits aussi extravagans que faux, que la malveillance des uns et la crédulité des autres ont concouru à répandre et à accréditer sur l'objet et les résultats des conférences de Troppau, les Cours Alliées ont jugé nécessaire de fournir à leurs Missions respectives dans les pays étrangers des informations authentiques propres à les mettre en état de dissiper les erreurs et les préventions qui ont pu se former à cet égard. La Pièce ci-jointe est destinée à remplir ce but. Il ne s'agit pas d'en faire l'objet d'aucune communication formelle; mais rien n'empêche qu'il n'en soit donné une lecture confidentielle. Ce même apperçu allant être adressée à MM. les Ministres de Russie et de Prusse vous voudriez bien concerter plus particulièrement avec eux l'usage que vous en ferez.

Recevez, &c.

Apperçu des premiers Résultats des Conférences de Troppau.

Les évènemens du 8 Mars en Espagne, ceux du 2 Juillet à Naples, la catastrophe du Portugal, devaient nécessairement faire naître dans tous les hommes qui veillent à la tranquillité des États un sentiment profond d'inquiétude et de peine, et un

besoin de s'unir et de se concerter pour détourner de l'Europe
tous les maux prêts à fondre sur elle.

Il étoit naturel que ce besoin et ce sentiment fussent plus
vifs dans les Gouvernemens qui naguères avaient vaincu la
Révolution, et qui la voyaient aujourd'hui reparoître tri-
omphante.

Il étoit plus naturel encore que, pour la repousser une troi-
sième fois, ces Gouvernemens eussent recours aux moyens qu'ils
avaient si heureusement employé dans la lutte mémorable où
l'Europe les avait vu briser le joug sous lequel elle gémissait
depuis vingt ans.   Tout autorisait à espérer que cette union
des principales Puissances, formée au milieu des circonstances
les plus critiques, couronnée des plus beaux succès, perpétuée
enfin par les actes de 1814, 1815, et 1818—que cette union
qui a preparé, fondé, et complété la pacification du monde,
ayant délivré le Continent du despotisme militaire, exercé par
l'homme de la Révolution, le délivreroit également du pouvoir
nouveau non moins tyrannique, et non moins désastreux, du
pouvoir du crime et de la révolte.

Tels ont été les motifs et le but de la réunion de Troppau.
Les uns doivent être si généralement sentis qu'ils ne demandent
pas une plus longue explication.

L'autre est si honorable et si utile que tous les vœux accom-
pagnent sans doute les Cours Alliées dans leur noble entreprise.

La tâche que leur imposent les devoirs et les engagemens
les plus sacrés est vaste et difficile ; mais d'heureux présages
leur permettent de croire qu'elles parviendront à la remplir en
agissant sans aucune déviation dans le sens des traités par lesquels elles avaient rendu la paix à l'Europe, et établi une
alliance générale entre tous les États Européens.

Les Puissances ont usé d'un droit incontestable en se dé-
cidant de prendre des mesures communes de précaution et de
répression envers des Etats dont le bouleversement opéré par
la révolte, ne fut il considéré que comme exemple, serait déjà
un acte hostile à toutes les institutions et à tous les Gouverne-

mens légitimes, envers des États surtout, qui, non contents de
leurs propres malheurs, cherchent par leurs agens à les communiquer à d'autres contrées, et s'efforcent d'y faire naître les
troubles et l'insurrection.

La position et la conduite de ces États constituent une infraction manifeste du Pacte qui garantit aux Gouvernemens
Européens, avec l'intégrité de leurs territoires, le maintien de
ces relations pacifiques dont le premier effet est d'exclure
jusqu'à l'idée de se nuire réciproquement.

Ce fait irréfragable devait être le point de départ des Cabinets Alliés.   En conséquence, les Plenipotentiaires qui pouvaient recevoir à Troppau même les ordres de leurs Souverains,
ont arrêté entr'eux, et soumis aux délibérations des Cours de
Paris et de Londres, les principes à suivre envers les États qui
subissent une altération violente dans la forme de leur régime
intérieur, ainsi que les moyens, soit de conciliation, soit de
force, propres à ramener au sein de l'Alliance ceux de ces États,
sur lesquels on pourrait exercer une action salutaire et efficace.

Comme la révolution de Naples jette tous les jours des
racines plus profondes, comme nulle autre ne menace d'une
manière plus sensible et plus immédiate la tranquillité des
États du voisinage, ni ne peut être atteinte par des voies plus
directes et plus promptes, on a reconnu la convenance et la
nécessité de faire au royaume des Deux Siciles l'application
immédiate des principes qui viennent d'être indiqués.

Afin d'entamer à son égard les mesures de conciliation, les
Souverains présens à Troppau ont addressé à sa Majesté
Sicilienne l'invitation de se réunir avec eux à Laybach, dé-
marche dont le seul but a été d'affranchir la volonté de sa
Majesté, et de l'engager d'interposer sa médiation entre ses
peuples égarés et les pays dont ils compromettent le repos.

Décidés à ne point reconnoître les Gouvernemens enfantés
par la sédition, les Souverains ne pouvaient entrer en rapport
qu'avec la personne du Roi.   Leurs Ministres à Naples ont
reçu des ordres analogues.

La France et l'Angleterre ont été invitées à se joindre à cette démarche. Elles s'y refuseront sans doute d'autant moins que le principe, en vertu duquel elle a été faite, est strictement conforme aux traités solemnellement ratifiés par ces deux Puissances, et qu'elle offre le gage assuré des vues les plus justes et les plus pacifiques.

Le système concerté entre l'Autriche, la Prusse, et la Russie, n'est point un système nouveau ; il ne présente qu'une application fidèle des maximes consacrées par les transactions qui ont fondé l'alliance générale.

Loin d'affoiblir l'union intime des Cours qui forment le centre de cette alliance, ce système ne peut que la fortifier et consolider.

Elle s'affermira comme elle s'est établie, conçue par les mêmes Cabinets, et successivement adoptée par les Puissances qui en ont reconnu les avantages.

La réalité de ces avantages ne saurait être révoquée en doute. Il est d'ailleurs hautement démontré que ce ne sont ni des pensées de conquête, ni le désir de porter atteinte à l'indépendance des autres Governememens dans ce qui concerne leur administration intérieure, ni celui d'empêcher des améliorations sages et volontaires, conformes aux véritables intérêts des peuples qui ont dicté les déterminations des Puissances Alliées. Elles ne veulent que maintenir la paix, que préserver l'Europe du fléau des révolutions, que réparer et prévenir, autant qu'il dépend d'elles les malheurs qu'entraîne l'oubli de tous les principes d'ordre et de morale.

À ces titres les Puissances peuvent se flatter qu'une approbation unanime les récompensera de leurs soins et de leurs efforts.

Copie d'une Dépêche de M. le Secrétaire d'État, le Comte de Capodistrias, à l'Ambassadeur Comte de Lieven, en date de Troppau, le 15-27 Decembre, 1820.

M. le Comte—Par nos dépêches, en date du 30 Novembre,

(11 Decembre) nous avons communiqué à votre Excellence les
plus complètes informations sur la démarche faite par les
Cabinets réunis à Troppau, auprès de la Cour de Rome, dans
la vue d'engager sa Sainteté à se charger de l'office de média-
teur entre le royaume des Deux Siciles et les Puissances
Européennes, pour le cas où le Roi de Naples n'auroit pu accepter l'invitation qu'il avoit reçue de se rendre à Laybach. ·

Cette impossibilité qu'il étoit permis de craindre et nécessaire de prévoir ne s'est heureusement pas réalisé.   Le Roi va
arriver à Laybach, et l'Empereur nous a donné ordre d'adresser
à cette occasion aux Ministres de Russie la Circulaire ci-jointe
en copie.   Vous êtes invité, M. le Comte, à remplir les ordres
de sa Majesté qu'elle renferme, en autant qu'ils concernent
votre Excellence.

Je la prie de recevoir l'assurance, &c.

*Copie d'une Dépêche de M. le Secrétaire d'État le Comte du
Capodistrias à l'Ambassadeur le Comte de Lieven, en date de
Troppau, 15-27 Decembre, 1820.*

M. le Comte—L'Ambassadeur Britannique près la Cour
d'Autriche est arrivé à Troppau en même tems que le Courier
porteur des Dépêches de votre Excellence du 22 9bre (4 10bre).
C'est dans la journée du 19 que Lord Stewart s'est acquitté
des ordres de son Gouvernement.   Il a déposé aux Actes de la
Conférence la Note dont votre Excellence nous avoit transmis
une copie.

Cette Note n'a point eu, et n'aura pas, d'autre suite.   Les
Cabinets Alliés ont vu avec peine que le Gouvernement Britannique leur refusât sa coopération.   Ils n'en persévèrent pas
moins dans les résolutions que leurs droits les autorisoient à
prendre, et qu'un devoir sacré leur commande d'accomplir.

Il n'y a point de théorie qui ne peut être attaquée.   Le
témoignage des faits seul n'admet plus ni doute, ni réplique.
C'est donc aussi à l'expérience que les Cabinets Alliés en ap-
pelent, à cette expérience qui au mois de Mars de 1815, a si

hautement justifié leurs déterminations. Elle démontrera encore, ils en sont persuadés, que leur doctrine et leur système, loin de pouvoir être nuisibles, seront toujours bienfésans ; et, lorsque cette nouvelle preuve aura été acquise, ils espèrent que le Gouvernement Britannique lui-même leur accordera son suffrage.

Tel est le sens dans lequel vous voudriez bien, M. le Comte vous expliquer avec Lord Castlereagh au sujet de la Note citée. La présente dépêche a été communiquée aux Cabinets de Vienne et de Berlin, et nous avons lieu de croire que leurs représentans près la Cour de Londres vont-être munis des mêmes instructions.

　　　　　Recevez, M. le Comte, les assurances, &c.

Lord Clancarty to Lord Castlereagh.
　　　　　　　Bruxelles, December 26, 1820.

My dear Lord—The drafts of your despatches of the 16th to Vienna and Naples arrived with me by the last mail, and I yesterday communicated their contents to Nagell, who rejoices more and more at every line he reads of yours upon this subject. He has not yet announced to me when I shall have a private audience with the King, for the purpose of making a similar communication to his Majesty ; so that I shall keep the papers sent probably till next week.

Nagell read me a private letter from Baron Fagel, which conveyed your sentiments of the cautious line this Government should follow in consequence of the reclamation made by the Austrian, Prussian, and Russian Ministers, relative to an alleged supply of arms to the *de facto* Government at Naples from Liège. Nagell expressed himself grateful for your suggestions, and will follow them by playing the game of time-gaining.

The Princess Marianne is recovering. Your summons from us of Seymour has given us both pain and pleasure : the loss of his society will be much felt both by me and by every member of my family ; while, on the other hand, we cannot but rejoice that he is now about to bear a substantive part in public affairs, and this immediately under your own eye. You will find him, not in manners alone (in which, however, his character is well displayed) but to the bottom of the heart, a gentleman, perfectly to be confided in, able and willing to work; and, I have no doubt, when informed of the details of his duty, which he will not be slow to seize, he will afford you complete satisfaction.

I know not whether you will feel yourself called upon to replace him by some other at this mission: for the march of affairs here this will not be requisite, as our remaining hands are amply sufficient for the work we have to perform. You may, however, be pressed upon this subject; and, if so, you will always find me ready to relieve you: but, recollect, you have yourself rendered me somewhat difficult on this matter, as far as relates to approbation of the persons attached to this Embassy, by having hitherto sent me a set of young men, who are each and every one of them a great acquisition to our society, and who, zealous in the discharge of their official duties, are not less qualified to perform the same with credit to themselves and advantage to the public.

We shall send Seymour to you on Tuesday next, the 2nd of January, and we shall endeavour to console ourselves for his loss by considering the personal advantages he is about to reap from being withdrawn from us, and also by the reflection that we have still three fine young fellows left behind, whose talents, manners, and good dispositions, will not easily be matched anywhere, and which are well adapted to do honour to themselves and credit to their country, when, in their turn, they may hereafter be called into more ostensible situations.

Yours, my dear Lord, &c.,   CLANCARTY.

AFFAIRS OF SPAIN, PORTUGAL, NAPLES, GREECE, THE NETHERLANDS, RUSSIA—CONGRESS OF LAYBACH.

Extract of a private Letter from Lord Clancarty to Lord Castlereagh, dated Bruxelles, January 1, 1821.

I was to have seen the King on Friday last, for the purpose of communicating your despatches to Vienna and Naples of the 16th ult. to his Majesty. The dreadful conflagration which took place on that day, and which has completely destroyed the hotel of the Prince of Orange and that of the States-General, necessarily prevented this. On Saturday last, at a *private* audience, the instructions to Naples and Vienna were communicated to his Majesty. It was impossible for him not to be in the highest degree pleased with the line taken by our Cabinet, and with the irrefragable reasoning by which it is supported; and, certainly, during the reading, the progress was interrupted by strong expressions from him of applause and coincidence of opinion. Among these, it will be sufficient to report one, as virtually embracing all. He said it was a line of policy which did us credit, and which had this advantage to us, that, if known, it would rally round us every State in Europe of the second order as the only security of their own individual independence.

As this our course of policy is known to his Majesty, the conclusion, as regards him, seems clear, and is likely also to acquire additional strength (as it ought) from the persuasion, so well enforced in the principal despatch, that our internal system of government renders our resistance to this Fifth monarchy scheme, attempted to be forced on the world, a matter of necessity as well as of choice, and this affords the best assurance of its permanence. The papers were returned to Planta, in the box, as they came, without copy, notes, or extract, being made by any one, on Sunday last, by the messenger Meates.

The despatches, of which he was the bearer from Vienna, show clearly, however, that it is not only to the Courts of the second order that the influence of our reasoning and upright plan of policy, when developed, is likely to extend. The effect of the note of the 4th December seems to have been adequate, if not to have much surpassed what could have been expected from its first impression; and notwithstanding that, after the immediate disposal of the Neapolitan business, (still, as I conceive, likely to be attended with much delay and difficulty) the acknowledgment of abstract principles by Protocol is threatened, I think it probable that your excellent reasoning will have its operation with the Fifth-monarchists to prevent this—more especially when they consider that their scheme must now, *ipso facto*, be destroyed by it, and that England, separated from the rest, must carry with her possibly France, but certainly every other Power in Europe not of the three, and leave this then triple-headed monster unsupported otherwise than by its own ill-assorted combination.

Sir Charles Bagot to Lord Castlereagh.

St. Petersburgh, December 22, 1820 (January 3, 1821).

My dear Lord—Everything is stagnant here, and, excepting the occasional arrival of a courier from Troppau, with such information as it may be thought fit to afford to the public of St. Petersburgh, nothing happens to interest or agitate this capital. This will account for the meagreness of my reports, which, if it be true that the Emperor will probably not return till the middle or end of February, may perhaps become yet more meagre.

The circular despatch of the 6th of December, addressed from Troppau to the Ministers of the respective Sovereigns there assembled, and which has been communicated, or rather shown, to the Ministers of all the Courts here, seems to have given great satisfaction to some of them. An idea was certainly prevalent that the affair of the Semenoffsky regiment of Guards would have the effect of making the Emperor give his sanction to much less moderate measures than appear likely to be adopted; and this idea was rather increased by an event which has taken place more recently. This event may be worth relating.

It appears that a certain M. de Karamsin,[1] a Conseiller d'Etat, a literary man with a very exalted imagination, had formerly made himself conspicuous here by some writings or sentiments not exactly calculated for this meridian. Upon his being then denounced to the Emperor, the Emperor, instead of taking any measures against him, admitted him to his presence, and finding that he was a mere enthusiast, without any dangerous connexions, and with some abilities, he encouraged him to address his opinions upon different matters immediately to himself.

·· I believe that he soon exercised this privilege to a tiresome extent, and was latterly little attended to; but, upon the revolt of the Semenoffsky Guards taking place, he thought fit to address a letter to the Emperor, saying that the time was now come when a Constitution must be given to the people, and calling upon him to give one. Upon this he was arrested,

[1] Karamsin was not only one of the most eminent Russian writers of his time, but had the merit of producing the first history of Russia ever published, in twelve volumes octavo. For this purpose all the archives were thrown open to him, and the Emperor Alexander assisted him with 60,000 rubles, and appointed him Imperial Historiographer. In the brief biographical accounts of Karamsin that I have seen, I find no mention of the circumstances here related: but it is said that, at his death, in 1826, a pension of 50,000 rubles, granted shortly before, was transferred to his widow and children.—EDITOR.

and a seizure was made of his papers, amongst which were
said to be found some brouillons, which had very much the
appearance of being parts of papers intended to be distributed
among the troops. It is not believed that he has any asso-
ciates; but the Emperor is reported to have been very angry
upon the subject; and, though he is not harshly treated, he
has been sent a prisoner to Kexholm.

The Aide-de-Camp, General Ouwarrow, arrived here about
ten days ago from Troppau, but he had passed by Warsaw,
and had been long on the road. It is said that he is to return
to the Emperor, which makes it believed that he came upon
some special and urgent business; but, if it is so, the nature
of it has not transpired.

I ought not to omit to tell your lordship that nothing can
be more gracious than the manner in which the Court continues to *accueillir* this Embassy. In the absence of the
Emperor, the occasions of doing so are necessarily less frequent;
but no opportunity is omitted of manifesting the most perfect
good-will and friendly disposition to us.

I have no accounts from England later than the 8th of
December, but, from what I observe in them, I hope I may
congratulate your lordship upon the improved aspect of affairs
in England, and upon the better sentiments which are beginning to make themselves heard in the country.

> I have the honour to be, &c.,   CHARLES BAGOT.

Extract of a Letter from Lord Castlereagh to Lord Stewart.

> Cray Farm, January 5, 1821.

I long for the next accounts from Vienna, combining Stuart's
Report of the instruction to Castelcicala with the immediate
movement of the Sovereigns for Laybach. It would seem as
if King Ferdinand was fully prepared to throw himself into
their arms, and to vote the whole *non avenu*. It is not our
part to give opinions, and, in truth, at this distance, it is

sufficiently difficult to form sound ones; but, after all his
Majesty's doings and undoings, if I was Metternich, I had
rather not mix my cause with such a tissue of duplicity and
equivocations as his Majesty's life must abound with, if now to
be retraced. I very much agree with à Court, both as to the
King's position and the inexpediency of returning now to the
old system after all that has passed.

I still think Metternich has essentially weakened his position
by making it an European instead of an Austrian question.
He might have had the same European countenance upon a
much more intelligible case of interference. He would have
carried public opinion (especially in this country) much more
with him, had he stood simply upon the offensive character of
a Carbonari Government to every Italian State, than embarking himself on the boundless ocean on which he has preferred
to sail. In placing *his* effort boldly on its strong Austrian
grounds, Russia and Prussia might have infused the general
interest into their declarations of adherence, without diluting
the main question to their own remote interest. But our friend
Metternich, with all his merit, prefers a complicated negociation to a bold and rapid stroke.

C——GH.

Lord Clancarty to Lord Castlereagh.

Bruxelles, January 5, 1821.

My dear Lord—To you, who are acquainted with the
manner in which this country is governed by separate departments, without mutual consultation or even communication, it
will be no surprise that, notwithstanding Nagell's signature of
the note to me of the 9th November, wherein a right is asserted
by this Government of continuing the trade in Slaves, except
directly with Africa, he should now agree with me in thinking
it clear that the Treaty of 1818 forbids all such right. Considering that my *energetic* note of the 23rd December,
endeavouring to enforce this latter interpretation, had been

sufficiently long before this Government, I called upon him on Wednesday last to urge the issue of an early and favourable answer, when he told me that he quite agreed in the view I had taken upon this subject, and requested me to talk the matter over with Falck, with whom he also would take an early opportunity of conversing upon it.

I accordingly went immediately to M. Falck. He at first talked of the necessity of a new treaty, in order, if it should be found fit, to explain the intention of the parties in the enlarged sense upheld by us; but I immediately told him the existing treaty was already so clear as not to require any explanation; that there could be no doubt of the fulness of the construction as advanced in my note; and that no words, however strong, could render the sense clearer than it already appears, as conveyed by those adopted by the treaty. M. Falck lowered his tone on this, and promised to look into the matter, so as to return an answer without unnecessary delay.

Though M. Falck did not couple the matters together, or attempt to make the one dependent on the other, yet I cannot help suspecting his abortive proposal of a new treaty originated in a hope that, if this business, in which he knows we are much interested, should be again thrown open, it would give an advantage to him in another, on which this Government is extremely anxious, viz., the settlement by Convention of the rights of trade and establishment, particularly in the Indian Archipelago, and generally in the seas eastward of the Cape.

Upon this subject (though, as I said before, without being at all blended with the other) I had some conversation before I left him, with M. Falck: he showed me two private letters, the one from Lord Hastings to M. Capellen, the Governor of Java, the other, the answer to it, dated in April last, from both of which it appears that the two writers expected, and the last particularly, with expressions of some anxiety, at that time speedily to receive the result of the negociations between the two Governments on Eastern concerns.

These papers were professedly, and I believe really, shown me by M. Falck for the purpose of proving that neither of the two Governors-General conceived that these negociations were to depend, for their commencement, on any fresh advices from either of them from India; and I must confess they seem to me (Lord Hastings' letter particularly) fully to bear out this conclusion. Be this as it may, in the event (which, however, I can scarcely believe will be realized) of any further difficulty being interposed to the admission of our construction of the Treaty of 1818, on the Slave Trade, you may perhaps be of opinion that some advantage may be derived by us on this point, from the great anxiety of this Government to proceed to a settlement on the other; probably, therefore, you may think it advisable, if applied to on this score before the Slave Trade point shall be determined, to answer that, desirous as we anxiously are to have all floating questions finally set at rest between the two Governments by Convention, it must still be confessed that this desire has not of late been increased by the manner in which the clear words of a subsisting treaty have been misconstrued by the Netherlands' Government.

> Yours, my dear lord, &c.,   CLANCARTY.

Three mails due from England.

Claims of British Officers, lately in the service of Portugal, on the Government of that Country.

It is unnecessary to state in much detail the circumstances in which those officers entered into that service, but undeniably they were such as took away all pretext for doubting their motives, and gave to them the greatest claim that individuals can hold upon a nation's gratitude.

Those officers volunteered their services to Portugal in its utmost need, as no nation could possibly be more critically circumstanced or in more imminent danger, and in a cause whereon no difference of opinion existed, in which all were unanimous, and it may truly be said to have been a national cause. It was also at a time when, it must be remembered, that, by the departure of the King for his Transatlantic dominions, by the then recent occupation of Portugal itself by the French, and by consequent emigration, from these united causes, of great numbers of officers, and especially by the marching of a considerable corps of Portuguese troops into France, during the occupation of the country by General Junot, she had been abandoned by all her officers in whom she herself had any confidence, and was left without any of experience, if she had any previously.

It will be also recollected that it was the Government of Portugal that first requested his Britannic Majesty's Government to supply that nation with a Commander-in-Chief to its army, and subsequently for the incorporation of a proportion of British officers into its forces. Those officers entered into the Portuguese service under the considerations that, besides the advantages accruing to them from the Portuguese service, they were to have during the war the advantages that would accrue to them according to their respective ranks in the British army, as promotion, honours, &c.: that the British officers in the service of Portugal well earned any reward it is in the power of that country to bestow on them, the result of the contest is the most evident proof; and the returns of the killed will show that the survivors have some claims not only upon the justice but upon the generosity of that nation, and still more when it is believed that few if any of those survivors are without wounds, acquired in the defence of the very existence of that country as an independent nation.

During the war, the necessity of the case, arising from the causes enumerated, called for the employment of more British officers in the army of Portugal than would have been desirable under other circumstances; and when the peace came, a new view and consideration of the case was made, and his Most Faithful Majesty judged it expedient still to retain a limited number of British officers in his service as a permanent arrangement, and the officers so to be retained were selected from those who had served the country during all its perils, through six campaigns; and those officers, in adopting the service of Portugal as a permanent service, were under the necessity of relinquishing their effective situations in the British army, as the advantages of promotion, &c., in it, which they had until then enjoyed.

By those who are acquainted with the nature of the British service, the sacrifice made by those officers will be appreciated, by being placed on half-pay, when all their promotions ceased, and so long as they remain so, and each must come in again youngest of his rank, and most must remain unemployed. This was an arrangement or understood agreement made by the then legal authority of the State with those officers, who came into it under the understood condition of participating in all the advantages of the Portuguese service, according to long usage, and under the guarantee of the justice and honour of that Government. It was not necessary to the protection of the interest of those officers that they should have made any sacrifices in their own service, (as they did, and large ones) it was sufficient that they entered into the Portuguese service, and were admitted into it by the legal authority to serve therein, permanently to ensure them all the usual advantages, as by it they bound themselves to all the disadvantages and penalties incident either by law or custom to that service.

It must be here observed that it has ever been the custom in Portugal for foreign officers entering permanently into that service to receive double pay, and which was enjoyed by some English officers who had previously entered that service when those officers whose interests are now advocated entered it, but which, neither during the war nor since, was ever claimed by them, or has been ever received when the new arrangement for the permanent service of the British officers in the Portuguese army took place; that is, after the peace of 1814. His Most Faithful Majesty's Ministers at the Rio de Janeiro adopted the principle and understanding that they were to serve under the same conditions and circumstances as the native officers, consequently with all the advantages, and his Most Faithful Majesty, at a late period in June, 1820, more fully explained this by a decree or law. Since the revolution which has taken place in Portugal, the ruling Power there has judged the services of the British officers in the Portuguese army unnecessary and inexpedient, and has dismissed them all. The employment or non-employment of any classes of officers, and particularly of foreigners, must ever be at the discretion of the Government under which they were employed, and no complaint can be or is made for the simple fact of that Government dispensing with the services of those officers; but it does appear a very great injustice to adopt respecting them a new and *ex post facto* arrangement, and to cut them off from the pecuniary advantages which the immemorial custom of the service gave them a right to expect, or that was secured to them previously to that revolution by express resolutions of the legal authority.

The determination come to respecting those officers by the Cortes of Portugal would probably be considered by the movers of them, on more deliberate consideration, to have been both hasty and a little *ex parte;* though it must be admitted such determination does not appear to have been influenced in the least by any feelings of dissatisfaction with or enmity to the British officers. But no one was ever heard on their behalf; and it is obvious that, referring to the situations of those who judged this matter when the engagements of the Portuguese Government were made with those officers both in 1809, and in 1814 and 1815, that they could not be acquainted with all the circumstances and bearings of the case.

There are three distinct grounds on which this business

might have been settled, all consonant to former practice—the first to have given them the double pay during or for the time they had served; the second to have given them their reforms on the full pay of their respective ranks, a case usual when the services of officers are dispensed with, without fault or crime on their part; and the third, what is called *reformado* (reformed) according to the number of years of service, and according to the terms of his Majesty's decree of 1820. To this latter it is presumed they have an absolute right, unless some crime is alleged and proved against them, as, when given, this decree was considered as a law. The second would be the most liberal and obviously the most just; for, if officers have not served the regular period to be entitled to the full pay of their ranks, according to the decree of 1820, it is not their fault; they were willing to conform to it and to serve, and they had already on their part made the sacrifices, with the expectation of remaining permanently in the service.

The decision come to by the Cortes is, that each officer shall receive so much pay, or for so long a time as he may have served in the Portuguese army during the war. It is impossible to guess on what ground such a condition has been made, as there is nothing to warrant it in the history of Portugal. It was, in truth, after the war that those officers made the sacrifices, and hence lost all the opportunities of advancement and employment in their own service, on the strength of the faith of the then legal Government of Portugal, and certainly the three, four, or five years of Portuguese pay that they may now receive, will be no adequate remuneration for such losses. If, besides, the services of the British officers are to be remunerated during the war only, then there are a great number of other officers (at least as many more) who are entitled to such remuneration, and either this mode, or the first, that of now paying up the twelve years of double pay to those officers, would be infinitely more onerous than that of allowing those officers who still continued in the Portuguese service at the

period of the revolution to retire on the full pay of their
respective ranks, which, in justice, they are undoubtedly
entitled to.   Surely a Government can no more do away debts
of this nature than any other pecuniary debts of the nation,
or, at least, whatever they may see fit to do with their own
subjects, they must keep faith with those whom they have now
declared foreigners, and who belong to an independent nation;
and it is to be hoped that the property of British individuals,
gained by their blood and labour, and under the sanction of
their own sovereign and country, whether in the shape of pay
or of pension, or of grants of any other nature, acquired and
given by the legal authority of the State, will as much deserve
the protection of the British Government as that of merchants,
traders, or any other class gained in the way of their lawful
calling.   The labour and the risks of the first are not certainly
less than those of the latter; and the result, that is the gain,
must equally, it is presumed, be considered as British property.

It will be further seen that the interest of those officers must
most justly come under the protection of their own Government, as well from the circumstances under which they, first
in 1809, and during the war, entered into the Portuguese service, as from those which induced them to remain in it at the
conclusion of the peace.   They did not, as adventurers, or as
persons having no employment, seek for it where it might be
found; but they acted with the consent and under the encouragement of their own Government, both during the war and
again when a new arrangement was made at the peace, and, as
it has been said, they all made great sacrifices at this latter
epoch, as well under the faith of the Portuguese Government,
as from being sanctioned by their own, and expecting its
protection.

It is hoped that the foregoing simple statement of the
case of the British officers lately serving in the Portuguese
army will suffice to induce his Majesty's Government to
interfere with that of Portugal, that they may be treated

with that equity and justice which they have so fair a claim
to expect.

It may be necessary to observe that, in addition to the
trifling pecuniary remuneration proposed to be given by the
Cortes to the British officers, they have decreed that each
officer of the rank of Brigadier shall have the commandership
of the Tower and Sword, and under that rank the small Cross
of the same order. This is thought not exactly a manner to
acquire honours, or that the acceptance, under such circumstances, would be sanctioned by his Majesty, as it would diminish the value of those honours already received by other
officers for particular services, and therefore, besides that this
additional remuneration would only be to a few, and as it could
not even to them be sanctioned, it would be of no avail at all.

Sir George H. Rose to Lord Castlereagh.

Berlin, January 6, 1821.

My dear Lord—Lest you should fear I might be inefficient
for some time, I contrive to write, to say that I shall undoubtedly be up in a few days. I was fairly knocked down,
and made to faint, (for the first time in my life) by pain by
lumbago, in an extraordinary degree instantaneously. I am
very much better, have had no fever, and hope to be on my
legs within a week at the farthest.

I am, my dear lord, &c., G. H. ROSE.

The Hon. F. Lamb to Lord Castlereagh.

Frankfort, January 6, 1821.

Dear Lord Castlereagh—In my last I omitted thanking you
for leaving your despatches open; but you will easily believe
how grateful I am to you for it. The suite of papers which
you have allowed me to see upon this subject, form a perfect
and most useful code upon the difficult question of foreign
interference.

I have reason to think that Capodistrias is the man to whom the line taken by England will give the greatest plea-sure. Many passages in his private letters have been shown to me, and from them I am led to conclude that his real object from the beginning has been to prevent the expedition to Naples. Before the Congress met, his language was, " que l'Autriche se trompoit fort si elle croyoit que la Russie l'aide-roit à aller à Naples, pour en faire un fief Impérial." This note has since changed, and it now is, " que l'on ne remonte pas l'esprit avec les bayonettes—que l'emploi de la force pour-roit avoir les suites les plus funestes, et que, pourvu que l'Angleterre tienne bon dans son système de neutralité, on espère parvenir à les empêcher." He has evidently had much difficulty in managing the Emperor, and one means which he employs is to send to Anstett a sort of theme upon which to work, who then writes a despatch in the most piquant style he can, to be laid by Capodistrias before the Emperor, as if he had known nothing of it beforehand.

Langenau, on the other hand, tells me that the Austrian military do not wish to act till they have 150,000 men in Italy, which force will not be collected there till the beginning of March ; so that, up to the present time, Metternich and Capodistrias may both have been playing the same game—delay.

Metternich has been making another attempt at Troppau to get Anstett removed from hence, which has only produced a letter to him to tell him to avoid giving any hold of himself, but not to change his system of conduct. I have seen the letter. At the same moment he was doing this, Metternich sent him an extra magnificent box for the Récès de Francfort, with a highly complimentary letter, which, being sent back the same day in original to the Emperor, crossed upon the road with the letter from Capodistrias, announcing that his removal had been demanded. What weakness to attach such importance to the presence of an individual, and to fall into

such contradictions in trying to get rid of him ! There is
nothing to write from hence.

                          Believe me, &c.,   F. LAMB.

Sir William à Court to Lord Castlereagh.

My dear Lord—I feel infinitely obliged to your lordship for
your kind letter of the 16th ultimo, as well as for the highly instructing and important papers you were so good as to send me.

The King having left Naples before the arrival of the
courier, I received no invitation to attend him, but I have
little doubt but that, as soon as he knows (as he will do from
other quarters) that I am authorized to follow him, he will
immediately urge me to join him at Laybach. Any such invitation I shall decline, for the reasons pointed out in my
despatch No. 4 ; and, in doing so, I am confident that I shall
act in the spirit of your lordship's instructions. As it is necessary my intentions in this respect should be known to your
lordship as early as possible, I have deemed it advisable to
send a courier with the present despatches.

Six weeks or two months will bring this unfortunate business to a conclusion, whether it be settled by the pen or the
sword, after which I shall naturally be desirous of rejoining
my family, from which I separated myself upon the sole consideration of the public service. I sent them to England that
I might be quite a free agent here. I shall, therefore, be truly
grateful to your lordship, if you will grant me a conditional
leave of absence, to return to England in the spring, provided
everything be settled here, and the public service should not
require my presence. Your lordship will, I am certain, do
me the justice to believe that I shall make no use of such
leave of absence, should there exist the slightest, the *very
slightest* reason for my remaining at my post.

I also cannot help indulging a hope that some arrangements

may be made to prevent my returning to Naples. Putting out
of the question what my own wishes may be, the public service
would henceforward undoubtedly be carried on with more
facility and smoothness by any other man than myself. I
have been here too long not to have imbibed prejudices and
predilections, which are probably reciprocal. My position
henceforward will evidently be a false one. I shall naturally
see everything in a wrong point of view, and my actions will
be liable to an equally false construction. Your lordship will
see. all this as clearly as myself, and relieve me, I am sure,
from so irksome a situation, and one where I can render so
little service to my country.

I have the honour to be, with the greatest respect, &c.,

WILLIAM À COURT.

Mr. Edward Ward to Lord Castlereagh.

Lisbon, January 14, 1821.

My dear Lord—All eyes are now fixed upon the Constella-
tion of Laybach, which is destined to guide our movements ;
and though our revolutionary watches, if left to themselves,
would run far beyond all regulation, yet, under the domi-
nation of that great planetary body, we are now fain to keep
them from the striking point until it shall have passed its
meridian.

The prevalence of very tempestuous weather has, by flood-
ing the roads, rendered the progress of the Deputies towards
Lisbon very slow. There are not yet a sufficient number (two-
thirds) arrived to enable them to open the Cortes. How the
councils of that body will be directed, God knows ! but I find
the hopes of the Moderates rising every day, and their courage
in proportion. The nobility have drawn up a protest, which
it is intended to present at the commencement of the session :
their object is to obtain a separate Chamber.

When I speak of Moderates, I believe I name the most
ultra set which is to be found ; for I have never met with any

ultra Royalists, according to the French acceptation. In fact, I believe the noblesse are by no means displeased with the prospect of a system which will enable them, in some measure, to get rid of the state of dependence in which the Crown has always considered it its policy to keep them, and which may perhaps wholly free them, by settling in their families the lands or rents which they now enjoy (and which constitute their chief revenues) during pleasure only.

I find they all reckon upon the interference of England, in the way of a demonstration, to support the appearance of the Prince Royal in his dominions, and then they do not doubt of a complete counter-revolution. The seeds of it are already sown, especially in the army: 180 Captains have been passed by in the late promotions, and many more subalterns—sufficient grounds for discontent, without taking into the account those who have been disappointed with less reason for their hopes of advancement.

They are proceeding to distribute some regiments along the coast, whether really under the idea of defending it, or only to endeavour to keep alive the notion of danger from foreign attack, I cannot say. Their means are scanty, and their courage nothing at all. Under the present peculiar circumstances, and with the temperament of this people, intimidation can effect almost anything.

The Prince will probably stay his voyage at the Azores, in order to make himself acquainted with the state of parties here, (I hope he will have good advisers) but, in order to give the *élan* to the Royalists, he must come into the country. Lisbon would not, I think, be desirable, as his *coup d'essai*: north or south he would succeed better: indeed, I am told that Oporto and the northern provinces would be the most eligible. It would have a fine moral effect if he were to succeed there where the revolution first broke forth.

Spain seems to be growing too weak to carry through the mischief she had planned and still wishes to execute, in co.

operation with her party here ; but I think this party is losing strength apace.   I hope things will soon admit of Matilda and the children coming out to me.   Pray instruct me what to do in the event of an open rupture with the royal authority.

Believe me, my dear Lord, &c.,

EDWARD WARD.

I find the Russians talking against the temporizing diplomatic measures.   The journals treat the Emperor with a good deal of abuse, and the Russian Chargé d'Affaires is very angry with them.

<hr>

Lord Castlereagh to Sir William à Court.

Foreign Office, January 19, 1821.

My dear Sir—I send you, in great confidence, a copy of a letter which the King has received from his Sicilian Majesty, with the enclosure to which it refers.   My object in doing so is that I may receive, in equal confidence, your private remarks upon the statement it contains.   It would be desirable that I should learn, in the most authentic manner, how far the facts alleged in the enclosures to the King's letter are open to contradiction, or are likely to be questioned.

I also send you, in the same confidence, the copy of a despatch which I have addressed to Lord Stewart, in reply to the queries put to me by him.   It may not eventually be necessary for Lord Stewart to enter into any explanations upon either subject; but I have thought it best to apprise you of the nature of the language his lordship is directed to hold on both these subjects.

CASTLEREAGH.

<hr>

Mr. T. Musgrave to Maréchal-Général Beresford.

Lisbon, January 20, 1821.

My Lord—I can hardly give you a just idea of the dissatisfaction which now prevails in the Portuguese army, and which has been occasioned principally by the partiality with which the late extensive promotion has been carried into effect. An immense number of officers, whose equal or superior pretensions to be promoted are undeniable, have solicited, and some have even insisted upon, their dismission. Requirimentos, drawn up in terms which nothing but the strongest feelings of indignation could suggest, have been presented to the Government in overwhelming numbers, and many officers, under an impression that their claims might best be personally urged, have presented themselves and stated their pretensions, with all that proud and haughty demeanour that a feeling of unmerited degradation is well calculated to inspire. The officers that anxiously desire your lordship's return are daily increasing in number. They have already their appropriate designation of Mareschalistas; and your lordship may anticipate a large accession to this party, from their ready assumption of the title, and from the natural consequences of progressive dissatisfaction: for all of this class now compare the injustice to which they are exposed with the firm and equitable distribution of military distinctions with which the fair claims of merit and services were rewarded, while the army, which owes its very formation and existence to you, was under your administration.

The political aspect of affairs in this country corresponds with the portrait which I have exhibited of the state of its army. A variety of circumstances, and some of a political nature, have still delayed the arrival of a sufficient number of members for the installation of the Cortes. This ceremony will now probably be delayed till the end of this month.

Party spirit is in a state of mischievous activity even before the meeting of the Deputies: it will, in my opinion, burst forth with great violence when they do meet. The Deputies for Estremadura are deeply infected with principles of republicanism: those for Beira affect a constitutional monarchy, and are anxious that the Duke of Cadouval should be temporarily invested with the presidency of the Government. This intelligence reaches me indirectly from Francisco Xavier Monteiro, at whose house the question to whom the Presidency should be offered has been discussed. The same question was agitated in a more general meeting of the Deputies, and the Duke of Cadouval, the Marquis of Abrantes, the Marquis of Castel Melhor, and the Conde de Sampayo, were all mentioned as persons to whom the Presidency might be confided; but they were all rejected for the following reasons: the first, because the nomination would not fail to give the greatest umbrage to the King; the second, because he was too immoral; the third, because he was too bigoted; and the fourth, because he was too weak. This information cost the Russian Consul (who communicated it to me) a bribe of two peços, but I doubt its accuracy, because it was at the same time mentioned to him that the Archbishop of Evora was considered by them as preferable to the rest for the Presidency of the Government. Now, it is so well known that everything emanating from the regular and secular clergy is held in such abhorrence by a large proportion of the Deputies, that it is less likely that the name of the Archbishop should ever have been mentioned in their deliberations. In short, they are, my lord, in the state in which you have so accurately described them to be—without one single man of talents in the whole nation equal to the direction of public affairs, or one single individual looked up to as of sufficiently prominent merit to possess the respect and confidence of the country. From such a state of things confusion, and nothing but confusion, can arise.

M. de Borel, the Russian Chargé d'Affaires, with whom I have much confidential communication, has put into my hands all his correspondence with this Government on the subject of an attack made on the Emperor of Russia in Nos. 6 and 7 of the "Portuguez Constitutional." By the next packet, I shall send your lordship a copy of the whole. You will very much approve of the dignity and firmness with which he conducted himself. The consequence of his proper assumption of this tone has been such as he himself anticipated—a most humble apology made to him by the Government, and general directions given to the censors of the press to permit nothing to be printed that may be deemed offensive to those States between which and Portugal friendly relations continue to prevail. One of the effects of this proceeding on the part of M. de Borel your lordship will see in the " Diario de Governo" of the 10th inst. A communication similar to that which has been sent to M. de Borel has also been made to Mr. Ward and all the other Chargés d'Affaires in this capital. I regret that I have not time to send you a copy of it by this packet.

On Sunday last, shortly after the packet had weighed anchor, Viana gave me a note, of which a copy is enclosed, conveying the substance of the intelligence which he had on that day been able to collect from Dr. Leal, the passenger in the Treize de Maio, to whom the Prince Royal confided the letter for Pedro José Cauper. This letter has not yet been published, but I still think that I may possibly be able to procure a copy of it. I understand that it is the determination of the Deputies not to avail themselves of the disobedience of the son in order to sanction their own acts of disobedience to the authority of the father. Should the Prince, therefore, clandestinely effect his escape from the Rio, he will most probably, on his arrival here, find no party whatever in the least disposed to invest him with any branch of the regal authority. It is conjectured that a deputation may very probably be sent from the Rio, in order finally to adjust the constitutional limits under which the royal prerogative is to be restrained. But this consideration places aside the influence which the decisions of the Sovereigns at Laybach must necessarily have on the future destinies of the Peninsula.

I had nearly forgotten to mention that the Bishops of Leiria, Aveiro, and Viseu, have declined to attend the Cortes, under various excuses ; and Manoel Paes de Sarde i Castro has also excused himself. There is, I am informed, a sort of protest or manifesto circulated in manuscript, expressing very forcibly the dissatisfaction of the Fidalgos at being excluded from the Cortes by the late elections. I suspect that the Conde de Sabougal is the author of it, and Dom Thomas de Mascarenhas, if I am not mistaken, avails himself of any good opportunity to make generally known these sentiments of well-founded discontent.

The day for the installation of the Cortes remains, as I have already stated, still undetermined. Their arrival appears to be delayed by circumstances more difficult to be vanquished than those which are supposed to obstruct their journey to the capital. Between the Deputies for Beira and those for Estremadura there seems to exist a difference of opinion, which does not promise an easy adjustment.

Believe me, my dear lord, &c.,   T. M. MUSGRAVE.

Précis of Russian Memoir on the Conferences in London, on the Slave Trade and the Barbary Powers.

The first paragraph states the questions to be discussed :

1st. *The abolition of the Slave Trade.*

2ndly. *The piracies of the Barbary Powers,* and the manner in which they arose.

The additional article to the Treaty of Paris, of 1815, having produced the agitation of the first, and the overtures of Russia occasioned that of the second—these separate and distinct questions were considered *together* at the request of England.

"Précis du Mémoire annexé au Protocole de la 7me et dernière Conférence et des communications qui s'y rapportent," —states the objects discussed in this paper to be—" Le projet d'une Ligue maritime temporaire fixée à sept années," which would have for its motive "le désir des Puissances de respecter les maximes d'humanité et des nations civilisées dans leurs relations avec tous les États d'Afrique," and the double object of which would be " l'abolition définitive, universelle, et efficace de la traite, et une défense mutuelle contre les piratéries des Barbaresques."

PREMIERE PARTIE.

De l'Alliance proposée comme moyen d'obtenir l'abolition définitive et universelle de la Traite des Négrès.

"1°. De cette Alliance dans ses rapports avec le système Européen"—states the great difficulties and complications which would take place in the execution of the system with respect to Spain and Portugal.

"2°. De cette Alliance relativement à son but? The military force of the Allies would be employed not against Spain and Portugal as Powers, but against their subjects carrying on the Slave Trade. Could this be done with impunity? Would not the different States themselves undertake it in their respective jurisdictions? If not, under what regulations could this be effected, and in common?

"3°. Exécution de l'Article additionel du traité du 20 Novembre, 1815"—recommends that the Conference should confine itself to things *stipulated*, and quotes this article as containing all that has been actually stipulated—recommends the course to be pursued to fulfil these stipulations, and annexes *projet* of a note to the Powers still authorizing the prosecution of the Slave Trade, demanding its abolition.

SECONDE PARTIE.

De l'Alliance proposée comme moyen d'abolir les Piratéries des Barbaresques.

Gives the object of the alliance against the Barbary Powers, as stated in the memoir of the Conference, and proposes the three following questions to their consideration:

1. Si le système défensif dont il s'agit est d'accord avec les principes de droit et avec les égards que chaque Puissance doit au maintien inviolable de ces principes?

2. Dans cette hypothèse, si les résultats de l'alliance proposée sont en rapport avec le but véritable qu'elle se propose d'atteindre ?

3. S'il n'y auroit point un mode à la fois plus légitime, plus simple, et plus sûr de faire cesser, d'un commun accord, les piratéries des Barbaresques ?

Will give explanation of these three questions.

I.—*Du Système Défensif contre les Barbaresques sous le point de vue de droit.*

The Barbary Powers are not independent States: they are and have always been considered as subjects of the Ottoman Porte. How, then, can you form an alliance against them, upon the "principes de droit ?" Still less can you do it upon a principle of common and reciprocal interest. You must first suppose a common and equal aggression on the part of the Algerines. And then how are some Powers to enter into this league, who would, by so doing, complicate their relations with the Porte, in consequence of engagements already existing between them and her ?

II.—*De ce Système relativement à ses moyens et à son but.*

Doubts whether the objects to be obtained will be worth the expenses to be incurred for the effort.

The pirates would have a right to recommence their depredations after the expiration of the seven years, especially towards those States who had not made peace with them during the interval. The Barbary Powers would not be civilized in that short space of time.

The solemn declaration of the cessation of Christian slavery would imply an acknowledgment of the previous right of the Algerines to enforce it.

And, after all, each Power would only gain the security which its own marine, if it had one, could procure for itself.

III.—*Mode de faire cesser, d'un commun accord, les Piratéries des Barbaresques.*

It is proposed by Russia—first, to decide "la manière d'envisager politiquement les Régences d'Afrique." To consider them as subjects of the Porte, whom she either *cannot* or *will* not control. The Porte will either allow or contest this.

If the first, offensive measures against the Barbary Powers would be legal; if the second, the Porte would guarantee their tranquillity. This guarantee must be one *of fact.*

Long experience having proved that the Porte cannot give such a guarantee, the Powers can then legitimately coalesce to procure it.

The mode of procuring it will be to deprive the Barbary States of all means of piracy, either by the authority of their Sovereign, or by the Allied Powers.

The naval force to be formed of contingents of all the Powers of Europe—contingents to be regulated.

The principles of the Alliance being thus decided, explanations will be demanded of the Porte, and whatever their answer may be, the first subsequent appearance of armed pirates in the Mediterranean will be the signal of the *casus fœderis* having arisen, and the naval forces will act.

The command of the naval force will be given to Great Britain.

One effort of this sort will be much less expensive than a league for seven years, and more likely to accomplish the end proposed.

Sir Henry Wellesley to Lord Castlereagh.

Madrid, January 27, 1821.

My dear Lord—I have determined to postpone my departure from hence for a short time, in order to see the effect produced here by the first proceedings of the Cortes at Lisbon, and of the Conferences at Laybach. I shall probably, therefore, not leave Madrid before the 20th of next month; and, if there should appear any necessity for it, I shall stay until the Cortes have assembled, which will be on the 1st of March. There can then be no further necessity for my continuance here, as my presence can in no way influence the deliberations of this body, and the agitations prevailing just now, in consequence of the intrigues of the Serviles and the apprehension of foreign interference, will probably cease when the Cortes have assembled.

I have thought it right to trouble your lordship with these few lines to inform you of the delay in my departure. I have no intelligence to communicate in addition to that contained in my despatches of this date.

I have the honour to be, &c.,   H. WELLESLEY.

The Hon. F. Lamb to Lord Castlereagh.

Frankfort, January 30, 1821.

My dear Lord Castlereagh—You will think I write a most unnecessary quantity about this Circular: but recollect the difference of opinion between the Allies was totally unsuspected here. Metternich employs here a blockhead, whom he thinks he can render harmless by trusting him with nothing; and when I administered the dose to him, he was so astonished, and found it so nauseous, and talked so much more nonsense than I will repeat to you, that I was afraid of his talking it to others as well as to me. For this reason I wrote the despatch to Stewart, and sent it to the Austrian Chancery, where all letters are opened, in order that the President may see what language he ought to hold, until he shall hear from Prince Metternich, and also to prevent the possibility of misrepresentation as to what has been done here.

I hope, by the next post, to hear that all difficulties in

England have been set at rest by a spanking majority, and am, my dear Lord Castlereagh, ever faithfully yours,

F. LAMB.

I enclose an extract which Anstett gave me an opportunity of making from his despatch upon the subject. The remainder of it was merely an account of the contents of the Circular.

[Enclosure.]

Extrait d'une Dépêche du Baron d'Anstett à sa Cour.

Mr. Lamb n'a donné connoître de la circulaire, qu'au Président de la Diète, parcequ'il lui a paru essentiel qu'il fut préparé à rectifier de fausses interprétations, lorsque la chose transpirait d'autre part, ce qui est inévitable ; et plus essentiel encore de prouver ce qui fait une partie capitale de la circulaire, que l'alliance entre les cinq Cours existe dans toute sa force, ainsi que dans ses bases fondamentales, et que rien n'y sauroit porter atteinte.

S'il m'étoit permis de joindre ici quelques remarques personnelles, j'observerais à votre Excellence combien il eut été facile à l'Envoyé de sa Majesté Britannique de profiter de cette circonstance pour rallier à l'opinion de sa Cour tous les États Allemands qui se placent vis-à-vis de l'Autriche. Je crois encore que la publicité, que l'apperçu des résultats des conférences a acquise, est due à la manière trop large dont le Baron de Binder a fait ses communications au Sénat de Hambourg. Il avoit oublié la peur dont les villes libres sont travaillées depuis quelque tems ; cependant c'est cette publicité qui a jeté probablement le Ministère Britannique dans la nécessité de faire une profession de principes dont la connoissance étoit au moins inutile au public. Lorsque l'on proclame, et l'on ne sauroit le faire assez, des principes légitimes parce qu'ils sont réparateurs, il semble superflu d'en soumettre l'autorité à l'indignation de la malveillance ; et c'est ce qui a été produit par un excès de confiance, sans doute. Je ne me permettrai pas d'y mettre un autre nom.

Lord Castlereagh to Sir William à Court.

St. James's Square, February 7, 1821.

My dear Sir—It being an object to which his Majesty's Ministers attach much importance to be enabled to make some reduction in the naval estimates of the present year, Lord Melville sends instructions for the return to England of one sail of the line and one frigate of the force now employed in the Mediterranean. As there will still remain one eighty-gun ship and four or five large frigates, I have not hesitated to give my consent to this measure, under present circumstances. The King's person being now placed beyond the reach of danger, I should hope the remaining force, acting in concert with that of France, will afford every necessary protection to the rest of the royal family.

We are yet without any intelligence from Laybach of the course of measures intended to be pursued.

· The British circular instruction, which has been laid before both Houses of Parliament, seems to have given satisfaction, and, I should hope, will discourage hostile discussion. The attention of the House of Commons has hitherto been exclusively occupied by a trial of party strength, founded upon the late proceedings against the Queen. The division of last night, of 324 to 178, seems to leave the issue no longer doubtful, and will, I trust, in conjunction with the display of loyalty which has shown itself both in addresses and upon his Majesty's late visit to the theatres, restore confidence and abate the popular fermentation.

I entirely approve of your determination to remain at Naples, and for the reasons that you have stated.

Sir Henry Wellesley to Lord Castlereagh.

Madrid, February 8, 1821.

My dear Lord—I have very little to add to my despatches of this day's date. It is said that the King was much agitated in the Council of State, while deliberating upon the measures to be pursued, in consequence of the occurrences of Monday. I see no salvation for him but giving his whole confidence to his Ministers, and I really believe that, if he had done so from the moment of their appointment, the affairs of this country would now have been in a very different state.

All the Ministers wish for a reform of the Constitution, which must no doubt happen sooner or later; but their differences with the King (which, I am afraid, must be attributed to him) only tend to throw delays in the way of it. I am informed that the Infant Don Francisco has recommenced his intrigues against his brother.

The town is now tranquil, but no one can say how long it will continue so. I think it probable that we shall have fresh disturbances before the meeting of the Cortes—I am sorry not to have received your lordship's despatch of the 19th ult. It might have been very useful to me just at this time.

I am, with great truth, &c.,   H. WELLESLEY.

Sir Henry Wellesley to Lord Castlereagh.

Madrid, February 8, 1821, 6 P.M.

My dear Lord—M. Gomez, the Portuguese Chargé d'Affaires, called upon me this evening, and showed me a note which he had received from the Infanta, wife of the Infant Don Carlos, written in her own hand, in which she asserts that the Ministers have sent emissaries into the Provinces, to endeavour to prevail upon them to declare in favour of a Republic; and that they have done this with the knowledge and sanction of the Ayuntamiento, the Captain-General Vilalba, and the two Colonels of the Foot Guards, the Prince of Anglona and the Marquis of Castel dos Rios.

I own I am not much inclined to give credit to this intelligence; and it may possibly have been communicated to M. Gomez with an insidious intention—that of inducing him to send it to M. de Saldanha; as it would operate as an additional incitement to the Allies to interfere in the affairs of this country; but, whether it be well founded or not, coming from such a quarter, I have not thought proper to withhold it from your lordship.

The Infanta likewise mentions in the same note the intrigues of the Infante Don Francisco.

I am, with great truth, &c.,   H. WELLESLEY.

Lord Burghersh to Lord Castlereagh.

Florence, February 21, 1821.

My Lord—I have delayed answering your lordship's despatch marked Circular, and dated the 19th of January, as I was in daily expectation of the return of the courier from Naples, who was the bearer of it. He has only this moment arrived, having been delayed six days at sea on his passage to Leghorn; and, as his communications are of moment, I shall delay him but for an hour.

In the concluding paragraph of the despatch above alluded to, your lordship leaves it to my discretion to make a communication on the part of my Government to the Courts to which I am accredited, regulating my language in conformity to the principles laid down in that document. This measure on my part was, however, to be dependent on the communication of the circular despatch of the Allied Powers which might have been made by the Ministers of Austria, Prussia, and Russia.

The Circular here alluded to, in the precise form in which it was transmitted to your lordship, had not arrived at Florence, but communications of the nature of its contents had constantly been made to the Tuscan Government by the Austrian Minister, and the language held by him, both in his official correspondence, and in his general conversation, was that England, though acting in a secondary line, was perfectly agreed both as to the principle set forth by Austria, and the measures about to be pursued by her; and further, that the British Government, by sending a fleet into the Bay of Naples, had adopted a line of conduct more hostile than any as yet resorted to by Austria; since the assembly of an army in Lombardy could not be considered as offensive to the Neapolitans as the presence of a fleet evidently destined to overawe them.

The same language was in a great degree held by the Russian Minister, and more particularly by M. D'Oubril, upon his return from Laybach, where he had received the appointment of Envoy Extraordinary to the Court of Naples. Under these circumstances, I felt that, in the execution of your lordship's instructions, it became my duty to present a note founded upon the despatch I had received; and I have the honour of enclosing a copy of the communication I transmitted to the Courts to which I am accredited.

The Hon. F. Lamb to Lord Castlereagh.

Frankfort, February 24, 1821.

My dear Lord Castlereagh—The Russian courier, who passed on to London with their Circular, brought letters here from Laybach: one semi-official, thanking Anstett for his communications, pointing out to him that his advice had been followed, not only as to its tenour, but almost in the very words, and inviting him, on the part of the Emperor, to continue to give his opinions on what is passing. Having seen his letter, I can speak as to the advice of his which is said to have been followed.

It was to ground their proceedings on the Holy Alliance, from which would flow, as a necessary consequence, the exempting Naples from any contribution. Upon this point you will observe a great difference between the Russian Circular and the Austrian Declaration; and this is the first blow which these *faiseurs* meditate against Austria.

The next letter was quite a private one from Capodistrias, in

which he finds great fault with the Austrian Declaration, but
washes his hands of it, and says that they have embarked,
and have only to go through with it.   The third letter is from
somebody, whose name I don't know, but who is evidently
very well informed, and who enters into much detail, and
clearly says that Capodistrias is without influence, and that
the Emperor is completely in the hands of Metternich.

I should not have troubled you with such a detail, if I had
not just received a letter from Bagot, in which I see he is of a
different opinion, and thinks Capodistrias is urging the
Emperor on.   I think it right that you should hear what there
is to be said on the other side.   I am the more convinced of
the truth of my opinion by Anstett's answers, which I happened not only to read, but to see sealed up and given to a
courier.

His despatch, in answer to the one communicating the
circular, states that he has communicated it as directed, but
that in this instance he has no merit but that of obedience, as
his opinion is completely at variance with the line they are
pursuing.   His private letter is headed by the motto, " that
in politics there is no longer any force but the force of opinion."   From this he derives and again insists upon the
necessity of levying no contribution upon Naples, whether she
submits in the first instance or not; and from this he deduces
a plan for the revival of the Alliance; which, he says, will
resume all its force, and acquire a fresh hold upon public
opinion, if it shows itself afresh for the purpose of assuring
the independence of Naples, and for making the Austrian
troops quit its territory within a reasonable period.   This is
perhaps true, but, coming from Anstett, it is, in fact, another
blow aimed at Austria.

There is a third letter from him, stating, and truly, that all
the Austrians here are dissatisfied with their own Declaration;
that they look upon it as a low apology for a line which did
not want one; and that the paragraph about Russia gives to

that Power the guardianship over Austria. All this is stated with bitter sarcasm, and putting into the mouth of imaginary persons every sort of *propos* which can the most pique the Emperor upon the part which he is playing.

Why do I trouble you with all this? For two reasons—first, because I am convinced that Anstett would not throw himself into the breach in this way, if he were not sure that he is playing the game of the Greek, and certain to be backed by him; secondly, because it is to be anticipated that this sort of battery will in the end have an effect upon the Emperor, who reads all these letters himself; or even if this fails, because, in the arrangements with Naples, it may be expected that Capodistrias will yet have influence enough to thwart, in some degree, the views of Metternich, and will not fail to exert it. As this part of my letter cannot be written without mentioning names, let me beg that it may be seen by as few persons as possible; and believe me, dear Lord Castlereagh, to be ever faithfully yours,

F. LAMB.

Sir Henry Wellesley to Lord Castlereagh.

Madrid, February 25, 1821.

My dear Lord—I am afraid that nothing will be done in the present Cortes towards altering the Constitution. There is not a thinking man in the country who is not convinced of the necessity of altering it, yet no one is willing to take upon himself the responsibility of proposing it. It must be admitted, likewise, that the conduct of the King and his friends is not calculated to inspire confidence, and this leads many people to doubt the wisdom of throwing more power into his Majesty's hands, or at least renders them less active in promoting a change than they would otherwise be. It is evident that the King and his friends are sanguine in their expectations that the proceedings in Italy will produce a good effect here. This may be the case, if the affairs of Naples are settled without bloodshed; but certainly not, if any resistance is made by the Neapolitans.

I still continue to think that the worst consequences would follow any foreign interference here. Their irritation at the declaration of the three Sovereigns, issued at Troppau, exceeds all bounds, and could only be removed by a public assurance that the Allies have no intention of interfering in their affairs. An assurance of this kind would, I think, lead them to turn their attention more seriously to the modifications so necessary in their system.

It is said that the conduct of the Ministers will undergo a serious investigation in the Cortes. Many disapprove their proceedings with respect to the King, particularly in the month of November last, when alarm was unnecessarily excited throughout the country. Many are likewise disgusted at the severe measure of removing the Gardes du Corps from the King's person, and at the little respect with which he was treated upon that occasion. Others say that his Majesty himself, being alarmed at the irritation manifested by the populace, desired that his Guards might be dissolved.

The alarming state of the finances is likewise a subject which must occupy the early attention of the Cortes. The Minister of Finance, it is thought, will be removed, and a new loan proposed to meet their most pressing difficulties.

I do not believe that any treaty has been concluded with Portugal, although it was reported lately that one had been concluded, the principal stipulation of which was, that each Power should furnish 25,000 men for the defence of the Peninsula.

I have the honour to be, &c.,   H. WELLESLEY.

The Hon. Robert Gordon to Lord Castlereagh.

Laybach, February 25, 1821.

My dear Lord—After much difference of opinion, which, contrary to usual custom, has terminated in the defeat of Count Capodistrias, the plan for reconstructing the Neapolitan

Government and communicating it to the Italian Plenipotentiaries has been decided upon by the three Cabinets. The plan in itself, although now unanimously adopted, seems to give but little satisfaction to many of the parties concerned. Prince Ruffo declares that the King's throat has been cut by forcing upon him a Consulta composed of too many members. Capodistrias feels that his Emperor is forfeiting all claims to be hailed as the general dispenser of justice—whilst the Italians have some fears that forms which are calculated to give little satisfaction at Naples may promote great evil in their own States, upon the score of example. The French Plenipotentiaries have only been withheld from expressing their disapprobation openly in Conference by a desire to preserve harmony, and hopes of a change when the King returns to Naples. All parties regret that he has remained so long at Laybach, and yet it is certain that, until the question of reconstruction was decided, the three Powers would not have permitted his Majesty's departure. His spirits have been much affected by the late news from Naples, and I am told he suspects his son of endeavouring to supplant him in the affections of his people.

It appears now quite determined that the Sovereigns will not even enter Italy; and the Emperor Alexander's desire to visit Naples has been allayed and postponed to next year. I ought to mention that one of the reasons alleged for fixing the reunion at Florence for the month of September in next year is founded upon an expectation that your lordship may be prevailed upon to join it; and this period has been chosen in order that your complying with the general wish might not interfere with your parliamentary duties.

M. de Saldanha, who remained here much longer than there seemed to be any occasion for, or than was prudent, left Laybach a week or ten days ago. I have been positively informed by the different Ministers who were privy to the object of his mission, that not only no encouragement was given, but no communication held with him upon it.

I am happy to observe that the discontent and *sharpness* which so unwarrantably existed, though but for a short time, on account of our circular, has entirely disappeared. The satisfaction given by your lordship's remarks in the House of Commons, upon the Neapolitan question, the triumphant majorities, and the reaction of a proper feeling amongst our public, have much promoted this change. The Emperor of Russia stopped me, the other day, in the promenade, to desire I would particularly express his congratulations upon the success in Parliament. I have even some difficulty in persuading Prince Metternich that our foreign are not in that degree intimately connected with our domestic politics as will permit of any change in our *attitude prise* upon the affair of Naples, which he almost expects as a consequence upon the successes of our Government at home.

Immutable as they have been and will continue to be, justice is gradually accorded to our principles in proportion as the Allies mark the inconsistencies of the French Government; for, notwithstanding Count Blacas' early assurances in Conference of the zealous co-operation of France, backed by letters from the Ministers of the Government at Paris, a short adherence to our line has been maintained, in point of fact, and as such held forth to Europe. The French Plenipotentiaries have now withdrawn their favourable countenance even from the Laybach Conferences: so that, on the part of the three Powers, there exists no slight dissatisfaction; and, in proportion as it increases, there is a disposition to be more satisfied with the relative and frank disposition of Great Britain. I consider my having been invited to the private Conference, which I have reported in my despatch No. 3, to be a proof of this.

Believe me, my dear lord, ever faithfully, &c.,

R. GORDON.

I understand Count Blacas has received instructions from Paris not to interfere to the extent which he had first engaged himself to.

Mr. Thomas Robinson to Thomas Lach, Esq.[1]

B. Sq., February 26, [18]21.

Sir—I am honoured by the commands of the Lords' Committee of Privy Council of Trade, signified in your letter of the 20th instant, enclosing a despatch from Sir William à Court, relating to the intention of the Government of Naples to impose new duties on trade in general, by which the interests of British merchants may be affected. And their lordships are pleased to request that I would report my opinion thereon, and with reference to the treaty of September, 1816, between Great Britain and Naples.

In obedience to their lordships' commands, I have the honour to report that the treaty appears to me to justify an expectation on the part of his Majesty's Government that the tariff there referred to should continue to be in force, if not permanently, at least for a very considerable time, and until the relations of commerce between the two countries might be revised and otherwise settled on terms of mutual agreement. The consent of his Britannic Majesty is recited, in the first Article, "to have been given with a view to provide for the security and *advantage* of the subjects and of the commerce of Great Britain;" but there is no other advantage in the treaty than the reduction of the tariff, which is made the price of the concession of former privileges on the part of his Britannic Majesty, which is the principal object of the treaty.

The 7th Article, which stipulates for a reduction of the tariff, reserves also a power to the King of the Two Sicilies of granting the same reduction of duties to other foreign nations.

The construction, therefore, cannot be, as suggested by Sir William à Court, to secure only a relative advantage to British merchants with reference to other nations. Nations are not

[1] This letter is endorsed: "Report of the King's Advocate on the Papers from Sir William à Court, relating to the intention of the Government of Naples to impose new duties on trade in general, by which the interests of British merchants may be affected."

usually considered to renounce the power of regulating their commercial duties otherwise than as they may be bound by specific engagements ; but, in the present instance, the want of an engagement in positive terms is supplied by almost necessary implications, as it is impossible to put any other interpretation on the treaty that would afford any equivalent for the privileges which are there relinquished.

I am humbly of opinion, therefore, that his Majesty's Government will be justified in maintaining that construction of the treaty, unless it should receive a different explanation from what passed at the time relative to this subject between the contracting parties.

I have the honour to be, &c.,   THO. ROBINSON.

The Hon. Frederick Lamb to Lord Castlereagh.

Frankfort, March 24, 1821.

My dear Lord Castlereagh—At such a crisis as the present, I shall make no apology for writing too much, but put down all I have to say.

A nephew of Capodistrias' arrived two days ago, *en courier*, from Laybach to Anstett. He brought the Russian circular of the 11th. I have seen it. But Anstett is not anxious to give it great publicity, as he says, and very truly, that, coming at this moment, it will be attributed to fear. It has appeared too late to be considered as a voluntary recognition of the principle put forward by England and France. He has replied by an Austrian courier, to say that the circular is worth nothing ; that it avoids the only word that can show a way out of the present difficulties—the word " Constitution ;" that the only thing the two Allied Powers can do is to force a way to Naples, and there to proclaim a Constitution, with two Chamqers, and with publicity in the finance and in the administration of justice, and to extend this system to all Italy.

The private letters to Anstett are, one from a Secretary of Capodistrias', stating that Nesselrode is the *intermediaire* be-

tween the Emperor and Metternich, and, in consequence, in
the highest favour; that Pozzo di Borgo, on his arrival, saw
this, attached himself to Nesselrode, and has, in consequence,
been named Ambassador at Paris, with 300,000 francs a-year
appointments, and other very large advantages. This letter
adds, that the first *coup de canon* fired in Italy was the signal
for the revolution in Piedmont; and that there is great apprehension at Laybach that the first shot fired there by the Russians
will be the signal of revolution in Prussia. It adds an opinion
that the Emperor must eventually recur to Capodistrias.

There is next a lamentable letter from Capodistrias himself,
saying that everybody has abandoned him, and expressing
his satisfaction to have found one honest man—Anstett—to
stand by him. He says that, since the month of October, all
the reports which he has laid before the Emperor have gone to
prove the certainty of a revolution in Piedmont, if the expedition against Naples were persisted in, and this with the certainty of geometrical demonstration. He expresses an anxious
wish that the issue of all this may be favourable, but adds, that
such a hope is contrary to the history of all human affairs.
He says that the Emperor still reads with pleasure all Anstett's
letters, because he has the talent to mix *l'utile avec l'agréable;*
but he advises him to be upon his guard, and not to push his
freedom of remark too far. I have already related how this
advice has been obeyed.

To turn to another subject—it appears to result, from a
most accurate examination of the returns of the Austrian army
in Italy, that its real numbers are as follows:—

	Men.
With Frimont	54,000
On his communications . . .	14,000
In the Milanese and Venetian States, gar- risons included	13,000

Of which about 80,000 are together under Bubna. This is
the result of Langenau's evaluation, counting them regiment

by regiment. The Duke of Wellington knows how far he is to be depended upon. I hope you have better authority for larger numbers, for the statement is alarming. He says there are regiments in Corinthia and the Tyrol which may possibly be concentrated as rapidly as the Piedmontese army, and has promised me a statement upon the subject, which unfortunately has not yet arrived.

With regard to this country, there is but one feeling in it, and the expression of it in favour of the Neapolitans is equally general and public. Yesterday there were reports in this town that symptoms of disobedience had appeared in more than one Prussian regiment. I cannot learn that there was the least foundation for it; but this sort of prediction tends to accomplish its own object; and there is a general avowal, even among the warmest Austrians, that no man has a right to be surprised if he shall hear at any hour of a Constitution having been demanded in Prussia. This may take place on the other side of the Rhine, either through the military or through the inhabitants. The latter, however, are less likely to move than if the question could be placed in the shape of separation from Prussia.

In the garrison of Mayence, disputes have taken place between the Austrian officers and those of Hesse-Darmstadt, in consequence of some of the latter boasting publicly that the Grand Duke had been forced to agree to the Constitution, in consequence of his knowledge of the disposition of the army. This is, however, the truth, and, with the knowledge of it, the Emperor of Russia sent, ten days ago, to recognize the notification of the Constitution, and to felicitate the Grand Duke on having granted it. Is this consistency? or are such distinctions worth the risk of a general war in Europe?

There is, of course, excessive anxiety as to the line which England and France are likely to pursue. My line in this place is so easy, that I do not wish to trouble you for an answer. Till you enjoin another language, I shall continue to say that I know nothing, but that individually I can perceive nothing to affect the principles on which our neutrality is founded, and that, having had the benefit of so much war single-handed, it is but fair that we should be spectators in our turn.

I forgot to mention, what perhaps it is unnecessary to state, that, in case of a revolution in Prussia, and a consequent attack upon her, it is to be expected that she will be supported by all Germany, and with an enthusiasm equal to any which has ever been seen. To this must be added the chance, in such a case, of a revolution in Poland, where the army abhors the Grand Duke Constantine, and where the only contradiction in the accounts is that the Russians say the discontent is greatest in the grand duchy of Posen, and the Prussians in the kingdom of Warsaw. My authority upon this subject is from many sources, and among others from Anstett, whose wife possesses large estates in Poland.

You will easily believe that I have no pleasure in writing so black a letter. It is the greatest proof I can give that I wish to be of real service, even at any personal risk. If there is a way (and I have no doubt that there is one) out of all these dangers and difficulties, it must be found by looking at them stedfastly, and allowing them their full weight. It is for this reason I so much deplore that Metternich should, at this moment, be at the helm.

One word as to the policy of Austria herself; for I much apprehend that her measures are not the best calculated to promote her own views. It is intimidation which she aims at, and the practical result in·this country is exaggeration and excitement of the passions. But the evil lies still deeper. She is striking with a material weapon against a spirit, and against one which is attacking herself where she least expects it. There have long been reports among the commercial houses here, as to the unwillingness of some of the Austrian regiments to march against the Neapolitans. It is only lately that I have thought them worthy of attention; nor can I learn that, in the above-mentioned shape, there is the least foundation for them.   The fact is, that a great number of the most active and the most distinguished officers in the last campaigns have been either laid aside entirely, or placed in inferior and unimportant situations.   At the head of this list are the Generals Bianchi and Jerome Colloredo, the latter much beloved by the army, and both put out of employment because the Emperor reckons them *reasoners*.   Can there be a more certain receipt for making a discontented man!   To this list of superior officers are to be added all the staff of the army, who, in the Austrian service, have greater weight than any other.   Among this class of officers, opinions are liable to run so high, that very lately a General Officer, at the head of a large Staff, called together all the officers of it, and notified to them that he was aware of the opinions they were in the habit of avowing upon Neapolitan affairs, and that, upon the smallest renewal of such language, he should send the offender as a prisoner to the nearest fortress.   This I can have no doubt about, as I know it from the General Officer himself.   My information about the general disposition of the Staff is almost as good.

It is perfectly true that these are but trifles in such an army as that of Austria; but it is the neglect of these trifles that leads to such deplorable results.   Who shall say how much of this spirit came back into Austria with her Armies of Occupation from France and Naples?   Who shall say how much more of it may be collected from a successful war and a subsequent occupation in Italy?

Let me end by begging that this long letter may be read with indulgence.   I have no wish to intrude my opinions or statements about countries and situations with which I have nothing to do, but these are so interwoven with what it is my duty to write, that it is not always easy to separate them.   Where my notions are wrong, they will be rectified by others, from better sources.   The only way in which I can injure the public

service is by omission. By writing too much, I can only
injure myself; and, of the two, this is the risk I prefer to run.

Believe me, &c.,   F. LAMB.

Lord Clancarty to Lord Castlereagh.

Bruxelles, March 27, 1821.

My dear Lord—Though I have not yet obtained an audience
from this King, for the purpose of remonstrating with him
upon the unreasonable delays of this Government, yet the
note verbale (a copy of which was transmitted in my letter of
27th February, marked private) has been apparently productive of this good, that it has at length elicited a satisfactory
answer upon the claims of the Commissariat contractors.

The principal object, however, of seeking this audience, viz.,
the necessity of obtaining from this Government a full admission of our true construction of the Slave Trade Treaty, in
accordance both with its spirit and letter, still remains unsatis-
fied; and, as I am quite clear that no other fair means have
been left untried by me to press an early and favourable decision on this most important point, and moreover feeling the
necessity of immediately urging the late violation of the treaty
which has occurred at Surinam on the consideration of this
Government, I have thought it expedient to accompany my
note to M. de Nagell on this subject (a copy of which you
will find in No. 13 of this date) by a second *note verbale*,
renewing my request for a private audience of his Majesty. A
copy of this I send for your information.

I am, however, privately informed that a favourable decision
has been made upon the construction of the Slave Trade Treaty.
If this second application for an audience shall hasten the only
proper satisfactory assurance on this head, it will quite answer
my purpose; if not, it is my intention to press this matter
still further, even to what may grow to a breach *between me
personally* and this Government, which, however much I sincerely hope it will not take place, as its result would hazard

my situation here, yet I shall consider it my duty to incur the
risk, rather than admit a point on the clear decision of which
the King and his Ministers are so much interested to be longer
held in a state of suspense.

Yours, my dear lord, &c.,   CLANCARTY.

[Enclosure.]

Copy of Lord Clancarty's Second Note to M. de Nagell.

Bruxelles, March 26, 1821.

Lord Clancarty presents his compliments to M. le Baron de
Nagell, and takes the liberty of referring him to his *note
verbale* of the 26th of February last, by which he sought a
personal audience from the King, for the purpose of pressing
his Majesty to direct that answers should be given upon some
points, (especially that relating to the construction of the Treaty
of May, 1818) and which, it appeared to him, had been left too
long in a state of apparent doubt between the two Governments.

Lord Clancarty, aware of the King's regretted indisposition,
has not hitherto urged an answer to this note, and had even
presumed to hope that the intermediate arrival to him of satisfactory answers upon these points might altogether have precluded him from the necessity of troubling his Majesty with
the renewal of a demand for a private audience.

Disappointed in this, having also recently received pressing
instructions from his Court, regretting the delays which had
hitherto occurred, and directing that an additional instance of
the infraction of the Convention for the abolition of trade in
Slaves should be laid before this Government, the substance of
which instructions M. le Baron de Nagell will find in the
accompanying official note; assured, moreover, of the happy
and entire recovery of the King, Lord Clancarty feels it to be
his duty to reiterate his request for admission to a private
audience of his Majesty, for the purpose of personally urging
what are not less the interests of his own than, rightly considered, they are of both Courts; and therefore solicits his

Excellency M. le Baron de Nagell to take the King's pleasure on this subject, and to acquaint him (Lord Clancarty) with the time when his Majesty shall be graciously pleased to receive him.

<hr />

Mr. W. Kenny to Lord Castlereagh.

43, Devonshire Street, Queen Square, March 31, 1821.

My Lord—The enclosed translation of Sir W. à Court's note to the King of Sicily, the tenour of which is so highly honourable to the character of the British Government, I was at first inclined to communicate to the public; but, it having occurred to me that its publication at the present moment might be detrimental, I deem it more advisable to make your lordship previously acquainted with the existence in this country of a copy of the same in the Italian language.

  I have the honour to be, &c., W. KENNY.

[Enclosure.]

Note presented to the King of Sicily by his Excellency Sir William à Court, Minister of Great Britain.

TRANSLATION.

The late fortunate events which have taken place in Europe having essentially altered the actual relations of Great Britain, with respect to Sicily, it becomes necessary for its representative to make known to his Majesty the sentiments with which the English Government is animated, and the views to which its attention is principally directed at the present moment. This is so much the more necessary, since, in the clashing of parties, the right of mediation has been on one side as much exaggerated as, on the other, it has been imprudently and unnecessarily blamed.

The sacrifices of Great Britain for the security and prosperity of this island give her a title to expect that her suggestions should be listened to with respect and attention: at least the moderation, with which she is disposed to exercise the privilege which the benefits conferred by her on Sicily have given her, ought to be considered a sufficient proof that she is little disposed to aim at the acquirement of an undue influence, incompatible with the principles of the Constitution and the dignity of an independent State.

It is not necessary to examine the causes whence originated the general manifestation of the desires of the nation for a reform in the Constitution of the country: this may be found in the progressive advancement of civilization, in the more general diffusion of knowledge, and in the insufficiency of every human institution to resist the abuses and deterioration to which they are naturally subject, and, in the midst of the changes of opinions and circumstances, to give the same degree of security to the happiness of the people, and which has continued to retain its original form.

But, although the wish for a change was almost unanimous, the determining the precise limits which ought to be established for the proposed changes was accompanied with the greatest difficulties. In this emergency, it was natural for the nation to turn its eyes towards a country which, not being of large extent, nor possessing a comparatively great population, had been able, nevertheless, not only to defend and preserve itself from the torrent that had overturned the principal kingdoms of Europe, but to extend everywhere a helping hand to those which were threatened or oppressed.

To these wise and excellent institutions of Great Britain it was readily seen that her splendour and prosperity were to be attributed, and hence it was hoped that the adopting a similar form of government would secure the like advantages to Sicily, whose insular position and primitive institutions afford a certain degree of resemblance with those of its powerful ally.

England could not be indifferent to the complaints (*riclami*) which had been made to her, and, whilst she had charged herself with the protection of Sicily from any foreign invasion, gave way, at the same time, to the invitation she had received, and became the protectress and supporter of innovations so just in themselves, and so honourable to those who had been their authors. Under such auspices commenced the formation of the Constitution, which, if in its progress it has encountered difficulties that could not be foreseen, if it has met with difficulties that may seem insurmountable, the greatness of the undertaking ought to be considered. It is necessary to remember the comparative effect (*facoltà*) with which various most important changes have been already accomplished, and, above all, it will be necessary to resist that debasing and discouraging spirit which leads people to condemn every attempt at amelioration as a vain and chimerical project. It is difficult, and it may be said almost impossible, to transfer from one country to another, without some previous modification, all its laws, forms, and institutions : the difference of customs, prejudices, religion, and education, offers an insurmountable barrier to such a total revolution.

Great Britain has never wished to impose this condition on Sicily ; being the friend and ally of the Sicilian nation, her wish was only to second the adoption of those parts of her own Constitution which, after grave and mature examination, should be conformable to the desires of its people, and deemed likely to secure its happiness and prosperity.   In the ulterior deliberations which may precede the completion of the Constitution, Great Britain is anxious to recommend to the serious consideration of the nation to leave an adequate proportion of power in the hands of the Executive Government ; and, on the other hand, would wish to hold up to the Executive Government the example of the King of France, who, on his restoration to the throne of his ancestors, has confirmed to the nation the privileges and advantages of a free Government, as far as they are compatible with the necessary authority of the Crown, the maintenance of order and tranquillity amongst the people, and with the customs and character of the French nation.

She would wish, further, to recommend a ready attention to

the code of laws, and the necessary measures to secure their
due observance; and also to call to remembrance that the
happiness of a people depends more on a pure and impartial
administration of justice, than on the degree of political power
with which they may be invested. The entire possession of
civil liberty is the only foundation on which political power
can be established.

England is very desirous that the Sicilian nation should
turn attention to the completion of this incomparable good,
which hitherto has been principally directed to objects of minor
importance. To every temperate and prudent modification of
the Government, England would with pleasure give all that
support and assistance which it may be in her power to afford.
As a condition on which this assistance would be granted, she
requires only that this should be done by the Parliament
itself; that it should be completed in a legal and constitutional
manner, as far removed, on one hand, from every indirect
influence and constraint, (*autorità comprimente*) as, on the
other, from every undue use of popular interference (*popolare
ingerenza*). Under no other point is she to be viewed than as
the most intimate friend and ally of his Sicilian Majesty.

The intention which has lately been shown of withdrawing
her troops from Sicily would be a sufficient proof (if proofs
were necessary) that England has not the most distant idea of
exerting a military influence on the councils of the King
and the nation. The attitude she was obliged to assume
during the war may have given rise to a variety of false
reports, to confute which the best argument is the well-known
uprightness of her conduct and her acknowledged good faith.

The continuance of a spirit of party in Sicily cannot be
sufficiently lamented. The views of Great Britain being
directed solely to the general prosperity of the island, nothing
can be farther from the intention of her Government than that
the English Minister in Palermo should appear at the head of
a party. But, in making this declaration, it will not be im-

proper to add that the English Government considers itself as
deeply interested in the fate of those individuals who have
supported the measures of the internal Government of Sicily
which the critical situation of the country during the last
three years obliged its (the British) representative to suggest.
The upright and honourable intentions with which these
individuals were actuated are well known, and it would,
under these circumstances, be inconsistent with the character
and dignity of the British nation to abandon them. It has an
incontestable right to insist that no one be molested, either in
his person or property, for the part he may have taken in
establishing and supporting the Constitution; and the perfect
security of these individuals is to be considered as the *sine quâ
non* of the protection and alliance of Britain.

The necessary relations of the two countries since the conclusion of the general peace have led to this declaration of the
sentiments and intentions of its Government. The influence
of Great Britain in the domestic affairs of Sicily never proceeded but from pure motives of disinterested friendship. She
will be amply compensated for all the sacrifices she has made,
if it shall be acknowledged that her efforts have contributed to
the well-being, happiness, and prosperity of the Sicilian nation.

The Hon. F. Lamb to Lord Castlereagh.

Frankfort, April 3, 1821.

My dear Lord—Although all demonstrations of the feeling
of this country have ceased, yet the foundation of it appears to
remain the same. I shall mention but two instances of this,
which have been furnished me by the Austrian Ministers
themselves.

The first is that the bulletin of the 20th, accompanying the
Convention of Capua, having been received here this morning,
has been published with the name of the Baron de Handel to
it; because, as he states to me, the former bulletin, in couse-
quence of the manner of its reception not being mentioned,

was universally disbelieved, both in Hesse-Darmstadt, where he is Minister, and here.

The other instance is contained in a report from the Austrian Minister at Hesse-Cassel, who states that the news of the submission of the Neapolitans was received with pleasure by the Elector, and by nobody else in that place.

I do not write these circumstances as indicating a state of feeling which is either necessarily permanent or at all important under the existing circumstances. But there is certainly a strong feeling in Germany that the delay of the attack upon Naples, and its slowness when made, with the apparent inadequacy of the force, had created a state of danger, from which we have but narrowly escaped.

I have the honour to be, &c.,   F. LAMB.

Mr. Edward Thornton to Lord Castlereagh.
Rio de Janeiro, April 3, 1821.

My Lord—It was in part from Count de Palmella, in part from M. de Pinheiro, and from those immediately about him, that I derive the loose and contradictory ideas which your lordship will observe in my public despatch of this date, No. 26. If I leave your lordship in uncertainty, it is no more than where I am left myself, and by the most intelligent and best informed people of this country.

Count de Palmella, though apparently an ex-Minister, is not the least well-informed, and has contrived to come to so good an understanding either with the Ministry of the 26th of February, or with the King, that he is on the point of returning to Europe, and of assuming the character of his Most Faithful Majesty's Ambassador at Paris, in the place of the Marquis de Marialva, who, of course, could hardly remain there after the Revolution in this country. This Count de Palmella told me yesterday, in a company where I dined with him, after an absence of some ten days or a fortnight; and he was even in a negociation, which failed, of embarking on board the present packet-boat for Lisbon. He promised me, indeed, that I should see him to-day, and that he would acquaint me with all his views upon public affairs; but he is not yet come.

In the mean time, it is utterly impossible for me to give your lordship any opinion further than I have already had the honour of laying it before your lordship. It would be premature to act in any manner on the supposition of the King's arrival in Europe, until he actually makes his appearance there.

I shall avail myself of every occasion, at this critical period, of keeping your lordship informed of passing events; and I beg your lordship to be assured of the truth and respect with which I have the honour to be, &c.,

EDWARD THORNTON.

Mr. Edward Thornton to Lord Castlereagh.

Rio de Janeiro, April 5, 1821.

My Lord—The delay of the packet-boat, on account of contrary winds, till this day, enables me so far to correct what I had the honour of addressing to your lordship on the 3rd of April, (in my private letter of that date) as I have had the advantage of seeing Count de Palmella himself.

He tells me that, some time ago, he addressed himself to his Most Faithful Majesty, with a request that he might retire from his Majesty's service, and that he might be allowed the usual pension of retreat—that, upon this circumstance, M. de Pinheiro was sent to him, for the purpose of informing him that, although his right to the pension was allowed in the fullest manner, yet the present circumstances of the country were such, that a concession of it would be very embarrassing; and that the King earnestly wished that he would continue to be employed in his Majesty's service—that, on account of the charge which the Marquis de Marialva held, that of Grand Ecuyer, the King would desire the Marquis's return to Lisbon, and that it was wished the Count de Palmella would assume his post at Paris, not, however, as Ambassador, but as Minister of the second order: to which rank, under present circumstances, it might be desirable to reduce all the foreign missions.

Your lordship will see in these circumstances, which Count de Palmella has mentioned, many points which render the offer by no means a very inviting one; but one of his motives for acceding to it, should he do so, is that of keeping aloof from the present scenes and from the jarring interests of Lisbon and Portugal, and to await, in a mission which has not many important relations to settle, more peaceable and fortunate times. He will endeavour to direct his course immediately to France, or at least by the way of England, rather than of Portugal, and to make his family join him there.

With regard to the period of the King's embarkation, I can give your lordship no better information than I gave two days ago. I had the honour of paying my court to his Majesty this evening, and I went as near as I could with propriety to the question of the day. The King, however, promised to give me due notice of it, and I, on my part, demanded permission, which was readily granted, to continue to present myself occasionally until the day of his departure.

I have some little ground to think that the French squadron in the Pacific may be shortly expected here.

I have the honour to be, &c.,

EDWARD THORNTON.

Sir Charles Bagot to Joseph Planta, Esq.

St. Petersburgh, April 10-22, 1821.

My dear Planta—As there are two messengers now here, and as I think that you must, at this moment, require a great many, I determine to send home Meates, although I have nothing to communicate by him which is worth his journey.

I congratulate you upon the Italian news. The business at

Naples seems to be finished, and that of Piedmont to be at
least in good train. I wish I could feel as secure about the
state of France. I hope, however, that the immense masses
of men who have buckled on their armour in this country, will
impose also upon that quarter. If. they do not, a huge
expense is being incurred here for little purpose. It is still,
of course, quite uncertain when we shall see the Emperor
again. His subjects are not more impatient for his return
than I am. When he is here, my communications to the
office must always have some interest ; but, at present, everything which is going on in the world (and this country has no
small share in it) is sooner known through old country newspapers than it can be through me.

· You will perhaps wonder why I send home officially copies
of the Secretary of State's letters to me, acknowledging the
receipt from me of copies of the King's letters to the Emperor.
It is to show that I have done everything I could about them
in the absence of the Emperor. Count Nesselrode once wanted
to make me send one of them (I think that announcing the
death of the Duchess of York) to Troppau, but I refused,
holding it to be " stuff o' th' conscience" in diplomacy, never
to deliver a royal letter but *en mains propres*. I have now
three undelivered.

I send in this bag a despatch from M. de Divow to Count
Lieven, and a small parcel, containing a diamond snuff-box, on
its road, I believe, to Rio Janeiro. Pray direct that they may
be safely delivered.

Has Stratford Canning ever sent home the report of a
Committee of Congress, presented last September to one of the
Houses of the Legislature upon the American Fur Trade, and
the expediency of making establishments upon the Columbia
river ? It has been sent to me from America, and it appears
to me to be a paper, deserving, on several accounts, both of Lord
Castlereagh's and Lord Bathurst's serious attention, as well
in respect to its immediate object as to its general doctrines.

You have never told me whether I am to expect further instructions and powers (as Mr. Middleton has led me to believe) upon the American Slave question; but I know how much Parliament must have taken up all your time and attention.

My latest letters and papers from England are of the 3rd of April, which I received yesterday. I observe that the celebration of the King's birthday is put off to the 3rd of May; but I suppose that this need not affect my celebration of it on the regular day, and therefore I give a ball to the English to-morrow evening.

Believe me, my dear Planta, yours always most sincerely,

CHARLES BAGOT.

PS.—I have just received a letter from Gordon, dated Laybach, April 5. It was brought by a Russian courier, who arrived from thence in the course of the night. I have added a postscript to my private letter to Lord Castlereagh, telling him what is brought by this courier.   C. B.

Lord Beresford to the Marquess of Londonderry.[1]

London, April 13, 1821.

My dear Lord—We have at length received news from the Brazils, and, by Mr. Thornton's despatches, you will be informed that the King has finally determined that the Prince Royal shall go to Portugal, in the quality of Constable. I annex the letter I have received from the Count Palmella, by which your lordship will perceive that the packet was despatched so soon as this resolution was made, and I know that it had been detained ten days waiting for it. We are, therefore, only informed of this prominent and principal fact: the detail of the consequent arrangements does not appear to have been brought into discussion; and the principal of these will be, who shall be nominated his councillors.

In the despatches of Mr. Thornton, your lordship will see

[1] On the decease of his father, in the month of April, Lord Castlereagh had succeeded to his title.

a request for a small squadron to be sent to Lisbon, which I trust you will be able to comply with, as it appears to be desired merely to give to the Prince a refuge for his personal safety, in case of necessity. But it will most certainly influence beneficially in other points of view. His Majesty has also sent an order that we should apply for the prize-money, in conformity to what was agreed upon with the Count of Palmella by your lordship; and he has directed the distribution immediately to all claimants out of Portugal, reserving the payment of the officers and soldiers there till a legal Government is re-established. I will have prepared a translation of this document, that you may be fully aware of the orders given on this head.

By the letter of the Count de Palmella, the Prince Royal may now be a month on this passage; and it is not impossible he may in a fortnight be in Lisbon. He ought to be there in three weeks, with a moderate passage.

I will not omit this opportunity of condoling with you on the melancholy loss you have so recently had, and which prevents my being the bearer of this news from the Brazils, not to intrude on such an occasion on your lordship's privacy, but am ready to attend you, should you desire it.

I have the honour to be, &c.,   BERESFORD.

PS. I will request of your lordship to return me the Count of Palmella's letter.

────────

Lord Clancarty to the Marquess of Londonderry.

Bruxelles, April 17, 1821.

My dear Lord—I write but a line, merely to solicit your attention to the postscript of my despatch, No. 16, of this date, and to its enclosure, where you will see confirmed (what has probably long been suspected by you) that the Netherland Monarch is endeavouring to evade the execution of his treaties with us relative to the Slave Trade.

This will not do, and must not be allowed. I have there-

fore to renew my request to you to do nothing which, on the
part of his Government, shall be asked of you by Fagel, and,
however kindly, as an individual, you may treat him, I pray
you that, as the representative of his master, he may not be
better treated than such a master deserves, till the master shall
learn to deserve better.

Most affectionately yours,   CLANCARTY.

Prince Esterhazy to Lord Castlereagh.

Vienne, le 4 Mai, 1821.

Mylord—Sensible à toutes les marques de bienveillance dont
Votre Excellence a toujours daigné me combler, et qui s'est
encore si hautement manifestée par l'envoi des béliers Merinos,
je le suis encore davantage, quoique bien péniblement à ce que
le soupçon de la plus grande négligence plane sur moi; informé par mon fils que la lettre que j'ai eu l'honneur de lui
écrire immédiatement après l'arrivée des Merinos, dans laquelle
je lui ai exprimé conjointement avec ma plus grande satisfaction mes remercimens les plus sincères, ne lui soit parvenue,
s'étant sans doute égarée par circonstance que je ne saurois
deviner.

Votre Excellence me permettra donc de lui réiterer encore ma
gratitude, que j'aurois souhaité depuis long-tems de lui renouveller verbalement, si tous les projets de voyage s'exécu-
teroient aussi facilement qu'ils sont conçus.

Mais comme enfin ce projet va se réaliser, ayant le bonheur
de remettre les vœux de sa Majesté Impériale au trône de sa
Majesté Britannique, je compte les instants qui doivent me
donner loisir de renouveller à Votre Excellence de bouche
tous les sentiments de sensibilité, et ceux de la considération la
plus distinguée avec laquelle j'ai l'honneur d'être, Mylord,
votre très obéissant et dévoué serviteur,

PRINCE ESTERHAZY.

Mr. Edward Thornton to Lord Castlereagh.

Rio de Janeiro, May 7, 1821.

My Lord—I had the honour of receiving by the February packet (which returns with this mail) your lordship's letter marked *most private, secret, and confidential,* of the 6th of February, with its several voluminous and most interesting enclosures; and I cannot sufficiently express the degree of gratitude with which I receive this high proof of the confidence which your lordship has been so good as to repose in my prudence and discretion. The only evidence which I can at present furnish of possessing any portion of these qualities, is by preserving a religious silence upon these papers; and I can venture to assure your lordship that, in all my previous conversations with the members of this Government and with the foreign Ministers, my colleagues, if I have not approached very near to that extended and enlightened policy which is laid down in these important State Papers, I have never held a language at all deviating from it, and much less one running counter to it.

On the Easter Tuesday, the 24th ult., on which the foreign Ministers took leave of his Majesty previously to his embarkation, the King told me that he wished to take leave of me in a more private and friendly manner in the evening, and that he would not write a letter, but would send a servant to say to me when and where. The message was accordingly given to me for the usual hour at the palace of Boa Vista (St. Christoval), from which his Majesty meant to embark the next morning in his barge, the bay being there but a short distance from the palace, and the position quite retired.

I believe I was the only one of the foreign Ministers to whom this distinction was shown, and I thought, of course, that his Majesty might charge me with some message to your lordship, such as, for example, the desire to have a small squadron of ships occasionally looking into Lisbon, or any other object of a similar kind, but none such was once in-

sinuated or hinted at; nor, of course, did I allude in any way
to it, however it may appear necessary by this demonstration
to keep the King up. His Majesty's object in calling me
appeared, by its effect at least, to be solely the desire of conversing with me at his ease, and with that sort of *abandon*,
which allows him to start or to depart from any subject,
according to his humour.

The conversation, therefore, was, for the most part, uninteresting for repetition, although it glanced occasionally upon
subjects of moment, such as his apprehension that a separation
between this and the mother country might take place ere
long. At one time, on a question of some of my latest letters
to M. Pinheiro, on the subject of the Slave Trade regulations,
the King asked me, with an apparent alarm and anxiety, whether I had received any new instructions upon the subject of
the abolition. His Majesty showed on this point, as it arose,
at least, his own feeling and humanity, by mentioning a circumstance that indicates a shocking want of both in another.

I have since heard, as a certain fact, that the King granted
their freedom to all the negroes, men and women, employed
about the King's apartments and his own person. This, however, his Majesty did not then mention to me, but lamented to
me, in an accent of great sorrow, and with tears in his eyes,
the conduct of the Queen. He said she would not take any of
her negresses with her; "And you know," said he, "that the
palace swarms with them." I observed to the King, that I
trusted her Majesty would mitigate this painful circumstance
at least by taking care that provision should be made for their
maintenance. The King dissented from this in silence, shaking
his head. "At least, then," I added, "her Majesty granted
to them all their liberty."—"*Ma foi*," replied his Majesty, in
a passionate exclamation, and the tears starting from his eyes,
"*elles ont été toutes vendues ce matin!*"

In order to know all the cruelty of this diabolical trait, (for
so I must call it) your lordship should be aware that these

poor creatures were employed in the apartments of the Queen, the Princesses, and the ladies of the palace, very idly, perhaps, and for no very useful or honourable purposes, but were lavishly maintained and well clothed; and I am told that many of them, if they occasionally went out of the palace, or were sent into the town on messages, were often followed by a white servant in livery, to secure them from improper treatment. But I have heard other instances of the wayward, selfish, and wicked character of the Queen; and her mischievousness and her courage are equally such, that I should not be surprised if the King were almost harassed out of his existence before the end of the voyage. She has embarked in the same ship with the King, in the sole view of gaining popularity by an apparent attachment and union subsisting between them.

I am aware that this trait, which is generally known, will be publicly mentioned in England with the detestation it merits: but I trust your lordship will not reveal the source from which I derived it, or that from which your lordship receives it: for that would be almost as disagreeable to me as to the former.

I am afraid I must defer until another occasion, or perhaps my arrival, to speak of the Prince's Government, since the departure of the King. It is at present very satisfactory, being temperate, extremely economical, (perhaps too much so) and having reformed many most gross and expensive abuses.

The King expressed his desire to see me at Lisbon, in my way to England, where I told him I should proceed, to take your lordship's orders. I promised to endeavour to pay my court to his Majesty there for forty-eight hours, if circumstances permitted, which I trust your lordship will be pleased to approve. His Majesty took a very kind leave of me, pressing me by the arm, and following me almost to the door of the Audience-room.

> I remain ever, &c.,   EDWARD THORNTON.

Laybach, May 13, 1821.

My dear Lord—*Les pièces de clôture* which have been brewing for the last ten days have at length appeared, and I have lost no time in transmitting them direct to your lordship. The declaration is of Pozzo's composition—the Austrian *dépêche* chiefly Gentz's.

The Cabinets are prepared to expect many attacks from the Liberals of all countries, and are not without some fears of the opinions which may be formed by our Government of their Budget, but in general they have assumed an air of boldness, which is evidently due to a determination on their part not to yield an inch to the cause over which they have triumphed with such facility in Italy, and to fight against the whole world, if necessary, in defence of their doctrine.

Austria could not speak with more decision if Russia had actually been transformed into a province of her empire, and confides as implicitly to her accord and support. On the other hand, serious apprehensions are entertained of the consequences which the Greek revolution may lead to; the worst of which look to the possibility of the Emperor Alexander being compelled by his own subjects to adopt a different line, and take up arms as defender of the Greek religion. An obstinate resistance to the unanimous voice of his people, it is feared, might seriously endanger the existence of his Government; and the Russian temper is already sufficiently soured by the countermand order given to the troops.

It is reported here to-day that the Patriarch of Constantinople has been murdered—an event which, if it be true, will not fail to increase the general apprehensions.

I confess that I have been much relieved by having it in my power to forward these last allied *travaux*, having been left in such perfect ignorance of the nature of them during their concoction. Although nothing vigorous has been lanced against

Spain, I am by no means certain that nothing is in preparation for the approaching Congress upon this head. Prince Metternich has a favourite theory that 10,000 foreign troops would suffice to overturn the Spanish Constitution, boasting, at the same time, that he has been able to prevent the Emperor Alexander from wishing to act upon it. The latter speaks, however, so positively upon the necessity of overturning it, that it is difficult to suppose that he has abandoned all thoughts upon the subject.

His Sicilian Majesty, by the latest intelligence from Rome, has promised, immediately upon his arrival at Naples, to repair the wrongs of the Provisional Government, and follow the advice given in Prince Metternich's letters to Prince Ruffo, and the counsels of General Frimont.

The Emperor of Austria leaves this place on the 21st inst.

   Believe me, my dear lord, &c.,   R. GORDON.

Sir Charles Bagot to the Marquess of Londonderry.

      St. Petersburgh, May 18-30, 1821.

My dear Lord—Since I wrote last, Chamberlain has continued, with the exception of a few hours the day before yesterday, when there was a slight reappearance of some of the former symptoms, gradually to recover; and Dr. Walker seems now to be of opinion that, barring relapse, of which there seems to be no prospect at present, he may be considered out of danger. He has had a miraculous escape, and complete recovery of all he has had to go through must be a work of time. He is, however, now in a fair way of being perfectly re-established, and I think that his friends need have no further anxiety about him.

Count Nesselrode arrived here yesterday morning, at three o'clock, having performed his journey from Vienna in nine days. In calling to inquire after him, I met him yesterday afternoon at his own door; but I have not yet had any opportunity of conversing with him upon matters of business. He brought me a despatch from Lord Stewart, and a private letter of the 19th, enclosing copies of two very interesting letters from Prince Metternich. The Emperor will certainly arrive at Zarskoë Zélo on Monday next.

I find that the Spanish Minister has not awaited the Emperor's return (as I had imagined he would) to give in the note which he has received orders to deliver. He has already presented it to M. de Divow, who has made answer that he had transmitted it to the Emperor. The declaration of the 12th of May, from Laybach, was published here yesterday morning.

I have the honour to be, &c.,   CHARLES BAGOT.

Sir Charles Bagot to Joseph Planta, Esq.

St. Petersburgh, May 21, (June 2) 1821.

My dear Planta—In my last despatch I announced the return of Count Nesselrode. Soon after I wrote he set out for Zarskoë Zélo, from whence he returned yesterday, and he will now, I suppose, immediately resume his functions.

I have nothing to send to you by this mail but two letters which I received the day before yesterday from M. Yeames. They are, however, very interesting, and may, I think, contain the latest intelligence which you will have received from Constantinople. I do not envy my brother diplomatists in that quarter, for it seems to me very doubtful whether it is in the power of the Turkish Government to give them the protection which they would be disposed to do.

I am happy to tell you that Chamberlain is recovering. He still keeps his bed, but I now think that he is so sure to do well, (at least so far as his last attack is concerned) that I shall not think it necessary to send any further accounts of him to Lord Londonderry.

I received no English mail by the last post. My latest accounts are to the 11th May. We go into the country on Monday, but my house is not five English miles from the barrier. Madame is getting much stronger and better than she was, and I think that before she has been in the country a month she will be herself again.

Our last revolutions are those of Brazil and Mexico.

Yours, my dear Planta, most sincerely,

CHARLES BAGOT.

Mr. Lionel Hervey to the Marquess of Londonderry.

Madrid, June 5, 1821.

My dear Lord—I have not alluded to the state of public affairs in my despatches ; as, in fact, nothing has occurred which I could communicate in an official shape ; and the complexion of the country varies so from day to day, that it is difficult to form a correct opinion of the probable course of events. Two portentous luminaries to guide the perplexed judgment in this wilderness of error exist, however, in the state of their Exchequer and of their public credit. In the former there is hardly a sixpence : and the latter is at so low an ebb, that Vales are at 80 discount, having fallen 30 per cent. within the last month, owing to the discovery that the value of the monarchal property has been excessively exaggerated. In this state of things, no one pays, and no one is paid ; and the natural consequence is, that the Government is neither feared nor respected, neither supported nor obeyed. The present Ministers have certainly had recourse to more vigorous measures than their predecessors, and seem more inclined to maintain the King's authority ; but I am afraid that their influence does not extend much beyond Madrid, where they have a large military force, and that they have no means of controlling the provinces.

M. de Bardaxi, however, told me yesterday that orders had been sent to the departments to remove all the public authorities who had exceeded their powers, and who had lent themselves to those arbitrary acts of oppression by which so many individuals have been unjustly and illegally forced into banishment. I know that very many moderate men and Deputies of the Cortes are much alarmed at the present aspect of affairs, and apprehend disturbances throughout the country, upon the prorogation of the Cortes; and the reports, upon which I can in a great measure rely, mention that, if Merino had arms, he would soon find himself at the head of several thousand men, and allege that Ministers have throughout made a false statement of all that has occurred in the disturbed provinces.

Whenever Ministers have appeared in the Cortes, they have conducted themselves with spirit and dignity, and they appear to stand upon better ground with that assembly than could have reasonably been expected; but I understand that the King does not repose that confidence in them which they appear to deserve. M. Casa Inigo was appointed Minister at Paris two days before the arrival of M. Bardaxi, and the Toison d'Or was conferred upon the Duke of Laval without the privacy of that Minister. These circumstances, and the suspicion that the Duke of Laval has prejudiced the King against him, do not tend to increase M. de Bardaxi's predilection for the French Ambassador and the French nation; and he never appears more animated than when he is abusing both the one and the other.

Whilst I am upon the subject of the Duke of Laval, I think it my duty to mention to your lordship that I have ascertained, beyond a shadow of doubt, that he has been intriguing against Sir Henry Wellesley, with the royal family here, in the most atrocious and malevolent manner, poisoning their ears with malicious and unfounded insinuations, and giving them to understand that Sir Henry was the avowed enemy of the Court and their party.

Whatever apprehensions may have been entertained of an offensive and defensive alliance between Spain and Portugal, there is now, I believe, little reason to fear such an event. I know that M. Bardaxi declared, the other day, that he could not enter into any negociation with the Portuguese Government until the arrival of the King at Lisbon.

It is believed that the King will refuse his sanction to the law respecting seigneurial property, and this makes the violent party in the Cortes, who have forced the law upon the nation, very anxious for the convocation of the Extraordinary Cortes; but, whatever may be his Majesty's decision, the mischief is already done, and is, I am afraid, irretrievable; for, the vote of the Cortes having been made known throughout the country, there will be no possibility of obliging the different tenants to pay their rents.

I have the honour to be, &c., LIONEL HERVEY.

Mr. Lionel Hervey to the Marquess of Londonderry.

Madrid, June 17, 1821.

My dear Lord—Notwithstanding what I had stated in my despatch of yesterday, I have no doubt that the King will give way, and that the Extra Cortes will be assembled either now or in the month of October. Bardaxi was the only one. of the Ministers who was against the measure; and his in-. fluence is not sufficiently powerful to sway the opinion of the. Cabinet. I am inclined to believe that he entertains a very different opinion of his situation to that which he had formed before his arrival at Madrid. He finds that the Cortes alone possess the confidence of the nation, and that the attempt to emancipate the Administration from their control would probably not succeed at present, and would only excite distrust on the part of that assembly and of the whole country. The language which he had used upon his arrival had tended to excite suspicion, and I conceive that he has found it necessary to conciliate and to endeavour to regain their confidence.

Something must have lately happened to influence the opinion of the Deputies upon the question of convoking the Extra Cortes for three weeks; since I was given to understand that there was a decided majority against the measure; and now two-thirds of the Members are in favour of their assembling. All the American Deputies support the proposition, as calculated to facilitate and expedite the proposed arrangement between Spain and her colonies. The violent party assert that the Constitution is in danger from the machinations of the Serviles, and that the prorogation of the Cortes will be the signal for carrying their plans into execution; and many of the moderate Deputies, from a conviction that the state of affairs requires that so long a period as eight months should not intervene between the prorogation of the present and the assembling of the future Cortes, and that the public tranquillity will be more effectually secured by the meeting of the Extra Cortes, have expressed themselves lately in favour of their convocation in the month of October.

The army are, generally speaking, devoted to the Cortes, and as the King thus stands isolated in his opinion, I have not ventured to give any encouragement to his Majesty's opposition to the counsels of his Ministers. Indeed, I am convinced that, if the King were to separate from the present Cortes upon bad terms, their influence in the provinces is such, that his Majesty would soon be obliged to convoke the Extra Cortes, from the impossibility of carrying on the Government and of enforcing obedience to the mandates of the Executive Power.

The American question will, I understand, be discussed in the Cortes on Tuesday next.

I have the honour to be, &c.,   LIONEL HERVEY.

Mr. Lionel Hervey to the Marquess of Londonderry.

Madrid, June 28, 1821.

My dear Lord—You will see by the last paragraph of my despatch marked "Secret and Confidential," that the King has given way. I much regret the whole transaction, and I tried my utmost to prevent the sensation which it has created, by advising that the King should listen to the suggestion of his Ministers, and not force the Cortes to discuss the question. His Majesty, however, preferred following the course of his secret advisers, and has again lowered himself in the public · opinion, and has increased the general suspicions of his inten- · tions and of his aversion to the Constitution.

What is most to be lamented is the breach which it has made between the King and his Ministers. All confidence on both sides must be completely destroyed; and I am afraid that they will not long be able to retain their situations. Incalculable mischief has been done by the Duke de Laval; and I am afraid that the Russian Chargé d'Affaires is not entirely free from the imputation he has subjected himself to, of intriguing with the Serviles. I must again repeat that I consider the safety of the King to consist in his reposing entire confidence in his Ministers, who, I am strongly inclined to believe, from conversations which I have had with M. de Bardaxi, are anxious to render him every service in their power. I apprehend that they have great reason to complain of the manner in which they have been personally treated by the King, both severally and collectively.

I have the honour to be, &c., · LIONEL HERVEY.

The Marquess of Londonderry to his Imperial Majesty the Emperor of all the Russias.

Foreign Office, London, July 16, 1821.

Sire—When admitted to take leave of your Imperial Majesty, previous to your departure in 1818 from Aix-la Chapelle, your Majesty condescended to permit me to address myself directly to your Majesty on any occasion when the interests of the European Alliance might justify me in having recourse to this indulgence.

That I have not hitherto availed myself of your Majesty's gracious permission is a proof that I have not been tempted to abuse this peculiar mark of your Imperial Majesty's favour and confidence.

In obedience to the King my Sovereign's commands, and under a deep sense of the importance of the present crisis, I now presume to address your Imperial Majesty upon the affairs of Turkey; and I do so with the less hesitation, as I feel an intimate conviction, however your Imperial Majesty may be pressed and embarrassed by local considerations and by the peculiar temper of your own people, that your Imperial Majesty's general view of these complicated evils will correspond with that of the British Government; and I entertain a not less sanguine persuasion that your Imperial Majesty, triumphing over every local impediment, will ultimately pursue that course of policy which will afford an additional but not an unexpected proof of your Imperial Majesty's determination to maintain inviolably the European system, as consolidated by the late treaties of peace. I am confident that the dreadful events which now afflict that portion of Europe are not regarded by your Imperial Majesty as constituting in the history of these times either a new or an insulated question. They do not originate exclusively in the conflicting and inflammable elements of which the Turkish Empire is composed; but they form a branch of that organized spirit of insurrection which is systematically propagating itself throughout Europe, and which explodes wherever the hand of the governing power, from whatever cause, is enfeebled. If its symptoms are more destructive in Turkey, it is because, in that unhappy country, it finds all those passions and prejudices, and, above all, those religious animosities, which give to civil commotions their most odious and afflicting colours. The limitrope position of your Imperial Majesty's States; the religious sympathy of the great mass of your Majesty's subjects with the Greek population of Turkey; the extensive intercourse which reciprocally takes place between the people of the respective empires for commercial and other purposes; and, amongst other causes, the ancient jealousies inseparable from the history of the two States, place your Imperial Majesty in the very front of this scene of European embarrassment.

It would be superfluous to waste your Imperial Majesty's

time by arguing that Turkey, with all its barbarisms, consti-
tutes, in the system of Europe, what may be regarded as a
necessary evil.   It is an excrescence which can scarcely be
looked upon as forming any part of its healthful organization ;
and yet, for that very reason, any attempt to introduce order
by external interference into its jarring elements, or to assimi-
late it to the mass, might expose the whole frame of our
general system to hazard.   The real question which presses.
for consideration is—how the danger shall be kept at a dis-,
tance from other States, and how the adjacent Powers can best
preserve their pacific relations with a people so convulsed.
The question presses most with respect to your Imperial
Majesty's dominions, and it divides itself into the two considerations :—

1st. What the risks are of the peace of your Imperial
Majesty's own provinces being disturbed by the insurrection
propagating itself in that direction ; and

2ndly. The injuries and indignities to which your Imperial
Majesty's servants or subjects have been or may be exposed
within the Turkish Empire during the continuance of these
troubles.

- With regard to the former, I should hope that little or
nothing is to be feared; and that, with the imposing force
which your Imperial Majesty can assemble on the frontiers,
the entry of the infection within the Russian territory may be
regarded as impossible.   The latter evil is of a more pressing
nature; and it is lamentable to observe, from the latest intelligence from Constantinople, to what trials your Imperial Majesty's forbearance may be exposed under this head.   To
expect or even to wish that your Imperial Majesty should not
at a proper moment assert the just rights of your Crown and
people, can form no part of the policy of this Government; but
in proportion as your Imperial Majesty's power is undoubted,
and, as the events of the late war have placed you on exalted
ground, your Imperial Majesty can afford to temporize, and to

suffer the tempest to exhaust itself. The Turkish State at this moment seems not only infected with all the poison of modern principles, but infuriated with all its ancient and distinctive animosities. The Government, as well as the population, have surrendered for the moment their ordinary faculties of reason and prudence, and have given themselves up to a fanatic madness, and to a blind spirit of internal and exterminating warfare. It is not at such a moment that wrongs can be satisfactorily inquired into, or reparation discussed. Your Imperial Majesty, it is humbly but confidently submitted, must wait for the moment of returning reason and reflection, unless you are prepared, Sire, to charge yourself with the perils and burthens of a military occupation, to be effectuated not amongst a Christian and tractable, but amongst a bigoted, revengeful, and uncivilized population.

No doubt humanity shudders at the scenes which are acting, as it appears, throughout the greater part of European Turkey; and it will require all the commanding authority of your Imperial Majesty's great name and character to reconcile the Russian nation to witness the ministers of a congenial faith so barbarously immolated to the resentment of a Government under which they have the misfortune to live. But it is in vain to hope that we can materially alter their lot, or deliver them from their sufferings, and preserve the system of Europe as it now stands. The hazard of innovating upon this consecrated work, and the reflection that, whilst we cannot refuse to the Greeks our sympathy and our compassion, they have been the aggressors on the present occasion; and that they have yielded to the hazardous and corrupting practice of the times, so reproved by your Imperial Majesty, may well reconcile your Imperial Majesty and your Allies to observe rather than to intermeddle in the endless and inextricable mazes of Turkish confusion.

The flame burns at this moment too ardently to be of long duration; a time must arrive, and that probably at no distant

period, when the Turkish Power, exhausted by its own convulsions, will be accessible to reason, and when your Imperial
Majesty's voice will be heard, and your wrongs be redressed;
and perhaps Providence, in the many trials to which it has
destined your Majesty in your eventful and glorious life, has
never presented an occasion in which your Imperial Majesty
may afford to your own times and to posterity a prouder
manifestation of your Imperial Majesty's principles than by
exercising towards this fanatic and semi-barbarous State that
degree of forbearance and magnanimity which a religious and
enthusiastic respect for the system which your Imperial
Majesty has so powerfully contributed to raise in Europe
could alone dictate under such provocations, and with such
means at your Imperial Majesty's disposal.

I presume to hope that the sentiments I have ventured to
express will neither prove unacceptable to nor be disavowed
by your Imperial Majesty. Whatever degree of divergence
of opinion may have occurred in late discussions on abstract
theories of international law, and however the position of the
British Government may have latterly been rendered distinct
from that of the three Allied Courts, by the line of neutrality
which the King thought it necessary to adopt with respect to
t alian affairs, there happily has hardly occurred an instance,
since the auspicious period which gave birth to the existing
alliance, of any point of grave, practical, political difference
between your Imperial Majesty's Councils and those of my
august master. I feel intimately convinced that each State,
avowing conscientiously in the face of all the world its own
principles, and at the same time adhering to its peculiar habits
of action, will nevertheless remain unalterably true to the
fundamental obligations of the Alliance, and that the present
European system, thus temperately and prudently administered, will long continue to subsist for the safety and repose
of Europe.

Your Imperial Majesty may rest assured that the King has

no object more sincerely at heart than to give to your Imperial Majesty and to his august Allies every proof of attachment which his sense of duty and the nature of his Government will permit; and that your Imperial Majesty may rely upon receiving, on all occasions as on the present, the most undisguised exposition of his Majesty's views.

I entreat your Imperial Majesty to interpret favourably the liberty which I have now taken, and that you will permit me, Sire, to seize this occasion of renewing to your Imperial Majesty the assurances of my respectful veneration and sincere attachment, and of the very deep personal sense which I can never cease to feel of your Imperial Majesty's gracious indulgence to me, whenever, in the discharge of my public duties, it has been permitted to me either to approach or to address your Majesty. It will always be my ambition to recommend myself to your Imperial Majesty's favourable opinion, and to labour to cement the connexion between the two States.

With the utmost deference, and with the highest consideration, I have the honour to remain, Sire, your Imperial Majesty's most humble and faithful servant,

LONDONDERRY.

Sir William à Court to the Marquess of Londonderry.

Naples, July 26, 1821.

Sir William à Court has the honour to enclose, according to Lord Londonderry's desire, a few remarks upon Lord W. Bentinck's speech upon the affairs of Sicily. His lordship will find the objection of the British subsidies clearly explained.

Sir William did not intend to have forwarded these remarks till he should have received from Sicily the most accurate information respecting the taxes, but he is unwilling to lose the opportunity of a courier, not knowing when another may offer. Should he receive hereafter anything which may strike him as being important, he will not fail to forward it to his lordship.

[Enclosure.]

Remarks on Lord William Bentinck's Speech upon the Affairs of Sicily.

The first point in Lord W. Bentinck's speech which affords any ground for remark, is the assertion that the Constitution established by him went on smoothly and prosperously. For information upon this subject, a reference may be made to the despatches of the late Lord Montgomerie, the Minister selected by his lordship to uphold the system during his temporary absence. If a higher authority be wanted, a faithful delineation of the state of Sicily may be found in the paper given in by Lord William himself to the Hereditary Prince, late in the year 1813, or early in 1814, under the title of *Les Rêves d'un Voyageur*, wherein he tells him plainly that it will be impossible to uphold the constitution without *foreign* assistance and interference, and therefore proposes to his Royal Highness to make over Sicily for a certain number of years to the British authorities, they guaranteeing to him an income equal to his Civil List, and to keep 10,000 foreign troops in the island. If it be true that the Constitution was in a flourishing state, what shadow of an excuse can be offered for this most extraordinary and most unconstitutional proposal?

Towards the close of the year 1814, when the evacuation of the island began to be contemplated, it is perfectly true that a memorandum was given in by the British Minister, explaining the nature of the future relations between the two countries, changed as they were in many respects by the prospect of a general peace. In this memorandum it was undoubtedly recommended that the modifications which, it was evident, must sooner or later be made, should be effectuated through the Parliament itself; but this was given, with many other recommendations, merely as advice, and never was by any means intended to imply a guarantee, or to bind England to an interference, should the advice be unattended to. The good treatment of those who had acted with the British authorities was the only stipulation made the *sine quâ non* of British protection and alliance.

During the Session of 1815, it was evident to everybody, and to none more than to the Constitutional party, that changes were absolutely necessary. With the view of affording the best chance of these changes being made with wisdom and moderation, the British Minister laboured to introduce into the Cabinet the most respected of the Constitutional party, namely, the Prince Vilhermosa. In this he succeeded. The Prince was called to the Council, and it was by his advice and with his assistance that the two Chambers were brought to petition the King to name a Commission for the purpose of effecting those changes, which they themselves were unable to accomplish. A Commission was named, composed of men of all parties, Prince Vilhermosa amongst the number; and the King submitted to it, a few days previous to his departure for Naples, a certain number of articles, extremely liberal in principle, which were to form the basis of its labours. The evacuation of the island followed, and *from that moment all responsibility on the part of Great Britain was completely at an end.*

The Commission, however, did nothing, notwithstanding the constant urging of the Hereditary Prince. The members fell off, the Constitutionalists giving the example in the person of the Prince Vilhermosa, who pleaded ill health. The end of the year 1816 was approaching, and, as the supplies were only voted for the year, the Government felt that it must either call the Parliament together without having effected any of the changes deemed necessary by all parties, or alter the system altogether.

It was then that the Union was resolved upon, and that a communication was made to the British Government of the King's intention to make some changes in the government of Sicily. It would have been free for England to declare that

the matter concerned her not, and that she could take no
further part in Sicilian affairs. There was neither engagement, guarantee, nor promise, to prevent such a reply. But,
though feeling that this would be the most prudent line to
take, the British Minister suggested to his Government that,
if England thus publicly declared her determination not to
interfere, it was to be feared that a species of reaction might
ensue, and nothing whatever be respected. With the view of
preventing this, the instructions of September, 1816, were
given, a communication of which to the Neapolitan Government would, it was hoped, be in some measure a check upon
its proceedings. These instructions, however, never went the
length of guaranteeing to the Sicilians any particular form of
Government, or their ancient constitution, as has been pretended. They merely stated that his Royal Highness the
Prince Regent might find it necessary to interfere, "if an
attempt was made to impair the freedom and happiness of the
Sicilians, as compared with what they formerly enjoyed."
And it must be recollected that these instructions applied
solely to the changes then in contemplation. It never was
intended to establish, in the person of the British Minister at
the Court of Naples, a perpetual rallying point for the discontented, the common organ of communication between those
who might be or who might fancy themselves aggrieved and
their Sovereign; or that kind of perpetual *surveillance* incompatible with the existence of an independent State, and which
would never have been looked upon but with the greatest
jealousy by other Powers.

Lord William, however, admits the wisdom of the instructions, but complains that they were not punctually executed.
This is best answered by the details of Sir William à Court's
interview with the Neapolitan Ministers, and by the note of
the Marquis Circello of the 6th of December, 1816, whereby
his Sicilian Majesty accepts and confirms the two reserves
pointed out in the instructions. In the proposed alterations,

it was not Sir William's province to look for a faultless scheme
of Government, as Lord William's arguments would seem to
imply.   He was simply to observe if the freedom and happiness
of the Sicilians were so materially affected, when compared
with their former situation, as to make an interference imperative on the part of the British Government.   In the execution
of this duty, he did not rely solely upon his own judgment.
The whole arrangements were as regularly transmitted to the
British Government as they were communicated to him.

His lordship next proceeds to particulars.   In its old form
of Government, Sicily had its Parliament, which the King
was bound to call together at stated intervals, in order to submit to it the wants of the State; and the Parliament had the
right of accompanying its grants by a Memorial containing a
recapitulation of any grievances of which the nation might
have to complain.   It had, however, no legislative powers, nor
indeed any power beyond that of voting and raising the supplies.   *British interference prevented the abolition of this institution;* but, by the new arrangements, the King was no longer
under the necessity of calling his Parliament together unless
he wanted supplies exceeding a *maximum* calculated according
to a former vote of the Parliament itself.   The right of accompanying its grant by a Memorial of grievances was never
taken away from it, as has been insinuated.   The repartition
of the taxes was certainly transferred from the Parliament to
the King, but this was done for the advantage of the people;
" for," as was truly observed by M. de Circello, "the experience
of ages proved that the poorer classes, notwithstanding all the
efforts of Government, were always overloaded, oppressed, and
sacrificed, in the repartition of taxes, beyond any just proportion."

The permanent Deputation was abolished, but its place was
supplied by the Supreme Chancery Council.   The repartition
of the taxes being placed in the hands of the King, it had no
longer any duties of importance to perform.

A considerable stress has been laid on the unfairness of including 560,000 ounces of British subsidy in the calculation of the *maximum*. A short explanation will be necessary upon this subject. The manner of voting supplies in the Sicilian Parliament was as follows: It first voted the amount of the sums which the wants and the exigencies of the State required, and this was called the *Patrimonio Passivo*. It then voted the ways and means of meeting these wants; and this was called the *Patrimonio Attivo*.

In the Parliament of 1813, the Patrimonio Passivo was fixed at 2,016,089 oz. 19 t. 6 g. In the Patrimonio Attivo, only 1,847,687 oz. 20 g. (which sum was adopted as the maximum) were at first voted; but in order to make up the deficit, other taxes were subsequently voted, viz., an increase of the fondiario, and a tax of two taris a barrel on wine exported, the probable amount of which was left blank in the budget, as an exact calculation could not be made, but it was understood that they would more than cover the deficit. The real Patrimonio Attivo, therefore, of the year 1813 was considerably above two millions, in which the British subsidy was certainly included; but as his Sicilian Majesty, in fixing the maximum, might very fairly have made his calculation upon the Patrimonio *Passivo* which the Parliament acknowledged by its vote to be what the exigencies of the State required, yet limited it to 1,847,687 oz. 20 t., (which, though it included the subsidy, did not include the amount of the taxes subsequently voted) the calculation did not appear open to any serious objection, considering it always as a *maximum*; 150,000 oz. also of this sum was allotted annually to the gradual extinction of the National Debt.

It cannot be ascertained from the papers in the possession of the British Mission that any budget was settled in the following Parliament, which appears to have been dissolved by Lord W. Bentinck, and the taxes levied upon the old scale, without any parliamentary authority.

In 1814-15, the Patrimonio Passivo was 1,925,823 oz., the Patrimonio Attivo was 1,946,083 oz., to which the Parliament added the County of Mascali, to be sold by the King for his extraordinary expenses. In this year's calculation, only about 150,000 oz. of British subsidy were included.

The Patrimonio Attivo fixed for 1815-16 was, it is true, only 1,407,886 oz., no subsidies included; but this sum, it is notorious, would have been rejected, as inadequate, by the King, had it not been presented to him on the eve of his departure for the recovery of the kingdom of Naples.

In fixing the maximum, therefore, it appears that the King neither took the highest nor the lowest estimate, even of the Patrimonio Attivo. He might have made his calculation upon the Patrimonio Passivo, and this would have brought the maximum considerably higher. As he satisfied himself with the former, and that not upon its most extended scale, it did not seem necessary to cavil upon the subject of the subsidies; for, after all, it was the principle of the maximum that formed the chief question, rather than its amount, provided that this was kept within the limits of the parliamentary votes. It is not the weight of taxation which the Sicilians complain of, so much as that its produce is not spent in the island, and this could only be effected by forcing the King to fix his residence at Palermo. Supposing the maximum to be exacted to the utmost farthing, (which the Government maintained, from its official documents, was very far from being the case) it would not amount to more than thirteen shillings of English money per head, taking the population of Sicily at a million and a half, which is the lowest calculation.

It is stated by Lord W. Bentinck that several new taxes were imposed, and he instances that upon the registry of mortgages and the introduction of stamps. The first was not objected to in a financial point of view, but it was extremely unpopular with the landed proprietors, as it obliged them to register the mortgages upon their estates, by which means the

mortgaging the same lands over and over again, (a constant
practice) and other frauds, were rendered impossible. The
introduction of stamps would have afforded perhaps a large
revenue, but the amount of each stamp was small; and as
they were introduced a few months only previous to the revolution, their produce was never clearly ascertained.

But as, in virtue of his power of repartition, the King introduced new taxes, so did he abolish several others, no allusion
to which has been made by Lord W. Bentinck. Some of
those voted by the Parliament being only of a temporary
nature, ceased of themselves. Others were removed by the
Government.

The tax of 30 per cent. upon the property of absentees was
diminished one-half.

The oppressive system of the Royal Caricatorj, the well-
known bane of the agricultural interests, was entirely done
away with.

The tax upon horned cattle was taken off, as was also another
upon horses.

Also a tax upon meat (*il macello*).

The extravagant fees, &c., paid in the tribunals under the
old system were abolished, and the expenses of the administration of justice defrayed by Government.

The duties upon the exportation of cattle were also re-
pealed, &c.

It is stated that the interest of the Sicilian debt was not
regularly paid. Abuses may have taken place; but it must
be observed that a specific fund was allotted for this purpose
in the decree of December, 1816.

" A new administrative system," says Lord William, " of
a very complicated and oppressive nature, was introduced,
which consumed the property of the communes, without being
productive of any advantage."

This is rather a vague charge. Abuses may certainly have
crept in, (a most difficult thing to be avoided, in so demoralized

a country) but the system was generally admitted to be good in itself, though it was made a little more expensive than was necessary, in order to gratify the general desire for peace and employment.

The conscription was certainly introduced into Sicily subsequently to the arrangement of 1816; but it was introduced in a modified form, the number of troops levied being limited to the same that Sicily had always supported, and only six years' service exacted. In the present state of Europe, it is evident that other means of defence must be had recourse to than those which did extremely well in different times. During Lord W. Bentinck's administration, when Sicily was guarded by British bayonets, the necessity of the existence of a strong national force was not so much felt, though nobody can know better than his lordship what difficulty existed even then, though with English pay and English bounties, to engage the Sicilians to enter into the military service. Voluntary enlistments, in 1816, were out of the question. The Government was obliged to decide whether it would introduce a modified conscription or an army of foreign mercenaries. It decided in favour of the former, and, in a constitutional point of view, it was the less objectionable decision. Forced services are exacted in countries where liberty most flourishes: England has its pressgang and its Militia ballot. The Sicilian army can hardly be considered in any other light than as a Militia.

Such are the chief objections to the new system which have been pointed out by Lord W. Bentinck. But his lordship appears carefully to have abstained from showing the more favourable side of the picture, and not to have made the slightest allusion to the advantages—the *inappreciable advantages*—which were secured to the nation by the introduction of a regular code of laws, to which all classes were equally subjected, and by the reform of its proverbially iniquitous tribunals. Instead of the lives and properties of the Sicilian subjects being made to depend, as heretofore, upon royal ordinances and despatches, having often a retrospective operation, a regular code was introduced, (modified from the Code Napoleon) just and wise in its principles, openly promulgated, and impartial in its operation, whether applied to the peasant or the prince. A royal despatch could no longer grant to a private nobleman the privilege of neither paying the principal nor the interest of his debts for seventy years. The feudal abuse of perpetual entails was done away. The nobleman was allowed to establish a fresh *Majorat*, after having had it duly proclaimed and registered; but he was obliged, in the first instance, to satisfy his creditors, and only permitted to entail that which was fairly and justly his own.

The independence of the judges was secured—the decision of causes expedited—the administration of justice in every respect simplified. It became no longer possible for powerful noblemen to influence the decisions of the Courts of Law, or to buy up doubtful causes, with the certainty of having them decided in their favour. Instead of the suitor being obliged to come to Palermo, from the furthest extremity of the island, to prosecute his cause, however small its object, judges were established in the principal towns of every district. The advantages accruing to the bulk of the nation from these reforms were incalculable; but the interests of the nobles and the lawyers were too much shaken, not to make them desirous of rendering the new system hateful. The distress experienced by the agricultural and commercial classes in Sicily, as well as all other countries, during the last few years, was extremely favourable to their endeavours. The *Union* was the great watchword of complaint; and national vanity, national prejudices, and national hatred, were all forced into action.

Taking, however, the good and the evil together, the loss of some parliamentary privileges, and the conscription, on one side; and the final abolition of the feudal system, making all men equal in the eye of the law, the publication of a fixed code,

the reform of the tribunals, and the acquisition of several personal privileges, on the other—it will hardly be affirmed that
the freedom and happiness of the Sicilians, *when compared with
what they formerly enjoyed*, were impaired in such a degree as
to render the interference of England imperative upon her.
It is not pretended that a perfect system was established, nor
was it ever contemplated to build up the old edifice exactly as
it existed previous to the British occupation.   However it may
suit Lord William's argument at present to extol that ancient
order of things, he ought to recollect that it was only by the
inherent vices of that system that he justified (and it may be
added *that he could justify*) the active part he took in over-
throwing it.   A detail of these views may be found in every
writer upon Sicilian affairs down to Mr. Leckie; and, if these
were falsely represented or imaginary, how could the General
of a friendly and allied Power reconcile it to his duty to assist
in pulling down what was in itself intrinsically good, in order
to substitute a speculative system, the success of which was
problematical even from the beginning ?

———

It may be well to subjoin a list of those who were acting
with Lord W. Bentinck, at the period of his departure from the
island, showing the offices they then held, and what has become of them since.   It will be seen that almost all have been
employed, or have had the choice of employment.   It may be
observed that the greater Barons, who originally acted with his
lordship, viz., the Princes Caparo, Aci, &c., had all abandoned
the cause long before this period, and were in the ranks of the
Opposition.

NAMES.	OFFICES HELD.	HOW EMPLOYED SINCE.
Prince Belmonte.	Councillor of State.	Died shortly afterwards.
Prince Vilhermosa.	Ditto.	Retains the same rank : was named upon the Commission to modify the Constitution, but declined from ill-health.

NAMES.	OFFICES HELD.	HOW EMPLOYED SINCE.
Don R. Settimo.	Minister of War.	Has the rank and pay of Admiral. As he was the personal friend of Lord W. Bentinck, it was particularly desired by the British Minister that a suitable place should be offered him in 1816. He was consequently appointed Director of the Chancery, but he declined the situation, which was immediately accepted by the Marquis Gurgello, who had also been Secretary of State.
M. Bonanno.	Minister of Finance.	A pension.
Duc de Serra di Falco.	Director of Posts and Chaussées.	The same situation: was subsequently promoted to be Director dei Bolli e Registri.
Prince Villafranca.	Secretary of State.	Not employed.
Prince Cazini.	Ditto.	Not employed, nor desirous of employment. His brother made Governor of Castelamare, which post he held till the Revolution.
Duke Lucchesi-Palli.	Ambassador to Spain.	Made Minister of Foreign Affairs, and afterwards a pension till his death.
D. Mestropaolo.	Procuratore Fiscale.	Director of Police — now Minister of State.
C. Airoldi.	Speaker.	Not employed.
M. Salva.	Under-Secretary of State.	Made a Marquis: destined to go to America as Chargé d'Affaires, but this appointment suspended for a reason not connected with politics.

Three other persons may be added, who, though not absolutely acting with Lord W. Bentinck at the period of his leaving the island, were brought forward entirely by the Constitution, and might therefore be supposed to be obnoxious, if it be true that any of the Constitutionals were obnoxious, viz., Duke Gualtieri, General Nazelli, and Marquis Ferrari. These were all continued Ministers of State in their several departments till the breaking out of the Revolution in 1820.

Lord Clancarty to the Marquess of Londonderry.

Bruxelles, August 3, 1821.

My dear Lord—I beg your attention to my despatch of this date, No. 41. I have found the King (for he stands alone in the business, as all his Ministers assure me) more obstinate than, with his well-known disposition, I had even expected him to be on the subject of the Slave Trade. With real deference to your better opinion, mine is that this point must not be relinquished; that, abstracted from the importance of the subject in itself, if we suffer his Majesty to triumph in victory over us on this occasion, he will not fail to wage continual war with us on every future opportunity.

I would, however, in the present instance, begin gently. It may be, as I have suggested in my despatch, that a point of pride withholds him from communicating to us the particulars of the instructions sent out, on which he professes himself so strongly to rely, and that these may be really framed with a view to prevent the future traffic in slaves; and this suggestion is certainly fortified by the fact that Falck, the Colonial Minister, desired Nagell to acquaint me that his report was quite favourable to our objects, and particularly to add that I might be well assured that the instructions he had sent out were amply sufficient to put an entire stop to all further importations of slaves into the Dutch colonies.

I should therefore propose that an instruction should be sent out to me, founded on Nagell's note of the 31st ult., and on the previous correspondence, directing me, both by an official note to the Minister of Foreign Affairs, and in a personal interview which I should be directed to solicit from the King, to assure his Majesty of the entire confidence placed by my Sovereign in the measures adopted by this Court for the execution of the treaty, subsequently to the decree of April 16 last, and that this confidence in the King my master was amply supported by those general assurances of their efficacy, which had been generally notified under the orders of the King of the Netherlands—that the form, however, of the British Government, the universal and anxious interest taken by the British public in this question, the circumstances of the details of every published document issued by this Government for the purpose of carrying the treaty on their part into execution, being manifestly insufficient for this purpose—these and other considerations had led my Government, without any distrust in their efficacy, to seek a communication of the instructions sent out to the Dutch subordinate authorities upon a subject in which both Crowns were equally interested, on which the most entire and unreserved confidence must necessarily be presumed to exist between them—a confidence which the Court of Great Britain would always be found ready in the fullest manner to justify by the communication of every law, instruction, or other proceeding for the complete execution on its part of the treaty, whenever such communication should be desired by this Government.

Such is the proceeding which I should suggest on this occasion; and, if the despatch shall be written so as to be communicated *in extenso*, so much the better. I have proposed that this should be done both by note and interview with the King—the former for obvious reasons common to all Governments—the latter, because the King here is his own Minister in every branch and department of the State, those called his *Ministers* being little more than mere *Chefs de bureau*, as is amply proved in this very identical case, in which all those styled Ministers, including the whole Council of State, are with us, the King alone against us.

If you should think this course worthy of adoption, and that it should succeed—well. If, having been promised, it should fail, other measures, which I have already suggested in former letters, will then be to be considered. Of these, should they become necessary, I will hereafter eventually write more at large. Sufficient to the day is the evil thereof.

Charles remains with us till Sunday : we shall lose him and his with regret.

Ever yours, my dear lord, &c.,   CLANCARTY.

Sir Charles Bagot to Joseph Planta, Esq.

St. Petersburgh, August 6-18, 1821.

My dear Planta—Chamberlain has had another attack, but he is now safe : it was not so severe as the last, but I was in considerable alarm for him for two days. It is now so clear that he must not stay here any longer, that, although he has not yet received a formal leave from Londonderry, I shall take upon myself to sanction his return home as soon as he is fit for the voyage. I hope and fully believe that he will be able to set out soon ; for it will be an object to avoid the equinoctial storms. He is a most excellent and honest fellow, and I wish that he could remain here, but his physician, and indeed everybody, is convinced that he must not. I cannot satisfy myself entirely as to the nature of his complaint ; but it is a very serious one. I sometimes think that it belongs to the genus gout, but, if so, it is of a strange sort.

A courier arrived here the night before last from Constantinople with despatches to the 28th July, N. S. These are no doubt the long expected answers to the instructions to Baron Strogonoff, which were communicated to the Allied Courts ; but both despatches, the Emperor's and the Minister's, are at Zarskoë Zélo, and nothing has yet been allowed to transpire. I shall despatch Aves as soon as I can give you any information upon this all-essential point. I only just save the post.

Yours always, my dear Planta, most sincerely,

CHARLES BAGOT.

Lord Clancarty to the Marquess of Londonderry.

Bruxelles, August 14, 1821.

My dear Lord—The Duke of Wellington arrived here on Friday last, the 10th inst., and left us yesterday morning, to

inspect the fortifications from Dinant to Maestricht.   He will
then go to Coblentz, and thence to Paris, for the French
King's birthday.

On his arrival here, he immediately communicated to me
your wishes that he should speak to this King on his Majesty's
conduct with respect to the Slave Trade Treaty.   His Grace,
however, expressed his unwillingness to do so, unless, indeed,
the King should first broach the subject with him.   Aware at
once of the immense benefit that might be derived from the
Duke speaking openly to the King upon this point, and conceiving his objection to arise merely from the delicacy of not
interfering with me, I fully assured him upon this subject;
and, having placed him in complete possession of the case as it
at present stands, he agreed to converse with the King about
it, either at the audience he was then about to have with him,
by his Majesty's appointment, or after dinner.

The accompanying Memorandum, which the Duke made
out for the purpose of being communicated to you, will show
you what passed at the audience, and that the King relieved
the Duke from one part of his difficulty by himself beginning
the subject.

I certainly augur much good from this conversation; for,
though the King did not promise to make known his instructions, yet I think if they are really of the nature that Falck,
through Nagell, assured me they were, that this will be the
result; and, if not, it is quite as well that we should at once
know this fact.   Some advantage, however, immediately
flowed from this conversation; the King having, after dinner
the same day, taken me aside, and, for near half an hour,
assured me of his anxious desire to be always on the most confidential footing with my Government; and personally complimenting me upon my conduct from the first hour at which I
was presented to him in London up to the present moment, in
terms which it would ill become me to repeat.

With the Algerine subject, stated in the Memorandum, I

have no other acquaintance than what I derive from Nagell, who, when he mentioned it, made no complaint, but rather praised the line of conduct of our Government upon it. He said that, called upon by Spain, under the Treaty of Alcala d'Honores, to support their demand for the liberation of the Spanish Consul, it became necessary to reinforce their naval squadron in the Mediterranean, and that, as the best means of notifying this fact to the two Governments, he had instructed the Fagels to acquaint you and M. Pasquier therewith, and at the same time to solicit the co-operation of the Consuls of Great Britain and France in the demand to be made upon the Dey—that the request for co-operation was declined by both Courts; but the attainment of the object immediately upon the demand being made at Algiers, furnished the fullest evidence that neither the English nor French Consul had in the slightest degree opposed it.

Upon the Slave Trade I should still recommend the line to be adopted which I had proposed to you in my letter of the 3rd inst.; and I think the sooner this can be done the better, in order that we may derive all the benefit which can be drawn from the recent impression made on this King by his late conversation with the Duke of Wellington.

Some three posts since, Nagell acquainted me that he had received advices from Fagel, stating your intention of forwarding to me certain communications to be made to the King on our notions respecting the events in Turkey, and their probable consequences. None have, however, yet arrived, and inquiries have been made from me by Nagell on this subject, which sufficiently denote the impatience of the King upon it. His Majesty, however, has personally assured me of his anxious desire for peace; and Nagell has further acquainted me that the latter instructions sent out to their Chargé d'Affaires at the Porte were in all things to take his tone and guide his conduct by those of Lord Strangford. Hatzfeld has, however, read me a despatch from Bernstorff to him, which states that a communication has already been made by Rose to the King of Prussia on this matter; and, as Hatzfeld is himself none of the most discreet, I own myself apprehensive lest he should make known this fact to Nagell, and that hence false conclusions should be drawn from the tardiness of our communication to this in comparison with that made to the Prussian Court. I should wish, therefore, to be furnished with those papers as soon as possible,[1] and if to these could be added some of a more recent date than those sent to Rose, as a ground for the delay, it may obviate jealousy.

The principal purpose for which Hatzfeld read me parts of Bernstorff's despatch to him was to show that he (Hatzfeld) had fulfilled a commission which he says you gave him, to make known your sentiments upon Turkish affairs to his Court, and that the Prussian Government entirely agree with you in your view of the subject, which fact is certainly deducible from those extracts read to me from the despatch in question.

Yours, my dear lord, most affectionately,

CLANCARTY.

[Enclosure.]

Memorandum by the Duke of Wellington of a Conversation between his Grace and the King of the Netherlands.

Bruxelles, August 12, 1821.

After I had been for some time with his Majesty, and was about to take my leave, he said that he was much concerned to find that he was not so well with the British Government as he had been; that he was pressed in an extraordinary manner upon the subject of the Slave Trade, while other Powers, such as Portugal, Spain, and France, were allowed to do as they pleased; that he had been left to himself in a recent discussion with Algiers, upon the subject of the Spanish Consul; and that all progress in the negociation regarding the

---

[1] These papers sent some time since.—Note by the Marquess of Londonderry.

East Indies was stopped.   He enlarged a good deal upon each
of these topics, but this was the substance of his discourse.

I assured his Majesty that he was quite mistaken, and that
the Government felt the same interest for his welfare and
prosperity that they had always felt; that he was likewise
mistaken in supposing that we had not pressed France, Spain,
and Portugal, equally with his Majesty, to the performance of
their treaties for the abolition of the Slave Trade; that we
certainly lamented that we were obliged to come, year after
year, before Parliament with statements of complaints of in-
fractions of the treaty for the abolition of the Slave Trade by
subjects of the Netherlands, which were unredressed; that it
was impossible for his Majesty, who governed a country in
which no public opinion against the Slave Trade existed, to
judge of the force of that opinion in England; and that, when
we pressed him to adopt measures to carry the treaty faithfully into execution, he ought to give us credit for the necessity
under which we were acting.

I then told him that it appeared to be admitted that the
law which had passed did not go as far as the treaty, and the
deficiency was supplied by an ordonnance of his Majesty.   The
ordonnance likewise was defective; and the Ambassador had
been informed that the deficiency had been supplied by an
instruction to the Governor of Surinam.   Before we pronounced any opinion on the case as it then stood, we asked to
see the instruction, but hitherto without effect; and we must
say, informed as we now were, that, as the law and the
ordonnance did not come up to the engagement made by his
Majesty by his treaty—

He here interrupted me, and said we ought to make trial
of what had been done before we pronounced—to which I
answered that it was not necessary to wait, for that his
Majesty, by sending out an instruction, which we were told
was sufficient, had pronounced that the law and ordonnance
were not sufficient till that instruction was issued.   All we

desired now was to see that instruction, which we were willing
to believe would place his Majesty, in relation to the Slave
Trade, exactly where he ought to stand.   But, situated as we
were, it was necessary that we should have in our hands the
proofs, to be able to produce them to Parliament, and to satisfy
the country not only that we had done our duty, but that his
Majesty had done everything in his power to perform his treaty.

In respect to the case of Algiers, I told his Majesty that I
did not recollect exactly what had passed upon it; but that I
was quite sure that, if we had not taken the case into consideration in the point of view which his Majesty wished, it
was because we were not aware of his wishes; that the British
Government might frequently be under the necessity of not
doing exactly what he wished; but, if we did not consider a
question in the particular point of view in which his Majesty
thought we ought to consider it, he had only to send for Lord
Clancarty and explain his wishes, and they would be immediately attended to.

In respect to the Indian question, I told him that I knew
nothing about it; that the Minister for India had been
changed, which might have occasioned some delay; but that,
at all events, I entreated his Majesty not to connect that
question with that of the Slave Trade, but enable us to prove
to the country that his Majesty had done everything in his
power to perform his treaty on the latter point.

He then entered into a discussion upon the details of the
question, and stated that the slaves, of whose importation into
Surinam we had complained, had been brought by a French
ship, and he asked why we did not prevent the French from
carrying these slaves.   I told him that these treaties all consisted of two points: 1st, there was an engagement that there
should be no trade in slaves; next, there were stipulations,
giving a right of mutual search, which were in fact nothing
more than providing means of carrying into execution the engagements to put an end to the traffic.

It was true that we had never yet been able to prevail on the King of France to adopt this particular mode of putting an end to the traffic, but his Majesty was much mistaken if he thought we had not pressed him upon that as well as upon all other points of the subject, as he would find, if he would take the trouble of reading the folio volumes which had been laid before Parliament last session.

He then talked of the importation of slaves from colony to colony, and said that we had last year refused to allow the importation from an island to the continent, although he conceived that each of the contracting parties had a right to transport slaves from colony to colony, whether continental or insular, and whether belonging to one of the contracting parties or not.

In answer, I told him that the treaty certainly left this transfer of slaves from colony to colony quite free, provided the two colonies belonged to the same Power; and this became the subject of regulation within the State itself, to which no other State had anything to say—that it was true that, in the last session, Parliament had refused to pass a private Act, to enable an individual to transfer his slaves from an island to the continent; but that this was done from motives of internal policy, and not from any supposed obligation of treaty; but that the treaty prevented the transfer of slaves from colony to colony, both not belonging to the same Power. That transfer was considered by both parties as a traffic in slaves; and the law and ordonnance of his Majesty, however insufficient, and lastly, his Majesty's instructions to the Governor-General of Surinam, had been calculated with a view to prevent it.

The conversation then turned upon the Indian question. His Majesty said that the negociation had been suspended in London, on the plea that further information was required from the Governor-General in India; and that at the same time Lord Hastings had informed the Governor-General at Batavia that, the two Governments in Europe having taken up the subject, he should discontinue the discussion of it. I repeated that I was quite ignorant of the question; that I neither knew how it stood, nor on what it had turned, but that it appeared to me there was nothing inconsistent in what had passed; as it was very probable that information was required from Lord Hastings, which he might be the only person capable of giving, at the same time that he should have broken off all discussion upon the subject with the Governor-General of Batavia.

The conversation having lasted above an hour, I took my leave, having left the King, as I thought, better satisfied and pleased than he had been; but he did not say that he should communicate his intentions to the Governor of Surinam, which I repeatedly urged him to do.

I must add, that before his Majesty began this conversation, I did not perceive any coldness in his reception of me or in manner or conversation.

Sir Charles Bagot to the Marquess of Londonderry.

St. Petersburgh, September 5-17, 1821.

My dear Lord—The Emperor's answer to your letter was sent to Baron Nicolai on the evening of the 10th. It has occurred to me that perhaps your lordship may accompany the King to Hanover, in which case, you will probably have left London before the arrival of the Russian courier. I therefore enclose to you a copy of this answer, which I think may possibly reach you before the original, as I direct Aves to proceed to Hanover, if he should learn at Berlin that your lordship is there. I regret very much that I should have been compelled to detain him so long, as I am sensible that great anxiety must have been felt to receive accounts from hence of the effects produced by Baron Strogonoff's abrupt departure from the Porte; but your lordship will see by my despatches that I have been kept from day to day without receiving the promised communications: and that, when they did arrive, I found that, according to the constant, but most inconvenient practice of this Government, they had been already forwarded to England. I am very glad that, having received them, I determined to wait till I had seen the Emperor. I hope that the language which he has held to me may be considered as some corrective of that held in the papers now communicated to the Allied Powers. Those papers certainly appear to be anything but conciliatory. They assume what is not true—that the answer of the Porte to Baron Strogonoff's note is a rejection of the Russian demands and an aggravation of its former conduct. They make no acknowledgment of the fact which, even at the time the papers were prepared, was in some degree known to them, that the Turkish Government had already begun to relax from their system of indiscriminate vengeance, and they take exactly the same ground, though with a higher tone, which was taken in the instructions to Baron Strogonoff and in the note which he was ordered to deliver to the Divan.

These circumstances and many expressions in the papers would naturally lead to the belief that a war was already determined upon, and that the demands of this Government were only the pretext under which it was to be justified. If this ever was the case, (which I do not believe) certainly the last intelligence received from Constantinople has at least deranged the scheme. Count Nesselrode, who is, I am sure, in his heart, most anxious to avoid a war, told me on the evening on which I had had my audience of the Emperor, and which was two days after I had received the communications, that he then began to think that there was an opening for conciliation. The Emperor, though he spoke less strongly of the intelligence received, referred to it more than once and in the same sense in which Count Nesselrode had done.

The papers now communicated have been long in preparing, and they have undergone repeated alterations. Had the last news received from Constantinople arrived before they had been issued, I feel confident that they would have undergone considerable modification. Your lordship will observe that Baron Strogonoff's proceedings are upheld and approved throughout. This I expected: indeed, it could scarcely be otherwise, when all the former Russian papers had been confessedly grounded upon his reports; but his conduct is not the less blamed by many, and it is felt that his departure was by no means an indispensable measure. I am sure, however, that the Emperor is right when he considers it a fortunate one.

I hope that I have not committed any indiscretion in taking upon myself to communicate both to the Emperor and Count Nesselrode the extract which I send by this messenger, of Lord Strangford's despatch to your lordship of the 26th of July; but besides that the reflections cast upon Lord Strangford required a prompt and most decided refutation, I thought it impossible to bring the argument on the Turkish side of the question before this Government so forcibly, and with so little risk of offence, as by showing the language held by the Reis Effendi in his conference with Lord Strangford.

I hope this Government is now sensible that Lord Strangford's conduct has not been what it has been represented to be. I ought to add, that I showed this extract to Count Lieven, whom I found so strongly prepossessed against Lord Strangford's supposed proceedings, that it had less effect upon him than I hope and believe it had both upon the Emperor and Count Nesselrode. Count Lieven has latterly been much with the Emperor, and the Emperor told me that he had spoken to him most fully upon the whole of the present state of affairs.

The despatches to Baron Lebzeltern, which brought the intelligence of the 18th of August from the Internuncio at Constantinople, brought also the copy of a note delivered by Lord Strangford on the 6th of August to the Divan. This note is still in Count Nesselrode's hands, and Baron Lebzeltern has not yet been able to show it to me; but I hear that it has given great satisfaction to this Government.

At my last audience of the Emperor, he repeated to me what he said at my former one—that he was much gratified by your lordship's letter to him, and that there was nothing which he so much desired as to encourage the fullest and most unreserved communications with the British Government; adding everything the most gracious as to the pleasure he always felt in transacting affairs with your lordship. He could not have received your lordship's letter in better part. I find that Count Nesselrode has read the Emperor's answer to it to the Austrian, French, and Prussian Ministers; but it was only to myself that he gave the opportunity of taking a copy of it.

There has been a movement of the Imperial Guards from Witepsk to the neighbourhood of Minsk, but it is scarcely to be called a forward movement, and has, I believe, been caused only by the necessity of putting them into a more fertile country, and for their more convenient inspection by the Emperor. There has been also a dislocation of some of the other corps, but nothing which indicates any immediate hostile movements. Preparations, however, are naturally making towards the Turkish frontier; and, if a war should arise, it will certainly be carried on upon a scale very different from that to which the Turks have been accustomed.

I have the honour to be, &c.,   CHARLES BAGOT.

Sir George Rose to the Marquess of Londonderry.

Berlin, September 22, 1821.

My dear Lord—I have hitherto received no order to correspond with you in duplicate, but I think it safer to write to you by Baron Ompteda, who goes to Hanover, setting off this evening or to-morrow morning.

My despatch of this date, on Russian matters, would have but little interest, inasmuch as the communications sent hither from Petersburgh, and thus long expected, and which arrived here yesterday morning, will also be made in London, and I

therefore only advert to them; but, as you will not see them
necessarily for some time, I think it safer to apprise you of
what I have learnt respecting them. When I saw Count
Bernstorff, however, yesterday evening, he had not seen the
papers, which Count Alopeus told him were so voluminous
that he had not had time to peruse them all. Count Bernstorff only knew what Count Alopeus had related to him.

Count Bernstorff had expected that these papers would not
have been sent off until the Emperor of Austria's reply to the
Emperor of Russia's letter should have been received, and
until the line of conduct to be adopted upon it should have
been determined on; but it seems that, just at the end of
M. d'Alopeus's last despatch, it is stated that the Emperor of
Austria's letter had just arrived, and that it would cause
modifications in the line taken as to Turkey; and it notified
to him that consequently another messenger would be sent to
him in the course of a few days.

Besides new matter, the present communications embrace
the papers some time since communicated to the foreign
Ministers at Petersburgh, the whole correspondence of Baron
Strogonoff with the Porte, in his last negociation with it.
Count Alopeus has stated that the present communications are
not decisive on the question of peace or war; that Baron
Strogonoff's return does not necessarily involve the latter;
that a distinct refutation of the arguments in the Grand
Vizir's letter has been sent to the Porte; that the demand of
the Porte that the Greeks who have taken refuge at Odessa
should be given up to it, the compliance with which would be
incompatible with the Emperor's feelings of justice and religion, is positively rejected.

Count Bernstorff understands that the most interesting
document in these communications is this answer to the Grand
Vizir; in it, in order to prevent Baron Strogonoff's cause
being separated from that of his Court, it is affirmed that
every part of his conduct was held under orders from home;

and, as a lower tone cannot now well be taken than that hitherto employed, and, as the great object is to frighten the Turks, it is supposed to be conceived in terms sufficiently harsh and peremptory; all the old demands are renewed, though not exactly in the same shape. Count Bernstorff told me that the accustomed recourse of the Russian Court is had to the expedient of declaring that the Allies must deal with this question, of which the decision is mainly made over to them.

I observed to him that I was very glad to see this matter, all things considered, thus nearly in the state which M de. Lebzeltern said it would assume, and particularly to learn the line thus taken of such complete reference to the Allies. Count Bernstorff said he thought with me as to this reference, in either supposition, whether the Russian Court is sincere in making it or not. He agreed with me that the Allies must act as assuming it to be perfectly sincere. I said I believed the Emperor to be sincerely desirous of avoiding war; that he finds himself in a very embarrassing minority at home on this question; and that, by this reference, he seeks support in the opinions of his Allies: and the Count was inclined to agree also in this opinion. He said that, as the Turks are constantly making new efforts to avert war, intelligence will have been received at Petersburgh, since these letters have been expedited, of fresh measures adopted by them, which diminish considerably the grounds Russia had alleged as tending to compel her to take up arms. He regretted Lord Strangford and Baron Lützow did not feel authorised to take upon themselves to guarantee to the Porte that Russia would not occupy the principalities of Moldavia and Wallachia, if the Ottoman troops were withdrawn from those provinces; but he felt how natural, especially on the part of Lord Strangford, it was to demur to take on themselves so great and fearful a responsibility.

I now expect the messenger Aves from Petersburgh hourly, and, in order that you may be enabled to apprise his Majesty

in the most expeditious manner of the intelligence he brings,
I intend to direct him upon Hanover, ordering him, if you are
not already there, to proceed to meet you, going towards
London by Frankfort sur Maine. If I sent him the usual
road by Leipzig, he might easily pass through Frankfort after
you had left it for Hanover, through Cassel, the road his
Majesty is to take. In this way, Aves, if even he meets you
beyond Frankfort, will only have made a circuit of about
fifteen or sixteen German miles : you are thus sure of receiving
Sir C. Bagot's despatches ; and the Government in England
will know all that is now essential from the Russian Envoy,
long before Aves could arrive there, proceeding even in the
straightest line of road. Of course if, before Aves arrives, I
receive directions from you repugnant to or incompatible with
this plan, I shall abandon it. If Aves meets you at Hanover,
he is then in the straightest road hence to London—that by
Helvoetsluys—if you prefer that road for him.

In conversation with Count Bernstorff yesterday, I adverted to the matter of my private letter of the 19th inst.,
stating how confidently I anticipate the satisfaction which his
Majesty will experience on learning the measures his Prussian
Majesty has taken to ensure, as far as time will allow, his
precautions to take effect, his Majesty being received everywhere in his dominions in the manner the most conformable
to his wishes. Prince Wittgenstein had observed to him on
the absence of notification of the King's intention to pass
through the Prussian Rhine provinces; and the Count replied
that when a journey lay through distant provinces, and was
not made near or through the capital, this omission of notice
appeared to him a matter of small moment. It seems that
Prince Hatzfeldt has anticipated the instructions sent to him
by estafette on the evening of the 19th inst., by the Count,
under his Sovereign's directions, as he has written to the
Count that, as soon as he has certain knowledge of the time
at which the King will reach the Prussian territory, he shall

send orders to the civil and military authorities to prepare
everything for his reception. Count Bernstorff said to me
that his Prussian Majesty has abstained from inviting the
King to Berlin purely through a feeling of delicacy, under the
anxious wish to avoid embarrassing him by so doing, but that
his Majesty's coming here will be most highly gratifying to
his Sovereign. I told him that, on this last point, I had
already ventured to give you a positive assurance, and he said
he was very glad I had; that I am entirely warranted in so
doing.

I do not think I ought to anticipate by detailing the measures taking to prepare for the King's reception. It is probable that the Duke of Cumberland, who means to be at
Hanover before the King's arrival there, will have occasion to
speak of them.

Count Zichy received yesterday morning a letter from the
Archduke Ferdinand, dated at Jüterbock, on the road to
Dresden, from this place, which he left the day before. His
Imperial Highness states in it, that he had written to the
Emperor of Austria that, being already out of the Austrian
dominions, and only now about to proceed to Dresden, he had
the less scruple to solicit his permission to offer his respects to
his Majesty at Hanover. To this the Emperor Francis
replied, by directing him to proceed to Hanover, to compliment his Majesty in his name on his arrival in his German
dominions. This reply only reached the Archduke at Jüterbock; and he, in the letter to Count Zichy, directed him to
apprise the Duke of Cumberland of the whole of this matter,
and to say that he regretted much he could not do so in
person here, as it was not till after his departure hence that
he learnt these intentions of the Emperor Francis, and knew
that he was to proceed to Hanover. This the Count communicated to his Royal Highness yesterday.

When I wrote to you to know whether I ought to go to
Hanover during his Majesty's presence there, I explained that

I have in that matter no one other wish than to do that which should best testify my feelings of personal respectful gratitude for his great and wonted kindness to me. The Duke of Cumberland understands that a Chapter of the Guelphic Order will be held there by his Majesty, and tells me I ought to be at it to be installed. I have informed his Royal Highness that I am without orders on the subject, and that I cannot go to Hanover without your permission. I trust to your kind- to bear me safe, should my absence appear to subject me, in any degree, to the imputation of a failure in that dutiful attention to his Majesty which it is my most anxious desire to offer.

I am, my dear lord, &c.,   G. H. Rose.

Berlin, September 23, 1821.

PS. On the news of the delay of his Majesty's arrival in London, received yesterday, Baron Ompteda delays his journey. I therefore send this letter to the Duke of Cambridge, requesting his Royal Highness to be pleased to send it to meet you, not by estafette or by the post, but by any safe opportunity that may offer, not, however, despatching a messenger with it. Lieutenant Stapleton, of the Prussian Lancers of the Guard, takes charge of this letter as far as Hanover. This young Englishman, much protected by Lord Morley, is very honourable and singularly good-natured; allow me therefore to make him known to you.

G. H. R.

Mr. Edward Ward to the Marquess of Londonderry.

Lisbon, September 26, 1821.

My dear Lord—I hope you will, in reading my despatch of this date, respecting my discussion with Pinheiro, be good enough to appreciate the difficulty of sustaining the informality of my character (vide your Despatch No. 6, October 18, 1820), and of asserting my correctness in making official communications at the same time.

Pinheiro denies that such a thing can be; however, I cannot but believe that his object in doing this was to gain time, and prevent the coming on of the woollen question, which I know he has dreaded ever since he has come into office.

The Cortes are such a variable quantity that it is impossible to calculate with any certainty upon the manner in which the subject will be treated by them. They are, however, a little afraid of England, and of England only. But they think the Liberal Party is so strong amongst us, that the Ministry, however they may love despotism and legitimacy, cannot act against them.

I think the Liberal cause has made more enemies than friends, during the last six months, in Portugal; and I should nightly apprehend a reaction, were it not that I know the want of energy which characterises this people. The utmost vigilance is, however, exerted, and the guards and patrols are very numerous. In the country the depredations of robbers are increasing, and the cause assigned is, that the article of the Constitution, which provides that no one shall be arrested without certain formalities, incapacitates the constables from seizing these voltigeurs. They have not near got through the discussion of the Articles of their Constitution. They bring up about three or four Articles per week, in order to keep the poll open.

In the hope that you will be so good as to let me soon have your orders, I remain very faithfully and sincerely yours,

E. M. WARD.

Matilda and family are at Cintra. The Brazilians say that Lisbon is hotter than the Rio.

[Enclosure in Lord Clancarty's letter of October 8, 1821.]

Lord Clancarty to M. le Comte de Herdt.

Bruxelles, October 2, 1821.

My dear Sir—I have great pleasure in acquainting your Excellency that, when I took leave of the King, my master, yesterday at Sombref, I received his Majesty's special commands to return you his thanks for the active and zealous manner in which, under the orders of the King of the Netherlands, you had provided for his accommodation in your department during his stay at Bruxelles, and to add that it would have been impossible to have rendered this service more completely to his satisfaction.

His Majesty has further commanded me to present you with the accompanying box, with his Majesty's portrait enamelled thereon, of which he has deigned through me to request your acceptance, as a testimony of his gracious regard and approbation.

Give me leave, on this occasion, to express the grateful sentiments with which I am sincerely impressed for all your kindness at all times shown to me, and more especially during the period of my Sovereign's residence here. Believe me that it affords considerable satisfaction to my mind to have been thus made the instrument of conveying to you the so well merited thanks of my Royal Master, which will scarcely fail to prove agreeable to your feelings.

I remain, &c.,   CLANCARTY.

The Hon. Robert Gordon to the Marquess of Londonderry.

Vienna, October 3, 1821.

My dear Lord—Prince Metternich acquaints me, in confidence, this morning, of his desire to pay his respects to his Majesty at Hanover, and of taking the opportunity of conferring with your lordship upon many important questions, now that his Majesty has abandoned his intention of visiting Vienna. He gave me to understand that his sole reason for not having made up his mind upon the subject, was his fear lest, upon political grounds, the visit might embarrass you upon the score of its *éclat*.

In answer, I thought it my duty to state in plain terms my

opinion to the Prince, which was certainly not in favour of the visit. I told him I was convinced your lordship was as desirous as he could possibly be of enjoying the advantage of such an interview; but I thought you would consider this advantage as more than counterbalanced by the bad effects which would result from it in the way of false interpretations, of jealousies, and evil reports in other quarters. I am not aware of the decision which his Highness may take; but I shall be happy to learn that I have not risked your disapprobation by contributing to turn it against the proposed visit. The Emperor has resolved to send some person of distinction to compliment his Majesty; and the conversation then turned upon the difficulty of selection, which had, in fact, in some way, given the idea to the Prince of going himself. There is no military officer at present here fitted to be so employed. Prince Dietrichstein, a civilian, of the first rank and talents in this country, was named; but I am unable to speak as to the probability of the choice falling upon him.

The latest despatches from Baron Lebzeltern have put this Government in a better humour with the Petersburgh conduct. Even should this only promise a respite until next spring, so much reliance is placed upon the success which the Turks will gain over the insurrection in the mean while, that Prince Metternich looks with confidence to the preservation of peace.

The news of his Majesty having put off his visit to Vienna has caused a general disappointment. I confess myself to be one of the most disappointed. It would have been a real gratification to me to have had the advantage of seeing your lordship upon this occasion, and I would venture yet to ask permission to meet you somewhere on the road, if it should not be considered to interfere with the public service.

Believe me, &c.,   R. GORDON.

Lord Clancarty to Viscount Sidmouth.

The Hague, October 21, 1821.

My dear Lord—The Messenger Cloud has just arrived here with despatches from Hanover: those marked Nos. 8 and 9, to your lordship's address, were left open for my perusal and instruction.

The despatch of this messenger from Hanover, so as to arrive here more than forty-eight hours prior to the despatch of our ordinary couriers for England, the nature of the instructions of which he is the bearer respecting the future expedition of couriers for his Majesty from England, and a sealed bag, with which he is likewise charged for your lordship, with the contents of which I am quite unacquainted, have induced me to send him forward immediately, and to give directions that he should be passed over to England forthwith, by an extra packet from Helvoetsluys; and I should hope that, under the circumstances above described, your lordship will approve of the step I thus conceive it to be my duty to take in this instance.

His Majesty proposes, upon his passage through Bruxelles, to occupy the house of his Ambassador to the Netherlands: I shall therefore have the honour of meeting him there; and, for the purpose of having all things ready for his reception, it is my intention, unless I shall receive intimation to the contrary from Hanover, on Tuesday next, to set out on Wednesday or Thursday next for Bruxelles, there to remain till after his Majesty's departure. Mr. Chad will be left here, to conduct all matters relating to this embassy at the Hague, during my short absence, and also to put in execution the orders received from Hanover respecting the despatch of couriers to his Majesty's address, or to that of Lord Londonderry.

I remain, my dear lord, &c.,   CLANCARTY.

Prince Metternich to the Marquess of Londonderry.

Hannovre, 26 Octobre, 1821.

Mon cher Marquis—Je venois de vous écrire quand la dépêche ci-jointe de Berlin m'est arrivée. Vous y retrouverez une singulière preuve de la confusion qui règne dans la marche de l'administration Prussienne. Je dois vous avoir remis, parmi mes pièces, une dépêche à Lebzeltern, qui touche l'objet de la *publicité* des sentimens des Puissances dans l'affaire Grèque. Cette dépêche a servie de réponse à la communication Russe dont a fait mention M. d'Alopéus. Voici, au reste, le fait.

J'ai écrit à Petersbourg, au mois d'Août, qu'un grand mal étoit le système de mensonges et d'erreurs, qu'avoit adopté le parti désorganisateur, et le silence du bon parti—que ce mal se trouvoit en grande partie lié à la position intermédiaire, dans laquelle se trouveroient placé les Cours, aussi longtems que la Russie n'auroit pas trouvé moyen de prendre un parti décidé, et déterminé à être avoué franchement.

C'est à cela que le Comte de Capodistrias a répondu par l'une des dépêches du 13–25 Septembre que vous avez entre les mains. Il prouve, par cette même pièce, qu'il désire que l'eau reste troublée jusqu'au moment où il n'aura plus l'espoir de pouvoir empêcher qu'elle ne s'éclaircisse. Ma réponse est également entre vos mains.

Aujourd'hui la Gazette de Berlin renferme un article plein de vérités et d'imprudences. Confrontez la avec la dernière note du Comte de Bernstorff, et vous vous convaincrez que rien ne se ressemble moins que ces deux rédactions. Capodistrias sera furieux contre le Chancelier et surtout contre Schöll.

Par une faute typographique singulière, la Gazette de Hannovre, du 24 Octobre, renferme le même article, sous la rubrique *Irlande*, tandis que dans celle de Berlin elle est cotée *Inland*, c'est-à-dire *Intérieur*.

S'il n'étoit pas prouvé que l'on n'invente plus facilement *deux* Dieux, nous verrions l'un de ces jours en paroître *deux* dans quelque pièce Prussienne.

T. à v.   METTERNICH.

Veuillez me renvoyer la dépêche de Vienne, quand vous n'en aurez plus besoin.

The Marquess of Londonderry to Sir Charles Bagot.

Foreign Office, December 14, 1821.

My dear Sir—In reflecting upon the present state of affairs in Greece, as connected with those of the rest of Europe, and one may say of the world, it is impossible the Emperor of Russia should not be struck with the critical nature of the course which he has to pursue. I shall endeavour shortly to state the case, as I see it, and upon which his Imperial Majesty will have to decide. It is, however, a subject upon which I do not wish to enter officially. I shall treat it shortly in a private letter, and if your Excellency should think fit to touch upon it with the Emperor, I submit that it will be best done in conversation.

The first point that deserves the Emperor's attentive consideration is the wide and increasing spread of the revolutionary movement throughout the American as well as the European Continent. The events of the last few months in Mexico, Peru, the Caraccas, and the Brazils, have nearly decided that both the Americas shall swell the preponderating catalogue of States administered under a system of government, founded upon a Republican or Democratic basis. The like spirit has been advancing in Europe with rapid strides; Spain and Portugal are in the very vortex of a similar convulsion. France fluctuates in her policy between extreme views and interests, both, in their very nature, seriously and perhaps equally menacing to her internal tranquillity: and Italy, including the King of Sardinia's dominions, though, for the time, recovered from the grasp of the Revolutionists, is held only by the presence of the Austrian Army of Occupation, and makes but very slow progress, as it is to be feared, in reconstructing such a native system of Government as may be competent to maintain against the Revolutionists an independent existence.

The same spirit has deeply mixed itself in the affairs of Greece. The insurrection throughout European Turkey, in its organization, in its objects, in its agency, and in its external relations, is in no respect distinguishable from the movements which have preceded it in Spain, Portugal, and Italy, except in the additional complications and embarrassments which it presents from being associated with the evils and mischiefs of another system of misrule, under the odium of which it seeks to cloak its real designs, to excite an interest, and thus to effectuate its final purpose.

In short, it is impossible that the Emperor should not see that the head of this revolutionary torrent is in Greece, that the tide is flowing in upon his southern provinces in almost an uninterrupted and continuous stream from the other side of the Atlantic; and it is upon this principle, and not upon local views of policy, that his Imperial Majesty will, I doubt not, as a statesman, regulate his conduct.

I am not now about to say what the British Government would do in such a case, because the principle upon which we must always act as a State is that of non-interference pushed even to an extreme; but sure I am that, if what is now passing in Greece, especially in the Morea, under the management of foreign adventurers, had shown itself in any other countries limitrophe to Russia, the Emperor would, ere this, have acted as he did when at Laybach, and no question with the Turks would have induced him to hesitate in opposing himself authoritatively, and in the first instance, to the common and more formidable enemy.

If I am right in regarding the revolutionary movement in Greece as the true danger, and that all the questions between

Russia and Turkey ought in truth to be regarded, at least for the moment, as merged in and subordinate in real importance, the question is, What course ought the Emperor in wisdom to pursue? I have said above, that, in any other case, his Imperial Majesty would decide at once, and, if necessary, act against the Greeks and in favour of the legitimate authority of the country.

In the particular case, that is more than can be expected or advised; nor could a Russian army move into Turkey to abate revolutionary danger, as the Austrian army did into the kingdom of Naples, without being involved in hostilities both with Turks and Greeks. If, then, the Emperor, in the special case, cannot repress by his own means the evil, it is an additional reason why his Imperial Majesty should not interfere to prevent the Ottoman Power from extinguishing the revolt, which menaces the general tranquillity not less than its own authority as a Government.

In contemplating the relative tendencies of the contending parties, whatever may be the views of the Turkish Power, it is, at least, exempt from the revolutionary danger. The cause of the Greeks is deeply and inevitably tainted with it, nor can it well, at least in these times, be separated from it. With all deference, the Emperor of Russia ought to disavow the Greek cause, as one become essentially revolutionary. His Imperial Majesty should rather favour than distract the exertions of the Ottoman Government for its suppression, and he ought to regard his differences with the Porte as of secondary importance, at least till the prevailing rebellion is suppressed. Then, and then only, can the Emperor safely bring the Turkish Government to an account, when his Imperial Majesty, without fostering revolutionary principles, may obtain redress for his own wrongs, as well as extend protection to the Greeks, no longer acting in open resistance to the sovereign power of their own State.

You may, if you think proper, read this letter in confidence to the Emperor; but I must entreat his Imperial Majesty to receive it with even more than his usual condescension and indulgence, that it may be regarded as conveying nothing more than my own hasty reflections, and consequently as entitled to no other consideration than the mere reasoning may appear to his Imperial Majesty to deserve.

I remain, my dear Sir, &c.,   LONDONDERRY.

Mr. Lionel Hervey to the Marquess of Londonderry.

Madrid, December 18, 1821.

My dear Marquess—The occurrences of the last ten days in the Cortes have, in the opinion of all moderate men, thrown indelible disgrace on that body, and the want of courage, want of good faith, want of judgment, of many Deputies have excited the disgust of all the real friends of their country. The Comte de Toreno, particularly, has acted with the greatest duplicity towards the Ministers, and, after having given them to understand that he would support them if they should apply to the Cortes for assistance, has left them in the lurch. Several others have acted in the same way. The whole rebellion of Cadiz and Seville was got up at Madrid, and the cry of alarm was the destitution of Riego. The reason, I believe, why the Ministers never gave any explanation on that head was, that he was implicated in the plot of Villamor, and that they wished to avoid any further discussion with the French Government, which had demanded that all the circumstances of that conspiracy should be made known to them, and that all the persons engaged in it should be brought to trial.

The circumstance most to be deplored in all this affair is the triumph of the violent party; for they have gained their object, which was to overthrow the present Administration; and every man of principle and of consistency should have voted with the Government, if it had been only to prevent the establishment of so dangerous an example. If the ensuing

Cortes were tolerably composed, the King might resist, but the great preponderance of the violent party in that body would render such an attempt very dangerous.

Mina has resigned his command at Corunna, and the authority of the Government is again completely established throughout the whole province of Gallicia. If the Ministers had possessed a little more courage, and had sent troops against Cadiz and Seville, instead of appealing to the Cortes, the same result might, I think, have been attained; but, as I before observed, they were decoyed into the net.

I have the honour to be, &c.,   LIONEL HERVEY.

MISCELLANEOUS.

Lord Clancarty to the Marquess of Londonderry.

The Hague, January 18, 1822.

My dear Lord—My despatch No. 5, of this date, will show you the result of all our endeavours to procure the detailed instructions of this Government to its Colonies. These, with some remains of that restiveness which has accompanied his Netherland Majesty through the whole of these discussions, he insisted should be furnished to me in Dutch. The translations accompanying them may, however, be relied upon, as they have been finally revised and corrected by M. Falck.

Falck is very anxious that these documents should not be laid before Parliament; and this is not to be wondered at, as more sorry pieces could scarcely have been composed. I therefore expect that, as soon as he shall have seen the King, so as to procure his sanction thereon, he will make me a proposal to apply to you to keep them back; but, as they were applied for for the very purpose of satisfying the Parliament and public of the loyalty of this Court that, on his authorized and full assurance to me of the King's intentions in all things hereafter to execute the treaty according to ours, its plain construction is that I should write a despatch to you to this effect, which he will probably propose should be laid before Parliament in lieu of the instructions.

This, *as far as I am concerned*, I shall be willing to comply with, notwithstanding the responsibility; because, from the solemn assertions I have already received from Falck privately that, as long as he shall be Minister of the Colonies, no breach of stipulation shall occur, and from similar assurances from Nagell, I really believe they mean in future to execute the treaty in all its parts. We shall see whether the King will chime in with Falck in authorizing this proposal; if he does, it will furnish an additional guarantee.

Ever yours most sincerely,   CLANCARTY.

Lord Clancarty to the Marquess of Londonderry.

The Hague, January 22, 1822.

My dear Lord—I have not yet heard anything further from Falck, about keeping back the instructions on the Slave Trade question from Parliament; so that, if he has seen the King, his Majesty has not condescended to his request. In fact, as Nagell acquaints me, the King imagines that Falck's anxiety to suppress these instructions proceeds merely from the reference made in his report to a private letter of the 22nd June, and of which his Majesty is aware that Falck has no copy to produce; and therefore, with that sub-acid humour by which his Majesty is sometimes governed, he has not the least wish to have his Colonial Minister spared from the humiliation of being shown up, for having referred to a private document in a public report, and to a private document of which he does not possess a copy. His Majesty seems quite to overlook the exposure of his own backwardness, or awkwardness, in the execution of his engagements, sufficiently apparent on the face of these papers. The papers are therefore quite at your service, to be laid or not to be laid before Parliament, according to your good pleasure.

Old Spaen writes from Vienna that the Porte is coming round to the terms of Russia. Consent has been given to the evacuation of Moldavia and Wallachia, as soon as the Russian forces shall be ready to retire from the frontier on their side; the re-establishment of Hospodars promised, when this can be done with safety, but that, from the present state of Constan-

tinople, the form and ceremonies made use of on these occasions
would be hazardous; the re-building of the Greek churches
likewise acceded to, as soon as the suppression of the rebellion
shall enable the same to be performed, &c.

He further writes that an instruction has been sent to the
Comte de Lieven, in answer to your despatch to Bagot of the
28th October last, from Hanover. Possibly you may think it
advisable to have a copy of the correspondence transmitted to
me for confidential communication, rather than that perhaps
false impressions should be created concerning its substance,
by representations at second-hand.

The Portuguese Minister here, (under recall, but not yet
absolutely superseded) acquaints me that Austria and Russia
have refused to receive Chargés d'Affaires from his Court. I
know not on what authority he states this: his correspondence
with those his chiefs now in power has not been active, still
less, I believe, confidential, under the late newly erected order
of things. Should it prove true, the measure seems an absurd
one, not only from its impotence to effect good, but from its
evil tendency in marking a difference in political proceeding
with France and England respecting the Peninsular Powers,
under present circumstances.

We have no news from London later than the 15th instant.

Yours most affectionately,   CLANCARTY.

The Hon. Robert Gordon to the Marquess of Londonderry.

Vienna, March 25, 1822.

My dear Lord—Nothing could be more tranquillizing than
the language held by M. de Tatitscheff, after perusing the
Turkish note; and if he is sincere and well informed of his
master's sentiments, we have not much to fear from the communication of the said note at St. Petersburgh.

Owing to my confinement to the house for several days,
Prince Metternich made me acquainted with the result of his

interview with the Russian Ministers upon this subject, by the few lines which I take the liberty to enclose. They will show your lordship how perfectly satisfactory was M. de Tatitscheff's reply upon this occasion.

The good points in the Turkish Note, if any exist, have completely failed in their effect here. Lord Strangford's copy differs materially from that presented to Count Lützow, which has discomfited Austria and may inflame Russia. Whether the difference be owing to a personal respect for Lord Strangford, or to a personal disrespect to Count Lützow, (for such is known to be their relative positions with regard to the Porte) it is difficult to determine, but the evil consequences are the same.

It is difficult to form a correct idea upon what may be the results of M. de Tatitscheff's mission, or to regard what has yet passed between him and Prince Metternich as anything more than so much preliminary conversation. Your lordship will shortly receive more of the Prince's voluminous reports, all extremely satisfactory, and according to which M. de Tatitscheff seems to have abandoned one false position after another with consummate good-will; but his language in other quarters is anything but extremely temperate; and, until he gives proofs of his acquiescence in Prince Metternich's arguments by his signature, we can hardly calculate upon possessing all the good which has been promised to us from his mission.

Count Bernstorf is blamed here for having too precipitately bound himself to an agreement by protocol, in which he partially sanctions what will be refused at Vienna. It is admitted that the salvo of doing nothing but in concert with the Allies renders this step of the Prussian Cabinet sufficiently harmless, but Prince Metternich says it should not have been taken without previous recourse to this very concert. A long despatch, with much ingenious *raisonnement*, has been addressed to the Prussian Cabinet, which, with the despatches to Constantinople and St. Petersburgh, now in hand, will be forwarded all together to Prince Esterhazy in a few days. I have not thought it prudent to wait so long for an opportunity to forward to your lordship the intelligence which has given rise to them.

I have the honour to be, &c.,   R. GORDON.

[Enclosure.]

Prince Metternich to the Hon. Robert Gordon.

Vienne, 21 Mars, 1822.

Je m'empresse, mon cher Gordon, de vous informer du résultat de mon entretien de ce jour avec MM. les Envoyés de Russie.

Après leur avoir fait part des intentions de sa Majesté Impériale sur la question que vous connoissez, et que M. de T. a entièrement approuvée, j'ai engagé ces MM. à faire la lecture de la note Turque. Cette lecture finie, M. de T. me dit qu'il connoissait trop les vues et les intentions de l'Empereur son maître pour pouvoir assûrer, sans crainte d'être démenti par l'évènement que sa Majesté Impériale regarderoit, ainsi que nous, cette pièce comme non avenue ; que ce n'étoit pas dans la conduite diplomatique Ottomane que sa Majesté puiserait ses conseils, mais qu'elle se maintiendrait sur le terrain de ses Alliés pour arriver à la pacification, pourvu que ceux-ci ne l'abandonnassent pas.

En vous disant ceci, j'ai réduit en une phrase ce que M. de T. m'a dit ce matin, et ce qu'il m'a répété ce soir, quand je l'ai prévenu que j'allois me rendre chez l'Empereur, afin de lui rendre compte de notre entretien du matin. Je passerai chez vous demain, et vous rendrai un compte plus détaillé d'un entretien qui n'a pas un seul instant dévié de la ligne de la plus parfaite modération. Je n'ai pas voulu vous laisser vous creuser la tête la nuit, et c'est dans cette intention que je vous écris encore ce soir.

T. a. v.   ————————   METTERNICH.

Mr. Lionel Hervey to the Marquess of Londonderry.

Madrid, April 6, 1822.

My dear Marquess—The conduct of Alava and of the friends of order in the Cortes, without some explanation, may not appear to be distinguished by that moderation which they profess to make the rule of their actions; but the fact is that they are all exceedingly disgusted by the participation of the King in the different insurrections in the provinces, and his negociations with the French Government for their interference.

These circumstances are generally known, and have excited great alarm amongst all the friends of the Constitution. On the one side they are threatened with a counter-revolution, on the other with the triumph of the republican party—for a republic is, I believe, the ultimate aim of Riego's faction. Their distrust of the King, and his notorious aversion to the Constitution, prevent them from attacking this faction in the Cortes with all the arguments and all the force of which they might otherwise avail themselves; and the disturbances in the different provinces, which still continue, give a colour to all the assertions of the violent party as to the danger to which the Constitution is exposed, and as to the intrigues of the Serviles.

The conduct of the French Government is to me inexplicable, unless they have been deceived by the accounts which they have received from this country; for no measures could be more calculated to continue the anarchy which at present prevails here, and to prevent any modification of the Constitution, than those they have adopted. It is known to this Government that supplies in money, arms, and ammunition, have been sent from France, and that great encouragement was held out to the King of French interference, in the event of his being able to form anything like an army: and I must again repeat that, as long there is a possibility of foreign interference, Spain will not be tranquillized; nor can any attempt be made by those who are convinced of the necessity of such a measure, to revise and amend the Constitution.

I must say in confidence to your lordship that " the King—the King's to blame;" and that, until his Majesty can be induced to change his conduct, nothing will go on well. His Majesty is very angry with us at present, and he has been led to believe that we prevented the armed interference of France.

I have the honour to be, &c.,   LIONEL HERVEY.

Lord Burghersh to the Marquess of Londonderry.

London, April, 1822.

My dear Lord Londonderry—During the Congress of Lay-bach, I received a private letter from Gordon, in which it was stated that the Note I had presented to the Courts I was accredited to, and which set forth the declarations contained in your Circular of the 19th of January, 1821, having been transmitted from Modena to Prince Metternich, he had accused me of having *renforcé*'d the attack made against the Allied principles, and of having misrepresented your meaning in my translation. This story appeared to me to rest upon premises so entirely false, that, although I answered Gordon in a private letter, yet, believing the accusation could not seriously be intended, I did not think it worth while to give any official contradiction to it, or to write to you upon the subject.

I afterwards heard the same story from Pozzo di Borgo, when I contented myself with placing the document in his hands, as a satisfactory refutation. But à Court now tells me that the same history was related to him at Naples. It has, therefore, really acquired a consistency that, both in duty to myself and to you, whose faithful agent I have as yet flattered myself to have been, I feel I am called upon to bring this *tangible* accusation against me to some issue. I therefore enclose you a copy of the Note I presented, which exists in your office, together with the original Circular, and I beg of you to cast

your eye over it, and to judge whether the accusation is truly
or falsely made.   If the latter, I hope you will have the goodness to direct the matter to be cleared up at Vienna and at
Naples; for it is really a charge which, if not merited, I
should not be stained with.   I enclose you à Court's Note, by
which you will perceive that he heard the story from D'Oubril.

Believe me, &c.,   BURGHERSH.

[Enclosure.]

Florence, 8 Fevrier, 1821.

Afin d'éloigner toute impression erronée sur les sentimens
du Gouvernement Britannique, et qui peut avoir été produite,
quoique sans intention par une Note circulaire adressée par les
Cabinets d'Autriche, de Prusse, et de Russie à leurs missions,
sous le titre d' "Apperçu des premiers résultats des Conférences
de Troppau," le Soussigné, Ministre de sa Majesté Britannique en Toscane, a reçu l'ordre de signifier à son Excellence
le Chevalier Fossombroni, Ministre des Affaires Étrangères
de son Altesse Impériale et Royale le Grand Duc, que le Roi,
son Maître, s'est trouvé dans la nécessité de se dispenser de
devenir partie, tant à l'établissement des principes énoncés
pour le règlement de la conduite politique future des Alliés
dans la dite Note, comme aux mesures, qu'on se propose de
prendre en vertu de ces principes contre l'état actuel des choses
à Naples.

Ces mesures seraient en répugnance aux loix fondamentales
de l'Angleterre; mais, même si cette objection décisive n'ex-
istait point, le Gouvernement Britannique envisagerait les
principes sur lesquels elles reposent, comme de nature à n'être
point admis comme système de lois pour régler les affaires
entre des nations indépendantes.   Il est d'opinion que leur
adoption sanctionnerait, et, dans les mains de souverains moins
bienfaisans, pourraient ci-après donner lieu à une intervention
plus fréquente et plus étendue dans les transactions intérieures
d'autres États; qui, certes, n'est l'intention des augustes Souve-

rains, par lesquels leur adoption est aujourd'hui réclamée—
intervention qui ne saurait se réconcilier ni avec la dignité ni
l'autorité efficace de Princes indépendants.

Le Gouvernement Britannique ne regarde point l'Alliance
comme ayant le droit, en vertu des traités existants, de se
revêtir sous leur caractère d'Alliés de pouvoirs aussi illimités
que ceux que viendraient à sanctionner les principes énoncés.
Il conçoit aussi peu, que les cinq puissances, par une nouvelle
transaction diplomatique quelconque se puissent approprier une
influence si extraordinaire sans s'attribuer une suprématie incompatible avec les droits des autres États (ou même étant
investies de cette influence par l'accession spéciale de ces Etats)
sans introduire en Europe un système fédératif, lequel non-
seulement deviendrait par son extension ingouvernable et
inefficace, mais qui conduirait aussi à de graves inconvéniens.

Pour ce qui regarde le cas particulier de Naples, le Gouvernement Britannique n'hésita point dès le premier moment
à exprimer sa forte désapprobation de la manière, et des circonstances sous lesquelles cette révolution fut censée avoir
été effectuée, mais au même tems déclara expressément aux
Cours Alliées, qu'il ne se regarderait ni autorisé ni justifié à
conseiller l'intervention de la Grande Bretagne : il admet
cependant que les autres États Européens, surtout l'Autriche
et les Puissances Italiennes, pouvaient se trouver dans une
position différente, et déclara que ce n'était pas son intention
de préjuger la question comme elle pouvait leur affecter, ou de
s'entremêler des moyens que tels États pourraient juger nécessaires d'employer pour leur propre sécurité, pourvu toujours
que les assurances nécessaires fussent données qu'aucune vue
d'agrandissement subversive du système territorial de l'Europe
établi dans les derniers traités ne fut en contemplation.   C'est
sur ces principes que la conduite du Gouvernement Britannique
à l'egard de la révolution de Naples a été, dès le premier moment, uniformément basée.   En suite de quoi, les copies des
instructions envoyées aux autorités Britanniques à Naples

ont été de tems en tems transmises aux Gouvernements Alliés.

Dans la Note circulaire, mentionnée au commencement de cette dépêche, on paraît s'attendre à l'accession des cours de Londres et de Paris aux mesures proposées, fondées, comme on allègue, sur les traités existans.   Pour justifier sa bonne foi, le Gouvernement Britannique, en se dispensant d'y consentir, doit protester contre une telle interprétation de ces traités.   Il ne les a jamais regardés comme imposants de telles obligations, et en plusieurs occasions, aussi bien au Parlement comme dans ses correspondances avec les Cours Alliées, il a toujours soutenu la négative d'une telle proposition.

Qu'il a toujours agi explicitement à ce sujet paraîtra par les délibérations de Paris, en 1815; avant la conclusion du Traité d'Alliance d'Aix-la-Chapelle, en 1818; et dernièrement en certaines discussions qui ont eu lieu dans le courant de l'année passée.

Le Gouvernement Britannique, après avoir éloigné toute mésinterprétation à laquelle la Note circulaire aurait pu donner lieu, et après avoir déclaré qu'il ne peut adhérer aux principes sur lesquels elle est basée, déclare cependant qu'il est prêt à soutenir le droit qu'a tout État d'intervenir là où sa propre sûreté, ou ses intérêts immédiats sont mis en danger par les mouvemens intérieurs d'un autre État; mais comme il regarde l'adoption d'un tel droit comme ne pouvant être justifié et réglé, que par la nécessité la plus absolue, il ne peut admettre que ce droit soit appliqué en général à tous mouvemens révolutionnaires; ou que, sans égard à leur rapport avec d'autres États, ils puissent devenir prospectivement la base d'une alliance.   Il regarde l'exercice de ce droit comme une exception aux principes, de la plus haute importance, et qui ne peut naître que de circonstances immédiates.   Les exceptions de cette nature ne pourront jamais, sans le plus grand danger, être adoptées comme règle de la diplomatie ordinaire, ou introduites dans les Instituts de la Loi de Nations.

En faisant cette déclaration, le Gouvernement Britannique rend justice à la pureté des intentions, qui ont sans doute dirigé les Cours Alliées dans l'adoption des mesures qu'elles poursuivent : la diversité d'opinion qui existe entre elles et la Cour de Londres à cette occasion ne peut faire aucun changement dans la cordialité et l'harmonie de l'Alliance sur tout autre objet, ni ne peut diminuer le zèle avec lequel elle concourira au maintien de tous ses engagemens existans.

Le Soussigné saisit, &c.,   BURGHERSH.

The Rev. Dr. Poynter to the Marquess of Londonderry.

4, Castle Street, Holborn, April 9, 1822.

My Lord—By the advice of the Honourable Commissioners for liquidating the claims of British subjects on the French Government, I do myself the honour to address myself to your lordship, and to solicit your lordship's kind aid, for the purpose of removing an obstacle that retards their proceedings in liquidating a claim of great importance which I have regularly presented in the name of the Rev. John Daniel, British subject, the rightful claimant.

The object of the present claim is the recovery of property in the French funds, which was all purchased with English money, and which is destined for the education of Catholic clergy for England. It was formerly employed for that purpose in the English secular College at Douay, and is intended to be employed in like manner, for the future, in England.

The Honourable Commissioners, from whom I have experienced the most kind attention, inform me that certain certificates which they have called for, in order to enable them to proceed in settling this claim, have been refused them by the French Government.

It is understood that this refusal is grounded on the opposition made by a Board called the *Bureau gratuit*, which claims the administration of the property belonging to our British seminaries, which were formerly established in France for ecclesiastical education.

Although the Honourable Commissioners have declared that, in case I (who am the representative of the Rev. John Daniel, the claimant) should be deprived of this property by the effect of the opposition which is made, the property will never be awarded by them to the *Bureau gratuit*, which has raised the opposition, since that Bureau is not composed of British subjects, it has no documents to produce in favour of its claim, and it had no part in the administration of this property previously to the epoch of its confiscation, in 1793—still, under the present circumstances, the Honourable Commissioners wish to be favoured with your lordship's directions how to proceed.

I beg to observe to your lordship that the Presidents of the English secular College at Douay, who had the administration of this money till the period of the French Revolution, were never subject to the control of any Board, nor were they responsible for their administration to any authority in France —that this property was confiscated *as British property*, in consequence of a decree of October 10, 1793—that the *Bureau gratuit*, which now claims the administration of it, to the exclusion of English superiors, originated in the Bureau established by Bonaparte, in 1806, for the administration of the property, and for the government of English, Irish, and Scotch Catholic Seminaries in France, which he consolidated in his " United British Establishment," at the head of which he placed Messrs. Walsh, Ferris, &c.—that this Bureau has succeeded, by various means, in retaining sufficient power to keep possession of the immoveable property which *exists* in France belonging to our English seminaries, and is now pretending to the administration of this funded property which I am claiming through our Honourable Commissioners.

I beg leave to submit to your lordship that, as neither the French Government, nor any Board or authority established by the French Government, ever exercised or claimed any control over the administration or employment of this money before the Revolution, it seems peculiarly hard that, after the Government, at the time of the Revolution, had destroyed our English seminaries, had confiscated the property which was attached to them, and had imprisoned the Superiors, *because they were British subjects*, a new Board, which originated in Bonaparte's hostile views against England, which has alienated above £5,000 of our ecclesiastical British property from its proper destination, should now be allowed to stop the progress of my regular claim, under the pretence that it should have the administration of this money.

I conceive, my Lord, that by the arrangements made for the execution of the Treaty and Convention, for which we are so highly indebted to your lordship, this money, being British property, is now taken out of the hands of the French Government, and placed in the hands of our honourable British Commissioners, who will do justice to British subjects. It was proposed to me by the Honourable Commissioners, in the month of August last, in the view of obtaining the aid of his Majesty's Government for the recovery of this property, that the English Catholic Bishops, Vicars Apostolic, should make a declaration that this property which I am claiming shall in future be employed in ecclesiastical education in England, and not in France. I delivered a declaration to this effect, duly signed, to the Honourable Commissioners, without delay, that it might be presented to Mr. Hamilton. I received an answer that our declaration was completely satisfactory.

I therefore think myself justified in considering this important claim as being entirely in the hands of his Majesty's Government and of the British Commissioners, and in saying that the property claimed is in no manner subject to the control of any authority supported or allowed by the French Government.

In these circumstances, I most earnestly and confidently implore your lordship's aid and commands, to forward the proceedings of the Honourable Commissioners in liquidating this claim, and I pray that your lordship will be graciously pleased to inform our Honourable Commissioners in what light they should view the opposition of the *Bureau gratuit*, and to do what your lordship may deem proper to remove every obstacle to the justice of my claim.

My lord, I beg permission to represent to your lordship that this funded property in question comprises the greatest part of what all the English Vicars Apostolic have to depend upon for the education of their clergy. If we lose this, we shall be nearly ruined. We have been amongst the greatest sufferers from the French Revolution, in point of property; not to speak of our personal hardships, *quorum pars magna fui*. We have received no relief to indemnify us, as other sufferers have. The Irish Roman Catholic Bishops have been relieved by the liberal annual grant to Maynooth College. We do not ask Government or Parliament to relieve us from the public Treasury; we only ask that your lordship will be pleased to protect us, and to see justice done us in the recovery of what is our own. In full confidence in your lordship's liberal dispositions, and with sentiments of gratitude for the kind attention I have personally received from your lordship, I have the honour to be, respectfully, &c.,

WILLIAM POYNTER, V. A., London.

May I presume to request the honour of a few minutes' audience on this subject, on which I feel deeply interested, at any time most convenient to your lordship?

Robert Sutherland, Esq., to the Marquess of Londonderry.

Osborne's Hotel, May 2, 1822.

My Lord—I have the honour to enclose for your perusal the Proclamation of the President of Hayti, on becoming possessed of the Spanish part of Santo Domingo. This I had anticipated and stated in a former communication. This extraordinary revolution has been brought about without the firing of a shot, and there can be little doubt of the whole of that vast island continuing in a state of perfect tranquillity under its present Government.

It would be well that his Majesty's Government were acquainted with the true state of affairs in Hayti, inasmuch as it regarded its own character. I therefore think I cannot discharge a more faithful duty than that of placing it in your lordship's power to know some circumstances which may be of service to you in the event of the present state of St. Domingo becoming a subject of inquiry.

In the first place, I deny the possibility of France ever becoming possessed of that island. I also deny, from my intimate knowledge of their politics, the possibility of France making any arrangement with the Government of Hayti, without a distinct acknowledgment of their independence. In respect to a proposition which had been made through some indirect agents of France for the purchase of their independence, the Government of Hayti would never listen to it, knowing well that France cannot, either at the present or at a future period, make any successful attempt against them. It would, in my opinion, be the wisest policy for France to acknowledge their independence.

In regard to our own relations with that island, there is one particular point to which I beg to draw the attention of your lordship. The Haytians suppose that his Majesty's Government are inimical towards them; they even allege that the British Ambassador at the French Court entered his protest against the recognition of their independence by the French Government. This has been cautiously circulated amongst them by secret French agents. They go still further, and believe that the inimical views of his Majesty's Government are only thwarted by a certain party in this country, which the Haytians call Philanthropists, and which we know here by the appellation of Saints.

These impressions I always exerted myself to remove, but unfortunately circumstances justified in some measure their suspicions : for instance, the British merchants in that country are often engaged in contraband transactions, and do not, in many instances, submit to the laws under which they are bound to carry on their mercantile speculations ; and, when interfered with by the Haytian Government, the cry is always, I am an English citizen—these gentlemen supposing, because they are English citizens, they have the privilege of transgressing the laws of the country into which they have voluntarily searched for speculation ; and upon the Government of that country's enforcing an adherence to their laws, they (the merchants) immediately apply to the Admiral upon the Jamaica station for a man-of-war, who, ignorant of the true cause of the complaint, immediately interferes.　A man-of-war appears in the ports of Hayti to demand redress for grievances that, in fact, never existed, and grievances that the Government of Hayti have greater cause to demand redress for than the other party.　The consequence is that, after threats and exultation on the part of the merchants, his Majesty's flag leaves the ports of that country in a way more sufficient to excite contempt than any other feeling.

During my residence in Hayti, I have known circumstances of aggravation on our own part scarcely to be believed ; and, had not the Government of that country been of a mild—indeed, too mild—a disposition, we should have lost our friendly footing there long ere now.　I merely state myself in these strong terms to give your lordship an idea of the strong impression that our own conduct in that island had upon my mind ; and, instead of gaining their affections, we have considerably lost them, although the Haytians would prefer being on terms with us than any other nation.

I will now beg leave to contrast the conduct of the Americans with that of ours.　The Americans have always been detested by the Haytians, yet, by their conciliatory conduct, have they gained a friendly footing in Hayti, and are now looked upon as the only true and sincere friends the Haytians have. They (the Americans) have had an agent there for some years, and will, no doubt, in the course of time, have three millions sterling in their funds, which, if we had adopted the same policy, would have been before now in the British funds.

I shall now beg leave to call the attention of your lordship to the situation in which we shall be placed, in the event of a rupture with America. It cannot but be known to you that the Haytians are in possession of the harbour of the Mole, which is the finest and the most important in the West Indies, and the key to the Windward Passage, and which the Americans will, without doubt, as they are insinuating themselves into the affections of the Haytians, endeavour to turn to their advantage. Considering the present state of South America, considering the state and situation of our own colonies, I would most seriously recommend the present situation of Hayti to his Majesty's Government; and the least advance to them by us would be hailed by them with great satisfaction, and not fail to gain their esteem and attachment. In regard to their endeavouring to molest our colonies, it is totally out of the question: their policy is that of internal regulation and defence, and to any attempt of that kind they must be instigated by America. Their Constitution, to which they strictly adhere, forbids any interference beyond their own coast.

I would rejoice at his Majesty's Government showing some mark of attention and consideration to that rising country; and its going directly as a boon from the Government would remove many ideas derogatory to its character, which, amongst a people who have so successfully struggled for independence, which they are now able to maintain, may become, at a future period, of more consequence than we are at present inclined to attach to it.

Your lordship will do me the honour to admit this as a private and confidential communication.

My lord, I have the honour to be, &c.,

ROBERT SUTHERLAND.

Sir Charles Bagot to the Marquess of Londonderry.

St. Petersburgh, May 16-28, 1822.

My dear Lord—The Messenger Ellis, with your lordship's despatches of the 29th of last month, arrived at Berlin without hearing anything of Count Lieven's courier. He proceeded to Memel, where he waited for him some hours, and then came on to St. Petersburgh, where he arrived more than two days before M. de Smirnove, who, it appears, did not leave London till the morning of the 3rd. Notwithstanding this, your lordship will see by my despatches that it so happened that I had no opportunity of making any communication to Count Nesselrode of the contents of those which I had received by Ellis, till after this Government had received the despatches of Count Lieven, which, I believe, you had wished to be the case.

Your lordship will see, by my despatch to Lord Strangford, in what manner, but with how little effect, I had an occasion incidentally to press upon this Government the measures which I was instructed to suggest by your Lordship's despatches Nos. 7 and 8. Count Nesselrode's reasoning upon that subject is fully stated in my despatch No. 27. I hope, however, that the course which affairs have now taken here may make my failure in this point a matter of less regret.

I have little to add to my public despatch in explanation of the motives which have induced me to lend myself to the proceedings which are there reported. I hope that they may be found sufficient for my justification; but I may here say, what I could not say in a more official form—that, at the moment when Count Nesselrode made his proposal to me, I was, as I am now, so satisfied that, barring very unforeseen accidents, the determination of the Emperor was absolutely taken not to have war, that I felt that, under the general spirit of your lordship's instructions, it must be my duty to lend myself to any course which might afford the Russian Government a handsome way out of the difficulties into which their former language had brought them.

Your lordship will observe that, in my note to Count Nesselrode, communicating to him the substance of Lord Strangford's last despatches, I make mention of the information which Lord Strangford reports himself, in his No. 56, to have received— that the Turkish Government had already agreed to nominate a Plenipotentiary.

A private letter from Lord Strangford, of the 30th of April, tells me that he was far from thinking that matter to be sufficiently advanced, or sufficiently approved by the Divan, to enable him to reckon upon it with much certainty. I mentioned the circumstance to Count Nesselrode, in conversation, but we agreed in opinion that we had better not do so in my written communication.

Lord Strangford asks me, in his private letter, what is the correspondence with the Grand Visir, to which reference is made in his despatch No. 61 to your lordship. I am utterly unable to answer his question. I know nothing of it; but I can well conceive that it may have been connected with some intrigue of those, whose power upon this particular question is now no longer to be dreaded.

At the express desire of Count Nesselrode, I have written privately to Lord Strangford, to request that he will exert his influence in the choice of a Turkish Plenipotentiary, if the Porte should agree to send one, and that he will endeavour to take care that a person of becoming station and rank is selected for the office. Due attention will be shown to this point by the Emperor; and it is essential that no person of a subaltern description should be nominated by the Turkish Government.

· Mr. Gordon, in his private letter, of which mention is made in my despatch No. 30, seems to say that the proposals made by this Court to the Cabinet of Vienna respecting Spain are believed to be the work of Count Capodistrias, for purposes which, it is thought, are seen through. I believe that there is no real ground for this opinion. The idea, whatever it may be, is, I am well assured, the Emperor's, and his alone. It did not originate with any of his Ministers, and I am taught to believe that none of them are friendly to it.

> I have the honour to be, &c.,
> CHARLES BAGOT.

Captain Irby, R.N., to the Marquess of Londonderry.

2, Park Crescent, Portland Place, May 31, 1822.

My Lord—In laying the accompanying statement before your lordship, I have to assure you that I am actuated solely by a sense of duty towards those who have served under me, and whose interests I am bound to assist.

As an application is about to be made to the Lords of the Treasury on this subject, I have, from the above motives, to solicit your lordship's attention to the case, if brought forward, and have the honour to be, &c.,

> FREDERICK PAUL IRBY,
> Captain Royal Navy.

Statement of the Claims of certain Naval Officers employed on the coast of Africa in the years 1811, 1812, 1813, 1814, and 1815.

On the 19th of February, 1810, a treaty was entered into between Great Britain and Portugal, for limiting and restraining the Portuguese Slave Trade. From that time to the 22nd of January, 1815, when a new Convention was entered into on the subject, the above treaty continued

H H 2

to be communicated by the Lords of the Admiralty to
the different naval officers stationed on the coast of Africa,
as the rule which, in conjunction with our own abolition
laws, was to regulate their proceedings in suppressing the
Slave Trade.

The peculiar importance attached by his Majesty's Government to the effectual suppression of this trade, and the urgency
with which the attention of the naval officers on the African
station was directed to that object, will appear by the following
extract from the instructions addressed to them by the Lords
Commissioners of the Admiralty, viz.—

" You are hereby required and directed to employ yourself
and the vessels under your command very diligently in looking
into the several bays and creeks between Cape Verd and the
coast of Benguela, particularly on the Gold Coast, Whidah,
the Bight of Benin, and Angola, (except such settlements as
are in the possession of the Portuguese) for the purpose of
seizing such ships and vessels as are liable thereto, under the
authority of the several acts of Parliament above mentioned,
(abstracts of which, together with several other papers on the
subject, are sent herewith for your information) and which may
be discovered carrying on, or proceeding to carry on the traffic
in Slaves; and you are to use every other means in your
power to prevent a continuance thereof, and to give full effect
to the Acts of Parliament in question."

In consequence of these instructions, many foreign Slave
ships were detained by his Majesty's ships of war and colonial
armed vessels stationed on the coast of Africa, and were condemned in the Vice-Admiralty Court of Sierra Leone; the
Slaves found on board being condemned to his Majesty, and
the ships, with their cargoes, to the captors. In a great majority of these cases, however, the grounds of condemnation
were considered by the superior Courts of Prize in this country
to be invalid, and, on that account, not only has his Majesty's
Government refused to pay to the captors the bounty assigned

by Act of Parliament for Slaves so condemned, but the proceeds of the vessels and their cargoes have been appropriated to the Crown.

It must, of course, be assumed that the superior Courts of Prize, in reversing the judgments of the Court of Vice-Admiralty, and appropriating the proceeds of the captures to the Crown, as well as in refusing the bounties on Slaves, correctly interpreted the law of the case. The main difficulty in the construction of that law appears to have arisen from the ambiguity with which the Portuguese treaty above referred to was framed, and which rendered it difficult to fix its true import. The capturing officers, however, were not left entirely to follow their own views of its bearing. The Government, from whom their instructions proceeded, thought it right to explain what they conceived to be the line of duty required by these instructions, and more especially what they conceived to be the conduct prescribed by the Portuguese treaty.

This explanation was communicated to them by the Lords Commissioners of the Admiralty, and was contained in a letter addressed to their lordships by his Majesty's Secretary of State for Foreign Affairs, to the following effect, viz.—

                    "Foreign Office, May 6, 1813.

"My Lords—In consideration of complaints received from the Government of Portugal, respecting certain seizures of Portuguese ships employed in carrying Slaves from the coast of Africa, I am commanded by his Royal Highness the Prince Regent to desire that your lordships will be pleased to instruct his Majesty's cruisers not to molest Portuguese ships carrying Slaves *bonâ fide* on the account and risk of Portuguese subjects from ports of Africa belonging to the Crown of Portugal to the Brazils; but, by this instruction, it is by no means intended that vessels as hereafter described should not be brought in for adjudication, viz.—

"1. A Portuguese ship, bound from a Portuguese port in

Africa, with a cargo of Slaves, to any port not subject to the Prince Regent of Portugal.

" 2. Any Portuguese ship bound to, or having taken her departure, with a cargo of Slaves, from any port in Africa not under the dominion of the Crown of Portugal.

" 3. Any Portuguese ship, the property on board of which, being a cargo of Slaves, is other than Portuguese.

" 4. Any ship whatever, laden with Slaves, wherein the ship or the Slaves are, in whole or in part, the property of a British subject, or of a citizen of the United States.

" 5. Any ship bearing the Portuguese flag which shall have been fitted up for the conveyance of Slaves at a British port, or of which the commander or other superior officer shall be a British subject, or a citizen of the United States.

" In order to prevent any misapprehension of what is to be considered a Portuguese vessel, it will be necessary to add that the 5th Article of the Treaty of Commerce with Portugal, of 1810, which defines what shall be considered as a Portuguese ship, applies only to ships claiming entry in British ports, under the favourable duties stipulated in that treaty : it was never intended to confine the trade of Portugal in all parts of the world to ships of that description, much less to expose to capture, by that construction of the treaty, on the high seas all other ships claiming to be Portuguese.

" With respect to what is to be considered as Portuguese territory on the coast of Africa, your lordships will be pleased to direct the naval officers to attend as strictly as possible to the tenour of the 10th Article of the Alliance with Portugal, until some farther regulations shall be agreed upon between the two countries.

" I have the honour to be, &c.,

" CASTLEREAGH.

" To the Lords Commisssioners of the Admiralty."

It is obvious that every naval officer receiving such instructions was bound to conform himself to them, and that, if he had failed to do so, he would have justly incurred censure, as having neglected his duty.

Many vessels, however, were detained, in strict conformity, as is conceived, with the principles laid down in the above letter of his Majesty's Secretary of State, and condemned in the Vice-Admiralty Court, whose sentences have since been reversed by the superior Courts of Prize in this country, and the bounties refused, on the ground that the detention and condemnation were nevertheless illegal; those Courts explicitly declaring that their decisions could not be influenced by the construction which his Majesty's Government might put upon treaties, but must be guided solely by the view which they themselves took, not only of such treaties, but of the law of nations generally, as applicable to the case.

But although the decision of the Courts may show that the construction put upon the treaties by his Majesty's Government was erroneous, and that the captures, though made in strict accordance with such construction, were therefore illegal, yet some consideration seems due to the case of the officers and crews of his Majesty's ships, who punctually executed the orders they had received.

The officers and men engaged in this service were led to expect that certain rewards would follow the faithful and zealous performance of the duties entrusted to them. They relied not only on having the whole of the proceeds of their prizes distributed among them, but also on a bounty of £40 for each man, £30 for each woman, and £10 for each child, whom they might liberate, agreeably to the tenour of the Abolition Acts. Of these rewards, however, they have been entirely deprived, not through any fault of theirs, for, on the contrary, they adhered with the utmost fidelity to the instructions of their superiors.

Nor was the service on which they were employed a light and easy service: on the contrary, it was one of great and imminent peril, not only to health but to life. Many individuals fell victims, through their exertions on the coast and in the rivers of Africa, to the diseases of the climate, and many acquired there the seeds of maladies which have since continued to afflict them. In the case of his Majesty's ship Amelia, Commodore Irby, not only did the officers and crew suffer severely in their health, from the zeal with which they prosecuted the task assigned them by their superiors, but they had to sustain, on finally quitting the coast, and while in an enfeebled and emaciated state, an action with a French frigate of superior force, having a crew fresh from Europe and in high health; in which action every officer on board the Amelia was either killed or wounded, and a large proportion of the crew suffered severely. The opposing force consisted of two frigates of the largest class, one of which, however, struck upon a rock —a fact which (as the action took place in the night) was unknown at the time to Commodore Irby, who was in the expectation every moment of seeing her come up to the aid of her consort. Still, however, the consequence of this unequal conflict was that one of the French frigates was lost, and the other so disabled, that the whole purport of their mission was frustrated.

And, while the officers and crews of his Majesty's ships experienced such severe sufferings in this service, the country has reaped considerable benefit from their exertions. Through their means a very considerable number of Africans were liberated from captivity. Many of these served to recruit our regiments in the West Indies and Africa, and thus to provide effectually for the defence of those colonies, while they spared that lavish expenditure of European life which their defence would otherwise have occasioned, and the remainder were added to the population of the colony of Sierra Leone, where, while they have themselves become an industrious, moral, and thriving class of colonists, deriving freedom, and civilization, and Christian knowledge, from the change they have undergone, they have imparted to the colony the benefits of their strength and exertions, and have very materially contributed to its present growth and prosperity.

But, notwithstanding the sufferings thus incurred in the active and faithful discharge of their duties, and the national benefits which have flowed from their exertions and sacrifices, and although conscious of acting in strict conformity to their instructions, they were led to form a sanguine and not unreasonable hope of enjoying the rewards they believed to be attached to such services, they have hitherto derived from them no advantage whatever. The whole of the proceeds of their prizes have been appropriated to the Crown; all bounty on the Slaves they liberated has been refused; and they have been subjected besides not only to severe and bitter disappointment, but to actual loss, exclusive of any liability to damages for the presumed illegality of their conduct.

If, however, their conduct, though held to be illegal by the Courts of Prize, was, as is maintained, in strict conformity to the orders under which they acted, then, although they may have no legal claim to indemnity, their case seems one which calls peculiarly for the equitable and liberal consideration of his Majesty's Government. It is therefore submitted, under all the circumstances of their meritorious services, that, in every case of the detention of a Slave ship, in which it shall appear to his Majesty's Government that they have acted agreeably to the tenour of their instructions, and in particular of Lord Castlereagh's letter, above referred to, they may be entitled to a moiety of the proceeds which have been appropriated to the Crown, and to a bounty of £10 a head on the Slaves they have liberated.

Such a decision on the part of his Majesty's Government, though it would fall far short of the measure of the just expectations of the captors, at the time they were engaged with so much vigour and cordiality in carrying into effect the humane purposes of their superiors, would be received by them all with the utmost gratitude, while it would be the means of alleviating the sufferings of many of the officers and men, and of ministering to the wants of many a widowed and orphan family.

If his Majesty's Government should deem this case to be one which has a just claim to their consideration, it is further submitted that the most eligible means of providing for it would be to introduce into Dr. Lushington's Slave Consolidation Bill a clause to the following effect, viz.

Lord Clancarty to the Marquess of Londonderry.

Garbally, June 3, 1822.

My dear Lord—I received the letter of which the enclosed is a copy yesterday from Mr. Eliot, the father of one of my attachés. As it seems the subject has not yet been communicated to you, I think it right to apprise you of it as soon as possible.

We shall all regret young Eliot's absence from us, both as a companion and as an efficient co-labourer with us. I have so written to Lord St. Germans, at the same time interposing no obstacle on my part to the execution of the project, which, however, does not seem to have been hitherto communicated to the principal object of it, and who, when he comes to be made acquainted with it, may possibly consider himself entitled to remonstrate against it. Should this not be the case, (though the three remaining attachés are ample for the performance of all the business) yet, if you should have some *white-headed* boy, whom you are really anxious about, I shall be ready to receive him at your hands. But pray let him be good-humoured, clever, and a gentleman.

We are quiet here, and I am convinced there is no scarcity of food in Ireland ; but there is, and except in this immediate neighbourhood, almost every where in this country an almost total want of employment for the people, so that, generally speaking, those who do not possess subsistence themselves have no means of acquiring it from others. Our markets, not at any time extraordinarily high, for the season are now falling.

I hear of your health sometimes from Seymour, and latterly from Charles. It is a wonder to me how you withstand and overcome all.

Yours most affectionately,   CLANCARTY.·

[Enclosure.]
Mr. Eliot to the Earl of Clancarty.

May 28, 1822.

My dear Lord—Both my son and myself are so deeply sensible of your kindness to him during the three years he has been attached to you, that it must not be without your previous consent and approbation that I should take any measure that would lead to his removal from your Embassy.

I have thought it advantageous for a young man to see different countries, and to be versed in the different ways of doing business at different Courts. Sir W. à Court, an old friend and near connexion of mine, has·proposed to take him to Spain; and, in the belief that the young man's removal could not inconvenience you, I closed with his offer, on condition that you would not consider it as a desertion of his post with you, if he was at all useful there.

I am myself going with my family to reside a year or two on the Continent, and have left this matter in the hands of my brother, Lord St. Germans, to whom I should be extremely obliged to you to answer this letter. If you simply say you would rather the young man remained with the Dutch Embassy, nothing more will be done; but, if you agree with me that a change is advantageous to him, and not inconvenient to you, the business would be mentioned to Lord Londonderry, and he would quit Mr. Chad in the autumn.

Believe me, &c.

The Hon. F. Lamb to the Marquess of Londonderry.

Frankfort, July 4, 1822.

Dear Lord Londonderry—The Diet has declared its vacation for the 15th of July. As nobody will remain here from whom to pick up so much as a stray report, I think of travelling either on the side of Switzerland or of Spa and Paris, (I am not sure which) unless you should give me directions to the contrary. Let me beg for an answer, and believe me, dear Lord Londonderry, ever faithfully yours,

F. LAMB.

Mr. John Lowe to the Marquess of Londonderry.

27, New Broad Street, July 20, 1822.

My Lord—Filling the high situation you do in his Majesty's Government, your lordship will not be surprised that humble individuals like myself, having a common interest with the rest of my fellow-subjects, should presume to address you whenever they conceive that they can promote, even in a small degree, the interests of the nation.

I presume to address you, my lord, on the subject of trade to Columbia; and when I inform you that my attention has been directed to it in such a way as to be already in activity with that country, I trust you will pardon me if I state in how unpleasant a situation the commercial interest is placed by the doubts and uncertainties as to the measures which his Majesty's Government will adopt respecting it. Your lordship has had an opportunity to judge of the feelings of all parties by the sentiments made public at the late dinner; and, if you will examine further, you will find amongst manufacturers and merchants an intensity of interest which, it is apprehended, your lordship has not had a fair opportunity to judge of. Men who have thought on the only principles on which commercial relations with a country can be permanently maintained, who have had the benefit of the experience of the late lamentable and extraordinary changes in commerce, look forward with interest to the prospects of new openings for any interchange of our industry with the products of other countries, and they feel much anxiety that any advantage now in our reach should not be lost by vacillation or delay.

They have seen that when our manufacturers first got ascendency, they were supported by demands from countries with whom we have now no other connexion than simple relations of amity; and they have observed that these countries have ceased to take the produce of our industry very soon after we have adopted those restrictive measures which have deprived them of any benefit from a demand for theirs. Thus we and other nations have been occupied in diverting capital, to produce what we and they could receive cheaper from other countries, and which, I believe, may be regarded as one of the chief causes of distress which we have occasionally felt. The circumstances of the late war certainly gave an impulse, which for a time created abundance and prosperity, and wealth became heaped in masses, which, finding no advantageous employment in the legitimate and proper occupations of a mercantile people, has become the source of gambling [in the] Stocks, and of turning the attention of sober and considerate traders to wild schemes of profit to be derived from loans to needy and expensive Governments.

But, my lord, I fear that we have not yet seen the full effects of this restrictive system. It has been my lot to have much to do, and to live in districts abroad which direct their industry to manufactures; and I can state to you that it is become in many of them a primary object to become exporters of articles once received from us, and to receive direct the produce which they have hitherto in a great measure procured through our agency. They have already done this with much success, and at this moment various shipments are preparing from ports of the Continent, consisting almost exclusively of cotton manufactures.

With such a prospect before us, I would implore your lordship to reflect what had been the position of this country, had
not our industry and our perseverance opened to us new vents.
The chief of the European markets have been lost by our laws;
they have not only ceased to buy from us, but they are actually
beginning a competition in foreign markets in the articles
which we were once in the habit of selling to them. I would
entreat your lordship to reflect, too, what had been our position, had we left to commerce as much freedom as it ought to
have. We should probably have had Europe as customers,
and the New World would have added to our wealth, as it
now becomes necessary to our support. And, above all, I
would now entreat you to reflect how important it is to be
prompt in every measure which can secure to us any lasting
trade. Our manufacturers possess everything necessary to
maintain their position, if protected and left to themselves;
and the country has enterprise and capital enough to maintain
its advantages, if not thwarted by inactivity or impeded by
restrictions.

If your lordship will take a glance at the exports of British
manufactures to Jamaica and to other West India Islands,
you will find that they have been to an amazing extent. These
sendings have been made with a view to supply the markets of
the main land, and they have been disposed of for those markets. Now, however, that we discover the possibility of a
direct intercourse, we look forward with satisfaction to the
increased demand which must ensue from additional prosperity,
and we are anxious not to saddle our sendings with unnecessary expense by sending to intermediate ports, and by incurring the delays which must be consequent on such operations;
and as regards Columbia, that Government has reduced the
duties on direct imports by five per cent., and we have reason
to believe that they would be even more reduced by proper
representations on the part of this Government. There is, my
lord, on the part of that Government, a feeling which is pro-

nounced in favour of this country : our constitution, our laws, and our national character, are admired and held up for admiration ; and it behoves us to profit by such a feeling, to cultivate kind offices and a friendly intercourse. The characters of the men at the head of affairs in that country have been developed, and we have seen a moderation and steadiness which would forebode a respectable, a liberal, and a regular order of things, which would promise security in our dealings with them ; and we have discovered a spirit of resistance to oppression and tyranny, which must convince us of a love of liberty and a free Government, which will for ever preclude Old Spain from exercising the power which it once exercised over them ; and, if we are convinced that the power of Spain has ceased to have effect, to what system of politics, to what interests, to what feelings are we subscribing, in not acknowledging the independence of Columbia ? Spain may say, I had a right—but can she exercise it ? Spain may say Columbia was hers—but Columbia says, We now belong to no one : and can Spain, by efficient force, show to the world that she can enforce her laws, produce obedience and a conformity to her dictates ! If she cannot, we may subscribe to the facile dictates of her pen ; but we shall be like the dog and the shadow, for we shall grasp it instead of the substance.

I will admit, my lord, that it is a difficult thing to interfere between a parent State and its colonies, but there is such a thing as adapting our views to facts, and conforming our views to things as they are, rather than to the wishes or the policy of a nation that would maintain its pretensions in vanity, without the power to enforce them. And I would ask, my lord, whether the regulations adopted by Spain for its commerce have for a long time shown any of that liberality which would encourage foreign relations ; and whether the literal understanding of its laws has not amounted to a prohibition of all the articles which are the produce of our industry. We may, my lord, continue to subscribe to the wishes of Spain ; but

Columbia and the free States of South America will adhere to their independence; and we may gain the palm of fealty to old opinions, but we shall be deprived of the riches and the abundance which may be derived from cultivating the friendship of those who have an interest in our friendship, and who have a sincere wish to cultivate it.

If your lordship will take the trouble to inquire what the produce of Columbia has been, you will learn that it affords room for the most encouraging speculation; and, if it be true that a country is, in commercial policy, interesting in proportion to what it offers as an exchange for what it receives, Columbia must claim a very great share of our interest; and if we do not hasten to avail ourselves of our position, other countries will derive the advantages of which we shall be deprived by a vain policy and an adherence to our antiquated system, warranted only by a policy which, on broad principles, we none of us comprehend or admire.

I address you, my lord, with this plain feeling, that we ought not, because Old Spain wishes to exercise a power which she has not, to sacrifice a positive advantage. All parties, all classes of your countrymen feel the importance of the subject, and feel anxious that we should at once adopt a line of policy which will secure to us the friendship of countries which have the power to serve us. I will not say that I or they feel so strongly from pure motives of benevolence, but we may rejoice that our sense of interest is combined with the promulgation of principles, the dissemination of knowledge, and the advancement of a people to civil rights and a free exercise of opinion. When your lordship refers to the map, and reflects on the peculiar position of the country, you may discover what may, nay, what will, be the influence of the measures of Columbia over the commercial policy of Europe. When you find that the ports of Columbia command an intercourse with the Atlantic and Pacific Oceans, and that a freedom of trade and a liberal policy will enable them to draw the riches of India and offer their own, you will be sensible that we are not wishing for any vain measure which might originate in party feeling or party politics.

To your lordship, therefore, the commercial part of this country looks up, as to the man who, by policy and by influence, can disseminate the benefits which must follow from a friendly feeling and connexion with Columbia; and they trust that you will, earnestly and without delay, embrace the opportunity afforded now to establish and confirm it. The position in which we are placed is one of peculiar difficulty; for we cannot truly comprehend what it is. We are exposed to risks from uncertainty, which the prudence of commercial men condemns; and whilst merchants are convinced that the trade to indirect ports must cease, they are fearful to undertake a direct trade, from an idea of great and improper risk. This has been so much so, that a great portion of the cargo of a shipment by the Robert Neilson, from Liverpool to Maracaybo, containing manufactures to the amount of £40,000, was uninsured, and the vessel is lost. For a risk which under ordinary circumstances ought to be done from two to three guineas per cent., a premium of ten to fifteen is asked by underwriters—a tax on this trade which in itself is too burdensome—a tax which would be at once removed by decisive measures or declarations as to our trade with Columbia.

Another ship, the Mary, proceeding direct to Columbia, laden with British manufactures, is burdened with the same inconveniences; and whilst we find difficulties to cover the risk but at an exorbitant rate, we find that, within a few days, a privateer fitted out at Cadix, for the purpose, for what we know, of intercepting and seizing property belonging to British merchants, thus shipped, has proceeded to the Columbian coast, and has been insured by British underwriters. Thus our enterprise is destroyed, our commerce prevented; and it is only with your lordship and his Majesty's Government to give security and confidence in a trade which promises every thing on proper principles to the country.

I should conceive myself, honoured, my lord, in affording your lordship any information in my power.

I have the honour to be, &c.,

JOHN LOWE.

THE END.

Lightning Source UK Ltd.
Milton Keynes UK
UKHW022131310522
403811UK00003B/59